Contents

Global and Culturally Diverse Leaders and Leadership: New Dimensions and Challenges for Business, Education and Society

Building Leadership Bridges

The International Leadership Association (ILA) series, *Building Leadership Bridges*, brings together leadership coaches and consultants, educators and students, scholars and researchers, and public leaders and executives working around the globe to create unique topical volumes on contemporary leadership issues. This cross-sector, cross-cultural, cross-disciplinary series contributes to more integrated leadership thinking, practices, and solutions that can positively impact our complex local and global environments. The world needs better leadership and ILA's mission of promoting a deeper understanding of leadership knowledge and practice for the greater good aims to make a difference. Learn more at www.ila-net.org.

Forthcoming Title:

Evolving Leadership for a Sustainable Future: A Path to Collective Wellbeing, edited by S. Steffen, with S. Rappaport and S. Trevenna (2018)

Recent Titles:

Breaking the Zero-Sum Game: Transforming Societies through Inclusive Leadership, edited by Aldo Boitano, Raúl Lagomarsino Dutra and H. Eric Schockman (2017), ISBN: 978-1787431867

Grassroots Leadership and the Arts for Social Change, edited by Susan J. Erenrich and Jon F. Wergin (2017), ISBN: 978-1786356888

Creative Social Change: Leadership for a Healthy World, edited by Kathryn Goldman Schuyler, John Eric Baugher and Karin Jironet (2016), ISBN: 978-1786351463

Leadership 2050: Critical Challenges, Key Contexts, and Emerging Trends, edited by Matthew Sowcik, Anthony C. Andenoro, Mindy McNutt and Susan Elaine Murphy (2015), ISBN: 978-1785603495

Global and Culturally Diverse Leaders and Leadership: New Dimensions and Challenges for Business, Education and Society

Edited by

Jean Lau Chin
Adelphi University,
Garden City, NY, USA

Joseph E. Trimble
Western Washington University,
Bellingham, WA, USA

Joseph E. Garcia
Western Washington University,
Bellingham, WA, USA

United Kingdom – North America – Japan – India – Malaysia – China

Emerald Publishing Limited
Howard House, Wagon Lane, Bingley BD16 1WA, UK

First edition 2018

Reprints and permissions service
Contact: permissions@emeraldinsight.com

British Library Cataloguing in Publication Data
A catalogue record for this book is available from the British Library

ISBN: 978-1-78743-496-7 (Print)
ISBN: 978-1-78743-495-0 (Online)
ISBN: 978-1-78743-535-3 (Epub)

ISSN: 2058-8801 (Series)

ISOQAR certified
Management System,
awarded to Emerald
for adherence to
Environmental
standard
ISO 14001:2004.

ISOQAR
REGISTERED
Certificate Number 1985
ISO 14001

INVESTOR IN PEOPLE

Part 4 Future Directions...

List of Contributors

Marco Aponte-Moreno	School of Economics and Business Administration, Saint Mary's College of California, Moraga, CA, USA
Christie Caldwell	Aperian Global, Gloucester, MA, USA
Jennifer L.S. Chandler	Arizona State University, Tempe, AZ, USA
Po Chung	Hong Kong Institute of Service Leadership & Management, Hong Kong, China
Caroline S. Clauss-Ehlers	Graduate School of Education, Rutgers, The State University of New Jersey, New Brunswick, NJ, USA
Ed Cunliff	University of Central Oklahoma, Edmond, OK, USA
Brighid Dwyer	Program on Intergroup Relations, Villanova University, Villanova, PA, USA
Rob Elkington	University of Ontario Institute of Technology, Canada
Timothy Forde	Eastern Kentucky University, Richmond, KY, USA
Kem Gambrell	Doctoral Program in Leadership Studies, Gonzaga University, Spokane, WA, USA

Ralph A. Gigliotti	Center for Organizational Development & Leadership, Rutgers University, New Brunswick, NJ, USA
Nyasha M. GuramatunhuCooper	Department of Leadership & Integrative Studies, Kennesaw University, Kennesaw, GA, USA
Robert E. Kirsch	Arizona State University, Tempe, AZ, USA
Lina Klemkaite	Institute of Migrations, University of Granada, Spain
Konstantinos Koulouris	Gerson Lehrman Group, London, UK
Hema A. Krishnan	Department of Management & Entrepreneurship, Xavier University, Cincinnati, OH, USA
Hildie Leung	Department of Applied Social Sciences, The Hong Kong Polytechnic University, Hong Kong, China
Li Lin	Department of Applied Social Sciences, The Hong Kong Polytechnic University, Hong Kong, China
Yvonne R. Masakowski	The U.S. Naval War College, College of Operational & Strategic Leadership, Newport, Rhode Island
Afsaneh Nahavandi	University of San Diego, San Diego, CA, USA
Eddie Ng	Department of Applied Social Sciences, The Hong Kong Polytechnic University, Hong Kong, China
Tom Otieno	College of Science, Eastern Kentucky University, Richmond, KY, USA

Lynn Pasquerella   Association of American
                                 Colleges and Universities,
                                 Washington, DC, USA

Ethan Prizant   Aperian Global, Shanghai,
                                 China

Kristi Robertson   University of Central
                                 Oklahoma, Edmond, OK,
                                 USA

Kristina Ruiz-Mesa   Communication Studies,
                                 California State University,
                                 Los Angeles, CA, USA

Damini Saini   Institute of Management
                                 Sciences, University of
                                 Lucknow, Lucknow, India

Atoya Sims   University of Central
                                 Oklahoma, Edmond, OK,
                                 USA

Daniel T. L. Shek   Department of Applied Social
                                 Sciences, The Hong Kong
                                 Polytechnic University, Hong
                                 Kong, China

Jeanetta D. Sims   University of Central
                                 Oklahoma, Edmond, OK,
                                 USA

Sherwood Thompson   Eastern Kentucky University,
                                 Richmond, KY, USA

Elizabeth A. Tuleja   Mendoza College of Business,
                                 University of Notre Dame,
                                 Notre Dame, IN, USA

Melba J. T. Vasquez   Austin, TX, USA

Ian O. Williamson   Business School, Victoria
                                 University, Wellington,
                                 New Zealand

Foreword

It is a very exciting and challenging time to examine the current changes of leadership styles in society, especially given the rapidly changing demographic changes worldwide. Those changes result in a society where members may speak several languages; have a variety of customs and ceremonies; represent people of colors; display a variety of clothing; introduce a variety of foods; and display multicultural and feminist specific orientations to leadership. It is thus timely that Chin, Trimble, and Garcia provide us with an edited volume on diverse leadership that provides a new body of knowledge that is more relevant and applicable in today's world.

Leadership is defined in a number of ways, and numerous models of leadership are described in the literature Most models describe the various processes of interpersonal influence that use power and authority to encourage others to act to achieve goals. Chin and Trimble (2015) addressed the importance of diversity and leadership to arrive at more expanded models of leadership. Their work is foundational to this volume where authors are providing more nuanced understanding of such issues as authentic leadership, revisiting trait theory, and integrating critical race theory. What impact do different models have on those influenced by the leadership styles and approaches?

Traditional leadership styles have advantages and disadvantages. In their 2015 volume Chin and Trimble described research that identified the most important characteristics and styles out of 63 that are embraced and preferred by various populations, and the least important. Results indicated that the least important were those associated with the "alpha male" leadership style, including aggressive, conflict-inducer, dominant, self-centered, and status conscious. The more important endorsed descriptors included adaptability, integrity, authenticity, honesty, and communicator (Chin & Trimble, 2015; Trimble, 2015).

Since the 2016 presidential election, we have witnessed a traditional dominant leadership style of the U.S. President, who has the lowest approval rating of any chief executive since *Gallup* began tracking the initial months of a president's term in 1953. The rating is due to high disapproval among Democrats and independents, but there is considerable satisfaction on the part of many Republicans, including those who elected him (Yourish & Murray, 2017, March 20). It is clear that people follow different leaders; various styles may influence individuals and groups differentially. The American Psychological Association's *Stress in America* survey found that between August 2016 and January 2017, Americans' overall average reported stress rose from 4.8 to 5.1 on a 10-point scale. Also, more than half of Americans (57%) report that the current political climate is a very significant source of stress. Also, two-thirds (66%) say the same about the future of our nation, and nearly half (49%) report that the outcome of the election is a very or somewhat significant source of stress (APA, 2017).

Chin and Trimble (2015), Trimble (2015), and most of the authors in this edition propose that in a changing society, new leadership styles are emerging and preferred. Traditional western models of leadership may be less and less relevant for societies that are increasingly diverse and global. As our societies become more diverse, more diverse leaders with a variety of styles are more relevant and appropriate; it is vital that the citizenry not only tolerate, but appreciate the contributions that diverse leaders can provide.

Several years ago former Supreme Court Justice Sandra Day O'Conner conveyed the belief that diversity in leadership was a compelling interest in society. She spoke of the importance of a critical mass of racial and ethnic minority attendees in higher education in order to cultivate a set of leaders from those diverse backgrounds with legitimacy in the eyes of the citizenry. She thus supported affirmative action in universities because she believed that universities are partly in the business of training a leadership corps for society and that a society with racial and ethnic tensions can benefit tremendously from having a diverse and integrated leadership (*Gratz v. Bollinger*, 2003; *Grutter v. Bollinger*, 2003; Jayson & Rodriguez, 2003, p. A-1).

The different perspectives and insights provided in this volume provide a critically important understanding relative to traditional perspectives on leadership. The authors shed light on under-researched and under-examined areas related to evolving leadership approaches regarding *how* to lead, but also *what goals* leaders should attempt to accomplish. This contribution does indeed address the value of a diverse leadership in society, including at a global level, especially in the context of challenging leadership models that have historically omitted racial and ethnic groups in society. Authors describe how diverse representation promotes values such as collectivism, benevolence, and familial affiliations that have greater relevance, effectiveness, and applicability in today's world. Authors also describe leadership theories and research agenda that are more relevant to a growing multicultural population. This helps contribute to a knowledge base that allows for leaders to be more responsive to the evolving changes in societies. The knowledge base can help and support women, people from different racial/ethnic backgrounds as well as traditional leaders to avoid becoming or continuing to be like those already in the power elite. It provides opportunity for different lived experiences and worldviews to influence those leadership styles.

The opportunity for a citizenry to have diverse leadership is a social justice issue. Leaders with varying ideologies and values that include prioritization of social justice issues can have positive impact on issues such as racism, classism, sexism, poverty, and other oppressions. Perhaps one of the most intriguing themes among several authors is how social identity variables such as gender, race, and ethnicity influence leader behaviors. Some of the authors address values of equity and social justice, and how the lived experiences of those from diverse backgrounds may predispose them to be empowered to prioritize those altruistic values. This volume describes how worldviews and lived experiences influence leadership styles, and how the interaction of diverse leaders, diverse members, and diverse contexts shape the enactment of leadership.

The challenges of diverse leadership are also addressed, including strategies for addressing some of those challenges. Leaders who have indigenous backgrounds, who are racial and ethnic minorities, or are women or homosexual often deal with those who are accustomed to White, North American, heterosexual males, and traditional leadership styles, e.g., masculinized, individual oriented, dominant, and controlled. Destructive biases, either explicit or implicit can result in failure to accept the diverse leader and/or leadership style. The authors validate orientations that examine virtue from philosophical and ethical principles, collective orientations, collaboration as a leadership process, incorporation of inclusiveness, socially derived identities tied to leadership traits, and examination of how altruism influences goals and communication across groups.

The authors also provide valuable information in the context of theories and models to help guide the development and training of leaders in a variety of different settings, including educational institutions, and business, military, professional, and civic organizations. Great skill is required in balancing conflicting interests that emerge in most contexts and in most settings. Training can help leaders become aware of the factors that shape goals, including the leaders' personal values, the organizational context, and needs of the setting. The information has the potential to help leaders become more effective across a broad range of situations. Training can also help leaders from diverse background to develop skills to address forms of microaggressions and other challenges to their leadership.

Editors Jean Lau Chin, Joseph E. Trimble, and Joseph E. Garcia are to be congratulated for their selection of authors who contributed knowledgeable, insightful, thought provoking, and inspiring chapters. This is a significant contribution to the evolving literature and research on leadership and diversity. It challenges existing notions of leadership with a more global vision of society. I am enthused about this extraordinary contribution that helps bring to light how we can understand, develop, promote, and support a more inclusive, diverse, and effective set of leaders in the many contexts of society.

Melba J. T. Vasquez

Introduction

The rapidly changing demographic composition worldwide calls into question the relevance of leadership models that historically have omitted ethnic and racial groups or diverse groups within society or a country. Rooted in a North American and European tradition, this omission has fostered a research agenda that was ethnocentric, gender biased, and bound by time and place. Western models of leadership have remained dominant and sometimes inappropriately applied to leadership in diverse, multicultural contexts. This is no longer justified as we enter a world and societies that are increasingly global and diverse. We start this volume by asking the following questions:

- How well prepared will leaders be to lead a diverse workforce and provide products and services to a diverse clientele?
- What will we teach our increasingly diverse future leaders?
- How will leadership models build a knowledge base that can be generalized to the population as a whole and to be inclusive of diverse entities within an organization?
- How do we prepare ourselves, our communities, our constituents, and our leaders to live, work, and practice in these future realities?

This volume examines new ways of examining research, teaching, and practice to develop a body of knowledge on leadership that will have greater relevance, effectiveness, and applicability in today's world. While masculinized contexts of leadership have prevailed, 21st-century models should seriously include feminist and culturally specific orientations to leadership.

With growing population diversity and mobility in the United States and throughout the world, leaders and members will find themselves in more culturally heterogeneous settings, organizations, and communities than ever before. Leaders of tomorrow need to be prepared to lead a diverse workforce in ways that are culturally responsive and competent in meeting the needs of a growing multicultural population. This demands that leadership theories and research be more inclusive and robust if they are to remain relevant. How best can we do that?

People throughout the world will grapple with the question of who best can lead them. Must our leaders look like us and share our beliefs and values? Are there different styles that lead to greater cultural understanding and healthier leader-member relationships? How do we prepare ourselves to live, work, and lead in a world when we do not know the skills we will need or the environments we will face?

A majority of leadership models foster a research agenda that is ethnocentric, gender-biased, and bound by time and place (Chin, 2009, 2010; Chin & Trimble, 2015; Eagly & Chin, 2010; Turnbull, Case, Edwards, Schedlitzki, & Simpson, 2012). With the growing worldwide population shifts, leaders and followers will find themselves in more heterogeneous contexts within institutions and communities than ever before. Will leaders be prepared to lead a diverse workforce and provide products and services to a culturally varied clientele? What will we teach our future leaders as they and those they lead become increasingly diverse? How will leadership models build a knowledge base that can be generalized to our expanding global and diverse societies? Can leaders and leadership be responsive to change?

In this volume, we challenge existing notions of leadership. We use personal narratives and case studies of diverse leadership styles to illustrate the importance of diversity in our lives, communities, and workplace, and how it influences access to leadership positions and exercise of leadership. An "idealized" prototypic model of leadership often drives leadership training and prescribes conditions of leadership for corporate, higher education, science, and social and political sectors of society.

As more women and people from different ethnocultural backgrounds begin to emerge in leadership ranks, Zweigenhaft and Domhoff (2006) report that they often become more like those already in the power elite. The prevailing question then is: Is there room for diverse forms of leadership, or are new leaders constrained by the prevailing norms?

Existing leadership theories often draw their case examples and narratives of those already in leadership positions, i.e., White, North American, heterosexual males, representing a narrow range of the potentially rich and diverse examples of leadership. As we develop leadership paradigms for an increasingly global and diverse society, we need to expand our examples with narratives reflecting the diverse experiences and social identities of leaders who understand and live amidst different paradigms of effective leadership.

In this volume, we give needed attention to ethnocultural diversity and leadership styles that reflect more inclusive theories of leadership applicable to the exercise of successful leadership in unique and diverse cultural settings. We include the use of personal narratives and case studies to offer new paradigms and identify new dimensions in the study and practice of leadership — to examine diversity in the minds and actions of successful leaders. We hope it will offer insights to challenge our existing notions of leadership and generate a post-industrial, post-colonial, diverse, and global view of leadership. Through the use of narratives and case studies we will emphasize:

- How the different worldviews and lived experiences of leaders influence leadership styles.
- How social justice, ethical, and cultural values are often manifest and included in dialogues about leadership.
- How social identities of leaders (e.g., gender, race, and ethnicity) intersect with leader identities and may result in biases that influence perceptions, shape leader behaviors, and influence appraisals of a leader's effectiveness.
- How the exchange between diverse leaders and diverse members and between leaders and diverse contexts shape the enactment of leadership.

Part 1: A New Look At Leadership: Overview

Western styles and models of leadership currently dominate the leadership literature. New global and diverse perspectives of leadership can begin to include non-dominant views where collectivism, benevolence, and familial affiliations are given greater prominence. This might include an attention to different perspectives of the same phenomenon which some might find to be anathema to long-held beliefs, e.g., examining virtue in leadership from philosophical and ethical principles as opposed to empirical validation; comparing effective leadership using collective vs. individual orientations; using non-Western metaphors, such as Daoist principles, to define the process of leadership; considering how alternative construals of the self as interdependent might influence the image of leaders; collaboration as a process; leader traits as identities which are socially derived; incorporating inclusiveness and difference as goals; examining power and its relationship to altruism, dominance, and control; and communication across groups and cultures.

Although leadership theories have evolved to reflect changing social contexts, they remain silent on issues of equity, diversity, and social justice. In these chapters, the authors challenge existing theories of leadership and move toward viewing leadership via a global view of organizations in their societal contexts. Others incorporate principles of leadership that are inclusive, multidimensional, and address group differences through the voices of those who have experienced cultural challenges rather than those who are privileged. In redefining leadership as global and diverse, the authors impart a new understanding of who our leaders are, the process of communication, the exchange between leaders and their members, and the contexts that shape the exercise of leadership.

1. Theory Leadership from Africa: Examples of Trait Theory — Nyasha M. GuramatunhuCooper
2. The Case for an Indigenous Collectivist Mindset — Kem Gambrell
3. Cross-cultural Dimensions of Personal Stories in Communicating Authentic Leadership — Marco Aponte-Moreno and Konstantinos Koulouris
4. How the Communal Philosophies of Ubuntu in Africa and Confucius Thought in China Might Enrich Western Notions of Leadership — Rob Elkington and Elizabeth A. Tuleja

Part 2: Ethnocultural Contexts

People around the world increasingly recognize their discontent with leadership models that derive from a Eurocentric or North American perspective. As more diverse leaders are recognized in the world (they exist in many different countries not viewed as among the powerful Western nations), or enter the ranks of leadership viewed to be the power elite, they are looking to be inclusive and multidimensional. Indigenous perspectives, once relegated to the exotic, less powerful, and unessential are now empowered to be perspectives worthy and useful in their own right. Chapters in this section provide examples of these alternative approaches among different populations, and open a dialogue on a more balanced view of how leadership is viewed and exercised.

1. Influence and Global Leadership: China, India, and the Multinational Corporation – Christie Caldwell and Ethan Prizant
2. Indo-European Leadership (IEL): A Non-Western Leadership Perspective –Afsaneh Nahavandi and Hema A. Krishnan
3. Current and Emerging Patterns of Muslim Leadership – Lina Klemkaite

Part 3: Application of Global and Diverse Perspectives in Different Contexts

As we urge paradigm shifts to develop and expand leadership models that are inclusive of all groups, responsive to difference and diversity among leaders and members, and attentive to the interaction of lived experiences, social identities, and leader-member exchange, chapters in this section apply these principles to different contexts in which leadership is exercised. The five chapters examine the different sectors of service to communities, social justice, military, and higher education from both the leader's and student's perspectives. While Part 2 examines ethnocultural contexts from the standpoint of populations and how their cultures influence and intersect with leadership, Part 3 is about the culture of organizations and institutions which shape how leadership is exercised. These chapters introduce the sense of vision and purpose that challenge our exercise of leadership and the values we bring to bear on how we lead.

1. Service Leadership under the Service Economy – Daniel T. L. Shek, Po Chung, Li Lin, Hildie Leung, and Eddie Ng
2. Reinvigorating Conversations about Leadership: Application of Strategic Choice Theory to the Social Justice Organizational Leader – Caroline S. Clauss-Ehlers and Lynn Pasquerella
3. Probing Leadership from Racio-Ethnic Perspectives in Higher Education: An Emergent Model of Accelerating

Part 4: Future Directions...

We end with visions of future directions for studies of leadership and how leadership is central to advancing society and promoting social change. As we examine the influence of different worldviews and lived influence leadership, how social justice, ethical, and cultural values emerge in our vision, goals, and exercise of leadership, how social identities of gender, race, and ethnicity intersect between diverse leaders' identities and diverse members, and how that exchange shapes the enactment of leadership, we emerge with new perspectives with an emphasis on cultural competence and promoting change. Saini emphasizes concepts of benevolence and ethics while Thompson et al. emphasize sustainable cultural competence as a catalyst for effective and excellent leadership. Chandler and Kirsch introduce a critical lens to examine the patterns of oppression and domination to challenge the power relations and social processes of leadership and to promote change.

Jean Lau Chin
Joseph E. Trimble
Joseph E. Garcia
Editors

References

American Psychological Association. (2017, January). *Stress in America 2017 snapshot: Coping with change*. Washington, DC: Author. Retrieved from http://www.apa.org/news/press/releases/stress/2016/coping-with-change.pdf

Chin, J. L., & Trimble, J. E. (2015). *Diversity and leadership*. New York, NY: Sage. ISBN-13: 978-1452257891, ISBN-10: 1452257892.

Gratz v. Bollinger (2003). 539 US 244.

Grutter v. Bollinger (2003). 539 US 306.

Jayson, S., & Rodriguez, E. (2003, June 24). Affirmation action in colleges upheld: UT official hails ruling, saying "Hopwood is dead". *Austin American Statesman*, A1–A5.

Trimble, J. (2015, August). *Discussant at Symposium: Race/Ethnic relations and the Obama presidency: Perspectives of some leaders in the field*. Presented at the annual Convention of the American Psychological Association, Toronto, Canada. Comments also available at: Trimble, J. (2015, April). *Bid farewell to the Alpha leadership style*. Available on *YouTube*. Retrieved from https://www.youtube.com/watch?v=fuHj3jsBdKE

Yourish, K., & Murray, P. (2017, March 20). The highs and lows of President Trump's approval ratings. *New York Times*. Retrieved from https://www.nytimes.com/interactive/2017/02/28/us/politics/the-highs-and-lows-of-trumps-approval.html

Chin, J. L. (2009). The dynamics of gender, race, and leadership. In R. H. Klein, C. Rice, & V. L. Schermer (Eds.), *Leadership in a changing world: Dynamic perspectives on groups and their leaders* (pp. 47–66). Lanham, MD: Lexington Press.

Chin, J. L. (2010). The road to leadership roles. In C. Rayburn, F. Denmark, M. E. Reuder, & A. M. Austria (Eds.), *A handbook for women mentors: Transcending barriers of stereotype, race, and ethnicity.* (pp. 251–260). Santa Barbara, CA: ABC-CLIO, LLC.

Chin, J. L., & Trimble, J. (2015). *Diversity and leadership*. Thousand Oaks, CA: SAGE Publishing.

Eagly, A., & Chin, J. L. (2010). Diversity and leadership in a changing world. *American Psychologist, 65*(3), 216–224.

Turnbull, S., Case, P., Edwards, G., Schedlitzki, D., & Simpson, P. (2012). *Worldly leadership: Alternative wisdoms for a complex world*. New York, NY: Palgrave Macmillan.

Zweigenhaft, R. L., & Domhoff, G. W. (2006). *Diversity in the power elite: How it happened, why it matters*. Lanham, MD: Rowman & Littlefield.

PART 1
A New Look at Leadership:
Overview

1

Theory Leadership from Africa: Examples of Trait Theory

Nyasha M. GuramatunhuCooper

Leadership from Africa: Examples of Trait Theory: Introduction

Written from a Leadership Studies educator's perspective, this chapter highlights and challenges the Western bias of leadership theories, and disrupts this ideological ethnocentrism by presenting leadership trait theory through the experiences of contemporary African community leaders. Using one of the most recognizable theories in leadership studies, this chapter proposes reimagining trait theory by presenting examples of skills, abilities, and qualities of leadership by contemporary leaders from Liberia, Cameroon, and South Africa.

By using examples of leadership in African countries, this chapter demonstrates that the Western bias of leadership is artificial because its theories, particularly trait theory, can be successfully employed to discuss leadership in non-western contexts in ways that prize the differences in culture and societies.

Current leadership theories need not be forsaken in favor of creating new Afro-centered leadership theories. It is possible to explore the attributes, skills, and abilities of trait theory using examples from places around the world that have typically been excluded as viable places to study leadership. To heed the call for inclusive leadership, particularly in a global society, it is crucial that Leadership Studies educators intentionally examine how leadership theories can be taught by exploring different ways of knowing and being. Failure to do so undermines the complexity of leadership and Leadership Studies, which transcend a single worldview.

This chapter presents an opportunity to explore leadership trait theory beyond typical examples from the West. Valuable lessons about leadership skills, abilities, and traits, can come from parts of the world that have been excluded from the leadership studies canon.

The objective of this chapter is to bring Africa into Leadership Studies education by demonstrating how Western theories of Leadership Studies can be studied and taught using Africans as examples of theories. The secondary objective of this chapter is to prompt leadership educators to think about expanding their understanding and examples of leadership by intentionally seeking leadership voices and experiences from different parts of the world.

With an aggregate population of almost one billion, the African continent is an important part of the global marketplace, with imports and exports in the form of goods and services worth billions of dollars (Nwosu in Deardoff, 2009, p. 158). Africans are creating and participating robustly in a world that has seen widespread shifts due to trade, technology, and migration (p. 159). This assertion is hardly new, yet Africa is noticeably and frequently excluded from conversations that explore the study of leadership. As Bangura (2011, p. 133) noted: "no one would deny that the continent of Africa is intimately involved when the disciplines of Geography, History, Political Science, Linguistics, Economics or Anthropology" are examined. However, the same cannot be said for the Leadership Studies canon. African voices and experiences have been excluded from the intellectual pursuit of leadership. This exclusion of Africa in Leadership Studies harkens back to the ideas advanced by 19th-century European thinkers who wrote and spoke of Africans "as objects unworthy of study, as lacking history, as lacking culture" (p. 133). Yet the rich and complex precolonial, colonial, and postcolonial histories of Africa's 55 recognized states show leadership in nuanced forms.

Exclusion from the Leadership Studies canon is not unique to Africa. The global south is noticeably absent in leadership theories and approaches that dominate academic curricula, international policy, and models of governance. The emergence of Leadership Studies as a discipline in the last 60 years has shown the pervasiveness of a Western, particularly North American lens (Den Hartog & Dickson, 2012). The result has been a discursive imperialism of sorts, wherein the West is positioned as the authority on the concept and practice of leadership, and leadership that occurs outside of this particular framework is not legitimate or noteworthy. In an effort to counter the problematic ethnocentrism in leadership theory, I call for intentional inclusion of non-Western experiences and perspectives in Leadership Studies education.

In this chapter, I propose a reimagining of trait theory by highlighting examples of young Africans who are influencing and advancing their communities: Arthur Zang, Fatu Kekula, and Sizwe Nzima. Arthur Zang, a Cameroonian engineer, invented the Cardiopad: "a touch screen medical tablet that enables heart examinations...to be performed at remote rural locations while the results of the test are transferred wirelessly to specialists..." (Nsehe, 2012). Fatu Kekula from Liberia saved her entire immediate family from the deadly Ebola virus (Cohen & Bonifield, 2015). Sizwe Nzima from South Africa started Iyeza Express: a medication delivery service (Kelto, 2014). The achievements of these three remarkable leaders show a kind of leadership that Masango (2002) designated as life giving and innovative. Moreover, these exceptional individuals exhibit some of the oft-cited desirable traits in leadership trait theory: intelligence, determination, and integrity (Northouse, 2015). Ultimately, this chapter serves as a resource for leadership educators to explore some of what Africa has to offer Leadership Studies education.

Before presenting the leadership stories of Arthur, Fatu, and Sizwe, I begin by discussing the positioning of Leadership Studies as a Western concept, followed by a brief overview of trait theory. The chapter ends with a discussion of the implications of shifting trait theory from a Eurocentric lens to a more global perspective that considers cultural and social context, which ultimately invites different voices and experiences in Leadership Studies education.

Locating Personal Interest

Sikes (2010, p. 19) noted that in maintaining a standard of ethics regarding their work, scholars must clearly present "where they are positioned in regard to their work." Explaining one's position includes revealing the origin of interest in the topic, and how the topic relates to personal experience (p. 19). I am a Leadership Studies educator. Teaching at the undergraduate level, my work in the classroom is committed to guiding learners towards and through the complexity of leadership. Guided by a postmodern lens, I hold that leadership is socially and culturally mediated, and one's geographical positioning in the world affects perceptions and practice of leadership.

Born and raised in Zimbabwe, I navigate the world as an African woman. I respond to people, places, things, and events as an African woman. I know that the continent, in its rich yet complex state, is poised to contribute valuable ways of knowing and being when it comes to the study and practice of leadership. As a young African, I believe that there are many young Africans who are doing incredible work to uplift their communities to little or no fanfare. Their leadership is a powerful reminder of Masango's (2002) life giving and innovative leadership.

At this juncture, I will also note that though I am writing about African examples of leadership trait theory and specifically name the countries of Liberia, Cameroon, and South Africa, I also invoke the rest of the global south, for the exclusion in Leadership Studies extends to regions such Latin America, the Middle East, and parts of South Asia. One can also find powerful examples of leadership that are scarcely written about and given due designation as demonstrations of leadership as it is known in the discipline. Though I do not write specifically about the global south in this chapter, the point remains that this is a part of the world that is not included in the framing of Leadership Studies and in the way that leadership is taught.

Leadership as a Western Paradigm

In a *New York Times* opinion piece, Garfield and Van Nordern (2016) issued a poignant call to their colleagues in the field of Philosophy. In a clear and pointed critique, they highlighted the flaw in their discipline, noting: "the vast majority of philosophy departments in the United States offer courses only on Philosophy derived from Europe and the English-speaking world" (2016). This same critique is gaining momentum in Leadership Studies education, particularly directed at leadership theories and approaches. Works by Chin and Trimble (2015),

Schedlitzki and Edwards (2014), and Den Hartog and Dickinson (2012) extensively discuss a Western bias of leadership theory.

Presenting a history of Leadership Studies, Perkins (2009) advised that though there is a Western bias in leadership research, the study and practice of leadership is ancient and universal, meaning that the concept of leadership transcends borders and fixed time periods. For example, the concepts of leader, follower, and leadership have been pointed out in Egyptian symbols dating back to 5,000 years ago (Bass, 1995). Such resources interrupt the notion of the discipline of Leadership Studies as couched in Western civilization, with examples of ideal leadership often associated with the works of Plato and Aristotle (Wren, 1995).

Alvez, Manz, and Butterfield (2005) proposed that leadership has "long been treated as a global field of study, borrowing from Eastern and Western classic teachings" (p. 9). However, this is a narrow treatment of the term "global field" in that it excludes much of the world as contributors to the field. These Eastern and Western classic teachings on leadership are often limited to examples such as Aristotle, Confucius, Buddha, Churchill, and Gandhi. However, this leaves out too many parts of the world as valuable sources for studies and scholarship on leadership, particularly Africa. This vacuum led Jallow (2014) to proclaim that there is "a need for African Leadership Studies, Asian Leadership Studies, Latin American Leadership Studies, and Middle Eastern Leadership Studies" (p. 3).

Shifting focus from historical major figures, contemporary leadership scholarship increasingly examines societal and contextual issues such as power, gender, and ethics (Day & Antonakis, 2012). However, there is no explicit focus on worldview. The arena in which leadership is studied and practiced is vast, so it is concerning that Leadership Studies as a discipline discusses cultural and social influences on leadership as special issues rather than critical shapers of the discipline. For example, a review of widely used textbooks on leadership shows the topic of leadership and culture at the bottom of the table of contents, and/or covered within a single chapter. Peter Northouse's *Leadership: Theory and Practice* (2015), places leadership and culture as Chapter 16 out of 16 chapters. Similarly, Richard Daft and Patricia Lane's *The Leadership Experience* (2015) examines leadership and culture in Chapter 14 out of 15 chapters. By treating leadership and culture as a special interest topic, the implication is that cultural and social contexts operate at the periphery of the discipline. Ideally, such chapters should be at the beginning of popular textbooks because it is important to frame cultural and social contexts as critical shapers in assessing the strengths and weaknesses of leadership theories, particularly for learners who are new to the discipline. Texts such as Chin and Tremble's *Diversity and Leadership* (2015) underscore how global shifts in trade, technology, and migration have buoyed advocacy for the inclusion of cultural and social contexts as a focal point for leadership.

If students, scholars, and educators are to laud Leadership Studies as an interdisciplinary field, then collective and intentional work must be done to make it an intercultural field of study. What I am proposing is not radical. Scholars need not completely change the basis of current leadership theory in order to be inclusive. Instead, there are opportunities to contextualize existing leadership theories so that their tenets can be appreciated from a culturally relativistic lens (Jallow, 2014). Indeed, the intellectual space for this already exists. Leadership is the study of possibilities based on context, situations, and contingencies (Ayman & Adams, 2012). This view creates space to critique, advance, and reimagine the concept and practice of leadership while spanning geographical borders. This is the allure of Leadership Studies despite its current limitations in inclusivity.

With this perspective, I present trait theory in contemporary terms with African exemplars. Even though I have levied the critique that Leadership Studies is presented from a Western centric lens, this very same lens can be used to study leadership related to Africa in a way that prizes African voices and experiences. This follows Bangura's (2011) proposition that there are aspects of Africa that are common to any continent, therefore there is license to use Western theories of leadership to uncover these commonalities. As I pointed out in previous work (GuramatunhuCooper, 2014), the ability for scholars to discuss African leadership in social movements speaks to the versatility of African leadership in how it can be analyzed using different worldviews.

At this juncture, I acknowledge that there are several ways to approach this chapter. Scholars versed in Afro-centered ways of knowing and being may question my use of Western derived theories to present Africans as examples of leadership theories. Scholars in the tradition of the formidable Cheikh Anta Diop might assert that there is a distinct character of African sociocultural constructs, which cannot be correctly interpreted by a

Eurocentric (Western) mode of analysis (Bangura, 2011). I acknowledge that this is a limitation of this chapter. I concur: it is critical to place "African ideals at the center of any analysis that involved African culture and behavior" (Asante, 1987, p. 6). However the beauty of Leadership Studies is such that a post-modern lens allows for such scholastic pursuits wherein knowledge from one cultural base can share the same intellectual space with another: without contrast or comparison, but simply as knowledge. To attempt to come up with Afro-centered leadership theories in this chapter would be a gargantuan task that deserves skilled and disciplined study, and I am encouraged that scholars such as Jallow (2014) are championing this cause.

A survey of scholarship shows a dearth in Leadership Studies scholarship written by and for African audiences. As Jallow (2014) noted, scholarship on African leadership comes from historians, political scientists, and theologians, and often lacks "infusion of Leadership Studies theories" (p. 5). However, a qualitative study by Bolden and Kirk (2009, p. 14) suggested that "Africans aspire for leadership founded on humanistic principles, and a desire for more inclusive and participative forms of leadership that value individual differences, authenticity and serving the community." What I propose, as a Leadership Studies educator teaching at a Western institution of higher education, is limited in scope and less ambitious for now, however, it impacts Leadership Studies education in important ways. In my quest to expose learners to global experiences of leadership, I focus on my immediate sphere of influence. Presenting Africans and African experiences as examples of leadership theories adds to the work of disrupting the Eurocentric lens in Leadership Studies.

Trait Theory

At its core, trait theory of leadership thrives on the assumption that extraordinary personal attributes, abilities, skills, and physical characteristics are the markers of leadership (Glynn & DeJordy, 2010, p. 122). In other words, "one is born into a leadership role in society," creating a clear demarcation line between the destinies of leaders and nonleaders (Schedlitzki & Edwards, 2014, p. 22). Trait theory is also sometimes referred to as the "great man theory" as inquiry into the theory began at a time when "leadership was thought to be the province of males" (Glynn & DeJordy, 2010, p. 122). Research on trait theory between the late 1940s and the early 1990s focused on isolating characteristics and qualities that distinguished leaders from non-leaders, seeking to understand "why certain people were great leaders" (Rowe & Guerrero, 2016, p. 33). Among the eminent studies on trait theory (see Kirkpatrick & Locke, 1991; Mann, 1959; Stogdill, 1948, 1974), five traits are most frequently noted: intelligence, self-confidence, determination, integrity, and sociability (Northouse, 2015). But this aforementioned trait theory research highlights the Western gaze as the normative lens in Leadership Studies. Specifically, all these studies were carried out in Western contexts, focusing on Anglo males as examples, thus excluding other people, places, things, and events from other parts of the world that might have advanced research.

One of the intriguing things about Leadership Studies is that each approach and theory can be assessed on its strengths and weaknesses, which gives way to developing other contextually responsive ways of thinking about leadership. Since trait theory is leader-centric, one of the critiques levied against the theory is its limiting nature (Yukl, 2010). It is limiting in that while focusing on attributes or traits of a leader, it does not take into account social, political, economic, and cultural variables that impact perceptions of leaders and leadership. In earlier extensive reviews, scholars such as Stogdill (1948) and Mann (1959) have critiqued trait theory "as being insufficient to explain leadership and leadership effectiveness" (as cited in Zaccaro, 2007, p. 6). Similar critiques were noted by Ghiselli and Brown (1955), Secord and Backman (1974), Muchinsky (1983), and Baron and Byrne (1987). In more recent scholarship, Chin and Trimble (2015) discussed the limitations of trait theory as rooted in "a presumption of universal traits" (p. 37). This limitation ushered a failure "to note cultural variation and/or gender variation" (p. 88). The basis of these critiques is that singling specific traits as markers of leadership, without consideration of circumstances, is an unproductive pursuit. These critiques made way for "situationism perspective," which emphasizes that different situations call for different types of leadership, and it cannot be assumed that an effective leader in one situation will be effective in another, without consideration of individual leadership attributes (Zaccaro, Kemp, & Bader, 2004).

A notable example of an examination of a type of situationism perspective: leadership traits within cultural and social contexts, is the GLOBE Study (House, 2004). This longitudinal quantitative and qualitative study presents culture and society as the situational variables, and uses data to extrapolate traits or attributes of leadership from various cultures. Though there is room to critique its scope in other venues, the Globe Study informs my attempt to present leadership attributes or traits as those that individuals possess and use in response to areas of need in their societies and communities. Bolden and Kirk's (2009) work supports this culturally and socially based presentation of trait theory, noting that their "research in Africa has indicated that leadership begins with accepting and taking up one's role within a community (or social) context" (p. 13).

Model of Leader Traits and Leadership

Critiques of trait theory have lauded it as "too simplistic" (Conger & Kanungo, 1998, p. 38). In its simplicity, it is perceived as rendering a reductionism of leadership that presents it as a "passive status" or "mere possession of some combination of traits" (Stogdill, 1948, p. 66). However, a revival of the theory abounds. According to Zaccaro (2007), contemporary application of trait-based perspectives of leadership must be grounded in conceptually meaningful ways. Such a perspective assuages Conger and Kanungo's (1998) label of the theory being "too simplistic" in that traits and attributes are useful in assessing leadership performance and outcomes if contextually bound meaning is applied. In other words, Stogdill's (1948) assessment of the theory as the "mere possession of some combination of traits" is transformed when traits are viewed within the specific contexts in which they are used to influence and impact people, places, things, and events.

In introducing the model of leader traits and leadership, Zaccaro et al. (2004) provide a useful framework for categorizing leadership traits and attributes. The model is unique in that it does not just list a set of traits, rather, it provides "integrated sets of leadership attributes" that can be used to evaluate leader performance and impact (Zaccaro, 2007, p. 11). The attributes include "cognitive capacities, personality or dispositional qualities, motives and values, problem-solving skills, social capacities, and tacit knowledge" (p. 11). Illustrating advancement beyond simply listing traits associated with leadership, the model of leadership traits and leadership makes a distinction between distal and proximal attributes. Distal attributes such as cognitive capacities, personality or dispositional qualities, and motives and values are traits that individuals are born with, thus, relatively stable (p. 13). Proximal attributes: problem-solving skills, social capacities, and tacit knowledge, are learned and developed, and susceptible to social, cultural, and systemic influences (p. 13).

For the purposes of this chapter, I will focus on the proximal attributes of leadership as presented by Zaccaro et al. (2004) to illustrate how examples of leadership trait theory can be found across Africa and can be used to teach leadership theory in institutions across the world. Focusing on proximal attributes (leadership traits that can be developed) reveals my own perspective of leadership as an inclusive enterprise that is not limited to certain kinds of people. Rather, leadership can be informally and formally nurtured and developed in response to situations and needs. The examples of trait leadership presented in this chapter underscore this perspective, illustrating how young Africans used problem-solving skills, social capacities, and tacit knowledge (all proximal attributes) to respond to the needs of their communities.

Examples of Trait Theory in Africa

In 2014, the West African countries of Guinea, Sierra Leone, and Liberia reeled from the Ebola epidemic. Global health institutions issued dire warnings and death counts, signaling the rapid impact of a disease that had been previously thought to be curbed. Even Liberian president: Her Excellency Ellen Sirleaf Johnson, traveled to the United States appealing for resources to fight or at least slow down the spread of the disease (Cooper, 2014). On the ground in Liberia, Fatu Kekula (then 23 years old) treated and saved her entire family from Ebola "using nothing more than plastic trash bags, a raincoat bought in the market, boots, and a surgical mask and gloves" (Dixon, 2014). A detailed profile in the *Los Angeles Times* shows that Fatu cared for her father, mother, sister, and cousin because: "Doctors called and told me to leave them alone, and not go anywhere near them. I could not. They are my only family. No one came near me" (2014).

With limited medical knowledge, Fatu showed her problem-solving skills by creating a rudimentary isolation room with a raincoat, rain boots, and chlorine as her primary medical equipment (Dixon, 2014). Dispensing a mixture of medications such as blood pressure medication, antibiotics, and analgesics, and monitoring an intravenous drip, Fatu worked tirelessly to keep her family alive without sleep, telling herself:

> You have to be sorry for them. You have to put yourself in the shoes of that person and ask yourself, what if it were me? I was fighting for my family and their lives, I would do it for other people in the hospital, so I knew I could do it for my family. (2014)

Indeed, her family survived. That experience prompted Fatu to pass her tacit knowledge gained from caring for Ebola patients to other desperate families (Dixon, 2014). During this time of personal and national crisis, she exhibited social capacity by collaborating with Liberia's ministry of health to teach others how to use everyday resources when there was nothing else available. Fatu enrolled in the nursing program at Emory University in the United States, becoming a nursing student whose experience in medicine was beyond what any textbook could teach her (Cohen & Bonifield, 2015). Fatu is an example of a leader whose proximal leadership attributes where quickly developed in response to a deadly situation.

National Public Radio (Kelto, 2014) profiled South African social entrepreneur Sizwe Nzima: "the guy who delivers HIV medicine on his bicycle." Sizwe saw a need in his community that impacted the quality of life for his friends and family. In his community in Cape Town, South Africa, access to healthcare came with long waiting periods, long lines, and multiple trips to the clinic to get medicine for his grandparents (2014). Waiting at a clinic, he came up with the idea of starting a medication delivery service that would deliver medicine to people's homes instead of them waiting in line for hours at local clinics and pharmacies (2014).

The idea was not novel because other companies in Cape Town were already delivering medication to homes. But for Sizwe and his community, their location made a difference in being a part of this service. There were no companies delivering medication to low-income townships such as his where "most people lived in wooden or metal shacks" without street addresses and could not be found without "local knowledge" (Kelto, 2014). This dire need was the catalyst for Iyeza Express: Nzima's bicycle powered medicine delivery service. Nzima's business, an illustration of his problem-solving capacity and tacit knowledge, began with just two clients and expanded to 930 clients and a staff of six after a few years (2014). Not only was Nzima delivering HIV medication, but he also delivered medication for diabetes and epilepsy (2014). His services are offered at a low cost due to "support from a local business incubation program that provides free office space, including a telephone, computer, and wifi" (2014).

Nzima is an example of African innovation and problem solving. He saw a need for his community and stepped into a leadership role that improved the quality of life for members of his community. His social capacity allowed him to recognize the layered impact that long wait times for medication had on his community. Waiting in line for medication was not just an inconvenience, it was an issue of livelihood. Spending time in a clinic waiting for prescriptions meant "lost income and lost opportunities to look for work" (Kelto, 2014). Further consequences were that many people did not go to get their medication and thus failed to manage their treatment plans for conditions such as HIV (2014).

Lastly, Arthur Zang was named one of Forbes Africa's 30 under 30 in the best young entrepreneur category (Nsehe, 2012). This designation was for good reason. In Arthur's home country of Cameroon, just 30 heart surgeons, primarily located in the country's two economic hubs (Douala and Yaoundé), provide service for 20 million people (Nsehe, 2012). This means that in addition to a lack of specialists, people in rural areas were competing with residents in urban areas for access to the surgeons, and also lacked the financial resources to make the trip to get help. As with many African countries, access to healthcare is a cause for concern. Using his engineering knowledge and problem-solving capacity, Zang invented the Cardiopad: a touchscreen tablet that facilitates wireless transfer of examination results performed in rural locations to trained specialists in Doula or Yaoundé who can interpret them and recommend courses of action (2012). The Cardiopad shows the ingenuity of Zang in its capacity as a life-saving device. It is the first of its kind in Cameroon and Africa with a reliability rate as high as 97.5%, which has been validated by the local scientific community (2012). Zang used his social capacity and tacit knowledge of the needs in his country to create a solution for a social justice issue, enhancing the lives of patients in remote areas and removing barriers and burdens to the healthcare system.

Discussion and Conclusion

In support of the call for an inclusive Leadership Studies, I presented African examples of leadership as being compatible with and contributing to Western theories and approaches of leadership. As a Leadership Studies educator, I urge a curriculum-wide conscious awareness of what is going on in other parts of the world, using knowledge of people, places, and events to reimagine the discipline as culturally and socially responsive. The advice from Den Hartog and Dickson (2004, p. 277) is well taken: "We should not take for granted that models and theories developed in one place will work similarly in another." However Bangura's (2011) proposition of commonalities across continents provides a framework in which to explore trait theory highlighting African exemplars.

The achievements of the three individuals presented in this chapter show exceptional qualities extolled by trait theory in its general form. However, their location in the world, that is, Africa, prevents their exceptionalism from being included in the current Western centric forms of trait theory and leadership inquiry at large. Their achievements should show that Africa can and does contribute to Leadership Studies and is primed to advance the discipline alongside other worldviews. Perhaps instead of only citing Napoleon Bonaparte, George Washington, and Winston Churchill as examples of trait theory, those interested in Leadership Studies (as students and educators) will also begin to cite young people in Africa who are changing the lives of people around them as examples of desirable leadership traits that inspire across borders.

The task for students, scholars, and educators of leadership is to normalize leadership acts in Africa and any part of the global south as part of the Leadership Studies canon rather than human-interest stories in the media. In consuming these leadership experiences as human-interest pieces, members of the leadership studies discipline become complicit in denying space and voice to leadership acts that occur outside of the West. In this case, the designation of human-interest stories functions as a sort of orientalism (Said, 1993) that denies the addition of African experiences as important contributors to leadership theories simply because Africa has long been framed through a single story: known as a singular and deficient place marred by poverty, death, and war (Adichie, 2009). Normalizing leadership from

African experiences means disrupting the well-worn single story of Africa and the notion of the West as the gatekeeper of Leadership Studies by intentionally seeking and naming leadership experiences as just that, rather than human-interest stories. That is a small but important start.

The next step is to challenge scholars, educators, and practitioners to intentionally use examples from non-Western contexts in their work. Normalizing leadership from non-Western contexts might mean using the examples of Fatu, Arthur, and Sizwe alongside examples of Steve Jobs, Bill Gates, Sheryl Sandberg. The examples are available. There is no shortage of leadership in Africa. It is a matter of those interested in leadership to be intentional in learning about experiences beyond their own social and intellectual spaces. As a leadership educator with cultural and social ties to Africa, I want to see my part of the world included in Leadership Studies. To contribute in the effort of disrupting the Western bias of Leadership Studies, I intentionally use non-Western examples to demonstrate leadership theories in my teaching. My goal is to guide learners and colleagues to think about the vastness and nuance of leadership, rejecting the confines of a Western gaze.

To address the leadership needs and demands of a global society, Leadership Studies education must become inclusive. Being inclusive means availing the discipline and curriculum to various cultural and social contexts. With demonstrated growth in population, market share, and leadership impact, those who study and teach leadership cannot ignore the contributions of Africa and the global south at large. To do so is missing out on valuable leadership lessons and knowledge that will provide more resources in answering the call to and for inclusive leadership knowledge.

Discussion Questions

1. What factors have contributed to the Western bias in Leadership Studies, and in leadership theories?
2. Whose responsibility is it to ensure that experiences and voices from the Global South (nations in Africa, Latin America, the Middle East, and parts of South Asia) are featured and included in the study and theorization of leadership?

3. Can leadership theories, in their current forms, be used to examine leadership in non-Western contexts? What are the implications of this particular pursuit?

References

Adichie, C. (2009). The danger of a single story. Retrieved from http://www.ted.com

Alvez, J., Manz, C., & Butterfield, D. (2005). Developing leadership theory in Asia. *International Journal of Leadership Studies*, 1(1), 3–27.

Asante, M. (1987). *Afrocentricity*. Trenton, NJ: Africa World Press.

Ayman, R., & Adams, S. (2012). Contingencies, context, situation, and leadership. In D. Day & J. Antonakis (Eds.), *The nature of leadership* (pp. 218–255). Thousand Oaks, CA: Sage.

Bangura, A. (2011). Africancentric methodology. In A. Bangura (Ed.), *African-centered research methodologies: From ancient times to the present* (pp. 149–164). San Diego, CA: Cognella.

Baron, R. A., & Byrne, D. (1987). *Social psychology: Understanding human interaction*. Boston, MA: Allyn & Bacon.

Bass, B. M. (1995). Concepts of leadership: The beginning. In J. T. Wren (Ed.), *The leaders companion: Insights on leadership through the ages* (pp. 49–52). New York, NY: The Free Press.

Bolden, R., & Kirk, P. (2009). African leadership: Surfacing new understandings through leadership development. *International Journal of Cross Cultural Management*, 9(1), 69–86.

Chin, J., & Trimble, J. (2015). *Diversity and leadership*. Thousand Oaks, CA: Sage.

Cohen, E., & Bonifield, J. (2015, April 10). Fearless Ebola nurse trains at Emory University. CNN. Retrieved from http://cnn.com

Conger, J., & Kanungo, R. (1998). *Charismatic leadership in organizations*. Thousand Oaks, CA: Sage.

Cooper, H. (2014). Liberian president pleads with Obama for assistance in combating Ebola. *The New York Times*. Retrieved from http://nytimes.com

Daft, R., & Lane, P. (2015). *The leadership experience*. Stamford, CT: Cengage Learning.

Day, D., & Antonakis, J. (2012). *The nature of leadership* (2nd ed.). Thousand Oaks, CA: Sage.

Den Hartog, D., & Dickson, M. (2012). Leadership and culture. In D. Day & J. Antonakis (Eds.), *The nature of leadership* (pp. 393–436). Thousand Oaks, CA: Sage.

Den Hartog, D. N., & Dickson, M. W. (2004). Leadership and culture. In J. Antonakis, A. T. Cianciolo, & R. J. Sternberg (Eds.), *The nature of leadership* (pp. 249–278). Thousand Oaks, CA: Sage.

Dixon, R. (2014). In Liberia, one woman's singular fight against Ebola. *Los Angeles Times*. Retrieved from http://www.latimes.com

Garfield, J., & Van Norden, B. (2016). If Philosophy won't diversify, let's call it what it really is. *The New York Times*. Retrieved from http://www.nytimes.com

Ghiselli, E. E., & Brown, C. W. (1955). *Personnel and industrial psychology*. Columbus, OH: McGraw-Hill.

Glynn, M. A., & DeJordy, R. (2010). Leadership through an organizational behavior lens: A look at the last half-century of research. In N. Nohria & R. Khurana (Eds.), *Handbook of leadership and practice* (pp. 119–158). Boston, MA: Harvard Business Press.

GuramatunhuCooper, N. (2014). The warrior and the wizard: The leadership styles of Josiah Tongogara and Robert Mugabe during Zimbabwe's liberation struggle. In B. Jallow (Ed.), *Leadership in colonial Africa: Disruption of traditional frameworks and patterns* (pp. 101–113). London: Palgrave McMillan.

House, R. J. (2004). *Culture, leadership, and organizations: The GLOBE study of 62 societies*. Thousand Oaks, CA: Sage.

Jallow, B. (2014). *Leadership in colonial Africa: Disruption of traditional frameworks and patterns*. London: Palgrave McMillan.

Kelto, A. (2014, November 17). The guy who delivers HIV medicine on his bicycle. *National Public Radio*. Retrieved from http://www.npr.org

Kirkpatrick, S., & Locke, E. (1991). Leadership: Do traits matter? *Academy of Management Executive*, 5(2), 48–60.

Mann, R. D. (1959). A review of the relationship between personality and performance in small groups. *Psychological Bulletin*, 56, 241–270.

Masango, M. (2002). Leadership in the African context. *Verbum et Ecclesia*, 23(3), 707–718.

Muchinsky, P. M. (1983). *Psychology applied to work*. Homewood, IL: Dorsey Press.

Northouse, P. (2015). *Leadership: Theory and practice*. Thousand Oaks, CA: Sage.

Nsehe, M. (2012, February 9). Young African invents touch screen medical tablet. *Forbes*. Retrieved from http://www.forbes.com

Nwosu, P. (2009). Understanding Africans' conceptualizations of intercultural competence. In D. Deardoff (Ed.), *The SAGE handbook of intercultural competence* (pp. 158–178). Thousand Oaks, CA: Sage.

Perkins, A. (2009). Global leadership: A theoretical framework. *Journal of Leadership Education*, 8(2), 72–87.

Rowe, W. G., & Guerrero, L. (2016). *Cases in leadership* (4th ed.). Thousand Oaks, CA: Sage.

Said, E. (1993). *Culture and imperialism*. New York, NY: Vintage.

Schedlitzki, D., & Edwards, G. (2014). Studying leadership: Traditional and critical *approaches*. Thousand Oaks, CA: Sage.

Secord, P. F., & Backman, C. W. (1974). *Social psychology*. New York, NY: McGraw-Hill.

Sikes, P. (2010). The ethics of writing life histories and narratives in educational research. In A. Bathmaker & P. Hartnett (Eds.), *Exploring learning, identity and power through life history and narrative research* (pp. 11–24). New York, NY: Routledge.

Stogdill, R. (1948). Personal factors associated with leadership: A survey of the literature. *Journal of Psychology, 25,* 35–71.

Stogdill, R. (1974). *Handbook of leadership: A survey of theory and research.* New York, NY: Free Press.

Wren, J. (1995). *The leaders companion: Insights on leadership through the ages.* New York, NY: The Free Press.

Yukl, G. (2010). *Leadership in organizations.* (7th ed.). Upper Saddle River, NJ: Prentice Hall.

Zaccaro, S. J. (2007). Trait-based perspectives of leadership. *American Psychologist, 62*(1), 6–16.

Zaccaro, S. J., Kemp, C., & Bader, P. (2004). Leader traits and attributes. In J. Antonakis, A. T. Cianciolo, & R. J. Sternberg (Eds.), *The nature of leadership* (pp. 101–124). Thousand Oaks, CA: Sage.

2

The Case for an Indigenous Collectivist Mindset

Kem Gambrell

Introduction

A new understanding of collectivism is forwarded that expands the one proposed by Hofstede and Triandis. The intent of this work is to introduce the new version of collectivism, termed "Indigenous Collectivism Mindset" (ICM) and describe its implications. Using indigenous research methodologies, findings from interviews with Native Americans provides evidence towards an indigenous understanding of collectivism that cannot be explained through a mainstream, dominant cultural paradigm. Implications of how this collectivist worldview impacts leadership and leadership development are also given. Identifying nondominant societal paradigms presents the opportunity for deeper understanding of the complexities that leadership and leadership development encompass. Historically researchers have approached leadership from a Western paradigm operating from the belief that leadership conveys a central authority that controls not only the use of rewards and sanctions, but also the power over others. This proposed different worldview, ICM, challenges this dominant perspective and presents the possibility that there are not unequivocally successful leadership behaviors, but rather different ways of being and understanding relationships.

The chapter presents a nondominant cultural understanding of collectivism, and how operating in this paradigm can advance leadership scholarship.

The Case for an Indigenous Collectivism Mindset

In Africa one of the highest forms of praise that can be given to someone is in reference towards how they treat their fellow human beings – *umbuntu* (Tutu, 2007). This philosophy involves seeing others worth, and "in doing so my humanity is recognized and becomes inextricably bound to theirs" (Tutu, 2007, p. 3). Historically, however, leadership scholars have adopted a framework that has perpetuated an "other" mentality (Smith, 1999). This perspective has focused on the leader or the follower, and negated the multifaceted cultural complexities that are now only just being unraveled. Newer approaches have become conscious of this disparity, and are just beginning to reflect the complex nature of leadership (Uhl-Bien & Marion, 2009). "Understanding the different ways people make sense of their worlds, or, in other words, making sense of the wildly different psychological worlds different people inhabit" may be the key to the complex nature of leadership (Garvey Berger, 2005, p. 21).

Consequently, grasping how individuals understand the world around them, and how these views impact relationships, leadership and cultural responsiveness become more important (Garvey Berger, 2005). One challenge is understanding the degree to which people in a society are integrated into groups, how meaning is made within these groups, and where precedence of personal and group needs lies (Hofstede, 2001). Traversing these juxtapositional individualistic and collectivist worldviews is nothing short of complicated. However, the advantage of practicing a collectivist approach, specifically one similar to that traditionally practiced by indigenous peoples, may be one way to better address some of society's biggest challenges.

Indigenous people's ontology and how their cultural ways of being impact relationship with self, others, and the environment around them has shown a number of advantages over a more individualistic perspective (Wilson, 2008). Some of these advantages include higher organizational cooperation, shared leadership, and commitment (Brougham & Haar, 2013). For many Alaska Indian/Native Americans[1] (AI/NA), this "collectivist" axiology creates a worldview that many from a Western individualism schema can scarcely grasp, if understand at all. Given the complex challenges organizations and their leadership face, consideration of a more "Indigenous Collectivism Mindset" (ICM) might be the additional method needed for better success in working with others.

The intent of this chapter is to propose an indigenous variation on Hofstede's cultural dimension *collectivism* described as people who are "we-conscious." For collectivist oriented people, "identity is based on the social system to which they belong...collectivistic cultures are high-context communication cultures... in collectivistic cultures it is necessary to first build a relationship and trust between parties" (de Mooij & Hofstede, 2010, p. 89). While a great deal of research has been conducted on the differences between individualistic and collectivist cultures (e.g., see Hofstede and Triandis' work), little consideration has been given to under-represented groups such as AI/NA's, and even less thought exploring how this may be an advantageous leadership ability.

This adaptation of collectivism incorporates a holistic understanding of relationship as described from an AI/NA understanding (Gambrell & Fritz, 2011; White Hat, 2012), and was explored using indigenous research methodologies (Smith, 1999; Wilson, 2008). Relationship is defined as being associated in such a way that "encompasses many different communities" (Smith, 1999, p. 128) with concern and attention to connection and communal well-being as well as connectedness to place and earth (Treuer, 2012; Wilson, 2008). It is with this ICM that individuals and communities may be able to more effectively solve complex challenges.

Background

Racial and ethnic identity is complicated owing in part because human beings have multiple, intertwined identities that influence one another in ways that are not fully understood (Geertz, 2000).

---

[1]For this chapter, Native American, Alaskan Indian, and indigenous all refer to peoples that originally inhabited North America.

"The enactment and nature of an individual's multiple identities can be influenced by an individual's *lifeways* and *thoughtways*, which may be at variance with conventional expectations and proscriptions" (Trimble, 2003, p. 320). Thus, salience of identity is a life long journey and integrates different components of self-definition and self-understanding. Identity is learning one's place in the world with both humility and strength. It is, in the words of Vine Deloria (1999), "accepting the responsibility to be a contributing member of a society" (p. 139).

For many indigenous people, fundamental to the construct of ethnic identity development is one's understanding, commitment to, and sense of connection with his or her culture and community (Smith, 1999; Wilson, 2008). Sadly, literature addressing ethnic identity development among Native populations is sparse relative to other groups (Markstrom, Whitesell, & Galliher, 2011). What is understood is that many AI/NA people carry a very strong sense of ethnic identity, bound closely to community, shaping how they view and operate within the world around them (Smith, 1999; Wilson, 2008).

CULTURE

Hofstede, Hofstede, and Minkov (2010) comment that every individual "person carries within him or herself patterns of thinking, feeling, and potential acting that were learned throughout their lifetime" (pp. 2−3). This paradigm constitutes an ability to adapt to the external environment presenting a social group's shared strategy for survival, and entailing aspects of beliefs, ways of life, and mental schema's that form how individuals understand the world (Triandis, 1995). As such, a cultural perspective is developed and handed down through generations. Although culture has been defined as "civilization" or "refinement of the mind," on a superficial level, on a deeper level it is illustrated as "the collective programming of the mind that distinguishes the members of one group or category of people from others" (Hofstede et al., 2010, p. 4). Hence, identification to a group and its ethos is a learned phenomenon constructed from the systems formed and shared by those who live within the same social environment.

COLLECTIVISM

One such way of navigating the world is through "shared operating procedures and unstated assumptions," or how individuals relate to the groups and community in which they reside (Triandis, 2001, p. 908). One cultural dimension, individualism-collectivism, may be the most significant among cultures (Triandis, 1996). Studies have revealed variations in cognitive, emotional, and social functioning between individualist and collectivist societies, demonstrating the applicability of this framework in cross-cultural comparisons (Kim, Triandis, Kagitçibasi, Choi, & Yoon, 1994). Greenfield (2000) calls this component the "deep structure" of cultural differences. While there are innumerable cultural variances, this one seems to be significant both historically and cross-culturally. This sense of self involves distinct behaviors that are constructed from an individual's independent or interdependent worldviews (Hossain, Skurky, Joe, & Hunt, 2011). How people relate to others is influenced by the psychology that they are familiar with. These constructs have been discussed in many contexts in the social sciences (e.g., Kim, Sharkey & Singelis, 1994; Triandis, 1995) and predictions of behavioral patterns from these constructs have been successful (Wheeler, Reis, & Bond, 1989).

Bergmüller (2013) characterized collectivism as the "assumption that individuals are dependent on one another... and places great emphasis on the needs and values of the group rather than those of the individual" (p. 184). Triandis (1995) discussed collectivism as a "social pattern consisting of closely linked individuals who see themselves as parts of one or more collectives; are primarily motivated by the norms of and duties imposed by those collectives" (p. 2). In direct contrast to individualism, in a collectivistic culture, the self is considered interdependent with others. Thus, the group's goals take priority over individuals', and norms, obligations, and duties guide one's behavior. Furthermore, communal relationships are commonplace, and people attempt to resolve interpersonal problems in a way that will maintain relationships, accord, and harmony (Kim et al., 1994; Triandis & Gelfand, 1998).

Although the utility of these constructs is indisputable, there is still the tendency to conceive of individualism and collectivism in pure dichotomies. However, Triandis and Gelfand (1998) contend that individualism and collectivism may be defined by four attributes and different varieties of these constructs. These include: (1) Kind of self; (2) Fiske orientation; (3) Rokeach orientation; and (4) Political system (Triandis, 1995, p. 51). For example, the Fiske orientation posits that "people must use some kind of models of and for social relations to guide their own social initiatives and to understand and respond appropriately to the social actions of others" (Rossides, 1998, p. 270). In comparison, the Rokeach orientation focuses on human values described as "enduring prescriptive or proscriptive beliefs that a specific mode of conduct (instrumental value) or end state of existence (terminal value) is preferred to another mode of conduct or end state" (Mayton, Ball-Rokeach, & Loges, 1994, p. 3). Thus, Triandis and Gelfand (1998) posit that there are as many varieties of collectivism as there are collectivist cultures. To better explain these nuances, Triandis (1995) developed four types of cultural categories:

- Horizontal Individualist (HI), where people want to be unique and do "their own thing."
- Vertical Individualist (VI), where people want to do their own thing and also to be "the best."
- Horizontal Collectivism (HC), where people merge their selves with their in-groups.
- Vertical Collectivism (VC), where people submit to the authorities of the in-group and are willing to sacrifice themselves for their in-group.

These subcategories of individualism and collectivism begin to explain the idiosyncrasies of these dimensions, however, Triandis (1995) suggests that there are many more opportunities for clarification.

Indigenous Collectivism Construct

While authors discuss the differences between individualism and collectivism within dominant cultures, limited attention has been given to the AI/NA worldview. Consideration of the advantages of this paradigm for leadership purposes is also underdeveloped. To begin the discourse regarding this limitation, four aspects of a proposed model are given. This model is not intended to represent all AI/NA perspectives, rather, to begin the dialogue around ICM, forward understanding of collectivism, and present opportunities for future research. This model evolved from qualitative research findings of AI/NA peoples. These four aspects of ICM are: *We Are All Related, Through Stories, Everybody has a Gift,* and *Involve the People.* By adopting this paradigm and moving toward a communal oriented leadership perspective, progress

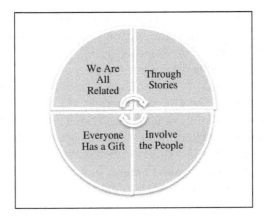

Fig. 1. Indigenous Collectivism Mindset.

may be made toward deeper connectedness with community. As Smith (1999) comments, "connectedness positions individuals in sets of relationships with other people and with the environment...to be connected is to be whole" (p. 148) (Fig. 1).

WE ARE ALL RELATED

As Chilisa (2012) states "postcolonial indigenous worldviews lean toward communities' togetherness, cooperation and connectedness" (p. 204). Historically however, this tendency towards community, extended family groups, or clans runs deep in the AI/NA cultural way of life. As an example, for the Lakota,[2] to understand the larger cultural underpinning of this relational philosophy, one needs to appreciate the *tiošpaye* system. In Lakota (Lakota Sioux[3]) *tiošpaye* means extended family, and in using this system, everyone is addressed by a relative term, such as aunt, brother, or cousin (White Hat, 2012). "We are all related" is a communal worldview that illustrates the idea of connection, and with this understanding, the treatment of others is based on cultural virtues of relationship (White Hat, 2012, pp. 87–88). In

---

[2]The Lakȟóta people are known as the prairie dwellers or plains tribes, who originally inhabited the upper Mississippi Region in present-day Minnesota, Wisconsin, Iowa, and the Dakotas.
[3]The word Sioux is derived from the Ojibwe term *Naadowesiwag* (a species of snake), and was a code word for "enemy." For the Lakota, Dakota, and Nakota, who are part of the Očeti Šakowiŋ (Seven Council Fires), this term is frowned upon (see Treuer, 2012; White Hat, 1999).

many AI/NA groups there is a strong connection to extended family and identity. Language, customs, traditions, and ceremony all reflect this tenet that everyone is related, and that placing others before oneself is the central focus.

This foundational ICM paradigm drives not just the actions of the individuals, but also how people are "chosen" for their various roles within the community. As one example, when considering skills and attitudes as employees or co-workers, priority is placed on how the individual interacts with others. The belief being that some things can be taught, but respect, love, and compassion towards others is foundational (White Hat, 2012).

For individuals with the ICM perspective, it is not necessary to focus on the self first, because one will be taken care of by the collective. This philosophy is evident in several contexts. For instance, in the Lakota *inipi* ceremony[4] and Sundance ceremony[5] (e.g., see White Hat, 2012), people are taught to pray for others first and foremost, and then only at the end, if need be, does one pray for themselves (White Hat, 2012). Historically, there are many examples of AI/NA working collectively to take care of the needs of the community (Deloria, 1944/1998; Eastman, 1918/1991; White Hat, 2012). Elders never go hungry, and children are never left alone or unsupervised, because everyone is a "relative," and being in community means that everybody has their basic needs taken care of (White Hat, 2012).

This philosophy of being interconnected extends to all living things – mother earth and all of her creatures, and has encouraged a more collectivist perspective by many AI/NA groups (Deloria, 2001). In addition, this worldview is interconnected to place and often embedded in the language. This is depicted in the Lakota statement of *"mitakuye oyas'iŋ,"* or "we are all related" with which prayers are always concluded (White Hat, 1999, 2012). "All *mitakuyepi* – are my relatives, that's how we address them when we pray," this includes all of creation, including the animal kingdom and mother earth (White Hat, 2012, p. 16). Additionally, other tribes such as the Anishinaabe[6] hold a worldview that is grounded in place and rooted in their language (Treuer, 2012).

---

[4]Purification or sweat lodge.
[5]Mails (1979) calls it a "celebration of thanksgiving, growth, prayer, and sacrifice" (p. 2).
[6]Also referred to as Ojibwe or Chippewa.

This construct of *We Are All Related* is a fundamental ICM virtue and is typified throughout history in a number of stories (e.g., Marshall, 2001; Mohatt & Eagle Elk, 2000; Young Bear & Theisz, 1994). Part of this philosophy includes understanding that care for others must be done genuinely and with a good heart. Because of this ICM worldview, there is a belief that there is always enough so that one's needs will be taken care of through relationships (Gambrell, 2009; Marshall, 2001; Mohatt & Eagle Elk, 2000).

THROUGH THE STORIES

Having a strong sense of traditions is not just something that ICM possesses or does, but involves deeper cultural norms that have been passed down for generations. While many authors have discussed traditional AI/NA virtues such as compassion, humility, respect, and generosity (Marshall, 2001; White Hat, 2013), these morals form a way of life that they are persistently following. For ICM individuals, these ideologies are vital to how collective understanding and its related behaviors are passed from one generation to the next. Through these teachings, not only does one learn how to operate in the world as part of community, but a strong sense of belonging is also developed (Marshall, 2001; Standing Bear, 1993; White Hat, 2012).

Generosity

Many AI/NA teachings discuss the fundamental aspects of morals such as generosity when in relationship with others. For example, many ICM practice the "potlatch" or "*wopila*" (to give thanks) tradition, which is marked by the distribution of gifts or property to demonstrate the honoring of an individual or event (Gambrell, 2009, p. 151). Not just is this an opportunity to honor a person, but it is the chance to practice gratitude as well. This act often shows the quality and meaning behind the gift; "I have made quilts for people and told them that the quilt was made especially for them. The next day they gave it away in front of me, and I had to realize they thought that much of it to give it to someone else." This way of life has been well-documented, and follows closely with a number of cultural traditions including honoring relatives, naming ceremonies, and the making of a relative (Deloria, 1944/1998; Marshall, 2001; Standing Bear, 1993).

Respect

As mentioned, respect is one of the core ICM virtues. While there are different words in AI/NA languages for respecting one's self and others, Marshall (2001) uses the Lakota word *wawoohola*, to hold someone in high esteem. To have *wawoohola* for another is described as respecting each other as human beings. ICM-oriented individuals' describe this as observing someone's heart through their actions and words. Therefore, if someone is being respectful, they don't manipulate others, instead, ICM's are truthful, compassionate, and forgiving. For ICM this means literally not just teaching or talking about one's values, but living them on a daily basis.

Humility

Called *uŋšiićiyapi* in Lakota, being humble translates into being modest and unpretentious in English, but actually is closer in meaning to "lowering yourself" (Marshall, 2001). This concept is often observed in the ICM as those individuals that "don't talk themselves up." Thus, if one consistently does good work, then others will recognize and honor the individual. There are a number of AI/NA historical stories of showing humility, and are accounts of great deeds which are told by others rather than the individual. One example in particular is that of Crazy Horse. In his writings, Marshall (2004) describes Crazy Horse as a painfully shy and unassuming individual who didn't seek out leadership roles and responsibilities. As Marshall (2001) recounts:

> The burden of humility is light because a truly humble person divests himself or herself of the need for recognition. The burden of arrogance, on the other hand, grows heavier day by day. In sharing the journey of life, travel with the humble person on the quiet path. (Marshall, 2001, p. 19)

As Marshall (2001) observes, "for the Lakota, a humble person is aware of other people and other things, while an arrogant, boastful person is only aware of him or herself" (p. 12).

Forgiveness and Compassion

To operate in a close community requires the essential practice of forgiveness and compassion. As White Hat (2012) observes, "there are all kinds of people...but like everybody else, we've had them from the beginning of time. Things like jealousy, frustration, cheating and anger — they've always been a part of every human being" (p. 87). Holding forgiveness and compassion, especially during times of personal hardship and struggle was also found to be deeply rooted in the ICM philosophy. As Echo-Hawk (2013) writes, "experts trace modern forgiveness practices derived from our religious scruples to our earliest ancestors who were more likely to survive if they responded with compassion to a friend in need or helped, and not hurt, a stranger suffering" (p. 260). One of the more prevailing examples of forgiveness and compassion was demonstrated in this story: a "medicine man's nephew had been murdered. He (the medicine man) went to the people that murdered the nephew and smoked the pipe with them and forgave them. He didn't condemn them, he showed them compassion" (Gambrell, 2009, p. 67). Additionally, ICM individuals understand compassion and forgiveness in dealing with others as a balance between the head and heart:

> We need the ability to have compassion for one another, genuine compassion, because as a child we were taught that we cannot think with our minds only. The Creator, *Tuŋkaśila*, gave us a mind to think, but that cannot work alone. They also gave us a heart to think with. So we must align our hearts and minds as one. (Gambrell, 2009, p. 68)

As Echo-Hawk (2013) reflected, "In the Indigenous World, the healing of wounds, forgiveness, peacemaking, and reconciliation are found in tribal ceremonies aimed at restoring balance in the world" (p. 261).

Thus, an ICM individual is one who applies these traditional teachings and practices. Furthermore, ICM people have the ability to pass on these sacred stories. This is part of the cultural identity that is embedded within the ICM (Marshall, 2001; Mohatt & Eagle Elk, 2000; Standing Bear, 1993; Young Bear & Theisz, 1994).

INVOLVE THE PEOPLE

Another aspect of ICM comprises involving and engaging people holistically. Successful ICM leaders consistently solicit input and engage others prior to making major decisions. This practice of a shared leadership has been observed at a much deeper level than individualistic oriented mindsets. One example involves the difficult decision a tribal leader had to make for the betterment of the community:

> He had to make a decision to let some individuals go because it was interfering with ceremony. So we went into the sweat lodge and he asked all of us. He had thought a lot about it, but he wanted us to be there and say how we felt. We were with him when he was making all of these decisions. He is the leader, yet he needs someone to support him. (Gambrell, 2009, p. 76)

This ICM practice has been documented in a number of settings including AI/NA councils coming together to discuss important community/tribal issues (Deloria, 1999; Marshall, 2004; Utley, 1994). A part of this process included asking the elders for guidance and involving the children because it was felt that they have a stronger connection with spirit and community (Gambrell, 2009). Consequently, decisions were made methodically with the input from a number of sources. While today in ICM the practice may lean towards consulting more with close advisors, there is a strong urge from ICM individuals for current leaders to work at involving a wide array of others regarding community decision making.

Being Diplomatic

An additional ability is to skillfully engage with others in the community. Findings showed that it is critical for all community members to handle difficult situations in such a manner as not to denigrate anyone involved. As one example, a leader trying to deal with an individual who was deeply impacting the well-being of the community was shared:

> He [the leader] had probably made all of the decisions, and didn't share them until the right time when we were in the sweat lodge when everybody was about to pray. In ceremony like that, it's a good way of confronting the person. In ceremony you can't get angry, cuss and stuff like that. Your mind is clear and that's when you are open to whatever. He didn't get angry or anything, he was just calm and clear and just put his concerns out there with his normal voice. (Gambrell, 2009, p. 77)

Another example of diplomacy is the tradition of talking circles. Such practices are intended to bring people together in an informal setting to talk about the needs of the community

(Marshall, 2004; Paul, 1997; Utley, 1994). Diplomacy is also seen as a key aspect in working with others and getting people to listen to each other's perceptions. This skill is very similar to the persuasive manner in which historical AI/NA leaders were portrayed as great orators, having had the capability to influence others through their use of patience, persistence, and logical arguments. Leaders such as Sitting Bull, Red Cloud, and others were alleged to have sat in council for days, listening to multiple perspectives before making decisions (Marshall, 2004; Paul, 1997; Utley, 1994).

EVERYONE HAS A GIFT

The last major premise observed in the ICM is the principle that all beings have unique talents to contribute towards community. For those practicing an ICM, identifying people who understand their skills and abilities and who are willing to look for ways to contribute are highly desired. Furthermore, people secure in their own gifts are also more willing to see and celebrate others contributions as well (Marshall, 2004; Paul, 1997; Standing Bear, 1993; Utley, 1994). This is a somewhat stark contrast to the more competitive nature of individualism (Triandis, 1995).

The willingness to attend and contribute to community is imperative to the ICM paradigm. For these individuals, the ability to see the potential and talents in others, and work towards developing those strengths begins with attending community gatherings. To understand others' strengths requires insight, patience, and a nurturing attitude. It also necessitates a patient teaching and mentoring mentality for which many AI/NA are known (Gambrell, 2009; Marshall, 2001). Learning from observation is an AI/NA custom that is still observed and practiced today (Reyhner, 1992, 2015).

Furthermore, ICM individuals understand that to learn and develop skills and knowledge individuals need to be able to practice (Marshall, 2004; White Hat, 2012). Often this is demonstrated by delegating tasks, with the insight that people can and will fail — this is part of the learning. For example, "I've worked with a lot of good teachers, and they gave me responsibility... I struggled and I failed sometimes, and I made mistakes. I just learned through practice" (Gambrell, 2009, pp. 80–81). As Deloria (1944/1998) observed, historically young children were often paired with relatives to help teach them a special skill that parents felt they had an aptitude for. Often in AI/NA traditions, individuals are taught to see talents and abilities in others, which they may not see in themselves (Crow Dog & Erdoes, 1995; Eastman, 1918/1991; White Hat, 2013).

Advantages to an Indigenous Collectivism Mindset

While there are some similarities to the collectivism model proposed by Triandis (1995) and others, the ICM offers several differences that may help leaders, and leadership dynamics. First, as proposed by Triandis (1995), horizontal collectivism "includes a sense of social cohesion and of oneness with the in-group. Vertical includes a sense of serving the ingroup and sacrificing for the benefit of the ingroup and doing one's duty" (p. 44). For those practicing a ICM paradigm, the sense of social cohesion runs beyond the ingroup, and as such, while there are moments of forgoing personal needs this is not viewed as sacrifice, but rather a deeper sense of relationship (see Table 1).

The second dissimilarity is in Fiske's (1990, 1992) orientation of social behavior. Fiske identified four basic forms of social behaviors that "occur in every culture, although the specific manifestation of the form can vary across cultures" (as cited in Triandis, 1995, p. 48). These main ideas are: sharing, hierarchy, equity, and proportionality (Fiske, 1990, 1992). According to the

Table 1.   Comparison of Vertical Collectivism, Horizontal Collectivism, and Indigenous Collectivism Mindset.

	Vertical Collectivism	Horizontal Collectivism	Indigenous Collectivism Mindset (ICM)
Kind of self	Interdependent	Interdependent	Interdependent
	Different from others	Same as others	Related to others
Fiske orientation	Communal sharing	Communal sharing	Communal sharing
	Authority ranking	Equality matching	Equality matching
Rokeach orientation	Low equality	High equality	High equality
	Low freedom	Low freedom	Medium freedom
Political system	Communalism	Communal living	Democratic communalism

premise, the first idea is discussed in terms of communal sharing, and entails sharing resources according to need, without regard to how much or how often (Triandis, 1995).

A third incongruity from the Triandis model is the perspective of collectivist oriented groups. Fiske (1990, 1992) proposes that resources are either shared by some degree of equity, or by hierarchical methods – depending upon who is ranked higher than another. For ICM, however, there is a third way practiced; elders and children are provided for first, then, everyone else is given what they need. Thus, while elders and children may get something initially, all get an equal portion (Eastman, 1991; White Hat, 2012). This third incongruity is from Rokeach's (1973) reflection on values. As Triandis (1995) reflects, "Rokeach's typology is strictly 'Western'" and he goes on to generalize how Vertical Collectivism and Individualism, Horizontal Collectivism and Individualism (see Table 1) may correspond (p. 50). Thus, in coming from a Western paradigm, one might argue that Rokeach's typology may be prejudicial. This opinion seemingly stems from a more Westernized mindset that negates the opportunity for the shared and collective leadership style often observed in many AI/NA traditions (see Marshall, 2004; Petrillo, 2007; White Hat, 2012). Therefore, this new model of ICM may provide a deeper understanding towards being in relationship with others, and how to do so with more of a collectivist verses individualistic worldview.

Conclusion

As Chin and Trimble (2015) observe, many leaders from a collective-oriented mindset show a high regard for humility, dignity, and a reverence to the group's well-being. Furthermore, these collective-oriented people perpetuate a deep reverence for compassion, forgiveness, and a diplomatic temperament that creates an energy of inclusion and group flourishing. As has been posit, this newer paradigm of ICM may help leaders better address the challenges that societies are facing. Desmond Tutu (2007) recounted:

> If we could but recognize our common humanity, that we belong together, that our destinies are bound up in one another's, that we can be free only together, that we can survive only together, that we can be human only together, then a glorious world would come into being where all of us lived harmoniously together as members of one family, the human family. (p. 36)

Individuals who have a cultivated perspective, taking others needs into consideration are often more advanced in constructive development, emotional intelligence, and other successful relational attributes (Gambrell, Matkin, & Burbach, 2011). Consideration of paradigms that are more collectivist oriented such as ICM may be an approach to encourage others to operate in a less self-oriented, individualistic manner. Future leadership exploration should consider not just using nonmainstream research methodologies, but also deliberate how alternative collectivist models may influence how people lead and relate to others, and operate in community.

Discussion Questions

1. Based on the reading, what are the advantages of having an indigenous collectivist mindset?
2. What are ways you believe an ICM can be learned?
3. How does the ICM model differ from other collectivist models?

References

Brougham, D., & Haar, J. M. (2013). Collectivism, cultural identity and employee mental health: A study of New Zealand Māori. *Social Indicators Research*, *114*, 1143–1160. doi: 10.1007/s11205-012-0194-6

Chin, J. L., & Trimble, J. E. (2015). *Diversity and leadership*. Los Angeles, CA: Sage.

Crow Dog, L., & Erdoes, R. (1995). *Crow Dog. Four generations of Sioux medicine men*. New York, NY: Harper Perennial.

de Mooij, M., & Hofstede, G. (2010). The Hofstede model: Applications to global branding and advertising strategy and research. *International Journal of Advertising*, *29*(1), 85–110.

Deloria, E. C. (1944/1998). *Speaking of Indians*. Lincoln, NE: University of Nebraska Press.

Deloria, Jr., V. (1999). *Spirit and reason*. Golden, CO: Fulcrum Resources.

Deloria, Jr., V., & Wildcat, D. R. (2001). *Power and place: Indian education in America*. Golden, CO: Fulcrum Resources.

Eastman, C. A. (1918/1991). *Indian heroes & great chieftains*. Lincoln, NE: University of Nebraska Press.

Eastman, C. A. (1991). *Indian boyhood*. Lincoln, NE: University of Nebraska Press.

Echo-Hawk, W. R. (2013). *In the light of justice: The rise of human rights in Native American and the UN Declaration on the rights of indigenous peoples.* Golden, CO: Fulcrum.

Fiske, A. P. (1990). *Structures of social life: The four elementary forms of human relations.* New York, NY: Free Press.

Fiske, A. P. (1992). The four elementary forms of sociality: Framework for a unified theory of social relations. *Psychological Review, 99,* 689–723.

Gambrell, K. M. (2009). *Healers and helpers, unifying the people. A qualitative study of Lakota leadership* (Doctoral dissertation). Retrieved from DigitalCommons@University of Nebraska-Lincoln. (http://digitalcommons.unl.edu/aglecdiss/17/)

Gambrell, K. M., & Fritz, S. M. (2011). Healers and helpers, unifying the people. A qualitative study of Lakota leadership. *Journal of Leadership and Organizational Studies, 19*(3), 315–325.

Gambrell, K. M., Matkin, G. S., & Burbach, M. E. (2011). Cultivating leadership: The need for renovating models to higher epistemic cognition. *Journal of Leadership and Organizational Studies, 18*(3), 308–319. doi: 10.1177/1548051811404895

Garvey Berger, J. (2005). Living postmodern: The complex balance of worldview and developmental capacity. *ReVision, 27*(4), 20–27.

Geertz, C. (2000). *Available light: Anthropological reflections on philosophical topics.* Princeton, NJ: Princeton University Press.

Greenfield, P. (2000). Three approaches to the psychology of culture: Where do they come from? Where can they go? *Asian Journal of Social Psychology, 3,* 223–240.

Hofstede, G. H. (2001). *Culture's consequences: Comparing values, behaviors, institutions, and organizations across nations* (2nd ed.). Thousand Oaks, CA: Sage.

Hofstede, G. H., Hofstede, G. J., & Minkov, M. (2010). *Cultures and organizations: Software of the mind* (3rd ed.). New York, NY: McGraw-Hill.

Hossain, Z., Skurky, T., Joe, J., & Hunt, T. (2011). The sense of collectivism and individualism among husbands and wives in traditional and bi-cultural Navajo families on the Navajo Reservation. *Journal of Comparative Family Studies, 42*(4), 543–562.

Kim, M., Sharkey, W. F., & Singelis, T. M. (1994). Relationship between individuals self construal's and perceived importance of interactive constraints. *International Journal of Intercultural Relations, 18,* 117–140.

Kim, U., Triandis, H. C., Kagitçibasi, C., Choi, S. C., & Yoon, G. (1994). *Individualism and collectivism: Theory, method, and applications.* Thousand Oaks, CA: Sage.

Mails, T. E. (1979). *Fools Crow.* Garden City, NY: Doubleday.

Markstrom, C. A., Whitesell, N., & Galliher, R. V. (2011). Ethnic identity and mental health among American Indian/Alaska native adolescents. In M. C. Sarche, P. Spicer, P. Farrell, & H. E. Fitzgerald (Eds.), *American Indian children and mental health: Development, context, prevention, and treatment.* Santa Barbara, CA: ABC-CLIO.

Marshall III, J. M. (2001). *The Lakota way: Stories and lessons for living*. New York, NY: Penguin Press.

Marshall III, J. M. (2004). *The journey of Crazy Horse: A Lakota history*. New York, NY: The Penguin Group.

Mayton, D. M., Ball-Rokeach, S. J., & Loges, W. E. (1994). Human values and social issues: An introduction. *Journal of Social Issues, 50*(4), 1–8.

Mohatt, G., & Eagle Elk, J. (2000). *The price of a gift. A Lakota healer's story*. Lincoln, NE: University of Nebraska Press.

Paul, R. E. (Ed.). (1997). *Autobiography of Red Cloud*. Helena: Montana Historical Press.

Petrillo, L. (2007). *Being Lakota: Identity and tradition on Pine Ridge Reservation*. Lincoln, NE: University of Nebraska Press.

Pickering, K. A. (2000). *Lakota culture, world economy*. Lincoln, NE: University of Nebraska Press.

Reyhner, J. (1992). *Teaching American Indian students*. Norman, OK: University of Oklahoma Press.

Reyhner, J. (2015). *Teaching Indigenous students: Honoring place, community and culture*. Norman, OK: University of Oklahoma Press.

Rokeach, M. (1973). *The nature of human values*. New York, NY: Basic Books.

Rossides, D. W. (1998). *Social theory, Its origins, history, and contemporary relevance*. Dix Hills, NY: General Hall, Inc. Publishers.

Smith, L. T. (1999). *Decolonizing methodologies: Research and indigenous peoples*. London: Zed Books.

Standing Bear, L. (1993). At last I kill a buffalo. In P. Riley (Ed.). *Growing up Native American* (pp. 107–114). New York, NY: Bill Adler Books.

Treuer, A. (2012). *Everything you wanted to know about Indians but were afraid to ask*. St. Paul, MN: Minnesota Historical Society.

Triandis, H. C. (1995). *Individualism & collectivism*. Boulder, CO: Westview Press.

Triandis, H. C. (1996).The psychological measurement of cultural syndromes. *American Psychologist, 51*, 407–415.

Triandis, H. C. (2001). Individualism- collectivism and personality. *Journal of Personality, 69*(6), 907–924.

Triandis, H. C., & Gelfand, M. (1998). Converging measurement of horizontal and vertical individualism and collectivism. *Journal of Personality and Social Psychology, 74*, 118–128.

Trimble, J. E. (2003). An inquiry into the measurement of ethnic and racial identity. In Carter, R. (Ed.). *Handbook of racial-cultural psychology and counseling: Theory and research (Vol. 1)*. New York, NY: Wiley.

Tutu, D. (2007). *Believe: The words and inspirations of Desmond Tutu*. Boulder, CO: Blue Mountain Press.

Uhl-Bien, M., & Marion, R. (2009). Complexity leadership in bureaucratic forms of organizing: A meso model. *The Leadership Quarterly, 20*(4), 631–650.

Utley, R. M. (1994). *The lance and the shield: The life and times of Sitting Bull.* New York, NY: Random House.

Wheeler, L., Reis, H. T., & Bond, M. H. (1989). Collectivism-individualism in everyday social life: The middle kingdom and the melting pot. *Journal of Personality and Social Psychology, 57*(1), 79–86.

White Hat Sr., A. (1999). *Reading and writing the Lakota language.* Salt Lake City, UT: The University of Utah Press.

White Hat Sr., A. (2012). *Life's journey: Zuya, oral teachings from Rosebud.* Salt Lake City, UT: The University of Utah Press.

Wilson, S. (2008). *Research is ceremony. Indigenous research methods.* Black Point, BC: Fernwood Publishing.

Young Bear, S., & Theisz, R. D. (1994). *Standing in the light. A Lakota way of seeing.* Lincoln, NE: University of Nebraska Press.

3

Cross-cultural Dimensions of Personal Stories in Communicating Authentic Leadership

Marco Aponte-Moreno and
Konstantinos Koulouris

Introduction

The purpose of this chapter is to shed light on the cross-cultural dimensions of telling personal stories to communicate authentic leadership. The chapter is based on findings from a research study conducted among aspiring leaders from 41 countries. The study consists of three stages: (1) analysis of responses from an interview aimed at testing whether authenticity is considered an important leadership trait across cultures, (2) analysis of findings from two experiments aimed at measuring the effectiveness of telling personal stories to communicate authentic leadership across cultures, and (3) discussion of written reflections by English and Chinese respondents on the role of personal stories to communicate authentic leadership in their respective cultures.

Authenticity seems to be an attribute that is valued across cultures. However, when trying to communicate authentically in leadership contexts, personal stories are likely to be effective in some cultures (such as the Anglo cluster as defined by the

GLOBE project) but not in others (such as the Confucian Asia cluster).

Limitations include the lack of demographic diversity in the samples (all respondents were students in their twenties), bias related to the fact that respondents in the survey measuring the importance of authenticity were applicants for a graduate program, the small sample for the analysis of reflections, the fact that non-native speakers of English were surveyed in English instead of their mother tongues, and the fact that the two cultural clusters used (Anglo and Confucian Asian) are overgeneralizations (ethnic glosses) of different ethnocultural groups.

The study provides a good foundation to understand why telling personal stories as a way to communicate authentic leadership may be effective in English-speaking cultures but not in other cultures.

Primary goal of the chapter: The main purpose of this chapter is to shed light on the cross-cultural dimensions of telling personal stories to communicate authentic leadership.

Secondary goals of the chapter: The chapter has two secondary goals:

1. To challenge the belief that telling personal stories to communicate authenticity in leadership contexts is universal;
2. To show that personal stories can work to communicate authentic leadership within the Anglo cultural cluster (as defined by the GLOBE project) but not in the Confucian Asia cultural cluster.

Telling personal stories has often been considered an effective way to communicate authentic leadership. In recent years, it has become an essential component in the teaching of leadership communication skills. Stories are said to provide followers with relevant information that allows them to connect with their leaders' authenticity (Shamir & Eilam, 2005).

However, the universality of storytelling in communicating authentic leadership is now being questioned. In her article "The Authenticity Paradox," Ibarra (2015) discusses the role of cultural factors in authentic leadership. She argues that telling a personal story as a way to communicate authenticity is not universal, but rather "very American." She describes it as a model "based on ideals such as self-disclosure, humility, and individualistic triumph over adversity," and suggests that it might not necessarily apply in other cultural contexts.

Ibarra's hypothesis seems consistent with Chin and Trimble's conclusions (2014) that culture and ethnicity play a key role in the way followers perceive leaders, and with Owusu-Bempah's (2013) findings, which show the existence of country-specific attributes related to authentic leadership. Ibarra's premise also corresponds well with Meyer's (2015) work, which argues that cultural differences can prevent a leader from communicating a message since people from different cultures operate under significantly different mental and perception frameworks.

The purpose of this chapter is to test Ibarra's hypothesis in order to shed light on the cross-cultural dimensions of telling personal stories to communicate authentic leadership. The chapter is based on findings from a research study conducted among aspiring leaders (graduate business students in a UK university) from 41 countries. The study consists of three stages: (1) analysis of responses from an interview aimed at testing whether authenticity is considered an important leadership trait across cultures, (2) analysis of findings from two experiments aimed at measuring the effectiveness of telling personal stories to communicate authentic leadership across cultures, and (3) discussion of written reflections by English and Chinese respondents on the role of personal stories to communicate authentic leadership in their respective cultures.

We will start our chapter with a review of the concepts of culture, cultural differences, and authentic leadership. We will then describe and analyze each of the three stages of our study: online interview, experiments, and reflections. Finally, we will provide our conclusions, including a brief discussion of the limitations of the study.

Culture and Cultural Differences

Culture has been defined in many different ways. In his book *Primitive Culture*, British anthropologist Tylor (1871), considered the father of cultural anthropology, argues that culture consists of the habits and skills that human beings acquire in the societies where they live. They include values, beliefs, knowledge, law, art, etc. American anthropologists Kroeber and Kluckhohn (1952) argue that culture consists of behavioral patterns acquired and communicated by symbols, which form the specific achievements of human groups. For them, traditional ideas and their attached values constitute the core of culture.

More recently, Ember and Ember (2010) defined culture as a group of learned ideas and behaviors acquired within a given society, including values, beliefs, attitudes, and ideals. The elements that form a culture vary individually depending on factors such as geographic region, religious beliefs, or professional background, to name a few. Thus, an individual can relate to more than one culture (Bauer & Erdogan, 2010). As human beings, we acknowledge that our culture is different from others when we realize that other people share common beliefs and behaviors that differ from our own (Ember & Ember, 2010).

Culture is not static but rather dynamic and complex; it changes constantly (Moua, 2010). Cultures can vary within a single nation. There are variations across regions, social classes, and time. In Spain, for example, we observe marked cultural differences between regions, which often have different languages (such as Catalan in Catalonia, and Basque in the Basque Country). In fact, the deep cultural ways of perceiving and interpreting the world can even vary within regions where people speak the same language (House et al., 2004).

Moreover, like in any other country, important cultural differences between social classes can be observed. Upper-class Spaniards show different values and beliefs from their working-class counterparts. This is interesting as often people from the same social class in different countries may have more in common from a cultural perspective than people from different social classes in the same country. For example, Indian elites may have more in common with UK elites (as a result of their past colonial relation, equivalent access to education, and similar socioeconomic backgrounds) than with the Indian working classes. In this respect, the British economist Maddison (1970) argues that British colonial rule brought major cultural changes at the top but few significant ones at the bottom.

Finally, cultures differ in time. The culture shared by Spaniards during Francisco Franco's military dictatorship from 1939 until 1975 was certainly not the same culture that exists in Spain today. The openness of Spanish society toward the world, allowing the arrival of new waves of ideas and people, brought changes in the culture. Beliefs, attitudes, and values toward, for instance, individual freedoms and gender roles, became much more open. As argued by American sociologist Landis (1935) in his seminal work on cultural change in the mining towns of Minnesota's Mesabi Iron Range, social changes and economic transformations contribute to changes in cultural patterns. This is also evidenced in Margaret Mead's seminal book *Growing Up in New Guinea* (1930), where she documents her encounters with the indigenous people of the Manus Province of Papua New Guinea, before they were in contact with missionaries and other influences from the West. However, it is important to note that culture tends to evolve rather slowly, especially among traditional societies which have been isolated from the modern world (Kroeber, 1917).

Despite the dynamic nature of cultures, scholars have attempted to create models to categorize and explain cultural differences. There have been many propositions, but Geert Hofstede's cross-cultural study is probably the most influential. Between 1967 and 1973, Hofstede distributed a survey, which measured and analyzed cultural differences among 116,000 IBM employees from 76 countries. This resulted in his Cultural Dimension Theory, which provides a framework of cross-cultural differences (Hofstede, 1980).

Hofstede proposes four dimensions intended to compare national cultures: uncertainty avoidance (level of avoiding and accepting uncertainty), power distance (strength of social hierarchy), individualism versus collectivism (orientation to individual or collective values), and masculinity versus femininity (task orientation vs. person-orientation). Later, in 2008, Hofstede added two additional dimensions: indulgence versus restraint (free vs. suppressed gratification of human needs related to enjoying life), and monumentalism versus flexible humility (pride and self-consistency vs. flexibility and humility) (Prosser, 2009).

Although Hofstede's framework provides a quick way to compare countries, it treats cultures as if they were static and homogenous, ignoring the fact that they change over time, and across social classes and regions. Also, by surveying the employees of a single company (IBM), the study fails to get a representative sample of the cultural system of an entire nation (Olie, 1995). Moreover, considering the complexity of cultures, it can be argued that six dimensions cannot possibly provide adequate data about cultural differences.

Between 1994 and 1997, House et al. (2004) from the Wharton School led the GLOBE (Global Leadership and Organizational Behavior Effectiveness Research) project. Based on Hofstede's findings, and collecting data from 17,300 managers in 951 organizations from 62 countries, his research team identified ten cultural clusters: Anglo cultures, Arab cultures, Confucian Asia, Eastern Europe, Germanic Europe, Latin

America, Latin Europe, Nordic Europe, Southern Asia, and Sub-Sahara Africa.

In addition, GLOBE identified nine cultural attributes, of which the first six were derived from Hofstede's cultural dimensions: uncertainty avoidance, power distance, societal collectivism, in-group collectivism, gender egalitarianism, assertiveness, future orientation, performance orientation, and humane orientation.

Finally, GLOBE identified six major global leadership behaviors, according to which the framework describes the leadership profile of each cultural cluster: Charismatic/value based, team oriented, self-protective, participative, human orientated, and autonomous. According to the study, only two leadership behaviors are valued in every culture: charismatic/value based behavior, which involves the communication of values and vision, and team-oriented behavior.

Although in this study we acknowledge that cultures within countries are not static and homogenous, we assume that there are certain characteristics that distinguish large cultural clusters from each other. This assumption is based on the findings from the GLOBE project, which is undoubtedly the most comprehensive leadership study ever conducted. Thus, in order to determine whether telling personal stories contributes to communicate authentic leadership across cultures, we will compare respondents' answers from two distinctive cultural clusters: the Anglo cluster and the Confucian Asia cluster.

Authentic Leadership

Authenticity can be defined as the quality of being real, genuine, or true. It is a trait that is attributed to both objects and people. We often refer to an object as authentic when it is not an imitation. On the other hand, people are said to be authentic when their words and actions reflect who they really are. According to the Canadian philosopher Taylor (1991), real authenticity should involve an openness to something larger than oneself. He cites benevolence and respect toward others and the environment as key elements in authenticity. Professors Goffee and Jones (2005) argue that authenticity is a quality that must be attributed by others. Leaders cannot be authentic on their own; they need to be perceived as authentic by their followers.

Authentic leadership is a relatively new area of research in leadership studies. It originated in the 1990s as a response to an increasing demand for a more responsible, ethical, and truthful leadership approach (Ladkin & Taylor, 2010). Its emergence is often linked to the many scandals of corruption and mismanagement that have taken place in recent years in corporations, banks, and the public sector. Some of the most famous cases include Enron, Lehman Brothers, and Volkswagen, where leaders and managers had intentionally deceived customers and investors. Bhindi and Duignan (1997) in their article *Leadership for a New Century* discussed how ethics within organizations can be restored by focusing on authenticity in leadership. They argue that this focus would make organizations more productive and better places to work.

The concept of authentic leadership can be understood in three different ways (Northouse, 2010). According to the first one, known as the intrapersonal perspective, the essence of authentic leadership is solely determined by leaders' own life experiences (which has made them truly who they are as individuals). This suggests that authentic leadership can be seen as a fixed trait.

The second viewpoint, known as the relational perspective, assumes that authentic leadership does not depend exclusively on leaders, but that it is created in the relations that develop between leaders and followers. In this respect, authentic leadership is seen as an interactive process determined by the leader–followers' relationship.

The third approach, known as the developmental perspective, is the one that has received more attention in leadership studies, and the one that we adopt in our study. According to this viewpoint, authentic leadership can be developed and nurtured over time. Defining life events such as career changes, accidents, illnesses, or other unexpected life changes often act as triggers to authentic leadership. Positive psychological capabilities and deep moral values can originate and be developed further from those critical life events, which at the same time will foster authentic leadership (Avolio & Gardner, 2005).

According to the developmental perspective, authentic leadership can be defined as a pattern of leadership behavior characterized by strong self-awareness, deep moral perspective, good capacity to process information with balance, and strong ability to be transparent when working with followers. This pattern of leadership behavior is strongly influenced by both the leader's positive psychological capabilities and by his or her deep moral values.

In this study we will look at whether personal stories help leaders, irrespective of their culture, to communicate authentic leadership. That is to say, to communicate according to their true selves (showing self-awareness, deep moral perspective, strong capacity to process information with balance, and transparency).

The Study

The study used both quantitative and qualitative data to answer three subquestions. These subquestions led to the answer of the main research question: whether or not telling personal stories when communicating authentic leadership is a universal tool. The subquestions were as follows:

1. Is authenticity an important trait in leadership across cultures?
2. Do personal stories contribute (or not) to communicate authentic leadership in two very distinctive cultural clusters: the Anglo cluster and the Confucian Asia cluster?
3. Why personal stories contribute (or do not) to communicate authentic leadership in these two cultural clusters?

Authenticity as an Important Trait in Leadership across Cultures

In order to determine whether or not authenticity is a leadership trait valued across cultures, a group of 90 respondents from 23 countries (from Asia, the Americas, Europe, Africa, and the Middle East) was asked two questions through an online video interview: (a) In your opinion, what are the characteristics of a good leader? And (b) rate how important authenticity is in leadership?

The nonprobability sample consisted of students drawn from a pool of applicants for a graduate program in management at a UK university. The data were collected from November 2015 through March 2016. Nine batches of ten applicants each were considered throughout the period. All students were in their early twenties. There were 48 females and 42 males. The two questions were part of a set of five questions aimed at measuring the applicant's suitability for the program. All respondents spoke English either as a first or second language.

Respondents received a link via e-mail, through a private company called WePow. When opening the link, a practice question appeared on the screen. This question was aimed at making respondents familiar with the process. After completion of the practice question, the actual interview started. For each question, respondents had 45 seconds to structure their answer and two minutes to answer the question.

The first question considered in the study ("In your opinion, what are the characteristics of a good leader?") was the fourth question in the application online interview. The second question in the study ("On a scale from 1 to 5, where 1 corresponds to 'strongly disagree' and 5 corresponds to 'strongly agree', rate how important authenticity is in leadership?") was the fifth question in the interview.

Using a Likert scale may cause cultural bias. For instance, Asian respondents tend not to choose extreme categories such as 1 or 5 (Trimble & Vaughn, 2013). Nevertheless, most respondents in our sample have lived and studied for many years in Western countries (during their undergraduate studies) where the scale is widely used. Thus, we assume that Asian students are likely to choose extreme categories (such as a 1 or a 5) just like their Western counterparts.

The purpose of asking students first to list the characteristics of a good leader was to see whether or not they thought of authenticity (or a related term) as an important leadership feature. The related terms included being truthful, genuine, honest, responsible, etc. The first three questions in the application online interview were not considered in the study; they related to academic preparation and personal interests and were only used as criteria for admission to the master's program in management.

Out of the 90 students surveyed in our study, only 13 listed authenticity or a related term as an important characteristic of a good leader. This represents only 14% of the sample. The most mentioned traits were "effective communicator," "good listener," "motivational," and "persuasive." However, when asked to rate the importance of authenticity (on a scale from 1 to 5, in which 1 corresponds to "strongly disagree" and 5 corresponds to "strongly agree"), the average response was 4.4, from a total of 88 respondents as two did not answer the question. It is important to note that in some cultures (including Chinese and other Asian cultures), authenticity is embedded in the concept of leadership. One cannot exist without the other (Whitehead & Brown, 2011). Therefore, respondents from these cultures might have not thought of authenticity as a separate characteristic when they answered the question.

The above results suggest that although authenticity does not immediately come to mind as one of the most important traits in leadership, the majority of respondents (regardless of their cultures) consider it very important when asked about it directly. In fact, half of respondents strongly agreed with the statement. These findings seem consistent with results from the GLOBE project, which indicate that charismatic/value based leadership, which stresses high standards, integrity, vision, and values, is an important leadership behavior in all ten cultural clusters identified in the project.

Despite these findings, we cannot overlook the fact that in the first question of our study, only 14% of respondents listed authenticity or a related term as an important characteristic of a good leader. Considering that authenticity and leadership are tied together in some cultures, and given the study's respondents were in a university interview situation, it is not surprising that they rated authenticity so highly when asked directly about its importance. Therefore, although the study suggests that authenticity is important in leadership across cultures (based on the 90 responses from students from 23 countries), its results are not conclusive.

Personal Stories in Communicating Authentic Leadership

Do personal stories contribute, or not, to communicate authentic leadership in all cultures? In order to shed light on this question, we conducted two experiments with a total of 190 respondents from 41 countries, and focused on two distinctive cultural clusters from the GLOBE project: the Anglo cluster and the Confucian Asia cluster.

In the first experiment, we asked 60 respondents to watch a one-minute video of a man delivering a persuasive speech on the importance of drinking sufficient amounts of water. The random sample was divided into two groups of 30 respondents each. The speech watched by the first group (called here "the story speech") included a personal story, in which the speaker spoke about the medical complications he suffered after not drinking enough water. The speech watched by the second group (called here "the standard speech") did not include a personal story. Instead, the speaker gave a compilation of facts about the importance of drinking sufficient amounts of water. Both speeches were delivered by the same person (who was a professional actor), they dealt with the importance of drinking water, and they lasted approximately one minute. Both groups were asked to rate (on a scale from 1 to 5, in which 1 corresponds to "not at all" and 5 to "very much,") how engaging, persuasive, authentic, and inspiring the person in the video was.

Out of the 60 respondents, we focused on two very distinctive cultural clusters as defined in the GLOBE project: the Anglo cluster (which includes native English speakers from Australia, Canada, Ireland, New Zealand, South Africa, the United States, and the United Kingdom); and the Confucian Asia cluster (which includes respondents from China, Hong Kong, Japan, Singapore, South Korea, and Vietnam). This reduced the sample for the first experiment to 32 respondents (19 from the Anglo cluster vs. 13 from the Confucian Asia cluster). All respondents spoke English. In both experiments, average responses were calculated for each category and cluster group. Moreover, t-tests were run to determine whether or not differences were significant at a 0.05 level.

Out of the 19 respondents from the Anglo cluster, 9 respondents (8 from the United Kingdom and 1 from the United States) watched the standard speech, while 10 respondents (7 from the United Kingdom, 2 from the United States, and 1 from Australia) watched the story one. Out of the 13 respondents from the Confucian cluster, 5 respondents (all from China) watched the standard speech, while 8 respondents (5 from China, 2 from Taiwan, and 1 from Korea) watched the story one.

Results of the first experiment indicate that personal stories do contribute to communicate authenticity in the Anglo cluster. This is evidenced by an average response of 4.20 for those respondents who watched the story speech, compared to an average response of only 2.89 for those who watched the standard one.

Results of the first experiment for the Confucian Asia cluster, on the other hand, indicate that personal stories do not contribute to communicate authenticity. This is evidenced by an average response of 3.38 for those respondents who watched the story speech, compared to an average of 3.80 for respondents who watched the standard one. It is interesting to note that among the

Confucian Asia cluster, the perceived authenticity diminishes with the personal story. In the last section of this chapter, we will be looking at possible reasons for this.

The experiment also measured three additional elements: how engaging, persuasive, and inspiring the speaker was. These three elements were selected considering how important they are in the leadership process. Our results show that respondents in the Anglo cluster also found the story speech more engaging (4.30) than the standard one (3.0), more persuasive (4.40 vs. 3.11), and more inspiring (3.60 vs. 2.22). Similarly, respondents in the Confucian Asia cluster found the story speech less engaging (3.63) than the standard one (3.80), less persuasive (4.60 vs. 3.75), and less inspiring (3.0 vs. 3.4). Tables 1a and 1b summarize the results of the first experiment.

In sum, the personal story contributes to communicate authenticity, engage, persuade, and inspire among the Anglo cluster, but not among the Confucian Asia cluster. This suggests that

Table 1a.   Experiment 1 — Average Responses per Category for the Anglo Cluster.

	Authentic	Engaging	Persuading	Inspiring
Story ($n = 10$)	4.20	4.30	4.40	3.60
No story ($n = 9$)	2.89	3.00	3.11	2.22
t-value	3.32925	3.10672	2.63349	2.76768
p-value	0.001986	0.003206	0.008714	0.006585
Significant difference at 0.05	Yes	Yes	Yes	Yes

Table 1b.   Experiment 1 — Average Responses per Category for the Confucian Asia Cluster.

	Authentic	Engaging	Persuading	Inspiring
Story ($n = 8$)	3.38	3.63	3.75	3.00
No story ($n = 5$)	3.80	3.80	4.60	3.40
t-value	−0.83948	−0.47087	−1.67654	−0.86726
p-value	0.209536	0.323466	0.060894	0.202161
Significant difference at 0.05	No	No	No	No

telling a personal story can be an effective tool in leadership communication in some cultures but not in others.

A second experiment was conducted to see whether the findings would be similar if instead of watching the video, respondents listened to it. This was done to account for any potential bias that could arise from visual cues such as gestures, body language, and ethnicity of the speaker.

The second experiment consisted of 130 respondents. A total of 80 listened to the story speech while 50 listened to the standard one. As in the first experiment, both groups were asked to rate (on a scale from 1 to 5 in which 1 corresponds to "not at all" and 5 to "very much") how engaging, persuasive, authentic, and inspiring the person delivering the speech was. Out of the 130 respondents, we focused again on the Anglo cluster and the Confucian Asia cluster. This reduced the sample for the second experiment to 85 respondents (16 from the Anglo cluster vs. 69 from the Confucian Asia cluster).

Out of the 16 respondents from the Anglo cluster, 10 respondents (all from the United Kingdom) listened to the standard speech, while 6 respondents (all from the United Kingdom) listened to the story one. On the other hand, out of the 69 respondents from the Confucian Asia cluster, 22 respondents (18 from China, 3 from Hong Kong, and 1 from Taiwan) listened to the standard speech, while 47 respondents (43 from China, 3 from Taiwan, and 1 from Korea) listened to the story one.

Results of the second experiment (in which respondents listened to the speeches instead of watching them) do not confirm that personal stories contribute to communicate authenticity in the Anglo cluster. The difference between the average response of 3.5 for those respondents who listened to the story speech, compared to the average response of only 2.8 for those who listened to the standard one, is not statistically significant at a 0.05 level. However, when it comes to the other three elements measured in the second experiment (being engaging, persuasive, and inspiring), respondents in the Anglo cluster did find the speaker in the story speech more engaging (3.83) than in the standard one (2.60), more persuasive (3.50 vs. 2.50), and more inspiring (2.50 vs. 1.70). In all three cases, the differences are statistically significant at a 0.05 level.

Results of the second experiment confirm that personal stories do not contribute to communicate authenticity in the Confucian Asia cluster. This is evidenced by an average response of 3.34 for those respondents who listened to the story speech, compared to an average of 3.35 for those who listened to the standard one.

Also, for these respondents, the personal story did not make any significant difference when it comes to the level of engagement and persuasiveness. However, they found the story speech more inspiring (2.68) than the standard one (2.18). Although it is not clear why there is a significant difference in the level of inspiration for the second experiment, the low scores in this category (below 2.68 for both groups in both clusters) show that no group found the speeches particularly inspirational. Tables 2a and 2b summarize the results of the second experiment.

In conclusion, both experiments show that telling a personal story as a way to communicate authenticity does not work in all cultures. Our findings indicate that it is an effective way to communicate authentic leadership in the Anglo cluster but not in the Confucian Asia one. Also, our findings suggest that the visual element associated with telling a story is important to communicate authenticity. This is evidenced by the fact that respondents in the Anglo cluster found that authenticity was conveyed when they watched the speech but not when they listened to it. In order to shed light on the possible reasons behind these findings, the next section will analyze written reflections of respondents from both

Table 2a.   Experiment 2 — Average Responses per Category for the Anglo Cluster.

	Authentic	Engaging	Persuading	Inspiring
Story ($n = 6$)	3.50	3.83	3.50	2.50
No story ($n = 10$)	2.80	2.60	2.50	1.70
t-value	1.22653	2.28962	2.29129	1.87083
p-value	0.120114	0.019046	0.018986	0.041209
Significant difference at 0.05	No	Yes	Yes	Yes

Table 2b.   Experiment 2 — Average Responses per Category for the Confucian Asia Cluster.

	Authentic	Engaging	Persuading	Inspiring
Story ($n = 47$)	3.34	3.26	3.02	2.68
No story ($n = 22$)	3.50	3.14	3.18	2.18
t-value	−0.72942	0.50583	−0.66651	2.0502
p-value	0.234145	0.307318	0.253687	0.02213
Significant difference at 0.05	No	No	No	Yes

clusters on the suitability of telling personal stories to communicate authentic leadership within their cultures.

Respondents' Reflections from both the Anglo and the Confucian Asia Cluster

The purpose of this section is to provide insight on why telling personal stories as a way to communicate authentic leadership applies to the Anglo cluster but not necessarily to the Confucian Asia cluster. For this purpose, in the spring of 2016, 58 students from 18 different countries in a graduate class on leadership communication were asked to form teams, read Herminia Ibarra's article "The Authenticity Paradox," and discuss in writing whether or not the following statement from the article applies to their own cultures: "a closer look at how leaders are taught to discover and demonstrate authenticity – by telling a personal story about a hardship they have overcome, for example – reveals a model that is, in fact, very American, based on ideals such as self-disclosure, humility, and individualistic triumph over adversity."

Out of all the teams (16 in total), we focused on the four teams in which all members identified with either the Anglo cluster or the Confucian Asia cluster. This resulted in one team from the Anglo cluster (with three British members), and three teams from the Confucian Asia cluster (with three Chinese members each).

In the first part of this section, we look at the extent to which the American model of telling personal stories described by Ibarra applies to the Anglo cluster. This is based on reflections from the team of the three students from the United Kingdom. In the second part, we address the reasons why the American model does not apply to the Confucian Asia cluster. This is based on reflections from the three teams of students from China.

Compatibility of the American Model within the Anglo Cluster

Respondents in the Anglo cluster team indicate that Ibarra's statement is very relevant to British culture because of the high level of individualism that exists in the United Kingdom. "British business culture promotes individualism, placing considerable significance and emphasis on personal career development, which leads to individuals being more concerned with personal progress rather than a common goal or objective," the Anglo team stated. These students argued that this individualistic orientation makes the notion of triumph over adversity (which is often present in personal stories) both powerful and inspirational for both British leaders and followers.

According to this team, another element in the American model that applies to UK culture is humility, which they loosely define as the quality of having a modest view of one's importance. "The British tendency to self-deprecate and be humble is somewhat seen as a social norm." Nevertheless, the Anglo team argued that humility in the United Kingdom is different from the United States. According to this team of UK students, in British culture there are certain topics that are considered distasteful and vulgar, even if they are addressed with a lot of humility. These include ambition, success, and financial achievement, which in the United States do not have a negative connotation.

The team noted that, unfortunately, this provokes a general disbelief in the self, which is spread across British schools and homes, limiting generations of children. "This is often cited by the media and politicians as one of the reasons for low levels of achievement in Britain." In contrast, the team noted that in the United States, success, ambition, and financial achievement tend to be celebrated, as can be seen in interviews and speeches of American business leaders and presidential candidates.

Respondents also indicated that a certain degree of self-disclosure, as mentioned in Ibarra's article, is also valued in the United Kingdom. "In Britain, it is common to reveal aspects about personal lives to each other as friendship and trust between individuals develop." They argued that self-disclosure can build trust considering its potential to find common ground.

However, they pointed out that self-disclosure in Britain seems to have narrower limits than in the United States and should be applied with care. "Too much information too soon into a relationship is somewhat frowned upon in Britain." They argued that in the United Kingdom, leaders who reveal intimate information are likely to increase the distance between them and their followers. In addition, considering how socially segmented Britain is, leaders have to be very aware of how they might be read by different social classes. "If a leader is of upper middle class, and discloses an aspect of his or her life to a working class subordinate which they have no understanding of, the disclosure may create more distance."

In conclusion, the American model as described by Ibarra does seem to apply to the Anglo cluster, as evidenced by responses from the three British students. This is mainly due to similarities between the two cultures (United States and United Kingdom) regarding the role of individualism, humility, and self-disclosure. Thus, personal stories seem to serve as an adequate tool to convey authenticity in both cultures. This is consistent with the results of our first experiments.

Within the Anglo cluster, however, the results also indicate that there are important differences between the United States and the United Kingdom that need to be taken into consideration when crafting personal stories in a UK context. Topics showing ambition, success, and financial achievement should be handled with care in the United Kingdom as they could be interpreted as distasteful and even vulgar. Similarly, self-disclosure seems to have narrower limits in the United Kingdom than in the United States. There are certain elements in the United Kingdom, such as intimate information and class differences, which have to be carefully considered to avoid misunderstandings in a British context.

Incompatibility of the American Model within the Confucian Asia Cluster

The first point raised by respondents from the Confucian Asia cluster is related to the collective focus of Confucianism. They argued that in China, for instance, personal achievements in a story are likely to be read as individually motivated actions with the potential of affecting the harmony and social order of the group. The team stated that in Confucian Asia individual actions and opinions are not valued as much as collective ones. Group members are expected to act according to what's beneficial for everybody. In a leadership context, followers in Confucian Asia are more concerned by common achievements instead of individual ones. According to our respondents, this is the reason why "Chinese leaders are more likely to use the pronoun 'we' rather than 'I' when communicating with followers."

Moreover, one of the Confucian Asian teams argued that while the American model implies that humility can be shown through telling a story, so that a leader comes across as authentic, humility is considered in Confucian Asia a fundamental character trait, cultivated by Zen Buddhism teachings, which cannot be shown purposely. It is a state of being, a natural disposition. According to the team, trying to show humility through telling a story would contradict the very essence of being humble. In an Asian context, realizing that a leader is telling a story to show humility would be perceived as unauthentic.

Another issue cited by one of the teams deals with the premise that in Confucian Asia words are not considered as important as actions. This is evidenced, for example, by Chinese popular sayings loosely translated as "act more, talk less" and "a man should act before he speaks." As the best way to show ability and build trust is through actions rather than words, the personal story might not be the best way to communicate authentic leadership.

One team also indicated that in Confucian Asia, where leaders are expected to assert their authority at all times, self-disclosure might not be the best way to build trust. Considering the high-power distance in China, a leader's self-disclosure through a personal story can be counterproductive, as it could cause loss of respect and lack of trust. Leaders' decisions are not questioned and their vulnerabilities are not discussed. Having a leader telling a personal story is likely to result in a lack of confidence on the part of the followers.

Finally, one team pointed out that given how prevalent avoiding "loss of face" and preventing embarrassment of self and others are in Confucian Asia, it is unlikely that telling a personal story in public would be an effective way to communicate authentic leadership. They argued that, in fact, it could be counterproductive as it may cause followers to feel uncomfortable with the story.

In conclusion, telling personal stories in a Confucian Asia context is unlikely to facilitate the communication of authentic leadership. This is related to various factors, including the collective focus of Confucianism, the fundamental value attached to humility, the importance of actions over words, the high-power distance (which prevents self-disclosure on the leader's part) and the potential of personal stories to embarrass both leaders and followers. These observations are consistent with the results of our experiments, which indicate that the American model as defined by Ibarra does not apply well to the Confucian Asia cluster.

Conclusions and Limitations

Authenticity seems to be an attribute that is valued across cultures. However, when trying to communicate authentically in leadership contexts, personal stories are likely to be effective in some cultures but not others. This is evidenced by the results of our study, which show that personal stories are likely to work in countries from the Anglo cultural cluster (as defined by the GLOBE project) but not in countries from the Confucian cultural Asia cluster.

A closer look at the possible reasons behind this difference, based on a comparison between the US model (as defined by Herminia Ibarra) and the case of the United Kingdom, reveals that people from both cultures tend to react positively to basic components of personal stories such as individualism, humility, and self-disclosure. However, in the United Kingdom there seems to be certain topics including ambition, success, and financial achievement that have to be handled with care in personal stories as they can have a negative connotation. Also, social class differences and issues about intimate information need to be carefully considered in UK contexts.

When comparing the US model with the case of China (the largest country in the Confucian Asia cultural cluster), we find various possible reasons why personal stories are not likely to be effective in communicating authentic leadership in a Chinese context. They seem to be related to the collective focus of Confucianism, the consideration of humility as a fundamental value, the importance of actions over words, and the high-power distance in China.

This study presents certain limitations including the lack of demographic diversity in the samples (all respondents were students in their 20s), bias related to the fact that respondents in the survey measuring the importance of authenticity were applicants for a graduate program, the small sample for the analysis of reflections, and especially the fact that non-native speakers of English were surveyed in English instead of their mother tongues. Moreover, the two clusters used (Anglo cluster and Confucian Asian cluster) are overgeneralizations of different ethnocultural groups. They can be considered ethnic glosses that hide differences among the groups within each cluster (Trimble & Bhadra, 2013). Nevertheless, the study provides a good foundation to understand why the communication strategy of telling personal stories as a way to communicate authentic leadership may be effective in English-speaking cultures, but is not universal.

We believe that storytelling is a fundamental element in human communication. After all, stories have been used as a way of passing wisdom, knowledge, and culture for thousands of years (Lockett, 2008). However, as suggested by this study, telling personal stories in leadership situations is culture bound and cannot be systematically applied in all cultural contexts. Personal information about a leader can serve to persuade and inspire followers in some cultures, but may have a contrary effect in others. It is important to acquire a deep understanding of a culture before deciding whether to tell a personal story aimed at communicating authentic leadership.

Discussion Questions

1. Discuss why personal stories seem to contribute to communicate authentic leadership in some cultures but not in others.
2. How could personal stories, which contribute to communicate authentic leadership in one culture, be adapted so that they contribute to communicate authentic leadership in another very different culture? Discuss specific examples.
3. Based on the results of the study, discuss to which extend personal stories need to be accompanied by a visual element (nonverbal communication) in order to effectively communicate authentic leadership.
4. Discuss cases of famous leaders from different cultures who are particularly good at communicating authentic leadership by using personal stories.

References

Avolio, B., & Gardner, W. (2005). Authentic leadership development: Getting to the root of positive form of leadership. *The Leadership Quarterly, 16*, 315–338.

Bauer, T., & Erdogan, B. (2010). *Organizational behavior*. Irvington, NY: Flat World Knowledge.

Bhindi, N., & Duignan, P. (1997). Leadership for a new century: Authenticity, intentionality, spirituality and sensibility. *Educational Management and Administration, 25*(2), 117–132.

Chin, J. L., & Trimble, J. E. (2014). *Diversity and leadership*. Thousand Oaks, CA: Sage.

Ember, C. R., & Ember, M. R. (2010). *Cultural anthropology.* (13th ed.). Englewood Cliffs, NJ: Prentice-Hall.

Goffee, R., & Jones, G. (2005, December). Managing authenticity: The paradox of great leadership. Harvard Business Review, 6, 87–94.

Hofstede, G. (1980). *Culture consequences: International differences in work-related values.* London: Sage Publications.

House, R. J., & Global Leadership and Organizational Behavior Effectiveness Research Program. (2004). *Culture, leadership, and organizations: The GLOBE study of 62 societies.* Thousand Oaks, CA: Sage Publications.

Ibarra, H. (2015, January). The authenticity paradox. *Harvard Business Review.* Retrieve from https://hbr.org/2015/01/the-authenticity-paradox.

Kroeber, A. L. (1917). *Zuni kin and clan.* New York, NY: Trustees.

Kroeber, A. L., & Kluckhohn, C. (1952). *Culture: A critical review of concepts and definitions.* Cambridge, MA: The Museum.

Ladkin, D., & Taylor, S. (2010). Enacting the 'true self': Towards a theory of embodied leadership. *The Leadership Quarterly, 21*(1), 64–74.

Landis, P. (1935). Social change and social interaction as factors in cultural change. *American Journal of Sociology, 41*(1), 52–58.

Lockett, D. (2008). *The basics of storytelling.* Taipei: CETC.

Maddison, A. (1970). *Class structure and economic growth: India & Pakistan since the Moghuls.* London: Routledge.

Mead, M. (1930). *Growing up in New Guinea: A comparative study of primitive education.* New York, NY: William Morrow.

Meyer, E. (2015). *The culture map: Breaking through the invisible boundaries of global business.* New York, NY: Public Affairs.

Moua, M. (2010). *Culturally intelligent leadership.* New York, NY: Business Expert Press.

Northouse, P. (2010). *Leadership.* Thousand Oaks, CA: Sage Publications.

Olie, R. (1995). The "culture" factor in personnel and organization policies. In A. Harzing & J. Van Ruysseveldt (Eds.), *International Human Resource Management: An Integrated Approach* (pp. 124–143). The Netherlands: Sage Publications.

Owusu-Bempah, J. (2013). Interpreting authentic leadership: A cross-cultural comparison of two universities in Ghana and New Zealand. *International Journal of Social Science Research, 1*(2), 59–74.

Prosser, M. (2009). Cross-cultural communication. In *Encyclopedia of communication theory* (pp. 248–252). Thousand Oaks, CA: Sage.

Shamir, B., & Eilam, G. (2005). What's your story? A life-stories approach to authentic leadership development. *The Leadership Quarterly, 16*(3), 395–417.

Taylor, C. (1991). *The ethics of authenticity.* Cambridge, MA: Harvard University Press.

Trimble, J., & Bhadra, L. (2013). Ethnic gloss. In *The encyclopedia of cross-cultural psychology* (pp. 500–504). New York, NY: Wiley Blackwell.

Trimble, J., & Vaughn, L. (2013). Cultural measurement equivalence. In *The Encyclopedia of Cross-Cultural Psychology*. (pp. 313–319). New York, NY: Wiley Blackwell.

Tylor, E. B. (1871). *Primitive culture*. New York, NY: J. P. Putnam's Sons.

Whitehead, G., & Brown, M. (2011). Authenticity in Chinese leadership: A quantitative study comparing Western notions of authentic constructs with Chinese responses to an authenticity instrument. *International Journal of Leadership Studies*, 6(2), 162–188.

4

How the Communal Philosophies of Ubuntu in Africa and Confucius Thought in China Might Enrich Western Notions of Leadership

Rob Elkington and Elizabeth A. Tuleja

Introduction

This chapter explores two communal philosophies of being, namely Ubuntu from Southern Africa and Confucianism from China, and seeks to contrast and compare how these ways of being inform and affect leadership theory in general, and Western individualistic notions of leadership, in particular.

The notions of Ubuntu and Confucianism are discussed within their historical context and original framework. This discussion then moves to contrast these two worldviews with the Descartian notion of individualism as a worldview. Finally, the history of Western individualistic leadership is presented briefly and then contrasted with Ubuntu and Confucianism with a view to enriching and enhancing Western leadership with the communal elements of these worldviews.

Leaders from the West can learn much from both Ubuntu and Eastern practices regarding communalism, benevolence, social norms, and integrity. Just as in the image of the sculpture in Fig. 1, Ubuntu is expressed as a family, a clan, a community, united and linked together since people can only exist because of what others do to sustain them. Ubuntu leadership is expressed in caring for and serving others as the foundation of life itself – just as the family in the sculpture is gathered around in an embrace, so too is the phenomenon of Ubuntu in practice. And, perhaps Western leadership also can take a lesson from the Chinese perspective and learn that there is more to "transmitter" communication that merely gets the message across in a clear and succinct manner; rather, "receiver" communication takes into account the feelings and emotions of the speaker and seeks to understand the essence of what might be, all the while attending to the kindness, respect, and moral integrity needed to interact in a harmonious society.

While utopian societies do not exist, we can hope for a better society by gleaning the best practices from multiple cultures. Western leadership has accomplished great things, but has also caused damage through the rugged individualism that might sometimes miss the interconnectedness of our world. Would a better leadership emerge if we could leverage the best of Western leadership learning with the beauty and richness of Ubuntu and Confucianism?

The African Ubuntu philosophy of, "I am because you are," and the Chinese Confucian philosophy of benevolence and virtue hold similar characteristics for inclusive leadership, which can provide an enlightened contrast to the Western notion of individual leadership. This chapter seeks to explore these ancient traditions and the contribution of each to the Western leadership discourse.

Primary Goal:

• The goal of this chapter is to introduce two non-western perspectives of leadership.

Secondary Goals:

• To understand the principles of Ubuntu, an African practice of communal leadership, which has as its basis the notion of: "I am because you are."

- To understand the principles of Confucianism, a Chinese philosophy of communal leadership, which has as its basis three primary virtues of benevolence, propriety, and virtue.

The African Ubuntu philosophy of, "I am because you are," and the Chinese Confucian philosophy of benevolence and virtue hold similar characteristics for inclusive leadership, which can provide an enlightened contrast to the Western notion of individual leadership. This chapter seeks to explore these ancient traditions and the contribution of each to the Western leadership discourse.

It Is Neither Old nor New Rather It Is an Integration of the Many with the Few

We live in rapidly changing times, what some might term *Terra Incognitae* (Lagadec, 2009). It now appears that in the globalized arena of the 21st century, no one leader has sufficient capacity in the modern turbulent environments to successfully navigate what has come to be known as "*vu jádè* (Day & Harrison, 2007, p. 370)." This is the opposite of dèjá vu, in which leaders realize, "I've never been here before, I have no idea where I am, and I have no idea who can help me." It may be that we need a different model of leadership to empower new ways of doing leadership and being leadership. For those of us who live and work in the West we might be acquainted with the trajectory (Komives & Dugan, 2010) of Western leadership thinking from the early notions of heroic and trait leadership through to the postheroic concept of leadership as a shared commitment to a common goal, in which leaders and followers interact in a dynamic process. A number of recent "post-industrial" (Komives & Dugan, 2010) leadership theories have emerged. These theories are aware of the need for new leadership models that provide capacity to thrive in the post-market "human economy" in which "prosumers" have little interest in competing for scarcity, and would rather collaborate in the creation of abundance. This notion of collaboration for mutual beneficence is a core tenet of Ubuntu, and it fits well with this new context that suggests new ways of seeing and understanding leadership.

Scholars in the West have developed new theories such as Distributed Leadership (Bolden, 2011), Leadership as Enabling

Function (Elkington & Booysen, 2015; Elkington & Upward, 2016), and the notion of Leadership as Gardener (Dervitsiotis, 2005), to name just three of many (Bolden, 2011). These leadership theories view organizations as complex adaptive systems, living organisms, and the leadership of the system as a "collective social process emerging through the interaction of multiple actors" (Uhl-Bien, 2006). This reframing of leadership theory and leadership understanding is helpful because, as Komives & Dugan suggest:

> Consequently, reframing the paradigm shift in the evolution of leadership theory as one that occurred largely for those in dominant societal positions is critical. It allows for more accurate and appropriate attribution of sources of contemporary theory to the marginalized communities that have often felt distanced from the term. The valuing of more inclusive leadership practices has widened the social construction of leadership and enriched the capacity of people in groups working together toward more effective outcomes. These views exist in dynamic reciprocity with the changing views of organizations from closed, hierarchical entities to open, dynamic, rapidly changing, interconnected systems. (Komives & Dugan, 2010, p. 113)

We agree with this assessment, but pause to add a further level of complexity, namely the Euro-West centric nature of leadership research and leadership thinking over the last twenty-five years. The vast array of leadership thinking and leadership research is centered within the North American and European contexts. This is not a bad reality, merely a limited one! As two authors (Bell & Metz, 2011) on the relationship of Ubuntu and Confucianism highlight, it is important to step outside of the myopic and parochial focus of North American and European comparisons on leadership. It is useful and helpful to include dialogues and exchanges between leadership theories in countries and cultures outside of this traditional area of focus.

In this chapter, we present two long-standing communal ontologies, or ways of being, namely the African concept of Ubuntu and the Chinese philosophy of Confucianism. These ancient communal philosophies are important because leadership is contextual and relational (Uhl-Bien, 2006), and we may need to find new leadership modalities and motifs in the post-capitalist collaborative economy (Lutz, 2009). This new emerging collaborative context might call for a leadership model in sync with all that we have learned from Euro-West centric leadership approaches, but now further enriched by the communal philosophies of Ubuntu and Confucianism and a leadership that is relational, communal, and collaborative. To illustrate the communal leadership philosophy of Ubuntu, I (first author) have inserted a picture of a soapstone carving I purchased in May of 2016 when I traveled to South Africa to meet with South Africans who endured the Apartheid era and to experience the art of Africa insitu. Whenever we mentioned "Ubuntu," the setting came alive with expectation and connection. One such moment arose when I (Rob) purchased a beautiful sculpture of a man, a woman, and three children. I asked the artist to explain how this sculpture represented Ubuntu and leadership. This is what the artist said:

> This sculpture represents Ubuntu in both its form and its formation. You see, everyone in my village worked together to produce this sculpture to sell to you to make money for food for the village. My son helped me carve it. The women in the village polished it. The men in the village went out to find the stone to carve and we all worked together to produce this art – that is Ubuntu in the formation of this carving. But, as you look at it, the carving also expresses Ubuntu in its form. A family, united, linked together, supporting each other in love and unity, but also distinct and individual. This is true leadership, a leadership that cares for the many and serves them in community whilst also allowing individual expression.

I have inserted a picture of my "Ubuntu" sculpture in Fig. 1.

Ubuntu Leadership a New Old Way

Ubuntu simply means "I am because you are." This is very different to Descartes's notion that "I think, therefore I am." The implication of Ubuntu for leadership is profound. It calls leaders into relationship, but also into humanness, inclusiveness, justice, compassion, and a sense of interrelatedness. As Du Plooy highlights Ubuntu means that I am a person by virtue of other persons, and that I cannot be a human alone or in isolation (du Plooy, 2014).

Fig. 1.   Soapstone Carving from Mutari, Zimbabwe.

Simply put, though, Ubuntu means: "I am what I am because of who we all are" (Dreyer, 2015). The notion of Ubuntu means that there is an ontological reciprocity in our humanness, or better; when you win, I win, and when you lose I lose. Ubuntu is far more complex than this simple notion of reciprocity, but benevolent reciprocity is a good starting place in the definition of Ubuntu. In fact, when thinking of Ubuntu as a worldview six core components comprise this notion of Ubuntu, namely:

> To be umuntu (according to ubuBemba as portrayed in Shalapo Canicandala) was an intricate interplay of the 14 values that culminated in the following attributes of ubuntu: (a) collective identity, (b) mutuality or interdependence, (c) morality, (d) unity, (e) humility, and (f) generosity. These were the non-negotiable attributes of ubuntu. (Mukuka, 2013)

What must happen for leadership in the postcommercial prosumer society to be characterized by these six attributes of Ubuntu? What would this Ubuntu leadership look like? Perhaps Ubuntu leadership is epitomized in the life of Nelson Mandela, as Claire Oppenheim remarks:

> The regent and the power of democracy helped nudge Mandela towards the realm of social justice through law, but the goal and driving purpose of Mandela's spiritual path, was the pursuit of a [*sic.*] making the South African community whole again, towards an Ubuntu equilibrium. (Oppenheim, 2012)

Mandela's sense of injustice stemming from the oppression of his community, his fellow South Africans, and his understanding that leadership means that a leader must "go out into his community" (Oppenheim, 2012), in a respectful, positive, and direct fashion, gave rise to his inclusive leadership style. This inclusive, Ubuntu leadership, is powerfully articulated in Mandela's Rivonia Trial speech:

> During my lifetime I have dedicated myself to this struggle of the African people. I have fought against white domination, and I have fought against black domination. I have cherished the ideal of a democratic and free society in which all persons live together in harmony and with equal opportunities. It is an ideal, which I hope to live for and to achieve. But if needs be, it is an ideal for which I am prepared to die. (Mandela, 1995, p. 378)

Nelson Mandela's message remained the same when he emerged from prison and when he gave his victory speech after winning the first democratic election in South Africa:

> ... Free at last! Free at last! I stand before you humbled by your courage, with a heart full of love for all of you. I regard it as the highest honor to lead the ANC at this moment in our history. I am your servant ... It is not the individuals that matter, but the collective ... This is a time to heal the old wounds and build a new South Africa. (Mandela, 1995, p. 619)

It is a profound question, but what if leaders today imbibed the spirit of Ubuntu and truly believed that it is not the individuals that matter, but the collective, that a leader's role, motivated by love, is to act as a catalyst for the good of the people? To have a sense of humanness, inclusiveness, and interdependence? To see the greatest wealth and capacity not in the heroic leader, but in the richness and diversity of the people? To quote Mandela again:

> Perhaps it requires such depth of oppression to create such heights of character. My country is rich in the minerals and gems that lie beneath its soil, but I have always known that its greatest wealth is its people, finer and truer than the purest diamonds. (Mandela, 1995. p. 622)

History is replete with the reality that society rises and falls on the quality of its leaders. Western leadership research has been bound up in a largely western milieu and Cartesian (Descartian) philosophical framework of individualism. This locus of leadership research grounded in the Western tradition is not a bad focus, but in a globalized world may simply be too narrow to effectively equip 21st-century leadership for a new world of *Terra Incognitae*, and *"vu jádè."* Ubuntu calls Western leadership to see the individual, but from a different ontological vantage point, namely, as an individual in a context, in relationship, and thus as primarily human. Ubuntu helps the leader to understand that in a postheroic era, the best leadership is an inclusive, inter-relational, and communal leadership. This is more than a theory of leadership, it is given form and meaning by one of its greatest exemplars, Nelson Mandela. It was Ubuntu that moved Nelson Mandela to move out into his community as a leader, and it was Ubuntu that caused him to grasp that his community was far more than simply the people who were like him, and who supported him. Ubuntu enabled him to see that his community included the White oppressors who were, like him, caught in a fallacious system that segregated rather than unified and that it would be all of the people who must restore that unity for all, not just the majority. In the end, Nelson Mandela was a catalyst to bring about a unified South Africa, because he understood that when the oppressors and the oppressed were set free, all would be free. To put it in the language of Ubuntu, when one group wins — all win, and when one group hurts, all are hurt!

If Ubuntu calls us to a different form of leadership that is postheroic and communal, how does this compare with the ancient tradition of Confucianism? How does the communal nature of Confucianism inform Western understandings of leadership? It is to these questions that we now turn our attention.

Confucius Leadership a New Old Way

If the Descartian view of individual leadership characterizes the notion of Western philosophy and the African principle of Ubuntu focuses on the interdependency of people, the ancient Confucian philosophy of propriety (also known as correctness of living) and one's proper role in society, informs the Eastern perspective of interdependence regarding leadership.

This next section explains the Confucian approach to leadership by discussing its historical and cultural roots in contrast to the Western form of communicating and relating, and then high-lights some of the most important concepts of Confucian philoso-phy that inform current Chinese values. Two points are worth noting. First, as China has modernized over the past forty years, old values have moved beyond the narrow roles as defined by Confucius, yet Chinese society is still influenced significantly by this age-old philosophy. Second, a main challenge at present is the need for developing non-Western models of leadership the-ory. With the abundance of Western methods that place empha-sis on contrasting dichotomies for cultural comparisons (Hofstede, 1980; Javidan, House, Dorfman, Hanges, & Sully de Luque, 2006; Kulich, Prosser, & Weng, 2012) it is beneficial to study the Eastern methods that employ a dialectic approach for blending opposites rather than separating them (Gallo, 2008).

All ontological perspectives are rooted in worldviews. The word, "worldview" comes from the German word, "*weltan-schauung*," which means "world perception," and throughout the process of enculturation (how a person learns the norms of culture and assimilates these into practices and values) all humans attempt to understand their place in the world and in relation to others. We define culture as the set of shared values, beliefs, attitudes, and practices that characterizes a group of peo-ple. In the field of intercultural communication, a worldview seeks to answer four basic life questions (Hills, 2002; Kluckhohn & Strodtbeck, 1961): Who are humans? What is reality? What is truth? What values are important? German philosopher, Emmanuel Kant, is credited with first using the term to describe a person's observations or perceptions about the world (Dicks, 2012). A worldview is one's belief about life and the universe — one's core assumptions of what is and what should be.

Almost a hundred years after Descartes but in keeping with an individualistic worldview, Kant lived during the 18th century Enlightenment and framed his particular worldview around the individual's ability for rationalism and empiricism. He believed that human reasoning was what contributed to understanding the laws of human nature and morality; the autonomous self ulti-mately guided a person to do right. Kant developed the categori-cal imperative that posited you should do something because it is the right thing to do (your duty) not because you want to feel good (Donaldson, 1992). This reasoning has influenced Western thinking and behavior over the past three centuries. However, while Kant's categorical imperative was new for his day, his line of reasoning started with Greek philosophers, in the 5th and 4th centuries BCE. Understanding this Western ontological foundation will help us understand the Eastern perspective.

Western Worldview of Agency

During the time of Socrates, Plato, and Aristotle the formation of personal agency focused on the individual versus the group. Greek personal agency was based upon the uniqueness of individuals who had distinct characteristics all one's own. Personal agency gave someone a sense that they were in control of their own lives and free to act as they pleased, which meant that one's personal fulfillment and satisfaction allowed an individual to pursue one's own destiny without interference from others. Greeks were also curious about the world and liked to categorize things by explaining observations of objects in terms of the underlying principles. Then they created rules to explain the principles; therefore, anything could be explained through personal inquiry and then categorization of underlying principles. Greeks believed the true, unchanging, fundamental identity of a thing is discoverable by inquiry (Nisbett, 2010). Such a focus played out in how leaders communicated and led at that time.

Eastern Worldview of Virtues

Whereas Western orientation is towards discrete objects, the Eastern philosophical tradition grew out of the need to explain observations in relation to the field (surroundings) of objects. Philosophers such as Confucius, Mencius, and Lao Tzu were influential in creating a foundation for Eastern thought. Confucius is credited with saying, "If I am walking with two other men, each of them will serve as my teacher. I will pick out the good points of the one and imitate them and the bad points of the other and correct them in myself" (Osnos, 2014; Violatti, Mark, Mark, & Cartwright, 2015). This is akin to the Ubuntu principle of communalism.

A classic yet contemporary example of this difference in Western and Eastern thinking is derived from social psychologist, Richard Nisbett, who did a study on how Asians (Chinese, Japanese, Koreans) and North Americans (Canadians and US

Americans) would respond to certain stimuli. In this definitive study, a moving picture of a fish swimming in an aquarium was used. When asked what they saw, the majority of Asians partici- pants focused on the environment (the "field") and the North Americans looked more at the objects individually. This meant that Asians (including Chinese) tended to focus on the environ- ment (the "field") and not just on the individual objects (Nisbett, 2010). It is an entirely different worldview and explains why Western and Eastern peoples focus more on task or relationship. In Asia, the emphasis on relationships begins at an early age as children learn to behave properly within their family unit. For example, Japanese mothers teach their children to consider the feelings of others. They use feeling-related words when their child misbehaves; Western mothers ask questions about the objects and then give information to describe them.

> The consequences of this differential focus on the emo- tional states of others can be seen in adulthood. There is evidence that Asians are more accurately aware of the feelings and attitudes of others than are Westerners...The relative sensitivity to others' emotions is reflected in tacit assumptions about the nature of communication. Westerners teach their children to communicate their ideas clearly and to adopt a "transmitter" orientation, that is, the speaker is responsible for uttering sentences that can be clearly understood by the hearer-and under- stood, in fact, more or less independently of the context. It's the speaker's fault if there is a miscommunication. Asians, in contrast, teach their children a "receiver" ori- entation, meaning that it is the hearer's responsibility to understand what is being said. (Nisbett, 2010, pp. 60–61)

In other words, Western style communication is low context, placing emphasis on the clarity of words, rules, and principles, whereas Eastern style communication is high context, placing emphasis on not necessarily what is said, but how it is said, or not said, in order to preserve relationships (Hofstede, 1991).

This coincides with the historical and cultural background of Asian societies, in general, that focus on harmony, collectivism, and uniformity. In particular, if we look at the foundations of Chinese culture, in contrast to the Western view of self (Triandis & Suh, 2002), Chinese personal agency equated harmony since a Chinese person was most importantly a member of several collectives (clan, village, family). This meant that an individual was not an encapsulated unit who maintained a unique identity across social settings; rather the person's identity came from one's association with a group. Chinese personal agency emphasized self-control for the sake of the group and one's social environment versus control of others. This ancient tradition developed twenty-two hundred years before European rationalism, a different form of thinking that evolved through the Chinese philosopher, Confucius, or Kung Fu Zu (Nisbett, 2010). Over the millennia this worldview has survived and is credited for being the framework of Chinese society (Lai, 2008).

Confucius was a philosopher and teacher who lived during a tumultuous time during the Early Autumn Era (6th–5th BCE). With the decline of the feudal system, landowners began to lose their power and instability crept in as warlords from different regions of China took advantage of the weakening social system. The era that followed is known as the Warring States Period where no dominant ruler had control over the vast empire. Wanting to help restore societal order and harmony he created a moral philosophy for human interaction based upon a system of social and political ethics meant to guide people towards proper behavior in everyday life (Lai, 2008). Confucius valued hierarchy, group orientation, and tradition and taught that it was important to hold to filial piety, kinship, and loyalty as an indication of the important obligations within hierarchical relationships – if this could be achieved, then harmony and peace would follow.

Confucius believed that, courtesy, generosity, honesty, persistence, and kindness were paramount to restoring order, bringing peace, and creating harmony within a society. He emphasized the following:

If you are courteous, you will not be disrespected.

If you are generous, you will gain everything.

If you are honest, people will rely on you.

If you are persistent you will get results.

If you are kind, you can employ people. (Analects 17:6; Lau, 1979)

Confucius's teachings included the five Constant Virtues. We will focus on three of them (see Table 1).

Table 1.   Three Constant Virtues.

Rén	仁	Humaneness, kindness, benevolence
Lǐ	礼	Correct behavior, politeness, social norms, propriety
Yì	义	Honesty, uprightness, justice, righteousness (virtue); duty, obligation

RÉN 仁 KIND BENEVOLENCE

Rén refers to the attitude of the heart, which means that one desires good for others. This inward focus of goodness and humaneness, benevolence and kindness is where all other virtues begin. Confucius believed that a person's integrity came from within and it was up to each individual to monitor her or himself within the context of relationship to others. Ren is the inward work of the heart and can best be summed up by Confucius's version of the Golden Rule: "What you do not want done to yourself, do not do to others" (Analects 15:23; Lau, 1979). Therefore, if one is aware of what is good for oneself and can extend this to others, one is virtuous, and this practice promotes harmony with others.

LǏ 礼 GRACIOUS BEHAVIOR

Lǐ is the outward behavior that focuses on propriety and ritual. If rén is the inner work of developing a kind and humane "heart" or attitude towards others, then lǐ is what puts rén to work. Lǐ deals with relationships that must be maintained via appropriate morality, proper etiquette, and adherence to customs (Jacobs, Guopei, & Herbig, 1995). For example, if you honor lǐ you will have strong relationships which are the glue that holds Chinese society together. Innate to rituals are protocols (procedure) whereby people are assigned a place in society and behave appropriately (decorum).

YÌ 义 MORAL CHARACTER

Yì translates into justice and righteousness which is the moral disposition of a person who wants to do good for others. Yì flows from the inner cultivation of benevolence (rén) and the outward manifestation of its practice (lǐ). Yì is not just following rules for the sake of rules but is the ability to see the big picture in order to balance what is necessary to deal with a situation

(Cheng, 1972). So, the person who demonstrates yì exhibits moral integrity and when faced with an ethical decision to do right or wrong does not have to dwell on the correctness of their actions because integrity comes from within. Confucius believed that rulers needed to strive for peace versus power because peace – not warring factions or rulers or people – was what constituted righteousness, and a ruler who adhered to a tight moral code and demonstrated virtue, humility, and benevolence was good to his people (Chan, Mandaville, & Bleiker, 2001).

Applications to Enrich Western Leadership

If Western notions of leadership are constrained by an individual-istic worldview, then Ubuntu and Confucianism enrich that worldview by challenging this individualistic core. The Western leader needs to put on a new lens through which to view the world and by which sense-making of different perspectives occurs. It is not merely a skillset that Western leadership needs to adopt, amidst an almost overwhelming list of emerging skillsets now in vogue. Rather, Western leadership will be greatly enriched by developing a mind-set infused with the filter of com-munalism as expressed in Ubuntu and Confucianism.

This mind-set calls the Western leader to a worldview that takes into account the individual, but does so within the context of that individual in close interrelationship to other individuals (Tuleja, 2017). To list the core tenets of Ubuntu once more: (a) collective identity, (b) mutuality or interdependence, (c) morality, (d) unity, (e) humility, and (f) generosity. These were the non-negotiable attributes of Ubuntu (Mukuka, 2013). And the core tenets of Confucius are similar: (a) humaneness and benevolence, (b) correct behavior and propriety, and (c) honesty, virtue, and duty (Ivanhoe & Van Norden, 2005). Table 2 highlights the mind-set change that Western leadership needs to embrace to move beyond the myopic focus of Western individualistic leadership.

While utopian societies do not exist, we can hope for a better society by gleaning the best practices from multiple cultures. Western leadership has accomplished great things, but has also caused damage through the rugged individualism that might sometimes miss the interconnectedness of our world. Would a

Table 2.   Moving from a Western Mind-Set to a Communal Mind-Set.

Western Individualistic Mind-Set	An Ubuntu/Confucian or Communal Mind-Set
Leadership is affected by certain Traits that cause the leader to stand out from the followers and thus above them (Northouse, 2016, p. 9)	Leadership is about mutuality or interdependence. How do I use who I am to benefit the collective, and thus move us toward mutual benefit and health? My Traits are useless if not deployed for the community (Mukuka, 2013). In Confucianism, the principle of yì means that a leader's self-interest is expected to be sacrificed for the good or the organization and enables a leader to pursue excellence without worrying about personal gain (Cheng, 1972)
I must have the Leadership Skills to solve problems. (Northouse, 2016, p. 48)	Problem solving occurs in community amongst the wise, this is our collective identity. Together in unity and humility we use our collective skills and wisdom to solve problems. (Mukuka, 2013). Effective leadership occurs when the community works together to problem solve rather than a lone heroic leader. In Confucian leadership, Benevolence — rén — is the foundation for inward reflection and cultivation of personal kindness ensures that those in charge act benevolently to others
As a Leader I have dyadic relationships with followers. Some are part of the "in" group and others are part of the "out" group. (Northouse, 2016, p. 138)	In Ubuntu leadership is not dyadic in scope but communal. There is no "in" group or "out" group. Everyone in the community has value and contributes to the health and wellness of the community. This speaks to both "unity" and "humility." In Confucian leadership, decorum (propriety) — lǐ — creates harmony. People innately understand that each person has a specific place in society which ensures the harmony and stability of the work environment

better leadership emerge if we could leverage the best of Western leadership learning with the beauty and richness of Ubuntu and Confucianism? Leaders from the West can learn much from both Ubuntu and Eastern practices regarding communalism, benevolence, social norms, and integrity. Just as in the image of the sculpture at the beginning of this chapter, Ubuntu is expressed as a family, a clan, a community, united and linked together since people can only exist because of what others do to sustain them. Ubuntu leadership is expressed in caring for and serving others as the foundation of life itself — just as the family in the sculpture is gathered around in an embrace, so too is the phenomenon of Ubuntu in practice. And, perhaps Western leadership also can take a lesson from the Chinese playbook and learn that there is more to "transmitter" communication that merely gets the message across in a clear and succinct manner; rather, "receiver" communication takes into account the feelings and emotions of the speaker and seeks to understand the essence of what might be, all the while attending to the kindness, respect, and moral integrity needed to interact in a harmonious society.

Discussion Questions

1. As you think through the implications of this chapter and the philosophies of Ubuntu, and Confucianism, would you define your perspective on life as "individualistic" or as "communal?" In other words, do you believe that in order to live a fulfilled life you need to take care of your own needs and priorities only, or the needs and priorities of others alongside your own?

2. As you reflect on your own leadership style are there ways in which you could transition from an individualistic approach to leadership to a more inclusive and communal approach to leadership?

3. Think for a moment about your communication style. Would you say that you are more "transmitter" oriented or are you also "receiver" sensitive? Do the feelings and context of the person, or people, to whom you are communicating matter as much as the content of what you communicate?

4. As you reflect on your outlook on life would you classify yourself as "fiercely independent" of others, or "willingly interdependent" with others? If you are fiercely independent, are you satisfied with this approach to life and to leadership? How could you develop meaningful interdependence in ways that enrich your life and your leadership?

References

Bell, D. A., & Metz, T. (2011). Confucianism and Ubuntu: Reflections on a dialogue between Chinese and African traditions. *Journal of Chinese Philosophy*, *38*(Suppl. 1), 78–95. http://doi.org/10.1111/j.1540-6253.2012.01690.x

Bolden, R. (2011). Distributed leadership in organizations: A review of theory and research. *International Journal of Management Reviews*, *13*(3), 251–269. doi: 10.1111/j.1468-2370.2011.00306.x

Chan, S., Mandaville, P., & Bleiker, R. (Eds.). (2001). *The Zen of international relations: IR Theory from East to West*. United Kingdom: Palgrave Macmillan.

Cheng, C. Y. (1972). On yi as a universal principle of specific application in Confucian morality. *Philosophy East and West*, *22*(3), 269–280. doi: 10.2307/1397676

Day, D. V., & Harrison, M. M. (2007). A multilevel, identity-based approach to leadership development. *Human Resource Management Review*, *17*(4), 360–373. http://doi.org/10.1016/j.hrmr.2007.08.007

Dervitsiotis, K. N. (2005). Creating conditions to nourish sustainable organizational excellence. *Total Quality Management and Business Excellence*, *16*(8–9), 925–943. http://doi.org/10.1080/14783360500163078

Dicks, I. D. (2012). An African worldview: The Muslim Amacinga Yawo of Southern Malaŵ. Zomba: Kachere Series.

Donaldson, T. (1992). *Kant's global rationalism: Traditions of international ethics*. Cambridge: Cambridge University Press.

Dreyer, J. S. (2015). Ubuntu. *International Journal of Practical Theology*, *19*(1), 189–209. http://doi.org/10.1515/ijpt-2015-0022

du Plooy, B. (2014). Ubuntu and the recent phenomenon of the Charter for Compassion. *South African Review of Sociology*, *45*(1), 83–100. http://doi.org/10.1080/21528586.2014.887916

Elkington, R., & Booysen, L. (2015). Innovative leadership as enabling function within organizations: A complex adaptive system approach. *Journal of Leadership Studies*, *9*(3), 78–80. http://doi.org/10.1002/jls.21414

Elkington, R., & Upward, A. (2016). Leadership as enabling function for flourishing by design. *Journal of Global Responsibility*, *7*, 1–21. http://doi.org/10.1108/JGR-01-2016-0002

Gallo, F. T. (2008). *Business leadership in China: How to blend best Western practices with Chinese wisdom*. Chichester: Wiley (Asia).

Hills, M. D. (2002). Kluckhohn and Strodtbeck's values orientation theory. Online Readings in Psychology and Culture, *4*(4), 1–13. doi: 10.9707/2307-0919.1040

Hofstede, G. (1980). Motivation, leadership, and organization: Do American theories apply abroad? *Organizational Dynamics*, *9*(1), 42–63. doi: 10.1016/0090-2616(80)90013-3

Hofstede, G. H. (1991). *Cultures and organizations: Software of the mind – Intercultural cooperation and its importance for survival*. New York, NY: McGraw-Hill Publishing Co.

Ivanhoe, P. J., & Van Norden, B. W. (Eds.). (2005). *Readings in classical Chinese philosophy*. (2nd ed.). Indianapolis, IN: Hackett Publishing Co.

Jacobs, L., Guopei, G., & Herbig, P. (1995). Confucian roots in China: A force for today's business. *Management Decision, 33*(10), 29–34. doi: 10.1108/00251749510100221

Javidan, M., House, R. J., Dorfman, P. W., Hanges, P. J., & Sully de Luque, M. (2006). Conceptualizing and measuring cultures and their consequences: A comparative review of GLOBE's and Hofstede's approaches. *Journal of International Business Studies, 37*(6), 897–914. doi: 10.1057/palgrave.jibs.8400234

Kluckhohn, F. R., & Strodtbeck, F. L. (1961). *Variations in value orientations*. Oxford: Row, Peterson.

Komives, S., & Dugan, J. (2010). Contemporaries leadership theories. In R. Couto (Ed.), *Political and civic leadership: A reference handbook* (pp. 111–120). Thousand Oaks, CA: Sage Publishing. doi: 10.4135/9781412979337

Kulich, S., Prosser, M. H., & Weng, L. P. (2012). *Value frameworks at the theoretical crossroads of culture* (Vol. 4). Shanghai: Shanghai Foreign Language Education Press.

Lagadec, P. (2009). A new cosmology of risks and crises: Time for a radical shift in paradigm and practice. *Review of Policy Research, 26*(4), 473–487. doi: 10.1111/j.1541-1338.2009.00396.x

Lai, K. L. (2008). *An introduction to Chinese philosophy (Cambridge introductions to philosophy)*. Cambridge: Cambridge University Press.

Lau, D. C. (1979). *The Analects [of] Confucius*. New York, NY: Penguin Group (USA).

Lutz, D. W. (2009). African Ubuntu philosophy and global management. *Journal of Business Ethics, 84*(S3), 313–328. doi: 10.1007/s10551-009-0204-z

Mandela, N. R. (1995). *Long walk to freedom: The autobiography of Nelson Mandela*. Toronto, Canada: Little, Brown and Co.

Mukuka, R. (2013). Ubuntu in S. M. Kapwepwe's Shalapo Canicandala: Insights for Afrocentric psychology. *Journal of Black Studies, 44*(2), 137–157. doi: 10.1177/0021934713476888

Nisbett, R. E. (2010). *The geography of thought: How Asians and westerners think differently...and why*. New York, NY: Simon & Schuster Adult Publishing Group.

Northouse, P. G. (2016). *Leadership: Theory and practice*. (7th ed.). Thousand Oaks, CA: Sage.

Oppenheim, C. E. (2012). Nelson Mandela and the power of Ubuntu. *Religions, 3*(4), 369–388. doi: 10.3390/rel3020369

Osnos, E. (2014, November 7). Confucius Comes Home. *The New Yorker*. Retrieved from http://www.newyorker.com/magazine/2014/01/13/confucius-comes-home

Triandis, H. C., & Suh, E. M. (2002). Cultural influences on personality. *Annual Review of Psychology, 53*(1), 133–160. doi: 10.1146/annurev.psych.53.100901.135200

Tuleja, E. A. (2017). *Intercultural communication for global business: How leaders communicate for success.* New York, NY: Routledge.

Uhl-Bien, M. (2006). Relational leadership theory: Exploring the social processes of leadership and organizing. *Leadership Quarterly, 17*(6), 654–676. http://doi.org/10.1016/j.leaqua.2006.10.007

Violatti, C., Mark, J. J., Mark, E., & Cartwright, M. (2015, June 17). Ancient Chinese philosophy. Retrieved May 10, 2016, from Ancient History Encyclopedia, http://www.ancient.eu/Chinese_Philosophy/

PART 2
Ethnocultural Contexts

5

Influence and Global Leadership: China, India, and the Multinational Corporation

Christie Caldwell and Ethan Prizant

Introduction

The chapter aims to explore the leadership transition of Chinese and Indian high potentials in multinational corporations from local leadership responsibilities to global leadership responsibilities. It focuses on influencing capabilities and the importance of verbal influencing skills in the global matrix organization.

This chapter presents a comparative analysis of three approaches of influence (verbal influence, structural influence, and relational influence) and explains how they differ culturally. The discussion is based on qualitative interviews with senior business leaders at multinational organizations.

The authors propose that verbal influence is a primary skill gap preventing the acceleration of Chinese and Indian high potentials into global leadership roles. The chapter highlights how Western multinational corporations prefer verbal influence over the more prevalent structural and relational influence styles found in China and Indian contexts. The findings link this primacy afforded to verbal influence to culture and the implicit leadership theories (ILTs) of Western multinational corporations.

The chapter presents a cultural explanation of why Chinese and Indian high potentials are not advancing into global leadership roles at Western multinationals.

The Shifting Center

As the global economic center rapidly shifts to the fast-growth markets of Asia, particularly China and India, multinational companies (MNCs) have pivoted their operations to both drive and capitalize on the growth potential of this region. For many organizations, this has been a transformative process, with China and India quickly making up an increasingly significant share of global revenue. This growth has increased the importance of these countries in the corporate portfolio, transforming organizations' employee demographic make-up by large proportions.

However, while these shifts are evident in both the corporate revenue and employee numbers, Chinese and Indian leadership representation from the region is far from proportional to either the revenue generated or the general employee population. In a 2012 study, CEOs in Western MNCs identified the ability to hire, develop, and retain talent in fast-growth markets such as China and India as "the main competitive differentiation" in today's market (PricewaterhouseCoopers, 2012). But numbers of Chinese and Indian nationals in global leadership roles lag far behind the revenue their countries generate. A recent survey of global executives reported that merely 2% of their top 200 employees were located in the fast-growth Asian markets that, in the years ahead, would account for more than one-third of global sales (Dewhurst, Harris, & Heywood, 2012). This paucity of Asian leaders is consistently cited by top business leaders as the biggest constraining factor for continued growth in the region. A Mercer survey on leadership found that only 51% of companies have strong successors in place for every critical role in the leadership pipeline and many still heavily rely on expatriates to fill top leadership positions in Asia (Mercer, 2013). This is a precarious position for global organizations whose primary growth trajectories depend on success in these markets. The rapid growth rate and the nascent state of certain industries within China and India both certainly contribute to the leadership imbalance.

Nevertheless, a consistent narrative among the corporations we studied cited a leadership talent gap among its Chinese and, to a lesser degree, its Indian high potentials. This gap was primarily identified at the point of transition from local leadership to global leadership responsibilities. This also corresponds to the leadership ceiling that most Indian and Chinese high potentials were unable to break.

At this critical juncture, recent studies investigating what differentiates local from global leadership identify a leader's ability to influence as the critical competency required to successfully transition past this inflection point (Corporate Executive Board, 2012; Gundling, Hogan & Cvitkovich, 2011). Our initial research corroborated this finding, with "lack of influence" being the most frequently cited factor preventing local leaders from transitioning into roles with global responsibility. However, both observation and investigation demonstrated that these local high potentials were both highly effective and highly influential within their home country context. If this was the case, how did influence change in a global context or how was it defined differently?

This research investigates how influence is defined and practiced within China and India within the local leadership context and juxtaposes this against the practice and definition of influence within the global MNC leadership context. Our findings show that influence is indeed defined and practiced very differently within these contexts. In order to differentiate between the types of influence being practiced and described, we broke down the term influence into three different subcategories: structural influence, relational influence, and verbal influence. The study identified the lack of verbal influence, versus other types of influence, as the primary gap preventing Chinese and Indian high potentials' transition to global leadership positions. This finding directly links to the cultures of China, India, and the West. While Chinese and Indian high potentials leverage a mix of the three influence types, the weight given to each of these influence subtypes was different, with verbal influence given the least weight out of the three. Conversely, Western leaders working within the global matrix organizational context privileged verbal influence above the other influence types. Culturally divergent forms of influence were found to be a key factor in preventing the transition of Chinese and Indian talent into global leadership positions.

Influence as the New Global Leadership Framework

In a 2011 study exploring what differentiates domestic leadership from global leadership, the ability to *influence across boundaries* was identified as one of the ten global leadership behaviors necessary for success in a global environment (Gundling et al., 2011). A subsequent study conducted in 2012 by the Corporate Executive Board (CEB) identified influence as the competency with the greatest impact on change in probability of being a great global leader (Corporate Executive Board, 2012). These results were markedly different from the competencies deemed most important for single country or domestic leaders. The CEB study demonstrated that, while influence is important for some single country market leaders, it is the *most* important competency for leaders with multicountry responsibilities. As soon as a leader transitions from single country to multi-country responsibilities, the ability to influence becomes the critical differentiator for success and the fundamental competency that leaders must possess to effectively inhabit global roles (Corporate Executive Board, 2012).

Both the aforementioned studies on global leadership link the importance of influence to the structural differences leaders encounter when assuming global roles. The CEB study identifies four structural challenges leaders face in transitioning to multi-country responsibilities: loss of direct authority, lack of accurate market information, increase in breadth of responsibility, and an increase in stakeholders (Corporate Executive Board, 2012). These challenges are indicative of the global matrix organizational structure within which the vast majority of global organizations currently operate.

Research Approach

This research took influence as the key framework to investigate the identified lack of Chinese and Indian leaders in global roles within multinational corporations. If influence is the critical competency enabling the successful transition from local to global leadership roles, then measuring this competency in Chinese and Indian leaders is an important first step in understanding the source of the transition challenge. To measure this, the authors conducted a qualitative study of 54 individuals across 22 organizations. The

22 organizations were all multinational companies headquartered in the United States or Europe with significant subsidiary operations in both China and India. 100% of the organizations involved in the study identified the number of Chinese and Indian leaders in "global leadership roles" as "below target" or "well below target." Similarly, 100% of the organizations identified the development of strong local talent pipelines for global leadership roles as "a top three global priority." These factors are critical to the study since they eliminate organizations for which Chinese and Indian leadership numbers may be low due to lack of prioritization or for which low numbers are not seen as an issue. All the participating organizations viewed low Chinese and Indian leadership levels as a problem and were actively seeking to address the gap.

The 54 interviewees selected were all senior business leaders in a position to evaluate high-potential leadership talent from India, China, or both countries. The interviewees all held one of the following titles: Human Resource Director, Learning and Development Director, or Business Unit Head. Of the 54 leaders interviewed, 18 specifically assessed Indian high potentials, 30 assessed Chinese leaders and six leaders were in a position to evaluate both Chinese and Indian high-potential leaders. These high-potential leaders were specifically being groomed to transition into global roles or were already in the process of transition. In these interviews, the senior business leaders were specifically asked through a series of structured questions to identify the key competency gaps for these high potentials as they moved from local leadership to global leadership roles. The interview questions were open-ended; at no time were interviewees fed a list of competencies from which to choose.

The findings corroborate the aforementioned studies (Corporate Executive Board, 2012; Gundling et al., 2011), influence being the most frequently referenced competency required for leaders transitioning to global roles. Influence was also identified as the biggest competency gap for Chinese and Indian high-potential leaders. 85% of interviewees identified "influence" as the key gap or one of the key development areas for high-potential Chinese or Indian leaders.

The numbers remained consistent when analyzing the two groups of high potentials separately. 84% of senior business leaders evaluating only Indian high potentials listed influence as a key gap or the key gap. For senior leaders assessing only Chinese high potentials, 87% identified influence as a development priority. Furthermore, 84% of senior leaders in the position to evaluate both Chinese and Indian high potentials mentioned influence as the primary competency requiring development. No other competency was identified with such a high level of frequency. In fact, of the three gaps mentioned most frequently after influence – global networking (22%), strategic thinking (16.67%), and global business acumen (16.67%) – none were mentioned by more than a quarter of the business leaders.

Influence and Culture

Having established influence as both the critical competency and also the primary gap preventing Chinese and Indian high-potential leaders from transitioning into global roles, the research sought to address the potential role of culture in both the competency gap as well as the assessment of that gap.

Previous research points to culturally informed, implicit leadership expectations as a possible source for the lack of Asian leaders in global leadership roles. A 2014 study posits that the low numbers of Chinese managers who actually progress to global-level leadership positions within MNCs can be attributed to misaligned ILTs (Wang, James, Denyer, & Bailey, 2014). ILTs "refer to the underlying constructions of leadership that people use to recognize leadership in others" (Wang et al., 2014) and are influenced by cultural values and norms and vary by culture (Lord & Maher, 1991). Schyn's study cited in Wang's research points to the broader impact of ILTs on any minority leader's career development within western MNCs. A person may not fit the ILTs of his or her supervisor and will therefore be disadvantaged in the promotion process even though he or she has the same capacity as the successful candidate (Schyns, 2006).

The interviewees who participated in this research were all in global leadership roles themselves. In addition, and perhaps more importantly, they rose to success within the context of a US-American or Western-European headquartered organization and therefore represent the ILT promoted within that organization. We can therefore interrogate the leadership culture of these organizations and their culturally embedded assumptions of what makes a good global leader as one potential factor obstructing the climb of local Chinese and Indian talent into higher global roles with more extensive global responsibilities.

The sudden and overwhelming identification of the influence competency gap by the current leadership of Western-based multinational organizations at the point where Chinese and Indian high-potential leaders begin to interact more frequently with the company's higher level leaders also raises questions. In addition to asking the question of whether influence is being defined differently by those assessing Chinese and Indian leaders, it is necessary to ask whether influence is practiced differently. A significant number of the interviewees noted that the high-potential Chinese and Indian employees were highly effective in their local environments. The influence gap only appeared when they moved out of their home turf and began interacting with global counterparts. Is there a different kind of influence being practiced between the local and global environment?

In order to understand how culture may be impacting both the definition and practice of influence, we first looked at how influence was described by the interviewees and then investigated cultural frameworks within the field of intercultural studies to understand the source of these discrepancies. We also conducted a second set of qualitative interviews with 34 identified Indian and Chinese high potentials working within 15 of the 22 multinational corporations used for the study.

Our study broke down the overarching concept of influence into specific descriptors, based on the words interviewees used to describe the influence gap. Significantly, the findings show that influence, as defined by the 54 senior executive interviewees was a very specific type of influence that, for the purposes of this study, we have termed "verbal influence." This form of influence is distinct from other forms of influence that we found more frequently practiced within Chinese and Indian cultural norms, namely "structural influence" and "relational influence." These three influence approaches are strongly linked to culture and therefore are rarely explicit within the leadership competency frameworks of the Western MNCs in which Chinese and Indian high potentials work. In fact, our findings reveal that the concept of "verbal influence" is more often embedded in the implicit leadership expectations of Western-dominated MNC leadership culture.

Defining Influence Approaches

VERBAL INFLUENCE

In our research, we define "verbal influence" as the ability to use language to persuade, convince or impact the outcome of a decision.

STRUCTURAL INFLUENCE

"Structural influence" is the ability to impact the direction or outcome of a decision based on one's positional power. This positional power can be afforded by an organization through a role or title, or an individual's place in the social or economic hierarchy, which provides them with some measure of authority or prescribes a certain behavior in response to their role.

RELATIONAL INFLUENCE

In the context of this study, "relational influence" is the leveraging of trust and ties of personal relationships to impact decisions and outcomes.

The research broke down the terms or phrases used by senior business leaders when describing the influence competency gap. These descriptors exclusively fall into the subcategory that we have designated as "verbal influence" (see Table 1).

The Influence Mix

Looking at the cultural frameworks underlying influence practices in China, India, Western Europe, and the United States, it is important to recognize that all three of these influence approaches exist and are employed in every country throughout the world. However, the cultural research shows that different influence techniques are given primacy across geographies in accordance with the particular cultural and historical evolution of countries. In short, the mix of influencing styles differs.

In India, for example, there is often a high level of proficiency in verbal influencing skills, as Indian culture greatly emphasizes debate, brainstorming, and verbal expression. However, in the Indian "influence mix," structural and relational influence are given more weight, often to the effect that hierarchy or lack of relationship can override one's capacity for verbal influence. An Indian high potential working for a global pharmaceutical company in Hyderabad cites the challenge of "influencing up" in his organization:

> At the global executive level, leaders need to continuously align with all the stakeholders, have debates over conflicting priorities and hold productive discussions to reach the ideal solution. But here, we are not capable of

Table 1. "Verbal Influence" — As Described in Our Interviews.

- Push Back
  - Challenge
  - Debate
  - Argue
  - Stand Firm
  - Hold Your Own
  - Take a Stand
  - Say No
  - Be Tough/Aggressive
- Speak Up
  - Voice Out
  - Raise Ideas
  - Have Voice Heard
  - Quiet
  - Express Yourself
- Lateral Influence
  - Influence Without Authority
  - Influence Up/Manage Up
- Make a Strong Case
  - Make an Argument
  - Make a Business Case
  - Articulate a Message
  - Get Ideas Across
  - Communicate with Impact
  - Persuading
  - Convincing
- Sell an Idea
  - Selling

- Sell Yourself
- Tell Your Achievements
- Make the Data Talk
  - Present Data in a Compelling Way
  - Turn Data into a Point of View
- Deliver a Succinct Point
  - Explain in a Simple Way
  - Get to the Point
  - Logical/Structured Arguments
  - Presentation Skills
- Engage and Align
  - Create Alignment
  - Collaboration
  - Engage Globally
  - Span Boundaries
  - Get On the Same Page
- Socialize
  - Socialize Ideas
  - Mingle with Global Counterparts
  - Be Visible
  - Informal Interactions
- Paint a Picture
  - Describe a Picture
  - Inspire People
  - Storytelling
  - Convey a Vision

driving these discussions with our counterparts in Europe because we just want to please them as we see them as our seniors. So we get frustrated because we are unable to create alignment and manage up.

In most situations and examples cited in the qualitative research interviews, hierarchy trumps verbal influence. Many Indian high potentials said they tend to "remain quiet" since it is "not my place to speak up."

In China, the influence mix is even more heavily weighted toward relational and structural influencing styles, with even what may be described as a deep historical and cultural distrust of verbal influence approaches. When citing the influence of Confucian ideology on Chinese business leaders, a 2011 study examining 100 Chinese CEOs finds that: "The modern Chinese business leader who manifests the ideology of Confucianism will portray a quiet, humble persona who earns respect based on a sense of relationship...The dominant metaphor of organization for these leaders will be that of a 'social network'" (McDonald, 2011). An oft-quoted saying by Chinese philosopher Laozi also describes the best leader as one who talks little and who people barely know exists. This preference for relational and structural influence over a verbal approach is also compounded by the fact that most of the verbal influencing conducted in global MNCs is in English. A business unit leader at an American-based automobile manufacturer echoed the challenge for Chinese high potentials to influence without authority, telling us:

> How can you forge a vision for people who are not directly under your control? You have to exercise a lot of indirect authority. China has a very high power-distance environment, so there's a great need to get used to this type of flat organization. This is a huge transition.

A Chinese high-potential working for a European consumer care company puts it this way:

> In China, the people we respect are those who get things done and don't need to say anything, because their work speaks for itself. If someone is talking all the time, we tend to think they are just self-promoting and not trustworthy. Here, the people with the real power don't have to say anything or convince people of their idea. They have the power because of their role or because they have a strong relationship with you. You trust them, so no words are needed, you just do it.

VERBAL INFLUENCE

In most Western countries verbal influence has become the predominant influence approach within the influence mix. These cultures often privilege verbal influence over relational or structural approaches because it falls in line with key Western values of objectivity and fairness. Historical roots harkening back to the Socratic Method, scientific inquiry, Descartes' rationalism, and the search for objective truth in the Age of Reason all reward a relentless line of inquiry into a black and white "truth". Methods of debate and deductive reasoning are designed to segment objective truth from the context of relationships in order to gain clarity and remove subjective personal sentiment. The current form of verbal influence prevalent within Western business culture evolved from these historical roots as a method for maintaining objectivity and ensuring that the best ideas are stripped of subjective influencers such as personal relationships, emotional attachments, roles, and social status.

This style of influence has been primarily practiced and rewarded within Western cultural contexts and links to key cultural dimensions and historical roots found there. Cultural assessment tools such as the GlobeSmart Assessment Profile, which merges the data of cross-cultural researchers such as Hofstede, Schwartz, McCrae and Inglehart with the assessment data of approximately one million users, can determine the average placement of countries and cultures along specific cultural dimensions. These tools place the headquarter countries of the 22 organizations we studied (Denmark, France, Germany, Israel, the Netherlands, Switzerland, the United Kingdom and the United States) further to the left side of the spectrum as, on average, more independent, task-focused, and direct in approach (see Fig. 1). Cultural tendencies attached to each of these dimensions create foundational links to Western cultures' proclivity toward verbal influence as the preferred method of persuasion. Independent cultures reward the voicing of independent thought, even when those thoughts diverge from the group; a component of egalitarianism is a high degree of comfort "challenging the views of superiors"; and direct cultures "come to the point quickly" and are "comfortable making requests, giving direction, or disagreeing with others" (GlobeSmart, 2016).

Erin Meyer's *The Culture Map* uses similar cross-cultural research sources to add the cultural dimension of "disagreeing" in which cultures can vary between confrontational or nonconfrontational (Meyer, 2014). The majority of Western countries analyzed were positioned as more confrontational (with the

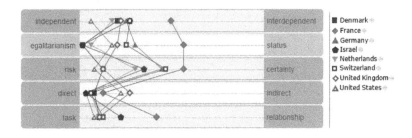

Fig. 1. GlobeSmart® Cultural Profile Averages for a Selection of Western Countries. *Source*: GlobeSmart® 2016.

exception of the United Kingdom and Sweden, which both fall in the middle) (Meyer, 2014). Cultures identified as disagreeing through confrontation typically view "disagreement and debate as positive for the team or organization" and see "open confrontation as appropriate" and without "negative impact on the relationship" (Meyer, 2014).

The importance of verbal influence for leading successfully in global MNCs today cannot be overstated. In our interviews with senior leaders from MNCs, the inability of Chinese and Indian leaders to effectively utilize verbal influence in the global organization was cited as the primary competency gap with negative impact on the organization and the individual's development. The director of a Research & Development team in India for an American-based technology firm expressed concern that his engineering high potentials were not getting their voices heard in the product-development process. The company was losing out on an important feedback loop and vital suggestions for product improvements. He complained that his team members "don't really make a strong case for what they think. They talk between themselves but don't make a business argument. Even though our Indian engineers are very good, they are not very confident and don't know how to make a business case for what they see and think to higher level global counterparts."

STRUCTURAL INFLUENCE

Cultures in which hierarchy provides the organizing framework for interaction often promote structural influence as their primary mode of influence. In hierarchical cultures, of which China and India are some of the most extreme (see Fig. 2, where China and India are both positioned far to the right on the egalitarian-status

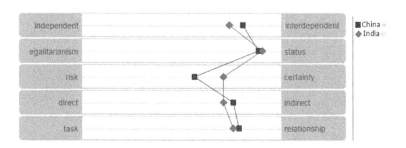

Fig. 2. GlobeSmart® Cultural Profile Averages for China and India. *Source*: GlobeSmart® 2016.

dimension), leaders are rarely, if ever, required to sell their decisions or ideas to their direct reports or peers. Generally, Indians and Chinese are "deferential to superiors" and "prefer not to challenge those above them," and frequently "adapt their behavior based on relative status." This is in direct opposition to egalitarian cultures wherein people "treat everyone the same" and "challenging the views of superiors" is seen as positive and natural (GlobeSmart, 2016). In India and China, decision-making is reserved for those at the very top of the hierarchy. As a Vice-President of Human Resources at an American-based healthcare company related, "Indians are socially wired to be hierarchical. If you look at the workplace, you have a large proportion of leaders who are deferential, more than OK to listen, accept, and execute rather than bring forward thinking to the table." Influence thus comes in the form of a position, and people are most comfortable operating in that type of work environment.

Furthermore, one's position and where one falls in the hierarchy also determine the validity of the decision. In China and India, a decision's inherent merit is almost never considered separately from the decision-maker. Because the roles in a hierarchy are so well-defined, the need to convince someone to do something through a well-honed argument or to hold one's own in a marketplace of competing ideas is seldom needed. This is illustrated by Terry Bacon's research into the frequency and effectiveness of influencing techniques in different countries (Lore International Institute, 2008). Bacon's research reveals that Indians frequently employ "push" influencing techniques that are intimately tied with hierarchy, such as stating and legitimizing. For leaders occupying high positions in corporate structures, a simple statement is often enough to solicit adherence, with no elaboration or explanation required. Legitimizing, or appealing to authority, is also commonly seen in India where people influence others by citing their positions in the hierarchy or by merely displaying accoutrements affiliated with positions of authority. The prevalence of both stating and legitimizing exemplify the power of structural influence.

The hierarchy also defines a leader's scope of power and rarely requires them to extend beyond their prescribed domain. Thus, collaboration or lateral influence skills that would allow them to impact decisions beyond their domain are rarely necessary. On the contrary, poking one's nose into another leader's sphere of control is often dangerous and generally discouraged.

RELATIONAL INFLUENCE

Ways of building and maintaining relationships can be extremely different in China and India but the role of relationships in both cultures as the sole arbiter of nonstructural power is highly similar. The GlobeSmart Assessment Profile places both China and India to the far right on the spectrum for the task-relationship dimension. Relationship-oriented cultures are defined as viewing "time building relationships as key to achieving good results" and thus people who are relationship-oriented "prioritize maintaining relationships over accomplishing tasks on time" (GlobeSmart, 2016). In China, one's network of relations is seen as equivocal to their level of "pull" in a particular sphere, whether social, professional, or familial (most often the lines separating these spheres are undefined, often viewed as arbitrary Western compartmentalization). Investing time or effort to build these relationships is often equated to putting money in the bank. Given the nature of obligation and reciprocity within Chinese relationships, if someone helps or offers a favor, the recipient is expected to acquiesce to future requests for favors from the same relation, leading to a perpetual cycle of give-and-take. In fact, as a Chinese leader, one's reputation and morality depend on one's ability to fulfill these relational obligations based on exchange.

Relational influence is used frequently by Chinese and Indians in the local organizational context to achieve goals and get work done. Terry Bacon found that of all the countries studied China had the highest frequency rating of exchanging, bargaining, or reciprocating influence behaviors and the second highest frequency for appealing to relationships and alliance building. India ranked 5th on exchanging and Indians use alliance building more than the global average (Lore International Institute, 2008). MNCs that recognize and use this influence mix get better results. "The private network is so strong, it helps the organization to be productive in China," said a senior leader from an American multinational insurance company. "We hire people because of the strong networks that we can tap into. We recently hired a well-connected guy high potential. He opens all the doors for us. He has allowed us to open up new branches in a shorter amount of time." This example illustrates the vital role that relational influence plays in the working environment in China. Whether one can verbally convince or persuade a government official does not matter, rather what matters in China is whether you have the relationship. Therefore, Chinese are much more likely to leverage these types of relations in their local work and are extremely efficient when doing so.

The New Emphasis on Verbal Influence in Today's Global Matrix

While generic influence is critical in any organization, the global matrix structure particularly emphasizes and requires "verbal influence" as the primary influence approach. When leaders rise in matrix global organizations, a key measure of success is the ability to work across multiple, complex boundaries, including functions, geographies, markets, cultures, business lines, and product groups, all of which are competing for the prioritization of their needs. What is required for success as a leader in a global matrix environment is often significantly different from what is required in traditional organizational structures. Indeed, PDI Ninth House identifies a completely different set of leadership competencies for what it terms as our "post-command and control world, where employee engagement, customer focus, and change are essential" (PDI Ninth House, 2012). Critical competencies for this flatter business environment include the abilities to foster open communication, promote collaboration, engage, and inspire, all of which are elements of verbal influence, rather than structural or relational influence (PDI Ninth House, 2012).

The matrix organizational structure is also a radical departure from the familial, societal and educational structures currently prevalent in China and India, which rely heavily on hierarchy to create order and stability and also on personal relationships to create "pull". As a result, leaders from cultures like China and India, for whom relational and structural influence styles are more often used, are potentially disadvantaged. In China, for example, the speaker's language, tone, and expressions are by and large dictated by the status of the listener and his or her place in the company hierarchy, as well as the intimacy and history of the speaker's relationship with the listener. These cultural norms and behaviors have resulted in different organizational structures. Chinese companies like telecom giant Huawei have rigid hierarchies, wherein decision-making power for almost all decisions rests with the CEO. This hierarchy is arguably even more present within China's state-owned enterprises. India's most famous business model, on the other hand, is its family

conglomerates, which leverage Indian society's strongest relational contract to create effective organizational structures in a
culture where strict social codes and relationship networks hold
more power and are more enforceable than law. Companies like
Tata, Mahindra, Aditya Birla Group, Reliance, and Arcelor
Mittal rely on this relational "pull" as well as the clear hierarchical structures within Indian families to impact decisions and
outcomes.

Global MNC matrix organizational structures effectively
strip leaders of the more formal forms of influence so important
in Chinese and Indian cultures. The matrix structure itself is particularly challenging for more hierarchical and relationship-based
leadership cultures. First of all, the model creates ambiguity
around who is in charge and the "leader" or decision-maker can
change on a project-to-project basis. Multiple reporting lines also
create competing priorities and confusion around who one
should ultimately seek to please. One Chinese high-potential
leader described the chaos of the matrix like this:

> In China, there is always a head and he/she is always the
> one with the authority. Everyone recognizes this. He/she
> is the one whose position is highest. But in Western coun-
> tries, the authority or the head isn't always the person
> with the highest position. Many times someone is given
> the title of project manager, facilitator or coordinator,
> and they have the authority in this certain situation or
> for this short-term project. Authority often shifts in a
> matrix environment.

Secondly, the matrix organization denudes Chinese and
Indian leaders of their local networks of relationships, requiring
them to do the same level of work by leveraging a group of foreign strangers they have never met face to face. In this scenario,
leaders must rely on their ability to influence without authority
or personal relationship, leveraging their verbal influence to
make the strongest argument, clearly articulate their ideas, and
fight for their priorities. One Indian high potential compared this
experience to having his limbs cut off. Similarly, when Chinese
enter the matrix environment and need to influence people outside of their networks, they find it challenging to do so, since
they are unable to utilize the relational influence derived from
shared experience and intimacy. An HR executive at an
American-based automobile manufacturer described the obstacles
Chinese leaders face when they are unable to leverage relational

influence: "The Chinese team relies more on face-to-face meetings and relationships as their core strength. But with our new project, they now need to establish those same relationships with people in Brazil. They are excellent in local business, but now we need the China team to act truly global and work in this environment where they have no confidence." As the HR executive states, the Chinese leaders essentially lose their "confidence" when they are unable to fall back on the relational influence techniques honed at home.

Implications and Conclusion

This study explored the global leadership gaps of Chinese and Indian high potentials in Western-headquartered MNCs. Our research reveals that influence, specifically verbal influence, is the critical competency gap preventing Chinese and Indian high potentials from successfully transitioning to global leadership positions within the Western-headquartered MNCs in our study. Our findings illustrate the cultural explanation for this gap and have significant implications for the assessment and selection processes of high-potential talent in MNCs.

Verbal influence is so deeply embedded within Western notions of leadership that it has become a central construct of "what leadership looks like" and an integral part of a majority of Western leaders' ILTs. The fact that 87% of senior leaders in this study identified verbal influence as a key development gap for Chinese and Indian high potentials strongly indicates that verbal influence is core to these leaders' definition of leadership. The primacy afforded to verbal influence in global MNCs often fails to take into account the specific influence mixes of China and India. Understanding these influence mixes, however, is critical both to companies performing well in these key markets and ensuring that the talent hailing from these markets is set up for success.

The results of this study do suggest that companies need to understand better the assessment bias at the organizational level and its role in blocking the rise of high-potential talent from China and India. Furthermore, our preliminary research asks companies to evaluate the rewarding of local influence behaviors in China and India. Finally, our findings highlight the critical need for MNCs to focus on developing "verbal influence" as a critical skill in their learning and training programs to enable

Chinese and Indian talent to work effectively in today's global matrix environment.

The senior leaders we interviewed for this study represent only a small pool of leaders in Western-headquartered MNCs and a rather broad cross-section of Western nations. Further research is needed to reinforce and corroborate the findings in this study.

Discussion Questions

1. How are expectations about "good leadership" informed by national cultures?
2. Why is verbal influence a critical behavior for global leaders at multinational corporations? How does it differ from structural and relational influence approaches?
3. What can corporations do to address the gap in verbal influence to ensure that their Chinese and Indian high-potential talent can progress into higher leadership roles?

References

Corporate Executive Board Company. (2012). *The global leader.*

Dewhurst, M., Harris, J., & Heywood, S. (2012, June). The global company's challenge. *McKinsey Quarterly*. Retrieved from http://www.mckinsey.com/business-functions/organization/our-insights/the-global-companys-challenge

GlobeSmart. (2016). Aperian global. Retrieved from http://learning.aperianglobal.com/portal

Gundling, E., Hogan, T., & Cvitkovich, K. (2011). *What is global leadership?: 10 key behaviors that define great global leaders.* Boston, MA: Nicholas Brealey.

Lord, R. G., & Maher, K. J. (1991). Leadership and information processing: Linking perceptions and performance.

Lore International Institute. (2008). *Cultural differences in influence.* Durango, CO: Terry Bacon.

McDonald, P. (2011). Maoism versus Confucianism: ideological influences on Chinese business leaders. *Journal of Management Development*, 30(7/8), 632–646.

Mercer. (2013). Asia pacific leadership development practices study: Report.

Meyer, E. (2014). *The culture map: Breaking through the invisible boundaries of global business.* New York, NY: Public Affairs.

PDI Ninth House. (2012). Can women executives break the glass ceiling?.

PricewaterhouseCoopers. (2012). 15th annual global CEO survey 2012: Delivering results, growth and value in a volatile world.

Schyns, B. (2006). The role of implicit leadership theories in the performance appraisals and promotion recommendations of leaders. *Equal Opportunities International, 25*(3), 188–199.

Wang, L., James, K. T., Denyer, D., & Bailey, C. (2014). Western views and Chinese whispers: Re-thinking global leadership competency in multinational corporations. *Leadership, 10*(4), 471–495.

6

Indo-European Leadership (IEL): A Non-Western Leadership Perspective

Afsaneh Nahavandi and
Hema A. Krishnan

This chapter moves beyond Western notions to expand our perspective on leadership by proposing Indo-European Leadership (IEL) as a distinct and divergent approach that originates in ancient India and Iran. The exponential Indian economic growth has garnered attention recently and the success of Indian organizations has been attributed partly to their unique management and business practices. We make the case that IEL is a unique leadership style that has contributed to the success of Indian organizations where leaders successfully blend social concerns and caring for stakeholders with Western business practices. IEL is a comprehensive and balanced approach to leading with a focus on integrity, action, moderation, accountability, kindness, and humility. It has been tested and has succeeded in ancient as well as modern dynamic and highly diverse environments that parallel many of the challenges global business and social leaders face today. The application of IEL to Western contexts is innovative in its performance and action orientation — that is, allows a focus on outcomes and the bottom line — while also taking care of people and demonstrating integrity and accountability. As businesses and economies worldwide continue to experience sluggish growth and face ethical and legal scandals in a highly diverse and global world, leadership models are being questioned and the need for innovative approaches has never been greater. IEL is one such proven approach that may point the way out of some of the current challenges.

The objectives of this chapter are to be able to describe and apply a non-Western leadership approach, IEL, to leadership, to

- Understand the roots of IEL; and
- Explore non-Western leadership principles.

Indo-European Leadership (IEL): A Non-Western Leadership Perspective

This chapter moves beyond Western notions to expand our perspective on leadership by proposing IEL as a distinct and divergent approach that originates in ancient India and Iran. Our current approaches to leadership are dominated by Western theory and research, many of which have self-interest and capitalism as their guiding principles. While such approaches may work in some environments, Chin and Trimble (2015) suggest that the changing global and local demographic contexts challenge existing Western-based models that assume that their approaches are appropriate in all contexts. Meanwhile, the success of many non-Western economies and organizations suggests alternative ways of leading. Specifically, the growth of the Indian economy and the success of many Indian companies provide a case in point.

On November 26, 2008, the Taj Mahal Palace hotel in Mumbai India came under a terrorist attack. What ensued was unimaginable bloodshed that left dozens dead and hundreds others wounded. Aside from analysis from numerous human and political perspectives, the attack attracted the attention of management experts because of the exemplary and selfless conduct of the hotel's staff members many of whom were recruited from villages and trained to focus on both people and profit. Deshpandré and Raina (2011) credit the staff's acts of bravery that saved numerous lives, to unique management practices of Tata, the hotel's parent company. This distinct management and leadership style was further explored in a comprehensive study of

105 leaders in 98 Indian companies (Cappelli, Singh, Singh, & Useem, 2010a; Cappelli, Singh, Singh, & Useem, 2010b; Cappelli, Singh, Singh, & Useem, 2015). The study identifies a strong focus on employees and training, putting people first, accountability to the organization rather than only to external stakeholders, integrity and maintaining one's reputation, an emphasis on long-term strategy, and involvement in broader social issues as key to the success of these companies.

The study of attack on the Taj and Cappelli et al.'s study make the case for a unique Indian leadership and management style and consider its applicability to Western organizations. What neither explores are the underpinning of these practices and the deep cultural traditions and roots that drive them. We propose that the success of Indian corporations is partially driven by a unique and divergent leadership approach we call IEL. IEL has been practiced throughout history in India and Iran and is celebrated and illustrated in the rich literary traditions of both countries. This chapter explores the cultural roots that underlie IEL and presents its six principles: (1) Integrity; (2) Action; (3) Moderation; (4) Accountability; (5) Kindness; and (6) Humility. We then consider the applicability of IEL to our current understanding and practice of leadership.

Roots of IEL

The success of Indian global corporations provides a glimpse into a unique leadership approach that dates back to Indo-European cultural, religious, and philosophical roots of India and Iran. The Indo-Europeans were tribes that migrated from the Pontic-Caspian Steppes of the Northern Black Sea to Central Asia, India, and Europe. While Iran, or Persia as it was officially known in the West until the beginning of the 20th century, is geographically considered part of the Middle East, its ethnic linguistic and cultural roots are deeply Indo-European. As a result, the country shares many cultural values with India. The shared historical, cultural, and philosophical roots between India and Iran are evident in the common origins of their languages (Proto-Indo-European; Mallory & Adams, 2006), and their religious traditions. Accordingly, modern cross-cultural research such as the GLOBE studies have grouped Iran in the South Asian cluster that includes India, rather than the in Middle Eastern cluster (House, Hanges, Javidan, Dorfman, & Gupta, 2004). Because of many factors that are beyond the scope of this chapter, India is well on its way to becoming one of the world's major industrial powers, while Iran has yet to achieve its potential. However, both countries are the cradle of civilizations dating back thousands of years. India and Iran both also have a treasure trove of literature, religious texts, and mythology that addresses leadership directly or indirectly, presents leadership guidelines and principles, and provides numerous historical examples of effective and ineffective leaders.

INDIA

Although practiced by millions of people throughout history and in modern India, Hinduism includes closely related traditions, but few unified sets of beliefs. The basic principles include realization of self through intense meditation and fulfilling moral and social duties with the recognition of the authority of the Indian sacred text (the Vedas), and its priests (the Brahmans), the principle of reincarnation, and the law of karma that determines one's destiny in this life and the next. For the common man or woman, Hinduism is simply a "way of life" and he/she should work toward the goals of "Humility, modesty, nonviolence, forbearance, honesty, service to Guru, purity, steadfastness, self-control and aversion towards sense objects, absence of ego, constant reflection on agony and suffering inherent in birth, disease and death" (Sarma, 2013).

The Bhagavad Gita, the 700-verse Hindu scripture, well-known in the West, emphasizes these goals and offers a clear focus on leadership. In the Gita, an effective leader is expected to demonstrate a high level of integrity and inner strength and be compassionate to all living beings especially when they are in distress. It is the leader's duty to fight injustice. Perhaps the most telling trait is the discourse in Gita on material possessions. A leader, or for that matter any human being, should not covet material things and should be satisfied with what he has been allotted in life. The Gita urges to "set thy heart upon thy work but never its reward" and to perform "work in this world, as a man established within himself – without selfish attachments, and alike in success and defeat" (Easwaran, 2007).

In more recent history of India, Mahatma Gandhi provides the most striking example yet of these leadership ideals. Gandhi, who lived his life based on the prescriptions of the Gita, has had a profound influence on the political, business, and social fabric of modern India with his message of peace and love rather than

war and destruction. He held that truth was the sovereign principle and he used it successfully in his struggle against racism, violence, and other social evils as well (Fischer, 1983). His actions
and teachings embodied integrity, kindness and compassion,
humility, fairness and justice, moderation, seeking knowledge
and accountability (Mahatma Gandhi, 2002). His vision of a free
India united all her people and they responded to his call of nonviolence and *Satyagraha*, or insistence on truth. Gandhi also
believed that India would never be completely free unless social
evils such as the caste system, the poor treatment meted out to
women, illiteracy, and poverty were eliminated. Gandhi's application of the Gita's prescriptions has made it easy for the common man or woman to understand the key principles of how to
conduct oneself in one's personal and professional life.

IRAN

Iranian literature presents a rich tradition of political treatise and
leadership advice. Ardeshir I (died in 242 AD), and Khosrow
Anoushiravan (531–571 AD), both of the Sassanid Dynasty
(224–651 AD) provided specific advice to kings that was clearly
influenced by the ancient Zoroastrian religion, a monotheist
religion that was dominant in Iran until the Arab invasion
that brought Islam to the country in the 7th century AD.
Zoroastrianism preaches free choice, battle against evil through
purity, good thoughts, good words, and good deeds (Brelian-
Djahanshahi, 2001). It is still practiced in modern-day Iran and
by the Parsis in parts of Northern India. Leadership lessons
can be found later in the writings of Nizam-al-Mulk (2002), an
11th-century scholar and statesman. Furthermore, Ferdowsi's
Shahnameh (*Book of Kings*, 2004), a masterpiece of Iranian literature that includes over 100,000 verses of Persian mythology
written in the 11th century, also offers many direct lessons
regarding leadership. Moreover, one of Iran's most renowned
authors, 13th-century philosopher Saadi, had a keen interest in
leadership and governance and addressed the topics specifically
in his writings (Saadi, 2536/1977). This rich literature presents
consistent leadership ideals and principles.

First, leaders are the indispensable drivers of the success of
any action. Kings are credited with the creation of civilization
and the rebirth of the country after its many invasions and wars.
Equality and being leaderless is tantamount to chaos (Ferdowsi,
2004; Nahavandi, 2009). An often told story about a general in

the army of Nadir Shah, the Iranian conqueror of India in the 18th century, who when asked why Iranians had failed so many times to conquer India, responded that while the army was always there, the King's presence is what made the difference in the final victory. Second, leaders carry the burden of their followers and are expected to be decisive and act when necessary. Saadi exhorts leaders into action: "You must kill the wolf in the beginning, not after all the sheep have been killed" (2036/1977). They are further expected to be kind, compassionate, and humble and dedicate themselves to serving those who have less power. "The one who does not serve others and does not help them does not deserve to rule and have the benefits of good fortune" (Saadi, 2536; 12) "The duty of masters is to serve their subjects. Additionally, their greatness comes from recognizing and expressing gratitude to servants without expecting anything in return" (Saadi, 2536, 88). Finally, integrity and reputation are paramount, and hubris is considered a fatal flaw (Nahavandi, 2009). While contemporary examples of leaders who embody and practice IEL are not available, the ideals of leadership have remained relatively unchanged for over 3,000 years (Nahavandi, 2012). The image of the benevolent, warm, and stern father figure is further documented in modern research about leadership in Iran (Ayman & Chemers, 1983; Chemers, 1969).

While some differences between the leadership traditions of the two countries exist, they share several key principles.

IEL Principles

Several unifying principles emerge from the review of Indian and Iranian literature and philosophy. These principles are the basis for an ideal leadership type in both cultures. While the focus of the literature and our review is on leaders and leadership, as powerful cultural memes, these principles and the words that express them are universal in India and Iran; they apply to everyone. However, leaders, because of their status and power, are expected to embody them, be role models, and conduct themselves such that all these principles coexist and are integrated.

Table 1 presents the principles, the Hindi and Persian equivalents along with their English translations. The Gita's original language was Sanskrit, a language no longer in daily use. Additionally, India currently has 14 major languages with Hindi as the official language spoken by 30% of the population. The

Table 1.   IEL Principles in Hindi and Persian.

IEL Principle	Hindi	Persian
Integrity	*Imaandari* (faith, noncorrupt) *Akhandtha* (honesty)	*Sedaghat* (integrity, wholeness)
		Dorosti (honesty)
Action-orientation	*Karya Anmukh* (action oriented)	*Amal Garai* (action oriented)
Moderation	*Sanyam* (restraint or moderation), *Santoolan* (balance)	*Miyaneh ravi* (walking between two roads)
		Ehtyat (prudence)
Accountability	*Zimadaari* (responsible for) *Javaabdehee* (responsible)	*Passokhgooee* (to answer to)
Kindness	*Dayaaluta* (generous) *Mehrabani* (noble minded)	*Mehrabani* (kindness)
Humility	*Vinamrata* (humble) *Namrata* (docile)	*Forootani* (humility)

business language in India is now primarily English. Modern Hindi and modern Persian are both highly similar to the languages found in each country's literature. As can be seen in Table 1, some of the Hindi and Persian words are similar (e.g., kindness), and in the case of accountability, "*javab*" (Hindi) is a synonym for "*passokh*" (Persian; meaning to answer), further demonstrating the common roots of the languages.

INTEGRITY

Integrity is the indispensable principle of IEL, its sine qua non. The themes of sound moral character, adherence to strong ethical practice, and maintenance of a good reputation are ever present in religious, cultural, and literary texts. In both Indian and Iranian writings, effective leaders have integrity, keep faith with their followers, and act based on consistent moral principles. When dealing with followers, they must remain true to their words and values. Integrity is a universal theme in leadership; however, its presentation as a key leadership factor in IEL is in sharp contrast with other classical writings such as Machiavelli's *The Prince* or Sun Tzu's *The Art of War* where deception and treachery are recommended as a means of achieving and retaining power. Moreover, leaders are also responsible for their advisors' and followers' behavior. If they surround themselves with dishonest people or tolerate lack of integrity in others, they themselves will lose legitimacy and will not be able to lead effectively.

ACTION-ORIENTATION

IEL is a call to action rather a passive observation of events. Leaders are seen as powerful and present. Leaders matter and they must act; they are defined by their actions and are required to take on the responsibilities of their role. Passivity is not desirable. A leader who fails to take action when possible and necessary, is ineffective and judged harshly. Leaders must be patient and prudent, but they must act. Followers expect them to make decisions and move things forward. Impetuousness is detrimental, but action is essential to IEL.

MODERATION

In IEL, action must be accompanied by moderation. Effective leaders shun extremes at every opportunity, carefully and patiently weigh all sides, show restraint, and avoid rash decisions and actions that can cause irreparable harm. Anything that is carried to its extreme, even courage, kindness, religiosity, and generosity, can have adverse consequences. The path to success is moderation, balance, patience, and careful slow actions that avoid extremes at all costs.

ACCOUNTABILITY

A leader's power, authority, and privilege come with considerable responsibility towards followers and other stakeholders and their community. In IEL, leaders are not only accountable to their followers, since they are their servants, they are, more importantly, accountable to a higher authority. They have to answer for their actions. Good deeds will be rewarded and transgressions punished, if not in the present, certainly in the future and in the after, or in another later life. Leaders must behave in accordance to IEL principles and are held accountable for two reasons. First, it is a source of power and legitimacy; second, applying these principles protects the leader against destiny. One's actions determine one's destiny, and therefore, must be carefully thought-out. When leaders act according to IEL principles, they not only become effective, respected, and loved, but they also protect themselves. The recurring themes of goodness for goodness sake along with threat of punishment and retribution provide strong incentives for leaders to act with integrity and to be accountable for their actions.

KINDNESS

Taking care of others is the cornerstone of IEL. The ideal leader is kind, generous, and compassionate to all regardless of their station in life. The leader is a strong and caring and benevolent father figure who advocates for followers and for those who are weak and powerless and cannot advocate for themselves. Leaders attend to their followers' needs to secure the latter's well-being and, as a result, assure their own success and salvation. Taking advantage of the powerless and weak is a fault and frowned upon. Cruelty and malice are considered fundamental flaws that are anathema to IEL. Leaders must show compassion when they can, and forgive mistakes, while they, themselves, are held to higher standards and must act without reproach.

HUMILITY

Humility and shunning pride are another essential IEL principle. The ideal leaders are humble and self-effacing servants to those they lead, not superior and overconfident. Leaders and followers are part of an integral whole rather than separate parts. One cannot survive without the other. When leaders mistreat their followers, they hurt themselves. Leaders must remain accessible and remember that their duty and the purpose of their power are to serve others. Power and glory must be used to help followers, not for the benefit of the leader. Arrogance, pride, and hubris are undesirable and likely to cause the fall of leaders. Leaders must do what is right without expectations for recognition. Their good deeds and accomplishments will speak for themselves — as will their mistakes.

Together, these six principles are the basis for a unique IEL approach. All are essential and must be integrated and balanced to lead effectively.

IEL, Far-Eastern Leadership Philosophies, and Modern Leadership

Some of the IEL principles are present in many other cultural traditions. For example, humility and caring are part of Far-East

Asian philosophies. Much like IEL's insistence on the need for humility, Chinese philosophy relies on it as a necessity for social order and happiness. Tsu (1989) states: "He who displays himself does not shine; he who asserts his own views is not distinguished" (24); "A skillful commander strikes a decisive blow and stops... He will strike the blow, but will be on his guard against being vain or boastful or arrogant in consequence of it" (30:3). The IEL principle of kindness is matched by Confucius' exhortation regarding the importance of benevolence: "Recompense injury with justice, and recompense kindness with kindness" (Confucius, 1979). Furthermore, the principle of moderation in IEL has strong similarities with the ideal of the golden mean or temperance discussed in Taoism, Confucianism, Buddhism. It is also echoed in ancient Greek philosophy and has even influenced American transcendentalism (Versluis, 1993), a movement that is based on a belief in the goodness of people and nature. For example, 19th-century American philosopher, poet and essayist Henry David Thoreau, a leading transcendentalist, cites Saadi as one of his sources of inspiration (Kramer, 2007), particularly in relation to living life simply and with humility (Crowley, 2011).

The IEL principles of integrity, compassion, and humility are in stark contrast to some Western leadership advice, such as that proposed by Machiavelli in the Prince. However, a connection to modern leadership theory can be found. The GLOBE findings on universal leadership ideals indicate that integrity is valued in most cultures and cruelty is unacceptable in most as well (Den Hartog, House, Hanges, Ruiz-Quintanilla, & Dorfman, 1999; House et al., 2004). Integrity is also at the heart of most current conceptions of leadership (e.g., Kouzes & Posner, 1993). Furthermore, strong action-orientation, as a general cultural value as well as a component for leadership, is certainly part of many Western cultures. Similarly, consideration of followers is present in all modern leadership theories in one form or another, for example, as part of charismatic (Bass, 1985; Burns, 1978) and authentic (George, 2003) leadership theories. Humility and service to others are at the heart of servant leadership (Greenleaf, 1998) where leading with strong moral principles, and service to, and sacrifice for others, are the focus. The concepts are also part of the growing spiritual leadership movement (e.g., Fry, 2003).

As the words Indo-European suggest, IEL bridges Eastern and Western cultural traditions and leadership ideals. It draws from both the Indian and the European cultures; it represents the middle ground between the East and the West. The examples of some successful India companies provide an illustration.

IEL in Action in Modern India

The rise of India as a global economic power provides recent examples of how IEL is at the core of the best-run Indian companies in modern-day India and can be practiced in modern organizations. Several well-run Indian companies have been quick to embrace and integrate the best practices from the Western world without compromising on India's cultural norms and traditions and have combined profitability with fairness and justice. Tata, one of the world's largest conglomerates and parent company of the Taj mentioned earlier, was founded on IEL principles in the late 19th century. Interestingly, the family that owns and runs Tata are Parsis, a religion based on Zoroastrianism. Birla another large conglomerate and other companies founded in the late 20th century such as Wipro, Infosys, and Aravind Eye Care have at their core a value system that was practiced and perfected by Gandhi. The philosophy also runs deep in Reddy's Laboratories and Godrej Consumer Products, to name a few. Finally, in recent years, this philosophy has also permeated some of the government-run enterprises such as NTPC (National Thermal Power Corporation) and the India Railway system.

Nobel Laureate Muhammad Yunus who hails from Bangladesh, a country in the Indian subcontinent, best known as the pioneer of Micro-Financing, is another example of IEL in practice. Yunus founded the Grameen Bank (village bank) on the principles of trust, solidarity, and independence with a business model based on the Gita and Gandhian leadership principles that show that "fairness and justice" and running a profitable enterprise are not mutually exclusive. Unlike the traditional banking system where the loan default rates tend to increase during a recession, more than 96% of the loans in the Grameen bank system are paid back (Khandker, 2005). Yunus' business model has helped uplift millions of women (and their families) living in abject poverty in the developing nations of Asia, Africa, and Latin America (Khandker, 1998).

Aravind Eye Care System, founded by ophthalmologist Govindappa Venkataswamy in 1976, is another case in point (Mehta & Shenoy, 2011). Venkataswamy's goal was to establish an alternate health system that could supplement the efforts of the government in combating blindness due to cataracts, a condition that afflicts millions of Indians. His business provides free treatment to patients who cannot pay, and high-quality yet affordable care for the rest. The profit generated from the paying patients is used to subsidize the free services for the poor. The company has a clear purpose (to cure needless blindness caused by cataracts), unique marketing (vision and extended distribution channels that tap into the networks of NGOs), highly satisfied customers (100% repeat customers), efficient operations (assembly-line style), and excellent human resource management and development (the technician force comprises primarily women from the rural areas; Govindarajan, 2012). Aravind's doctors perform 2,000 cataract surgeries a year, on average, without compromising on quality, whereas the global average stands at 400 (Mehta & Shenoy, 2011). Its lenses cost $10 a piece while the global average stands at $100. These practices tell the story of purpose-driven leadership that has a strong focus on employees training and development, is accountable to the organization rather than only to external stakeholders, values integrity and reputation, emphasizes long-term strategy, and is tightly involved in broader social issues.

The two brief examples profiled here, along with the case of the Taj (Deshpandre & Raina, 2011) and the study of Indian executives (Cappelli et al., 2010a, 2010b, 2015) reveal that adopting the IEL style can have far-reaching consequences and positive impact for both businesses and communities. By improving the financial well-being of millions of women, who remain the primary caregiver for their families, and by treating blindness, which contributes to securing family income and stability, the leaders of Grameen and Aravind are able to make a significant impact on society, and also turn a profit.

Application of IEL Western Organizations and Implications for Practice

IEL's strong action orientation draws and appeals to the West, and its emphasis on kindness, compassion, and humility connect with Far-Eastern approaches. IEL provides the middle ground that may make it both appealing and applicable to many cultural settings. It proposes that leaders are honest, moderate in their actions, decisive and daring, accountable to those they lead, kind to the weak and even enemies, caring of their followers, focused on action, and doing good and humble. Some of these themes are present in ideals of leadership in most cultures. However, the totality of these and the strong emphasis on kindness and caring, moderation, and humility while still focusing on action, are unique and offer a novel perspective on leadership. IEL is based on facing turmoil, adversity, and the inherent challenges of leading with unwavering integrity, moderation, action, kindness, and humility. The teachings have a strong religious and spiritual basis with the focus on purity, abstinence, repentance, and contentment as the means of achieving closeness to the Divine. However, the lessons can be applied and practiced in a secular manner in organizations.

IEL is characterized by duty, honor, compassion, accountability, and responsibility without selfishness, greed, and ambition. Some may argue that such ideals are archaic and outdated. Instead, what we need today are speed, innovation, and boldness, pushing the envelope in all areas; and those require individual rewards and recognition for leaders. However, integrity, compassion, accountability, and responsibility are principles that make a society civil and allow us to prosper and live in peace. They provide the essential order, predictability, organization, and accountability that allow communities and societies to thrive. They are what make us human, and allow us to aspire to be the best that we can be. The research about modern Indian industrial leaders and their unique style indicates that they are successful at blending these cultural roots and values with the managerial and economic demands of today's business organizations. They provide a case in point that demonstrates that the IEL principles can be used to run highly effective and financially successful organizations. Leaders who practice IEL create an environment where followers, along with the leader, will be dedicated to one another's well-being, be bold and look for solutions to problems, innovate, and address problems cooperatively.

IEL offers a fresh perspective that may be easier to implement in Western settings than Far-East Asian approaches. Indeed, leading U.S. businesses have already taken note of the IEL's promise as evidenced from the appointment of several leaders of Indian origin to the helm of their companies in the past decade: Indra Nooyi has served as the CEO of PepsiCo since 2006; and Satya

Nadella was appointed as the CEO of Microsoft in 2014; and in 2015, Sundar Pichai assumed office as the CEO of Google. Nooyi's leadership is dominated by her unwavering moral compass and relationship building skills with all constituencies, including the families of her employees (Kruse, 2014). Nadella has been described as a humble, collegial, and calming personality (Ovide, 2015). Both have a bias for innovation and action. Pichai is described as an even-tempered person devoted to his coworkers' achievement without drawing attention to himself (Lebowitz, 2016).

Innovation and action are not as much part of the Far-Eastern Asian leadership ideals that place a higher value on conformity to social order, and gradual and measured action. The strong emphasis on action that defines IEL fits well with many Western cultures that are also action-oriented. Leadership is about making decisions, taking action when necessary, being responsible for the community, organization, or state and being accountable for your actions. These tasks come with considerable privilege that can often go to the leaders' head or, at worst, make them corrupt and abusive. Staying humble and connected to followers and being well-grounded are probably the biggest challenges of leadership, especially leadership at high levels.

IEL provides a contrast to leadership styles that are practiced in many organizations and in many countries (including countries with Indo-European cultural roots). The focus of Western leadership is more often than not, on the leaders, their power, ideas, and actions. IEL is based on others; not the leader. Leadership is based on service and focus on the common good where leaders are accountable to those they lead and must act as shepherds and servants, rather than as powerful overlords who command their followers. They must be humble and focused on their primary role of helping followers since, followers are the ones who achieve results. Yet, IEL does not negate the importance of vision or leading change. The mythological and real leaders in these ancient countries have provided vision and managed change that is far more drastic than anything we face. However, the unique contribution of IEL is to focus on taking care of followers so that they can achieve the goals. So what can modern-day leaders learn and borrow from IEL?

- *Integrity matters.* No matter where and what the circumstances, integrity counts. "Walking the talk," being honest and truthful, and guarding one's reputation are essential to a leader's ability to be effective. Followers demand it and deserve it. No one trusts and follows — at least not willingly and not for long — a leader who lacks principles, lies, and cheats.

- *A leader must act.* The work of a leader is defined by his or her actions. Leaders must, and are expected to, act and help their followers, organizations, and communities move forward.
- *Take the road of moderation.* We live in times where extremes are sought out and valued. Many seem to hunger for increasing stimulation that comes from engaging in thrilling activities that start an unending cycle. Taking extreme risks, for potentially high rewards, has become the norm and is celebrated in Western popular culture. Leadership has not been immune from this trend. IEL strongly advocates the middle road, the Golden Mean instead. When you have responsibility for others' life and well-being, as leaders do, taking moderate actions is essential. The path of moderation does not shun innovation and creativity; it simply advocates careful and thoughtful action that is most likely to benefit the largest number of people.
- *Be accountable.* The power and privilege that come with leadership demand accountability to other. Leaders must accept responsibility for their actions, their successes and failures. Power does not allow leaders to act with impunity. If anything, they are held to higher standards than others. While followers are allowed mistakes and should be forgiven when they are committed in good faith, leaders do not have such a luxury. As role models, they have little room for error.
- *Kindness and caring for others are essential.* As a follower, most of us expect some degree of kindness and compassion. But we find many political and business leaders who disregard their importance. They argue that their job is to get things done, not take care of people. They are not parents; they are organizational or national leaders. Particularly in Western countries, compassion is not a word associated with leadership. IEL proposes a different approach. Being kind and compassionate is essential and necessary to good leadership. Leadership is not about things; it is about people. Without caring about people and without engaging them, nothing can get done, or at least nothing can get done well.

Being kind, compassionate, and forgiving does not make leaders weak; it makes them stronger and better.

- *Be humble*. The power that we give our leaders can be heady and one of the major challenges they face is not to let that power get into their heads. They must make every effort to remain humble and unpretentious. The arrogant leaders who show hubris and act with a sense of impunity do not start out that way; they acquire those behaviors as they gain power. Focusing on others, not oneself, is a key lesson from IEL.

Summary Conclusions

This chapter traces leadership lessons from two ancient Indo-European cultures, India and Iran, and discusses how their IEL principles can be applied to Western cultures and modern organizations globally. Calls for fresh leadership practices that address the challenges of a diverse and global world have been growing not only in Western organizations, but all over the world. For example, Ratanjee and Pyrka (2015) have highlighted the need to fill the leadership gap in Southeast Asian organizations with leaders with authenticity, transparency, and objectivity, all characteristics that are part of IEL. The IEL perspective has much to offer especially in a millennium when social and economic inequalities are on the rise and organizations in all sectors are tarnished by scandals. IEL has evolved and has been refined and honed over thousands of years. Perhaps the greatest contribution of this perspective is that one can balance ancient and well-tested traditions and cultures with the best practices of the West to create a new paradigm of leadership that can move nations and people forward. This paradigm, which has already been successfully implemented in some of the best-run companies of the world, reveals that improving the lot of societies and caring for people, and profit are completely compatible.

Western leadership philosophy is based on a version of capitalism that emphasizes self-interest and focuses on profit maximization as the most important goal for any firm. Interestingly, Smith (1776), who is recognized as the father of capitalism through his book *The wealth of nations*, suggested that while human being are selfish by nature, and that by pursuing their self-interests, they collectively can build a diverse and prosperous economic and social system, there is also a moral obligation to take care of society. In his earlier writings Smith discussed the morality of wealth and introduced the idea of the *Invisible hand* that tampers and moderates self-interest (*The theory of moral sentiments*, 1759). Smith suggested that without a good moral base, and without control from government, and self-control from individuals, capitalism cannot succeed. He proposed that a "prudent man" would go beyond self-interest and seek to benefit all of society with simplicity, sincerity, modesty, and frugality, and would act with caution (Smith, 1759). It appears that modern capitalism has focused on the self-interest aspect without considering the moral obligations that even Adam Smith believed would make society function fairly. The practice of IEL can successfully coexist with Smith's recommendations for capitalism, and his emphasis on prudence and moderation.

Unfortunately, many Western business and political leaders have, at best, paid lip service to the interests of other constituencies such as the employees or communities. The economic and political upheavals of the 20th century, along with increasing local and global diversity, suggest that capitalist solutions based only on individual self-interest that have roots in only one cultural tradition can no longer move nations forward. The IEL approach, as it has been successfully implemented in a few companies, reveals that serving broad constituencies is not inconsistent with free market principles that drive prosperous Western economies.

Discussion Questions

1. What are the underlying cultural roots of IEL?
2. Discuss each of the six IEL principles and their impact on leadership.
3. How can IEL principles be implemented in Western organizations?
4. What are the challenges and benefits of implementing IEL?

References

Ayman, R., & Chemers, M. M. (1983). Relationship of supervisory behavior ratings to work group effectiveness and subordinate satisfaction among Iranian managers. *Journal of Applied Psychology, 68,* 338–341.

Bass, B. M. (1985). *Leadership and performance beyond expectations.* New York, NY: Free Press.

Brélian-Djahanshahi, F. (2001). Histoires légendaires des rois de Perse *(Legendary History of the Persian Kings)*. Paris: Edition Imago.

Burns, J. M. (1978). *Leadership*. New York, NY: Harper and Row.

Cappelli, P., Singh, H., Singh, J. V., & Useem, M. (2010a). Leadership lessons from India. *Harvard Business Review*, March, 1−10.

Cappelli, P., Singh, H., Singh, J. V., & Useem, M. (2010b). *The India way: How India's top business leaders are revolutionizing management*. Boston, MA: Harvard Business Press.

Cappelli, P., Singh, H., Singh, J. V., & Useem, M. (2015). 12 Indian business leadership: Broad mission and creative value. *The Leadership Quarterly, 26*, 7−12.

Chemers, M. M. (1969). Cross-cultural training a means of improving situational favorableness. *Human Relations, 22*, 531−546.

Chin, J. L., & Trimble, J. E. (2015). *Diversity and leadership*. Los Angeles, CA: Sage.

Confucius (1979). *The analects* (D. C. Lau, Trans.). Harmondsworth Penguin Books.

Crowley, J. M. (2011). *Eastern past, Western present, and back again: Emerson, Thoreau, and Eastern philosophy*. Proquest − Umi Dissertation Publishing.

Den Hartog, D. N., House, R. J., Hanges, P. J., Ruiz-Quintanilla, S. A., & Dorfman, P. W. (1999). Culture-specific and cross-culturally generalizable implicit leadership theories: Are attributes of charismatic/transformational leadership universally endorsed? *The Leadership Quarterly, 10*, 219−256.

Deshpandre, R., & Raina, A. (2011). The ordinary heroes of the Taj. *Harvard Business Review*, December. Retrieved from http://hbr.org/2011/12/the-ordinary-heroes-of-the-taj/ar/1

Easwaran, E. (2007). *The Bhagavad Gita: A classic of Indian spirituality*. Berkeley, CA: Nilgiri Press.

Ferdowsi, A. (2004). *Shahnameh: The Persian book of kings*. New translation by Dick Davis. New York, NY: Penguin Books.

Fischer, L. (1983). *The life of Mahatma Gandhi*. New York, NY: Harper Collins.

Fry, L. W. (2003). Toward a theory of spiritual leadership. *The Leadership Quarterly, 14*, 693−727.

George, B. (2003). *Authentic leadership*. San Francisco, CA: Jossey-Bass.

Govindarajan, V. (2012). Profitable audacity: One company's success story. *Harvard Business Review*. January 25. Retrieved from https://hbr.org/2012/01/profitable-audacity-one-companys-success-story.html

Greenleaf, R. K. (1998). *The power of servant leadership*. San Francisco, CA: Berrett-Koehler.

House, R. J., Hanges, P. J., Javidan, M., Dorfman, P. M., & Gupta, V. (2004). *Culture, leadership and organizations: The GLOBE study of 62 societies*. Thousand Oaks, CA: Sage Publications.

Khandker, S. R. (1998). *Fighting poverty with microcredit: Experience in Bangladesh*. Oxford: Oxford University Press.

Khandker, S. R. (2005). Microfinance and poverty: Evidence using panel data from Bangladesh. *World Bank Economic Review, 19*, 263–286.

Kouzes, J. M., & Posner, B. Z. (1993). *Credibility: How leaders gain and lose it, why people demand it.* San Francisco, CA: Jossey-Bass.

Kramer, J. S. (2007). *I to myself: An annotated selection from the journal of Henry D. Thoreau.* New Haven, CN: Yale University Press.

Kruse, K. (2014). Why PepsiCo's CEO writes to her employees. February 6, *Forbes.*

Lao Tsu (1989). *Tao Teh Ching.* (J.C.H. Wu, Trans.). Shambhala Dragon Editions.

Lebowitz, S. (2016). The brilliant management strategy Google's new CEO used to become one of the world's most powerful executives. March 29, *The BusinessInsider.*

Mahatma Gandhi. (2002). The essential Gandhi: An anthology of his writings on his life, work and ideas. In: L. Fischer (Ed.). Vintage Spiritual Classics.

Mallory, J. P., & Adams, D. Q. (2006). *The Oxford introduction to Proto-Indo-European and the Proto-Indo-European World.* Oxford: Oxford Linguistics.

Mehta, P. K., & Shenoy, S. (2011). *Infinite Vision: How Aravind became the world's greatest business case.* California: Berrett-Koehler Publishers, Inc.

Nahavandi, A. (2009). Cultural mythology and global leadership in Iran. In E. H. Kessler & D. J. Wong-Mingji (Eds.), *Cultural mythology and global leadership* (pp. 242–256). Cheltenham: Edward Elgar Publishers.

Nahavandi, A. (2012). Iranian mystical leadership: Lessons for contemporary leaders. In G. P. Prastacos, F. Wang, & K. E. Soderquist (Eds.), *Leadership through the classics: Learning management and leadership from ancient East and West philosophy* (pp. 191–204). New York, NY: Springer-Verlag.

Nizam-al-Mulk. (2002). *The book of government* (D. Hubert, Trans.). London: Curzon Press.

Ovide, S. (2015). Microsoft's quiet office evolution under Satya Nadella. September 29, *Wall Street Journal.* Retrieved from http://www.wsj.com/articles/microsofts-quiet-office-evolution-under-satya-nadella-1443557059

Ratanjee, V., & Pyrka, A. (2015). Fixing the leadership gap in Southeast Asia. *Harvard Business Review,* May 27. Retrieved from https://hbr.org/2015/05/fixing-the-leadership-gap-in-southeast-asia

Saadi, M. (2536/1977). *Complete works of Saadi.* M. A. Forouqi (Ed.), (2nd ed.). Tehran: Amir Kabir.

Sarma, D. S. (2013). *A Primer of Hinduism.* Kindle Edition. Chennai: Sri Ramakrishna Matt Printing Press.

Smith, A. (1759). *The theory of moral sentiments.* Patianos Classics.

Smith, A. (1776). *The wealth of nations: Inquiry into the nature and causes.* Bantam Classics.

Versluis, A. (1993). *American transcendentalism and Asian religions.* New York, NY: Oxford University Press.

7 Current and Emerging Patterns of Muslim Leadership

Lina Klemkaite

Introduction

The chapter aims at providing a theoretical overview of Muslim authority and leadership and, to analyze the reasons behind the current pluralization of religious authority and emerging leadership patterns and challenges. The author argues that Muslim leadership shall be studied as reciprocal relationship, that is an interactive and dynamic process. In addition, it is discussed that understanding of leadership and the leadership process necessitates developing an understanding of leader, the follower(s), the context, the processes, and the resulting consequences.

The Weberian approach to leadership and to be more precise, three ideal types of authority can provide us with the analytical lenses for interpreting the complex networks of authority that have formed throughout the history of Islam and that, at the same time, are evident in the current Muslim societies.

Other sociological schools and/or approaches to leadership can provide further insights to understanding leadership dynamics within the community and the relationship among the leader and the led and so, offer series of overlapping insights.

This chapter aims at contributing to the construction of knowledge, theoretical as well as practical, about the processes during which the effective leadership can be built, able to promote the intracommunity dialogue (leadership within) and integration (leadership outside).

It is argued that Islamic authority and so, Muslim leadership should be approached and analyzed as a sociological concept and constructed on theoretical assumptions of classical sociology as well.

INTRODUCTORY NOTE

> The authority of much scholarship from the past has been rejected: the authority of the traditional interpreters, the ulama, has been marginalized. New claimants to authority have come forward with none of the finely − boned skills of traditional scholarship, indeed, for growing numbers of Muslims Islam has become a matter of individual conscience, individuals have come to interpret the faith for themselves. No one knows any longer, as the saying goes, 'who speaks for Islam'. There is in fact, a crisis of authority. (Robinson, 2009, p. 340)

The present chapter aims at providing a theoretical overview of Muslim authority and leadership. It will be argued that Muslim leadership shall be studied as reciprocal relationship, that is an interactive and dynamic process, whereby the leader influences the follower, the follower (who also fulfils active roles) influences the leader, and both are influenced by context surrounding leader−follower relationship. In addition, it will be discussed that understanding of leadership and the leadership process necessitates developing an understanding of leader, the follower(s), the context, the processes, and the resulting consequences.

First of all, it has to be highlighted that up to date, the majority of the studies undertaken on Muslim leadership in Spain and Europe were developed on an actor-centered approach, focusing on specific types of religious actors and/or institutions. On the other hand, a big amount of scientific literature, in both, theoretical studies as well as in elaborated proposals addressed to support political action (e.g., proposals issued by the European Agency of Fundamental Rights), have highlighted the importance of "leadership" in the constitution of Muslim communities, which is of crucial importance in leading and guiding the community, and especially, for the construction of dialogue and promotion of a positive image of Islam. According to the Abdulhaleem (2012), the role of Muslim representatives and leaders is decisive in building the bridges of understanding and promoting the common values between the community and host society. All in all, the chapter aims at contributing to the construction of knowledge, theoretical as well as practical, about the processes during which the effective leadership can be built, able to promote the intracommunity dialogue (leadership within) and integration (leadership outside).

Leadership as Reciprocal Relationship

The history of Islam reveals us a multiplicity of compelling patterns of authority, let alone the current and emerging patterns of competing Muslim leadership. It has to be highlighted here that critical literature and scholarship on the topic (particularly when it comes to the issue of Islamic leadership) is rather rare. Various scholars have fallen into the trap of biased analysis and interpretation by "praising" the Islamic leadership model and ethics, while providing models with wage theoretical assumptions (among others, Beekun and Badawi (1999)). A prevailing culturalist approach presents another methodological challenge.[1] Although the debate on what the Qur'an says might turn into a sterile one and support prejudices (Roy, 2004), it is indeed an insightful exercise to start with (though alone not sufficient) when studying the concept of religious authority in Islam and trying to understand the progressing crisis and fragmentation of Islamic authority and leadership. On the other hand, in terms of methodological limitations and challenges, it has to be said that many current studies on Islamic authority rather avoid the qur'anic conception of authority, being more focused in authority as a political or anthropological concept. Therefore, I would argue that Islamic authority and so, Muslim leadership should be approached and analyzed as a sociological concept and constructed on theoretical assumptions of classical sociology, to be more precise, with a Weberian approach.[2]

---

[1] As a result, *culturalist* approach which states that Islam is an "issue" provides a rather reductionist analysis, while looking at exclusively what does Islam or Quran say about certain study objects. Furthermore, *culturalist* approach reinforces a constant confusion between Islam as a religion and "Muslim culture."

[2] *Weberian* approach implies seeing the study objects in question in terms of ideal types and abstract categorical schemes, including the analysis of historical and cultural trends and a point of view of the situated subject (interpretative sociology).

Sociological perspective approaches leadership as a reciprocal relationship. Understanding of leadership and leadership dynamics implies developing an understanding of the leader, the followers, the context, the processes, and the resulting consequences (Pierce & Newstrom, 2011). As suggested by a number of social scholars, leadership is a social influence relationship interactive between two or more people dependent upon one another for the attainment of certain mutual goals, bound together within a group situation (*Ibid.*). Thus, leadership, as highlighted by Murphy (1941) is essentially sociological in its nature; is socially constructed through interaction, emerging as a result of the constructions and actions of both, the leaders and the led. In addition, other sociological schools and/or approaches to leadership can provide further insights into understanding leadership dynamics within the community and the relationship among the leader and the led and so, offer series of overlapping insights, among them: Social Identity theory of leadership, Symbolic Interactionism perspective on leadership, and "Dramaturgical approach" of E. Goffman.

A social identity theory of leadership views leadership as a group process generated by social categorization and prototype-based depersonalization processes associated with social identity. Group identification (as self-categorization) constructs an intragroup "prototypically" gradient that invests the most prototypical member with the appearance of having influence. As follows, the appearance arises because members cognitively and behaviorally conform to the prototype.[3] As Hogg and Van Knippenberg (2003, p. 189) puts it forward: "Leadership is more than passively being a prototypical group member; it involves actively influencing other people. One way in which this is made possible is through the social attraction process." In addition, social identity processes associated with leadership do not only apply to emergent leaders but also to enduring and structurally designated leaders. These ideas are a potentially rich source of conceptual explorations and provides a well-supported basis for the study of leadership effectiveness in a variety of areas.

---

[3]Depersonalization affects people's feelings about one another. They become based on perceived prototypically (social attraction) rather than idiosyncratic preferences or personal relationships (called personal attraction), which is the social attraction hypothesis (Hogg, 1999).

Symbolic Interactionism places primary value on subjective meaning and so, within the symbolic interactionism perspective or framework, the meaning placed on leader behaviors by followers is of importance in understanding the process by which leaders influence followers: the meaning-making process of followers mediates the influence of leader behaviors on subsequent follower behaviors. Symbolic leadership, as explained by Paul (1996) can influence followers' meaning-making processes in three ways: through the creation of shared meaning, through the creation of equifinal meaning, or through the creation of idiosyncratic meaning. Finally, symbolic interactionism as an individual-centered orientation focuses on individuals in interaction and within a group, as well as on the composition and development of the self and personality. Parker, Brown, Child, and Smith (1997, p. 2) defended this interpretative process, how it distinguishes behavior from action and "is made possible by a universe of symbols which links the individual to sets of ongoing socially constructed meanings." To put it in the words of Kotter (1999, p. 11): "Leadership is a supremely human activity where an emotional connection is created, trust is fostered and loyalty is strong. Leaders understand and resonate with the emotional needs and wants of people who follow them." Thus, leadership interpreted from the premise of symbolic interaction is a subject-orientated approach; it places emphasis on the subjective intention of individual wishes, motivations, situations, and interpretation of symbols.

Sociologist Erving Goffman's dramaturgical approach to human interaction provides insightful lenses to understand how impression management plays a critical role in the performance of leadership (Jacobsen, 2010). Considering social interaction as a performance, and the setting in which interaction occurs as the stage, the actors (the persons on the stage) play their parts to manage the impressions of others sharing the stage with them so that they may achieve their goals or objectives. The more skillful the actors, the more effective they are at convincing others that they are knowledgeable, trustworthy, and possess a charisma or dynamism that makes them a person to follow. Leaders use *framing*, specifically defining a scene or situation in a way that helps others interpret its meaning in the way the leader desires: by framing an action in a specific way the leader hopes to give followers a reason to offer him or her their support. In addition, leaders also use *scripting*, the identification of each actor's role in the scene: the leader convinces others on the stage that the leader needs them to play their roles as assigned so they can achieve the desired outcome. Finally, leaders use *engaging dialogue* – storytelling together with colorful and descriptive language and effective use of nonverbal cues – to guide the response of the other players.[4] It has to be added, that within the framework of Goffman's dramaturgical approach, *front-stage* is the area where the individuals (or actors) appear before the audience and where positive self-concepts and desired impressions are offered and constructed, while *back-stage* is the area where individuals can drop their social roles and identities (Goffman, 1974).

Weberian Approach to Leadership and Three Ideal Types of Authority

The theoretical assumptions and main postulate of Weberian approach to leadership refer to the three ideal types of authority (legal-rational, traditional, and charismatic) and the ways in which leaders can secure legitimacy for their rule. The leader's authority needs to be legitimate in the eyes of the led. Social and organizational structures shape leadership ideologies and their meaning (Guillén, 2010).

Rational-legal authority is based on the belief of the "legality" of patterns of normative rules and the right of those elevated to authority to issue commands, thus, "obedience is owed to the legally established impersonal order" (Weber, 1947, p. 328). Rational-legal authority involves impersonal order to which actions are oriented and the order in question consists of a body of generalized rules that are universalistic and applicable to all persons. It takes the form of "bureaucratic" structure ("purest type of exercise of legal authority" (Weber, 1947, p. 33)), when

---

[4]All these elements underlie the leader's performance. When engaged in performing, a leader makes a number of choices. For example, the leader can opt to use the technique of exemplification – serving as an example or acting as a role model for others to follow – or promotion – elucidating personal skills and accomplishments and/or a particular vision for others to value. The leader can engage in face-work – protecting his or her image by reducing the negative aspects of himself or herself visible to others – or practice ingratiation – using techniques of agreement that make others believe the leader to be more attractive and likeable and less threatening, harmful, or pernicious (Sage Handbook of Leadership, pp. 14–15).

rational-legal authority involves an organized administrative staff. Capitalism, though by no means alone, as defined by Weber (1947) is the most rational economic basis for bureaucratic administration that facilitates fundamental fiscal conditions. Together with fiscal conditions, communication and transportation becomes an extremely important dependent condition for the effective functioning of bureaucratic administration. In addition, "bureaucratic administration means fundamentally the exercise of control on the basis of knowledge" (*Ibid.*, p. 339).

Traditional authority, according to Weber (1947) is based on established belief in the sanctity of immemorial traditions and the legitimacy of the status of those exercising authority under them: "Obedience is owed to the person of the chief, who occupies the traditionally sanctioned position of authority and how is bound by tradition" (*Ibid.*, p. 328). Thus, the object of obedience in traditional authority is personal authority of the individual and is not owed to enacted rules. The system of order is treated here as having always existed and been binding. The order (here) in traditional authority systems contains concrete rules and may depend on the following: concrete traditional prescriptions of the traditional order, authority of the other persons above a particular status in hierarchy, arbitrary free "grace" open to incumbent. *Substantive rationality* marks a contrast between rational-legal and traditional authority, as observed by Parsons (1949). Moreover, "both the first two types of authority are, for Weber, modes of organization appropriate to a settled permanent social system" (*Ibid.*, p. 125). Like all human arrangements, they are subject to change; nevertheless, they are of particularly *"routine"* character, which marks the main difference from the third type of authority: the charismatic authority.

Charismatic[5] authority is based on devotion to the specific and exceptional sanctity, heroism, or exemplary character of the person. A charismatically qualified leader is obeyed by virtue of personal trust in him and his revelation or heroism/exemplary qualities.[6] "The term 'charisma' will be applied to a certain quality of an individual by virtue of which he is set apart from ordinary men and treated as endowed with supernatural, superhuman, or at

---

[5]As noted by Weber (1947), the concept of "charisma" ("the gift of grace") is taken from the vocabulary of early Christianity.
[6]Charismatic leadership usually stands for revolutionary force, challenging the stability of institutionalized order (Parsons, 1949).

least specifically exceptional powers or qualities" (Weber, 1947, p. 358). It is recognition of the followers (those subject to authority) that is decisive for the validation of charisma (legitimacy). Hence, charismatic authority refers to a claim to authority, which is actually, in conflict with the basis of legitimacy of an established order and as noted by Weber (1947, p. 361) is "specifically outside the realm of everyday routine and the profane sphere," therefore it cannot be stable until it is traditionalized or rationalized (*routinization of charisma*).

Three ideal types of authority can provide us with the analytical lenses for interpreting the complex networks of authority that have formed throughout the history of Islam and that, at the same time, are evident in the current Muslim societies. Indeed, Dabashi (1989) in his study *"Authority in Islam. From the Rise of Muhammad to the Establishment of the Umayyads"* provides an insightful account of the application of Weber's typology as a model – a point of departure to investigate Muhammad's charismatic authority: "Muhammad is a particular case that Weber's typology of charismatic authority illuminates" (*Ibid.*, p. xii). Dabashi (1989) discusses that Muhammad's charismatic authority was his personal quality. He was not to be followed by a similar figure of authority, being recognized as the last Prophet to be sent by the God. Within the framework of Weberian terminology, Muhammad as a charismatic authority had to confront the traditional patrimonial mode of Arab tribal authority. The death of the Prophet and thus, the end of his charismatic authority, initiated the inevitable process of disintegration. This process of disintegration, as Dabashi (1989, p. 3) explains: "manifested the complexity that the Islamic community had inherited after the death of its founding figure." This mode of all-encompassing personal authority was alien to traditional Arab tribal society. The division of the Muslim community after the Prophet's death is described by Dabashi (1989) as an institutionalization process that the legacy of this authority assumed. As follows, the institutionalization[7] resulted in three simultaneous processes, "which may be visualized as three horizontal lines moving along early

---

[7]"*The charismatic authority of the Prophet and the various ways in which it was sought to be institutionalized, overshadowed, to a considerable degree, the rest of Islamic history, which may be considered as a continuous effort to come to terms with the Prophetic authority of Muhammad*" (Dabashi, 1989, p. 16).

Islamic history, are then cut across by three vertical lines, known historically as the different branches of Islam" (*Ibid.*, p. 3). Sunni groups opted for the institutional preservation and continuation of the faith as the Prophet's legacy or routinization of the social economic life (what Weber called back to a more "normal situation"). Shiite groups attempted toward the preservation and institutionalization of the Prophet's charismatic authority, while the Kharijites advocated the preservation and continuation of Islam as a universal expression of the Muhammad's charismatic legacy (Dabashi, 1989, pp. 1–16).

As the history of Islam and to be more precise, the rise of Islamic empires revealed, the networks of authority over time became more complex. With the passage of time the successors of Muhammad (the *caliphs*) started to claim primary authority in both, spiritual and worldly affairs. Campo (2009) argues that this can be also seen in formal titles they (the successors) took: "God's deputy" (*khalifah Allah*) or even "commander (*amir*) of the faithful" or "God's authority on the earth" (*sultan*), rather than/instead of "deputy/successor of God's messenger" (*khalifat rasul Allah*). By the 10th century, due to the growing challenges to maintain the religious authority, the rulers had negotiated a division of legitimate power with *the ulama*, who over the course of history have been assigned multiple roles and functions, including: guardians of religious traditions, moral critics of the regimes, and/or legitimizers of regimes, etc. From the mid-18th century onwards the networks of authority became fragmented by a variety of historical forces, among them, worth noting: the breakdown of the Ottoman, Safavid, and Mughal empires and European colonial empires invasion to the Muslim lands, bringing multiple and frequently contending notions of authority at play (*Ibid.*).

Changing Roles of Traditional Authority: Postcolonial Legacy

Huge expansion of mass media and communications changed rapidly (and radically indeed) the socialization processes across the Muslims communities. As a result, all sources of books and information became widely available: "unknown spaces become known and the viewer become familiar with alternative ideologies" (Sutton & Vertigans, 2005, p. 107). At the same time, as

observed by Eickelman and Piscatori (1996), even though the
population on the Muslim countries outpaced educational expansion, we can observe a big increase of population able to con-
verse intelligently with religious and political authorities together
with the significant increase of the market for books, including
books about religion and society. Eickelman and Piscatori (1996,
p. 8) provides an insightful illustration of the above-described
process and its impact: "For example, consider 'The book and the
Qur'an: A Contemporary Interpretation', written by Muhammad
Shahrur, a Syrian civil engineer. To date, it has sold tens of thousands of copies. Even though circulation of the 800-page book
has been banned or discouraged in many Arab countries, photo-
copy machines and pirate editions (in Egypt among other places)
have allowed it to travel across official borders." Despite the great
impact of media and education, we shouldn't dismiss the fact that
mass schooling has also created a wide audience of people able to
read though not capable to interpret accordingly the religious literature. In terms of religious books and literature, we have also
faced an explosive growth of "Islamic books" — "many address
practical questions of how to live as a Muslim in the modern
world and the perils of neglecting Islamic obligations, and not all
appeal to reason and moderation" (*Ibid.*). In countries with liter-
acy levels still relatively low, TV and radio played a huge role in
the socializing process. On the other hand, it has to be highlighted
that the access of the information and information quality
depends on the extent to which media is state or privately owned.
Hence (in short), increasing offer and ongoing debates in newspa-
pers, magazines, journals, TV programs, and shows facilitated
an explosion of religious — political ideas and movements,
although it also has to be pointed out that many Muslim communities (particularly in Muslim nation-states) still lack access to
ICT technologies and usually rely on Internet Cafes (Sutton &
Vertigans, 2005).

It has to be added that a postcolonial replacement of the
Islamic legal systems with European models of nation — state
laws (post-colonial legacy) and transnational movements have
also had a huge impact on reducing the role and importance of
the *ulama*, leading to the crisis of authority (or "full-pledged
chaos," according to El Fadl (2001)) and "increasing fragmenta-
tions of authority as new methods of interpretation emerge"
(Robinson, 2009, p. 339). As a result: "virtually every Muslim
with a modest knowledge of Qur'an and the traditions of the
Prophet was suddenly considered qualified to speak for the

Islamic tradition and Shariah law – even Muslims unfamiliar with the precedents and accomplishments of past generations" (El Fadl (2005, pp. 38–39), as cited in Hammer (2011)). This "full-pledge chaos" or vacuum of authority facilitated new spaces for alternative voices to emerge and grow, including a *"cut-and-paste"* version of Islam (construction of religious knowledge, selecting from heterogeneous sources) or *"bricolage"* (do-it-yourself project), as named by Roy (2004). It can be argued that the loss of influence of traditional religious authorities and the reformulations of religious authority are leading to more individualized religiosity and accelerate the process of pluralization of religious authority structures.

External Context: New Identity Dynamics and Emerging Leadership Challenges

Although Muslim integration and accommodation pose similar challenges to many European countries, there is a range of instruments and models of accommodation, naturally, one could argue, due to the different nature of the hosting states and the different models applied. Consecutively, the accommodation models have a tendency to focus on immigrants' political rights, citizenship claims, labor demands, and civil rights and liberties; however, leaving apart the accommodation of religious practices and generally dismissing the fact that along the established Western European lines of secularization, Muslim religious rights and needs are key components of Muslim political demands – demands raised by diverse Muslim communities and demands that the new Muslim leadership is expected to answer.

Analyzing the external context and current integration policies, it has to be highlighted that the recent discussions about religious diversity management and migration are of distinct character. Bramadat and Koenig (2009) highlights two main reasons. First of all, it is due to the increasing non-Christian as well non-European Christian religious affiliations of the incoming migrants that raise new significant challenges to policy makers. Secondly, September 11th marked a shift in migration patterns and policies and thus, it is in the last 10–15 years that religion called special attention to the policy makers and scholars. Thus the 1990s marked a historical shift "when religion became a publicly more visible dimension of immigrants' claims for recognition, more complex analyses emerged from various models of believing and belonging among Muslims in Europe" (2005, p. 220). Besides, as Bramadat and Koenig (2009) puts it forward, we need to take into consideration the fact that for centuries in the West we were talking about accommodation of two major forms of Christianity, while recently we turned to the struggle about religious diversity governance; about accommodation of the different religious claims and denominations.

The association of Islam and immigration together with the securitization of Islam, as Cesari (2009) argues, has been followed by the restricted immigration policies and hardened national discourses on immigration. What is more, "European nations face a paradox: although they seek to facilitate the socio-economic integration of Muslims, anti-terrorism and security concerns fuel a desire to compromise liberties and restrict Islam from public space" (Cesari, 2009, p. 2). As a result, the integration policies are shaped by "culture talk." Muslim integration and interaction in secularized spaces "reopens" the question of the state–religion relationship that is strictly covered by the secularity. Within this context, Ferrari (2005) identifies a dual challenge: "on the one hand, for the Muslims themselves who have to find a means of integration in a reality (the secular state) that is culturally alien to many of them, and on the other, for the Europeans who have to understand how far the secularity of the state can go in integrating this reality" (2005, p. 12). On the other hand, Casanova (2004) questions and reveals that the "Islamic problem" is an indicator of disparity between liberal and nonliberal facets of European secularism. Cesari (2009) calls it "visibility of Islam," Casanova (2004) puts it as "religious otherness" explaining the challenges posed by Muslim integration. All together, we are dealing and reopening the question of the role of religion in the public space, "which European societies assumed they had already solved according to the liberal secular norm of privatization of religion" (Casanova, 2004).

As far as religious identity as a study object is concerned, when it comes to the recent multiculturalism and integration studies, there is a prevailing tendency to leave the religious identity aside, to the private sphere, focusing on the ethnicity "as the key factor responsible for a migrant group's persistence and survival in the new, different socio-cultural environment" (Baumann, 1999). Likewise, Modood (2000) also argues that theorists of multiculturalism ignored the religious dimension of identities in the framework of migration processes focusing on the claims for recognition of cultural and ethnical identities. Religion, according to Baumann (1999), "takes on a crucial role for identity re-construction and the maintenance of distinctiveness," thus in the modern and secular context, religious identity as a factor (that strengthens the feeling of solidarity and delineates the groups from its surroundings) should not be left apart as secondary. The inclusion of the religious identity in the public space not only challenges the above discussed established principle of secularity, it also comes to question various institutional arrangements of political organization, collective identity, and post national forms of citizenships.

Conclusion Remarks

The above-described integration trends and approaches represent a complex external context that the pluralized authority and Muslim leadership have to face. In addition, the increasing pluralization creates alternative spaces for new social and religious leaders to emerge. Furthermore, it could be argued that the increasing variety of voices and demands at the same time makes it difficult to distinguish who "speaks" or how and to identify the corresponding ideologies and rules – that remains one of the challenges of Muslim leadership research, while the relational aspect of authority and leadership adds a considerable complexity. Multidimensional approach to explaining leadership patterns and so, different sociological schools and/or approaches to leadership can bring new insights in understanding the complex leadership dynamics within the community and the relationship among the leaders and the fellowship.

Muslims as a community embrace a variety of cultural and ethnic diversities and thus, culture imposed values might stand as an important situational variable. On the other hand, current Muslim leadership is being faced with traditional leadership challenges: it must accommodate a problematic external context, a heterogeneous and demanding fellowship, the challenges of individualized religion, still remaining influence of imams and ulama, and the increasing role of women, young Muslims, and emerging intellectual leaders.

As observed by Dasssetto (2009), "one of the major problems Muslims in Europe face, except perhaps for UK, is the absence of religious intellectual leadership." He goes further and argues that Muslim countries must accept that Muslims in Europe will develop their own specific interpretation and autonomous way of Islamic thought. According to the Swiss Islamic scholar Tariq Ramadan, there are many leaders, in fact, but no leadership (Ramadan, 1999).

To put in a nutshell, Muslim leadership is not only of crucial importance for guiding the community (leadership "within" dimension), but also for constructing the dialogue and promoting a positive image of Islam (external leadership dimension). As highlighted in the report prepared by the European Parliament (2007) "Islam in the European Union: What's stake in the future?": "Indeed, the Muslim communities in Europe should be able to express intellectual and normative elaborations, adopting a European perspective able to deal with contemporary times and, above all, contemporary problems being faced by Islamic thought. This is nowadays a basic requirement in order to acquire a higher profile in public places for Islam. And this requirement should be fulfilled through the appearance of new leaders."

References

Adbulhaleem, H. (2012). *Musulmanes en el Pais Vasco: Perfil religioso, actitudes y creencias*. Vitoria – Gasteiz: Servicio de publicaciones del Gobierno Vasco.

Baumann, M. (1999). Multiculturalism and the ambiguity of recognizing religion. *Diskus (The on-disk journal of international Religious Studies)*, Vol. 5. Retrieved from: http://www.uni-marburg.de/religionswissenschaft/journal/diskus

Beekun, R. L., & Badawi, J. (1999). *Leadership: an Islamic Perspective*. Maryland: Amana Publications.

Bramadat, P., & Koenig, M. (Eds.), (2009). *International migration and the governance of religious diversity*. Kingston: Metropolis.

Campo, J. E. (Ed.), (2009). Encyclopaedia of Islam. *Facts on file*. New York, NY: An Imprint of Infobase Publishing.

Casanova, J. (2004). Religion, European secular identities, and European integration. *Eurozine*. Retrieved from: http://www.eurozine.com/articles/2004-07-29-casanova-en.html

Cesari, J. (2009). The securitization of Islam in Europe. *Ceps Challenge*, Research Paper No. 15. Retrieved from: https://www.ceps.eu/system/files/book/1826.pdf

Dabashi, H. (1989). *Authority in Islam: From the rise of Muhammad to the establishment of the Umayyads*. New Brunswick, NJ: Transaction Publishers.

Directorate General Internal Policies of the Union (2007). "Islam in the European Union: What's at stake in the future?" Policy Department Structural and Cohesion Policies, Brussels, Study: IP/B/CULT/ST/2006_061. Retrieved from: http://www.europarl.europa.eu/activities/expert/eStudies.do?language=EN

Eickelman, D. F., & Piscatori, J. (1996). *Muslim politics. Princeton.* New Jersey: Princeton University Press.

El Fadl, A. K. (2001). *Speaking in God's name: Islamic law, authority and women.* Oxford: Oneworld Publications.

Ferrari, S. (2005). The Secularity of the state and the shaping of Muslim representative organizations in Western Europe. In J. Cesari & S. Macloughlin (Eds.), *European Muslims and the secular state.* London: Ashgate.

Goffman, E. (1974). *Frame analysis: An essay on the organization of experience.* New York, NY: Harper & Row.

Guiller, M. (2010). Classical sociological approaches to studying leadership. In *Handbook of leadership theory and practice: An HBS centennial colloquium on advancing leadership.* Boston, MA: Harvard Business Press.

Hammer, J. (2011). Activism as embodied Tafsir: negotiating women's authority, leadership and space in North America. In M. Bano & H. Kalmbach (Eds.) *Women, Leadership, and Mosques— Changes in Contemporary Islamic Authority.* Brill: Leiden.

Hogg, M. A. (1999). *Social identifications: A social psychology of intergroup relations and group processes.* New York, NY: Routledge.

Hogg, M. A., & Van Knippenberg, D. (2003). *Leadership and power: Identity processes in groups and organizations.* London: SAGE.

Jacobsen, M. J. (2010). *The contemporary Goffman.* New York, NY: Routledge.

Kotter, J. P. (1999). *John P Kotter on what leaders really do.* Boston, MA: Harvard Business School Press.

Murphy, A. J. (1941). A study of the leadership process. *American Sociological Review,* 6, 674–687.

Parker, B., Brown, R. K., Child, J., & Smith, M. A. (1997). *The sociology of industry.* London: George Allen and Unwin.

Parsons, T. (1949). *Essays in sociological theory pure and applied.* Illinois: The Free Press.

Paul, J. (1996). A symbolic interactionist perspective on leadership. *Journal of Leadership and Organizational Studies,* 3(2), 82–93. doi: 10.1177/107179199600300207

Pierce, J. L., & Newstrom, J. W. (2011). *Leaders and the leadership process: Readings, self-assessments, and applications.* New York, NY: McGraw-Hill/Irwin.

Ramadan, T. (1999). *To be European Muslim. A study of Islamic sources in the European context.* Leicester: Islamic foundation.

Robinson, F. (2009). Crisis of authority: Crisis of Islam. *Journal of the Royal Asiatic Society of Great Britain and Ireland,* 19, 339–354.

Roy, O. (2004). *Globalised Islam: The search for a new Ummah.* London: Hurst & Co.

Sutton, P. W., & Vertigans, S. (2005). *Resurgent Islam: A sociological approach*. Cornwall: Polity.

Weber, M. (1947). *The theory of social and economic organization* (A.M. Henderson & T. Parsons, Trans.). New York, NY: The Free Press.

PART 3
Application of Global and Diverse Perspectives in Different Contexts

8 Service Leadership under the Service Economy

Daniel T. L. Shek, Po Chung,
Li Lin, Hildie Leung and Eddie Ng

Introduction

The economic structure of the world has transformed from an industrial into a postindustrial mode in the past few decades, with service industries taking an increasingly important role in most postindustrial societies (Chung & Bell, 2012; Rost, 1993). At the same time, manufacturing industries have gradually shrunk in the global economy. In 2014, the share of the service sector, including trades, transport, government, financial, professional, and personal services, was 79.7% of the Gross Domestic Product (GDP) in the United States, 78.3% in the United Kingdom, 79.8% in France, 71.4% in Japan, and 92.7% in Hong Kong (The World Bank, 2015).

The transformation of the economic structure has brought changes in organizational structure, human capital, and desired attributes of leadership. Unfortunately, traditional models of leadership do not fully encapsulate the leadership needs within the vast boundaries of the service sector. As pointed out by Chung and Bell (2015), "our educational institutions and company training programs put so little planning, effort, or resources into teaching people how to succeed in the Service Economy" (pp. 115–116). Based on the literature of leadership, religion, and social philosophies, as well as the successful experiences of companies, professionals, and his own business experience and

143

observations, Po Chung, the co-founder of DHL International, proposed the notion of "service leadership" and promoted service leadership education in Hong Kong. Service leadership was proposed to meet the global demand for service leaders while considering unique Chinese cultural emphases (primarily Confucianism) in practicing leadership. Service leadership was defined as "satisfying needs by consistently providing quality personal service to everyone one comes into contact with, including one's self, others, groups, communities, systems, and environments" (Chung, 2011). The notion of service leadership is not only applied to traditional service business such as catering, but to a wide range of industries and settings that involve production and transaction of service, such as financing, education, health care, public administration, and other industries where service transaction occurs.

Against the above background, the overarching objective of this chapter is to review a new leadership model for leadership practice and leadership development with reference to service economy – Service Leadership Model. There are two secondary objectives of this chapter – to highlight the differences between the Service Leadership Model and selected contemporary leadership models, and to introduce the Service Leadership initiative at The Hong Kong Polytechnic University.

As ideal types, there are fundamental differences between a manufacturing economy and a service economy, with different organizational structures and desired leadership qualities (Rost, 1993; Shek, Chung, & Leung, 2015b). In manufacturing economies, tangible goods are produced with the input of tangible raw materials and the production is quite standardized. Employees are simply expected to complete the task assigned by leaders without much individual input such as creative thoughts. In contrast, in service economies, intangible services have no physical presence and are produced with the input of intangible knowledge, skills, and innovation. Employees are expected to be knowledgeable, professional, creative, and innovative so that they can handle the diverse challenges in the knowledge-intensive industries and services (Bandt, 1999).

Besides, due to the standardization of the mass production process, little human interaction is needed in manufacturing economies. However, the production process in service economies is dynamic, in which service providers and recipients engage in personalized interactions, which vary across situations. Employees need to possess people skills and be apt to handle diverse situations flexibly. In manufacturing economies, production and consumption processes are separated, and thus the value of the product is primarily determined by the producers while customers have little say in the production process. In this case, service recipients' needs are less likely to be the priority. On the contrary, service production and consumption processes take place simultaneously and customers are actively involved throughout the service production process under service economies. In addition, creation and delivery of service are very complex and require multiple professional inputs which involve interaction of many people. A leader can hardly determine the value of the services and make decisions alone. Instead, the value of the services is co-created by employees, customers, and other partners who are involved in the service exchange (Lusch, Vargo, & O'Brien, 2007).

When service industries account for most of the economic development of a society, the socioeconomic environment changes. It is thus necessary to make a change in the organizational structure and leadership paradigm to promote service quality (Rost, 1993; Shek et al., 2015b). First, distributed leadership is encouraged in service economies. The ideal organizational structure for manufacturing economies is relatively centralized and hierarchical, in which all decisions are directly made by the management with the minimal empowerment of the subordinates. This top-down leadership style can ensure high efficiency and effectiveness in a mass production process. However, in a rapidly developing knowledge era, the goal of the group or organization is defined by the interaction between leaders and collaborators instead of merely leaders' individual wishes (Uhl-Bien, Marion, & McKelvey, 2007). A service business is more complicated and multidisciplinary, which calls for more communication, sharing, and collaboration among multiple stakeholders, including the leaders, followers, and other stakeholders (Lusch et al., 2007). Therefore, desired organizational structure in service economies is decentralized and less formalized where employees from top to bottom are allowed to contribute to the decision-making process. In addition, localized decisions become important, and thus every employee can be a leader.

Second, leaders in a service economy should be primarily people-oriented rather than merely task-oriented (Rost, 1993). In the service era, good employees are a human asset of an organization, and thus treating them as "a machine" does not result in good service quality. Third, the success of service business is not merely determined by a product while leaders' personal character becomes increasingly important. People are more likely to follow a leader who is moral, caring, and willing to serve rather than powerful and efficient but indifferent to others' needs. Empirical evidence suggests that leaders' morality and caring behavior enhance followers' trust in leadership and leadership effectiveness (Kalshoven & Hartog, 2009; Mahsud, Yukl, & Prussia, 2010). Thus, in addition to professional skills and competence, the importance of demonstrating soft skills such as integrity and empathy is heightened in a service economy relative to a manufacturing economy.

Finally, the increasing complexity of social and organizational settings calls for considering diversity (e.g., cultural values; ethnic identity) in the conception of leadership (Chin & Trimble, 2015). For example, the behavior of a successful leader in a Chinese society is closely linked with the Chinese moral values. Therefore, although there would be universally desired qualities of leaders (such as efficiency), one should be aware of the diversity of people and context when practicing leadership in the Chinese culture (such as the ability to maintain harmony).

Actually, leaders' morality and care have been strongly emphasized along with competence in the literature related to leadership and human development. By reviewing philosophical theories, psychological theories, and empirical research across history, Ciulla and Forsyth asserted that "leaders must be ever mindful of the morality of their choices, for a successful leader is someone who not only does the right thing but also does so in the right way and for the right reasons" (2011, p. 230). In her conception of "good leader", both efficiency and ethics are emphasized. Incorporating Gilligan's conception of morality (1993), Ciulla believed that leader's morality not only includes behavior aligned with moral principles such as justice and fairness, but also includes caring for others and taking responsibility for others (Ciulla, 2009). A global study with participants from 62 countries (Dorfman, Javidan, Hanges, Dastmalchian, & House, 2012) has also suggested that a prototypically successful leader is visionary, inspirational, and competent to lead an effective team, while behaving with integrity. In this study, "trustworthy, just, and honest" were found to be universally desirable leadership attributes. However, considering the economic structure, "doing the things right" (i.e., such as following "correct" procedures in the assembly line) is more important for a leader in a manufacturing economy while "doing the right things" (i.e., following universal and culturally specific "correct" values) is more important in a service economy.

With specific reference to Hong Kong, although service industries occupy a large proportion of the GDP, there is a lack of leadership education that addresses the needs of service economies. This is especially so for students in tertiary institutions, who probably will be the leaders of tomorrow in the service industries. Hence, there is a strong need for an innovative leadership ideology to guide the leadership practices and leadership education in the service era. Against this background, Po Chung proposed the Service Leadership Model. During the promotion of service leadership education, academia has endeavored to develop the theory of service leadership and identify its unique features (Shek, Chung, & Leung, 2015a).

With the transformation of the economic structure from manufacturing mode to service mode, the requirements of effective leadership have changed. The service era calls for leaders who are people-oriented, moral, caring, and able to satisfy the needs of different stakeholders. The notion of "Service Leadership" was proposed by Po Chung to address this paradigm shift in leadership in the service era. It highlights three essential components of effective service leadership, which include domain-specific leadership competence, caring disposition, and moral character. Guided by the Service Leadership Model, the Fung Service Leadership Initiative was implemented to initiate service leadership education among university students in Hong Kong. The work done and the impact of the project at The Hong Kong Polytechnic University are presented. Evaluation findings indicate that service leadership education is beneficial to the development of service leadership qualities amongst university students.

Service Leadership Model Versus Other Leadership Models

Although the Service Leadership Model is not completely new, it incorporates and goes beyond the propositions of previous leadership theories in the postindustrial era. Based on some related leadership models in the field, we highlight the similarities and differences in the following paragraphs.

SERVANT LEADERSHIP

Servant leaders are individuals who are motivated to serve and put the needs of others above their own (Greenleaf, 1970), including showing concern for and attending to the needs of others, behaving ethically by being fair and honest, and possessing skills such as knowledge of the tasks at hand. Service leadership model and servant leadership model are similar in two aspects. First, both models maintain that effective leaders should possess leadership competencies, moral competence, and a caring disposition. Second, the two models argue that all individuals have the potential to become leaders. Servant leadership is regarded as a life-long journey (Parris & Peachey, 2013) where followers can become leaders when the right opportunity arises (Hunter et al., 2013). While service leadership focuses on satisfying needs of the self, others, groups, and communities, the servant leadership model focuses predominantly on the needs of others and emphasizes that the best leaders are individuals who put the needs of their followers above their own (Greenleaf, 1970). The model does not focus on how service may be beneficial to the leader him/herself, or how it may impact on communities or systems. In addition, servant leaders are committed to the growth of followers (Spears, 2010), whereas service leadership emphasizes the personal growth of service leaders.

ETHICAL LEADERSHIP

Ethical leaders are ethical models who treat people fairly, actively manage morality, and demonstrate behaviors of conduct through personal actions and interpersonal relationships (Brown, Treviño, & Harrison, 2005). It is crucial for ethical leaders to possess both moral and technical excellence (i.e., a combination of both virtue and skill) as ethical leadership concerns both "being" and "doing" (Lawton & Páez, 2015). Hence, both service leadership model and ethical leadership model stress on moral character and leadership competencies. Both models have a service-orientation toward the self and others (Shin, 2012) and they both believe that leadership qualities are malleable (Demirtas, 2015). Ethical leadership involves self-transformation and character development of the leader (Mendonca, 2001), which is similar to that proposed by the service leadership model. However, the basic difference between the two models is that service leadership model emphasizes caring disposition, yet ethical leadership literature does not elaborate much on the role of care for others.

TRANSFORMATIONAL LEADERSHIP

Transformational leaders exhibit characteristics, including idealized influence, inspirational motivation, individualized consideration, and intellectual stimulation (Bass & Avolio, 1993). They serve as role models and demonstrate ethical behavior for followers to emulate to encourage transformation (Bass & Steidlmeier, 1999). Hence, service leadership and transformational leadership are similar in terms of their emphasis on moral competence. Besides, another major assertion of transformational leadership is that "to transform others the leader must be willing to change and develop" (Avolio, Waldman, & Yammarino, 1991, p. 12). The assertion is similar to the service leadership model that self-development is important and everyone has the potential to be transformed into leaders. Lastly, both service leadership and transformational leadership models are concerned about satisfying the needs of the self and others. Particularly, effective transformational leadership is a process that brings mutual elevation and stimulation to both leaders and followers. However, unlike the service leadership model, caring disposition and leadership competencies do not appear as essential components for effective transformational leadership.

SPIRITUAL LEADERSHIP

Spiritual leadership comprises "values, attitudes, and behaviors that one must adopt in intrinsically motivating one's self and others so that both have a sense of spiritual survival through calling and membership" (Fry, Vitucci, & Cedillo, 2005, p. 836). Characteristics of spiritual leaders include having a vision, hope, faith, and altruistic love, such as kindness, empathy, honesty, and trust (Fry, 2003). In terms of similarities, both models assert the prominent roles of morality and care in effective leadership. Second, leadership under both models attempts to satisfy the needs of oneself, others, as well as the group that one is embedded in. Third, both models hold the assumption that leadership can be nurtured. As such, different spiritual leadership programs have been developed and successfully implemented in various organizations (Fry & Matherly, 2006). Finally, Fairholm (1996) asserted that to become a spiritual leader, one must embrace values and attitudes for personal development and growth to become one's best self. This illuminates the final similarity between the two models, that is, the importance of seeking for continuous improvement. Regarding the differences, it is noteworthy that the spiritual leadership model places little emphasis on leaders' task knowledge or other related competencies, which is strongly emphasized in the service leadership model.

The Service Leadership Model

Despite its similarities to other postindustrial leadership models, Service Leadership Model has its unique features in the service economies. Specifically, Chung and Bell (2015) listed 25 principles that define successful service leadership practices in the service economy (see Table 1). According to Shek and Lin (2015a), these 25 principles are subsumed under seven core beliefs that form the conceptual framework for service leadership (see HKI-SLAM, 2016).

First and foremost, leadership is defined as "a service aimed at ethically satisfying the needs of self, others, groups, communities, systems, and environments" (Core Belief 1; Shek & Lin, 2015a). In sharp contrast to the notion that leadership is an instrument for increasing fame and wealth, service leadership regards service as the premise of leadership. Creation of personalized and high-quality service is considered to be the fundamental activity of service leadership. Specifically, "service leadership is about creating appropriate personal service propositions in real time and constantly striving to provide the highest quality service one affords to everyone one comes into contact with and whose lives are affected by one's actions or leadership" (Core Belief 5; Shek & Lin, 2015a). Chung and Bell (2015) believe that the drive for serving others and being served by others is evolved and hard-wired into human minds, and thus leadership that stresses on service can reach the hearts of people. This paradigm shift in leadership requires leaders to pay more attention to the wellness of others rather than simply personal interest.

Additionally, in contrast to the notion of "elite leadership," it is proposed that "everyday, every human occupies a position of leadership and possesses the potential to improve his or her leadership quality and effectiveness" (Core Belief 2; Shek & Lin, 2015a). In other words, for everyone, there is a moment when he/she is taking a leadership role. For example, when a salesman

Table 1.   Brief Description of 25 Principles.

Principle	Key Ideas
1. The principle of 15 minutes of leadership	• For everyone, there would be a moment that he/she takes a leadership role in the eyes of others
2. The principle of self-leadership	• The inner self can actively monitor one's interaction with others while interpersonal interaction helps purify the inner self
3. The principle of people leadership	• The skills to deal with people need to be nurtured
4. The principle of the server	• Service is a high-level human activity developed through evolution that deserves respect from others and self-respect
5. The principle of competence, character, and caring (the three C's)	• Competence, character, and caring are three essential determinants of effective service leadership
6. The principle of co-created service leadership	• Service is co-created by the service provider and service recipient, and thus communication becomes important for both two parties
7. The principle of knowing who you are	• A service leader needs to make self-reflection on his/her actions, attitudes, relationships with others and other personal attributes for self-improvement
8. The principle of personal ethics	• Personal code of ethics is essential to the establishment of professional and personal success
9. The principle of whom you hire	• Hire for character, train for skills
10. The principle of authoritarian leadership and distributed leadership	• A combination of authoritarian leadership and distributed leadership is the most effective approach to handling different issues in an organization
11. The principle of trust, fairness, respect, and care	• Trust, fairness, respect, and caring are the "hidden ingredients" that distinguish a successful service experience from an unsuccessful one
12. The principle of POS (personal operating system)	• A service leader needs to maintain the personal operating system working appropriately and ethically
13. The principle of personal brand	• A service leader needs to establish a good personal brand
14. The principle of relationship	• An excellent service is a characteristic of a healthy and mutually sustained relationship between the service provider and service recipient

Table 1.   (*Continued*)

Principle	Key Ideas
15. The principle of service	• The mentality of service is fundamental to the success of many professions in service economies
16. The principle of mentor–follower	• When training new employees, it is encouraged to adopt the mentor–apprentice model
17. The principle of historical service development	• The impulse to serve and be served is evolved from early human experience
18. The principle of tradable and nontradable service	• Nontradable service is more valuable than tradable service
19. The principle of a service mindset	• The success of many professions in service economies requires a service mindset
20. The principle of transformation and inspiration	• A true service leadership is able to provide transformative solutions to the problems, with a goal of making those being served becoming agents of transformation
21. The principle of global extension of service relationships	• Think globally and act locally in service provision
22. The principle of habitat management	• A service leader needs to take care of the work habitat
23. The principle of the diaspora mindset	• Maritime mindset, which underscores trust in relationship sustainability, is more suitable for service economies
24. The principle of Anna Karenina	• One unacceptable negative trait is sufficient to ruin a business
25. The principle of wrapped service (i.e., the hamburger principle)	• While a tangible product is like a patty, service is like the buns that wrap the patty into a hamburger; every product can be embedded in service

Source: Adapted from Chung and Bell (2015).

helps a customer in selecting a product, he/she serves as a leader influencing the choice of the customer. When a teacher receives a complaint that requires a quick response from a student, the teacher serves as a leader when making the decision on the spot. Even though in a case where there are no other people involved, one leads oneself in setting personal goals and attaining them. In this regard, everyone can be (and is) a leader. Adopting this belief instills confidence in individuals, which may motivate them to learn and practice leadership. Besides, this belief also indicates that everyone needs to take initiative and responsibility in his/her work and life rather than always waiting for others' decisions and shifting the responsibility to "leaders."

When practicing leadership, service leaders believe that "leadership effectiveness and service satisfaction are dependent on a leader or service provider possessing relevant situational task competencies plus being judged by superiors, peers, and subordinates as possessing character and exhibiting care" (Core Belief 3; Shek & Lin, 2015a). Chung and Elfassy (2016) proposed 12 areas of qualities needed for a service leadership, namely functional, social, mental, spiritual, moral, emotional, physical, economic, care, visual, leadership, and life-long learning dimensions. Three determinants are summarized from these 12 dimensions, which are domain-specific competence, moral character, and caring disposition. In short, effective service leadership (E) is a function of one's moral competence (M), competencies (C), and caring disposition (C) (i.e., $E = MC^2$).

While conventional leadership models often emphasize competencies such as professional knowledge, administrative skills, and strategic planning skills, Service Leadership Model places greater importance on the role of the moral character and caring disposition in determining leadership effectiveness. These two components are both closely tied to the trust of followers in their leaders. Service leaders believe that acting ethically, for example, maintaining integrity at work and showing care toward others such as nurturing the growth of followers, increases the trustworthiness of a leader in the eyes of his/her followers, which renders followers more willing to work for them. Reversely, immoral and indifferent leaders would repel their followers. This belief echoes Chinese traditional wisdom about leadership in The Analects, "He who exercises government by means of his virtue may be compared to the north polar star, which keeps its place and all the stars turn towards it." (*"wei zheng yi de, pi ru bei chen, ju qi suo er zhong xing gong zhi."*) Due to the influence of Confucianism, Chinese people believe that great leaders possess Chinese virtues such as benevolence (*"ren"*), righteousness (*"yi"*), propriety (*"li"*), wisdom (*"zhi"*), and trustworthiness (*"xin"*) (Shek, Sun, & Liu, 2015). People choose to follow a leader because of his/her virtues rather than simply power and authority. For example, a leader who ensures him/herself to do the right thing even at the cost of self will be admired for his/her righteousness. In this case, when it comes to the moral character of a leader, Service Leadership Model not only addresses the qualities that are universally desired such as integrity, but also incorporates virtues that are highly upheld in Chinese culture.

To improve leadership effectiveness and service quality, continuous self-development is required. Specifically, service leaders believe that "service includes self-development efforts aimed at ethically improving one's competencies, abilities, and willingness to help satisfy the needs of others" (Core Belief 4; Shek & Lin, 2015a). Such self-development effort is worthy physically, psychologically, and even financially, because "now and in the future, high-paying, high-status positions and management promotions will go to people who have domain-specific knowledge and skills plus service leadership competencies, appropriate character strengths and a caring social disposition" (Core Belief 7; Shek & Lin, 2015a). Service leadership is regarded as the "oldest, most competitive and longest serving business model" (Core Belief 6; Shek & Lin, 2015a). Accordingly, the Service Leadership Model is assumed to be universal across time and service industries, while taking the specific cultural context into account (Table 2).

Service Leadership Education in Hong Kong

With the support of the Victor and William Fung Foundation, the Fung Service Leadership Education Initiative was launched in eight University Grants Committee (UGC) funded institutions in Hong Kong in 2013. The Hong Kong Polytechnic University (PolyU) is a key player to move forward the service leadership education and initiative in Hong Kong (Shek & Chung, 2015).

Drawing on the SLAM framework mentioned above, PolyU has developed both credit-bearing subjects and non-credit-bearing programs to promote the knowledge and practices of service leadership among university students (Shek et al., 2016). For credit-bearing subjects, 2-credit and 3-credit subjects on Service Leadership were developed to enable students to gain knowledge on the theories and concepts related to service leadership. In addition to the typical "classroom-based" approach, a subject entitled "Service Leadership through Serving Children and Families with Special Needs" was also designed, employing a service learning approach and utilizing both classroom and service-oriented strategies. Students had to make use of the service

Table 2.   Comparison between the Service Leadership Model and Existing Leadership Models.

Characteristics of the Service Leadership Model	Leadership Models			
	Servant leadership	Ethical leadership	Transformational leadership	Spiritual leadership
Effective service leadership is a function of one's:				
Moral competence	✓	✓	✓	✓
Leadership competencies	✓	✓	×	×
Caring disposition	✓	×	×	✓
Core Belief 1: Service is aimed at satisfying the needs of self, others, groups, communities, systems, and environments	×	✓	✓	✓
Core Belief 2: Every day, every human occupies a position of leadership and possesses the potential to improve his or her leadership quality and effectiveness	✓	✓	✓	✓
Core Belief 4: Service includes self-development efforts aimed at ethically improving one's competencies, abilities, and willingness to help satisfy the needs of others	×	✓	✓	✓

Source: Adapted from Shek et al. (2015a).
Note: ✓ = Discussed/applicable to the model; × = rarely discussed/non-applicable to the model.

leadership concepts and skills in their community-based service activities. The community services in which the students engaged involved those with various needs, including boys with behavioral and emotional problems in Society of Boys' Centres, pre-school children with mental retardation, and developmental disorders in Heep Hong Society, students with drug addiction or social and economic deprivation in Christian Zheng Sheng College (Shek et al., 2016).

Besides credit-bearing subjects, a modified version of the Service Leadership course (30 hours in 4.5 days) was offered to students joining the two-year Global Youth Leadership Program jointly organized by PolyU and Peking University in Beijing in July 2013 (Shek & Lin, 2016a). In 2015, another condensed course on service leadership (21 hours in 3.5 days) was offered to students joining the one-year Silk Road Youth Leadership Program jointly organized by PolyU, Peking University, and Xi'an Jiaotong University (Shek, Zhu, & Lin, 2017). In addition to the credit-bearing subject on service leadership, visiting and serving in various ancient Silk Road cultural sites, meeting and interacting with government and voluntary organizations along the Silk Road in China were also in place.

To test the impact of our courses and programs, multiple evaluation studies, including objective outcome evaluation, subjective outcome evaluation, process evaluation, and qualitative evaluation for both the credit-bearing subjects and non-credit-bearing programs have been conducted (Shek & Lin, 2015b). Several studies have shown that students changed in the positive direction after joining the courses (Shek, Lin, & Leung, 2016; Shek, Yu, & Ma, 2014) and programs (Shek & Lin, 2016a) in different developmental outcomes, including indicators of positive youth development, life satisfaction, and service leadership (i.e., self-leadership, caring disposition, character strengths, and service leadership beliefs). Besides, subjective outcome evaluation findings also showed that students had positive perceptions of the program and its effectiveness (Shek & Li, 2015; Shek, Lin, & Liu, 2014). Additionally, evaluation of classroom processes from two independent observers was favorable (Shek, Lin, Liu, & Law, 2014a). Finally, positive qualitative evaluation findings, where many students described the subject/program as enjoyable and useful, were obtained (Shek, & Lin, 2016b; Shek, Lin, Liu, & Law, 2014b). These evaluation findings suggest that service leadership education at PolyU is able to promote qualities needed for successful leaders in the service economies. Of course, future studies are needed to test the pivotal hypothesis of $E = MC^2$ in real-life settings.

In summary, since the inception of the Service Leadership Initiative at PolyU, not only more than 1,400 students have been nurtured to become service leaders in the process through participation in credit-bearing subjects and non-credit-bearing programs but the impact and influence of the subject on the students have been also shown to be impressive (Shek, Chung, Yu, & Merrick, 2015a, 2015b).

Conclusion

Due to the transformation from manufacturing economy to service economy locally and globally, a service leadership model was proposed to address how to act as a successful leader in service economies. Although incorporating some ideas from previous postindustrial leadership models (e.g., servant leadership, transformational leadership), Service Leadership Model has its unique features, such as its emphasis on service and three determinants of effective leadership (i.e., competencies, moral character, and caring disposition), the belief in everyone's potential and capacity to be a leader, highlight on self-leadership, and inclusion of Chinese philosophy. The implementation of service leadership education at PolyU showcases that the notion of service leadership is worth spreading and service leadership education benefits the university students who will become the leaders of tomorrow.

Discussion Questions

1. Why does the transformation of economic structure from manufacturing economy to service economy demand for a paradigm shift in leadership?
2. How can we promote the notion that "everyone is (and can be) a leader?"
3. Are there any universal moral character attributes for effective service leadership across cultures?
4. How can we assess service leadership attitudes and behavior in an objective manner?

Acknowledgment

This book chapter and the Service Leadership Education project were financially supported by the Victor and William Fung Foundation.

References

Avolio, B. J., Waldman, D. A., & Yammarino, F. J. (1991). Leading in the 1990s: The four I's of transformational leadership. *Journal of European Industrial Training, 15*(4), 9–16.

Bandt, J. D. (1999). The concept of labour and competence requirements in a service economy. *Service Industries Journal, 19*(1), 1–17.

Bass, B. M., & Avolio, B. J. (1993). Transformational leadership: A response to critiques. In M. M. Chemers & R. Ayman (Eds.), *Leadership theory and research: Perspectives and directions* (pp. 49–80). New York, NY: Free Press.

Bass, B. M., & Steidlmeier, P. (1999). Ethics, character, and authentic transformational leadership behavior. *The Leadership Quarterly, 10*(2), 181–217.

Brown, M. E., Treviño, L. K., & Harrison, D. A. (2005). Ethical leadership: A social learning perspective for construct development and testing. *Organizational Behavior and Human Decision Processes, 97,* 117–134.

Chin, J. L., & Trimble, J. E. (2015). *Diversity and leadership.* Thousand Oaks, CA: Sage.

Chung, P. (2013). *Your second skin: Managing the 12 dimensions of your personal brand for the service age.* Unpublished manuscript.

Chung, P., & Bell, A. H. (2012). *Service reborn.* Hong Kong: Lexingford Publishing.

Chung, P., & Bell, A. H. (2015). *25 principles of service leadership.* Hong Kong: Lexingford Publishing.

Chung, P., & Elfassy, R. (2016). *The 12 dimensions of a service leader.* Lexingford Publishing.

Ciulla, J. B. (2009). Leadership and the ethics of care. *Journal of Business Ethics, 88*(1), 3–4.

Ciulla, J. B., & Forsyth, D. R. (2011). Leadership ethics. In A. Bryman, D. Collinson, K. Grint, B. Jackson, & M. Uhl-Bien (Eds.), *The SAGE handbook of leadership* (pp. 229–241). London: Sage.

Demirtas, O. (2015). Ethical leadership influence at organizations: Evidence from the field. *Journal of Business Ethics, 126*(2), 273–284.

Dorfman, P., Javidan, M., Hanges, P., Dastmalchian, A., & House, R. (2012). GLOBE: A twenty year journey into the intriguing world of culture and leadership. *Journal of World Business, 47*(4), 504–518.

Fairholm, G. W. (1996). Spiritual leadership: Fulfilling whole-self needs at work. *Leadership and Organization Development Journal, 17*(5), 11–17.

Fry, L. W. (2003). Towards a theory of spiritual leadership. *The Leadership Quarterly, 14,* 693–727.

Fry, L. W., & Matherly, L. L. (2006). *Spiritual leadership and organizational performance: An exploratory study.* Paper presented at: Academy of management meeting. Atlanta, Georgia.

Fry, L. W., Vitucci, S., & Cedillo, M. (2005). Spiritual leadership and army transformation: Theory, measurement, and establishing a baseline. *The Leadership Quarterly, 76*(5), 835–862.

Gilligan, C. (1993). *In a different voice: Psychological theory and women's development.* Cambridge, MA: Harvard University Press.

Greenleaf, R. K. (1970). *The servant as a leader.* Indianapolis, IN: Greenleaf Center.

HKI-SLAM. (2016). *HKI-SLAM's core beliefs (CB1-7) about service leadership and management.* Hong Kong: Hong Kong Institute of Service Leadership and Management. Retrieved from: http://hki-slam.org/index.php?r=article&catid=2&aid=27

Hunter, E. M., Neubert, M. J., Perry, S. J., Witt, L. A., Penney, L. M., & Weinberger, E. (2013). Servant leaders inspire servant followers: Antecedents and outcomes for employees and the organization. *The Leadership Quarterly, 24*(2), 316–331.

Kalshoven, K., & Hartog, D. N. (2009). Ethical leader behavior and leader effectiveness: The role of prototypicality and trust. *International Journal of Leadership Studies, 5*(2), 102–120.

Lawton, A., & Páez, I. (2015). Developing a framework for ethical leadership. *Journal of Business Ethics, 130*(3), 639–649.

Lusch, R. F., Vargo, S. L., & O'Brien, M. (2007). Competing through service: Insights from service-dominant logic. *Journal of Retailing, 83*(1), 5–18.

Mahsud, R., Yukl, G., & Prussia, G. (2010). Leader empathy, ethical leadership, and relations-oriented behaviors as antecedents of leader–member exchange quality. *Journal of Managerial Psychology, 25*(6), 561–577.

Mendonca, M. (2001). Preparing for ethical leadership in organizations. *Canadian Journal of Administrative Sciences/Revue Canadienne des Sciences de l'Administration, 18*(4), 266–276.

Parris, D. L., & Peachey, J. W. (2013). A systematic literature review of servant leadership theory in organizational contexts. *Journal of Business Ethics, 113*(3), 377–393.

Rost, J. C. (1993). *Leadership for the 21st century.* Westport, CT: Praeger Publishers.

Shek, D. T. L., & Chung, P. (2015). *Promoting service leadership qualities in university students: The case of Hong Kong* (1st ed.). Singapore: Springer.

Shek, D. T. L., Chung, P. P. Y., & Leung, H. (2015a). How unique is the service leadership model? A comparison with contemporary leadership approaches. *International Journal on Disability and Human Development, 14*(3), 217–231.

Shek, D. T. L., Chung, P., & Leung, H. (2015b). Manufacturing economy vs. service economy: Implications for service leadership. *International Journal on Disability and Human Development, 14*(3), 205–215.

Shek, D. T. L., Chung, P., Yu, L., & Merrick, J. (Eds.) (2015a). Service leadership curriculum and higher education reform in Hong Kong. *International Journal on Disability and Human Development, 14*(4), 297–406.

Shek, D. T. L., Chung, P., Yu, L., & Merrick, J. (Eds.) (2015b). Service leadership Education for university students: Experience of Hong Kong. *International Journal on Disability and Human Development, 14*(3), 203–293.

Shek, D. T. L., & Li, X. (2015). Evaluation of an innovative leadership training program for Chinese students: Subjective outcome evaluation. *International Journal on Disability and Human Development, 14*(4), 393–400.

Shek, D. T. L., & Lin, L. (2015a). Core beliefs in the service leadership model proposed by the Hong Kong Institute of Service Leadership and Management. *International Journal on Disability and Human Development, 14*(3), 233–242.

Shek, D. T. L., & Lin, L. (2015b). Evaluating service leadership programs with multiple strategies. In D. T. L. Shek & P. Chung (Eds.), *Promoting service leadership qualities in university students: The case of Hong Kong* (pp.197–212). Singapore: Springer.

Shek, D. T. L., & Lin, L. (2016a). Changes in university students after joining a service leadership program in China. *The Journal of Leadership Education, 15*(1), 96–109.

Shek, D. T. L., & Lin, L. (2016b). Service leadership education in the global youth leadership programme: A qualitative evaluation. *International Journal of Child and Adolescent Health, 9*(2), 245–252.

Shek, D. T. L., Lin, L., & Leung, H. (2016, January). *Objective outcome evaluation of service leadership education at The Hong Kong Polytechnic University.* Paper presented at the International Conference on Service Leadership Education in Service Economies, Hong Kong.

Shek, D. T. L., Lin, L., & Liu, T. T. (2014). Service leadership education for university students in Hong Kong: Subjective outcome evaluation. *International Journal on Disability and Human Development, 13*(4), 513–521.

Shek, D. T. L., Lin, L., Liu, T. T., & Law, M. Y. M. (2014a). Process evaluation of a pilot subject on service leadership for university students in Hong Kong. *International Journal on Disability and Human Development, 13*(4), 531–540.

Shek, D. T. L., Lin, L., Liu, T. T., & Law, M. Y. M. (2014b). Service leadership education for university students in Hong Kong: Qualitative evaluation. *International Journal on Disability and Human Development, 13*(4), 523–529.

Shek, D. T. L., Sun, R. C. F., & Liu, T. T. (2015). Character strengths in Chinese philosophies: Relevance to service leadership. *International Journal on Disability and Human Development, 14*(4), 309–318.

Shek, D. T. L., Sun, R. C. F., Lin, L., Leung, H., Yu, L., Ma, C. M. S., … Law, M. Y. M. (2016, January). *Service leadership education at The Hong Kong Polytechnic University.* Paper presented at the International Conference on Service Leadership Education in Service Economies, Hong Kong.

Shek, D. T. L., Yu, L., & Ma, C. M. S. (2014). The students were happy, but did they change positively? *International Journal on Disability and Human Development, 13*(4), 505–511.

Shek, D. T. L., Zhu, X., & Lin, L. (2017). Evaluation of an intensive service leadership course in Mainland China. *International Journal of Child and Adolescent Health.*

Shin, Y. (2012). CEO ethical leadership, ethical climate, climate strength, and collective organizational citizenship behavior. *Journal of Business Ethics, 108*(3), 299–312.

Spears, L. C. (2010). Character and servant leadership: Ten characteristics of effective, caring leaders. *The Journal of Virtues and Leadership, 1*(1), 25–30.

The World Bank. (2015). Services, etc., value added (% of GDP). *The World Bank*. Retrieved from http://data.worldbank.org/indicator/NV.SRV.TETC.ZS/

Uhl-Bien, M., Marion, R., & McKelvey, B. (2007). Complexity leadership theory: Shifting leadership from the industrial age to the knowledge era. *The Leadership Quarterly, 18*(4), 298–318.

9

Reinvigorating Conversations about Leadership: Application of Strategic Choice Theory to the Social Justice Organizational Leader

Caroline S. Clauss-Ehlers and
Lynn Pasquerella

Introduction

A review of the literature indicates a lack of scholarship that simultaneously examines leadership, social justice, cultural values, and ethics. The lack of research that jointly explores these concepts is startling given demographic changes in our increasingly global society. The following chapter seeks to encourage a national dialogue about what represents effective, inclusive leadership through the lens of strategic choice theory. The concept of the *social justice organizational leader* is introduced. This construct refers to a leader who identifies organizational cultural values, relevant moral distress situations, and through such identification and understanding, bases leadership decision-making on principles of social justice and ethical practice. The notion of the social justice organizational leader focuses on equity as central to the leadership role. Real world examples provide case material that illustrate the social justice organizational leader in action. A model is presented that highlights process and outcome variables for the social justice organizational leader.

PRIMARY CHAPTER GOAL:

The chapter seeks to provide the reader with key concepts relevant to the introduction of the social justice organizational leadership style. Strategic choice theory provides a framework for this type of leadership style. Consideration of equity in decision-making is presented.

A literature review of journal articles from 2005 to 2015 using the key words "leadership," "social justice," "cultural values," and "ethics" in the general data base of a research university, identified a mere 15 publications (Fehr & Gelfand, 2012; Martin & Dagostino-Kalniz, 2015). The dearth of scholarship that considers these key components of leadership is striking (Feng-I, 2011). Demographic changes in our increasingly global society raise the question: What type of contemporary leadership is deemed effective, and what is the relationship between effective, culturally competent, and ethical leadership? Despite the critical importance of this query, the lack of literature in this area suggests a gap in knowledge and understanding. Indeed, social justice, ethics, and cultural values are at times omitted from our mainstream, national dialogue about what represents effective, inclusive leadership (Shoho, Merchant, & Lugg, 2005).

Ethical Leadership Characteristics: A Historical Overview

The notion of ethics and leadership has long-standing philosophical and historical foundations. From Plato's wise and virtuous philosopher king who places the interests of others above his own immediate self-interest (Plato & Lee, 1974), to Kant's categorical imperative that leaders treat all others always as ends in themselves and never as means to an end (Kant, 1785), philosophers have weighed in on what constitutes good leadership. Yet, when addressing the question of whether good leadership necessarily comprises both effective and ethical leadership, political philosopher Niccolò Machiavelli comes to the fore.

Largely exempting leaders from the constraints of individual morality, Machiavelli insists that leadership can, at times, require moving past the confines of moral dictums applied to private lives to promote the general welfare using any means necessary. According to Machiavelli, leaders must act in accordance with the demands of a much broader scope of responsibility (Machiavelli, 1909–14). This does not mean, however, that there are no limits on their behavior. Indeed, though he is famous for his assertion that it is better to be feared as a leader than loved, Machiavelli urgently warned against a leader engaging in acts that would foster hatred, since this would foment rebellion (Pasquerella & Killilea, 2005).

While we are not seeking to defend Machiavelli's approach to leadership, his words do serve to remind us that ethical decision-making often requires more than simply choosing right over wrong. In almost all cases, it involves a more complex assessment of internal and external factors, including context, culture, and role responsibilities, along with a consideration of whether there are circumstances under which a leader's service to a given institutional mission is sufficiently valuable to override any given individual's rights.

Appeals to role responsibility as justifying otherwise unethical behavior rest on an argument from strong role differentiation, which holds that one's professional role carries duties that not only permit, but morally require one to act in ways that would otherwise be morally unacceptable. For instance, given the value ascribed overall to the system of justice, lawyers are considered justified in keeping their clients confidences and providing the most zealous advocacy, even when the client has confessed.

As this example illustrates, the ethical challenge created by an appeal to role responsibility follows from the fact that a morally good institution may mandate that its leaders and officers act in a manner that would otherwise be considered wrong. The success of an institutional excuse for the individual's behavior depends upon a justification that the institution is itself good. In turn, role obligations are justified by showing that they are essential. Finally, the act is justified by exhibiting that the role obligations require it. Nevertheless, the acceptance of strong role differentiation under certain circumstances does not imply that all institutional excuses are sufficient to justify otherwise unethical behavior; nor does it eliminate the need to determine what constitutes unethical behavior in the first place (Pasquerella & Richman, 1996).

Ethics, in its most general sense, is the study of correct conduct – of which acts are right and which acts are wrong. Right actions are those that are done in accordance with correct moral principles. Wrong acts are those that are in violation of these principles. Thus, the primary challenge for moral theorists is to justify which principles are the correct ones to guide our actions. Traditionally, ethical principles are thought of as falling into two broad categories: deontological principles and consequentialist principles. The difference between the two types of theories can be understood by examining how they respond to the question, "Are there certain acts that are right or wrong regardless of the consequences, or is the rightness and wrongness of acts solely dependent upon the consequences?"

Deontologists emphasize acting out of a sense of duty to certain moral rules, believing that the rightness or wrongness of acts can be determined without considering the consequences of following the principles deemed correct. In other words, certain acts are right or wrong, regardless of the consequences. Thus, Immanuel Kant, the most notable of deontologists, contended that acts are good if and only if they are done out of a sense of duty to his Categorical Imperative: "One should act only in accordance with those maxims through one can will them to become a universal law of nature" (Kant, 1993, p. 30).

Consequentialists, on the other hand, assess the moral permissibility of actions based on whether or not they will produce the greatest good or least amount of bad for everyone involved. Consequentialists Jeremy Bentham (1996) and John Stuart Mill (1901) propose a theory of utility according to which no actions that are good or bad, in and of themselves. Instead, the rightness and wrongness of acts is determined solely by their consequences – interpreting goodness as pleasure or happiness and badness as displeasure or unhappiness, respectively.

Though deontologists and consequentialists are sometimes at odds regarding the correct course of action, this is not necessarily the case. Considerations of utility might lead to the same course of action as considerations of duty or justice. In fact, on a practical level, most of the time decision-makers appeal to both types of theories when ethical dilemmas arise. In fact, ethical dilemmas by their very nature are such that no matter what action one takes, some ethical principle will be violated.

The first step toward resolving a dilemma is to identify the various issues that need to be addressed before a decision can be made about the right thing to do. In applying principles such as respect for persons, autonomy, beneficence, justice and fairness in resolving dilemmas, leaders have an ethical base from which to function. Still, despite these historical guideposts, the literature lacks empirical data concerning what constitutes ethical leadership (Robicheau, 2011). At a time when the complexities of ethical leadership regarding day-to-day decision-making are more visible than ever, given the advent of social media, the dearth of research in this area is particularly noticeable.

This is not to suggest that there is no scholarship on ethical leadership. Management theory, for instance, contains an examination of notions of justice and fairness in organizations, which includes three "dimensions": distributive justice, procedural justice, and interactional justice (Rhodes, 2012, p. 1312). *Distributive justice* refers to the extent to which organizational members perceive that resources are allocated in an equitable (or nonequitable) fashion. *Procedural justice* refers to the extent to which organizational members feel that the procedures used to allocate resources are equitable. Finally, *interactional justice refers* to the extent to which organizational members feel they are being treated fairly in their interactions with others (Cropanzano & Stein, 2009; Deutsch, 1985; Thibaut & Walker, 1975).

However, what much of the managerial research indicates is that when leaders in pursuit of the common good enact justice, it is done to promote productivity rather than equity and fairness. Hence, the goal of such efforts is better outcomes rather than justice per se. Says Rhodes (2012):

> The managerialist logic of leadership justice is laid bare – beneath the veneer of claims that justice is undertaken for others, it is evident that justice is really valued because it makes people work harder in pursuing non-justice-related organizational imperatives. As a corollary, leaders should pursue justice not as a goal in its own right but as a means through which to achieve 'effectiveness' (Cho & Danseraau, 2010). In other words, justice is subordinated to managerial power and organizational success through a rational and instrumental formulation where justice is the means, and organizational effectiveness is the end that is truly valued. (Rhodes, 2012, pp. 1313–1314)

The result of this approach appears to be that justice is manipulated — what is viewed as the greater good — in reality is about the effective outcomes desired by those running the organization. Hence, "justice is used as a means to enhance organizational self-interest" (Rhodes, 2012, p. 1315).

STRATEGIC CHOICE THEORY

How does the approach taken by a social justice leader differ from justice as a utility? One answer can be found through an examination of strategic choice theory. Child's (1972) concept of *strategic choice* refers to the notion of choice in the context of organizational operation, performance standards, and organizational structure, where the latter is defined as "the formal allocation of work roles and the administrative mechanisms to control and integrate work activities including those which cross formal organizational boundaries" (p. 2). Strategic choice is presented in the context of Child's contention that organizational change research is needed in response to the simplistic manner in which many models discuss associations between organizational structure and contextual factors. In their simplicity, these models also fail to consider "the agency of choice by whoever have the power to direct the organization" (p. 2). Says Child (1972):

> At the present time, some of the most influential models of organization explicate little more than positively established associations between dimensions of organizational structure and 'contextual' (i.e. situational) factors such as environment, technology, or scale of operation. These models proceed to the simplest theoretical solution, which is that the contextual factors determine structural variables because of certain, primarily economic, constraints the former are supposed to impose. (p. 2)

Nearly 50 years later, Child's (1972) analysis is equally applicable, especially in relation to the concept of strategic choice as an alternative to promoting justice exclusively as a means. Implied in Child's (1972) analysis is that organizational members carry unequal weight in their determination of organizational features and operation. The term "decision-makers" refers to the "power-holding group on the basis that it is normally possible within work organizations to identify inequalities of power which are reflected on a differential access to decision-making on structural design" (p. 13). The agency embedded in the concept of strategic choice supports the notion that organizational outcomes can result not merely in organizational responses to system needs associated with the environment, technology, and organizational size, but from individual choices.

Including strategic choice in organizational theory acknowledges the "operation of an essentially political process in which constraints and opportunities are functions of the power exercised by decision-makers in the light of ideological values" (Child, 1972, p. 16). And while Child did not engage in a consideration of the social justice organizational leader, our contention is that strategic choice theory provides the theoretical underpinnings for a proposed model of such a leader.

Leading with Social Justice: Key Concepts

A central tenet of strategic choice as it relates to the social justice organizational leader is that leaders play a key role in their organizations by exercising agency and influencing their organizations through a political process. This is quite different from merely responding or reacting to structural demands. By having agency and engaging in conversations about choice, the social justice organizational leader is encouraged to make decisions that consider the greater good and not just those that promote organizational performance.

Our definition and differentiation of the social justice organizational leader is presented in the following section. First, we examine the status of the literature on strategic and social justice leadership. A first glimpse indicates that, decades after Child's (1972) publication, the literature continues to lack consideration of strategic leadership, ethics, power, and politics (Glanz, 2010). Glanz (2010) seeks to fill this gap by viewing strategic leadership through the lens of *social justice* and *caring*, especially in relation to the role of school principals, where much of the strategic leadership research is focused. Even more specifically, current research is focused on high stakes leadership, or leadership within an accountability environment (e.g., testing, achievement). Here we see an issue raised by Child (1972) when context is not considered – a recognition that the high stakes environment itself coerces the leader in a manner that upends the capacity to lead.

Glanz (2010) presents an ethical framework for strategic school leadership that promotes student success in a caring and fair environment. Through strategic planning, data-driven decision-making, and mediating the political environment, the principal engages in activities to transform schools (e.g., "leading for social justice," "building relationships") that promote high achievement for all students. In the framework's second phrase, four stages move the model into action. These include *articulation* (i.e., the principal discusses strategies with others); *building*, in which the principal encourages support; engaging in *creative ways* to have a dialogue with others about the strategic plan; and taking steps to *define outcomes* and strategies to accomplish them.

The role of social justice and multicultural education in educational leadership has also been explored in efforts to identify alternatives to mainstream education (Santamaría, 2014). Through her study of educational leaders in K-12 schools and institutions of higher education, Santamaría (2014) examined ways in which leaders accessed aspects of their identities in efforts to be responsive to issues of social justice and educational equity. Nine leadership characteristics were identified.

These characteristics include: being willing to have *critical conversations* with others, and in particular, conversations about difficult topics; considering perspectives through a *critical race theory lens* that acknowledges white hegemony; using *group consensus* to build support, often through personal talks and in meetings; being aware of *stereotype threat* and its impact; engaging in *academic discourse*, or the importance of contributing to research about underserved groups; *honoring constituents* by being inclusive of all the voices of the community, including those often unheard; *leading by example* and, in so doing, bringing issues associated with race, gender, social class, and ethnicity to the forefront of the conversation; *building trust with the mainstream*, meaning that educational leaders sought to gain the trust of those not necessarily committed to issues of equity in education; and *servant leadership*, the sense that there was a call to lead. Santamaría (2014) concludes that her study "reveals some of the implicit strategies leaders of color use in their applied work toward social justice and educational equity to address diversity in different learning environments, as well as strategies they use to navigate dual and multiple cultures" (p. 378).

Likewise, Goldman and Kirsch's analysis of women, leadership, and social change (2005/2006) details the experiences of two women with little political power, making connections to contemporary issues. Their study shows how Mercy Otis Warren and Dr. Mary Bennett Ritter ushered in social change, despite being viewed as "powerless," by implementing four identified strategies: subversion; moral righteousness; networking; and systematic research. The authors conclude by making connections between the strategies used by the two historical figures and contemporary leadership questions for women. For instance, Goldman and Kirsch (2005/2006) talk about the importance of networking for women and how this is a tool for career enhancement. Similarly, they demonstrate how systematic research can be a powerful tool for demonstrating institutionalized inequity.

HAVING THE CONVERSATION: DIFFERENTIATION OF THE SOCIAL JUSTICE ORGANIZATIONAL LEADER

In contrast to environmental determinism, that holds the leader will respond to environmental pressures in decision-making, strategic choice theory assumes that leaders are free to make choices and engage in proaction rather than simply re-action (Ng & Sears, 2012). In relation to the choice to champion diversity as a means of promoting social justice for the communities and organizations they serve, Ng and Sears (2012) examine three factors as possible influences on leaders' strategic choices to promote diversity: CEO leadership style, whether transformational or transactional; values; and age at the time when diversity practices are implemented. In keeping with strategic choice theory, Ng and Sears (2012) found that CEO leadership style plays a critical role in the implementation of diversity practices. These results emerged outside of institutional and environmental factors – thus further supporting the important role of the CEO in determining diversity outcomes within the organization.

The framework for the social justice organizational leader builds on findings by the Ng and Sears (2012), Santamaría (2014), and Goldman and Kirsch (2005/2006) studies. This level of justice is not about outcomes or performance only, but rather about making intentional decisions with regard to the best course of action to take for the larger collective. Says Rhodes (2012):

> The implication for leadership is that justice is not about ensuring that people report that they are treated fairly, but is about engaging in and taking responsibility for the heated ethical dilemmas entailed in trying to be just. This

justice is not a state of being that can be achieved in the cold comfort of self-righteousness, but is a motivating force that calls into question and troubles the practice of leadership in all its dimensions. (p. 1325)

Our contention is that leaders often lack the disposition and willingness necessary to develop a language and interpersonal skill set to have difficult conversations about topics that include race, ethnicity, and gender, among other reference group identities. If they are not experienced in naming and describing phenomena related to reference group identities, leaders may avoid the conversation rather than engage in it. Because having values as central to one's work is increasingly viewed as strong leadership, the mentoring pipeline needs to include training focused on how to engage in what the leader may perceive as difficult conversations (Clauss-Ehlers & Pasquerella, 2014).

DISCUSSION OF EACH PHASE OF THE MODEL

In our view, there are three tiers, each with multiple interlocking levels to the model of the Social Justice Organizational Leader. Fig. 1 illustrates the three tiers and the relationships among them.

Tier 1 consists of two levels. The first is *Understanding Cultural Expectations of Leadership*. Just as leaders bring their own cultural background and values to the organization, so too does the organization have its own culture and way of being. To engage in strategic choice, it is critical that leaders understand organizational pressures and identify what the culture expects from its leader. This is not to say that the leader has to go along with what the culture says it expects the leader to do. Quite the opposite. By understanding what those expectations are, the leader can exercise strategic choice more clearly.

The notion of cultural expectations for leaders has profound implications for social justice efforts. If, for example, there was a consistent cultural expectation that the leader would undervalue a group in the organization, and the leader went along with this pressure, the group would consistently be undervalued. This expectation would then become a part of the culture. Through an understanding of expectation and outcome, the social justice organizational leader can initiate the challenging conversation about how this marginalization became a reality for the organization.

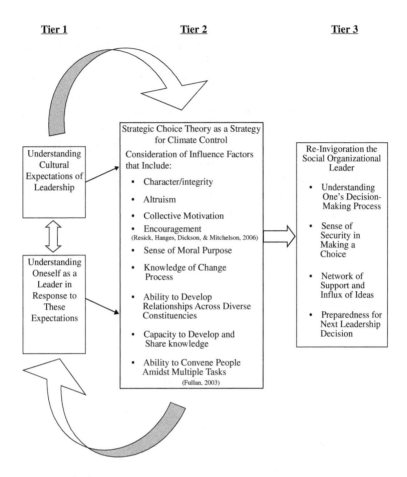

Tier 1   **Tier 2**   **Tier 3**

Fig. 1. Social Justice Organizational Leader: A Three-Tiered Model.

The second level in Tier 1 is *Understanding Yourself as a Leader in Response to these Expectations*. In keeping with strategic choice theory, this second level refers to understanding oneself in response to cultural expectations. Self-reflection is important because it encourages the social justice organizational leader to take a step back from organizational dynamics, rather than get pulled into them. Part of this reflection is for the leader to consider the values s/he communicates (e.g., espoused theories) and the values that s/he acts upon (e.g., theories-in-use; Senge, 1990). Is what is communicated consistent with what is acted upon? Is what is acted upon consistent with what the leader communicates to him/herself as reflecting his/her values?

Fig. 1 depicts a double arrow between both levels of Tier 1. This arrow indicates the ongoing dynamic relationship between

understanding cultural expectations of leadership and understanding oneself as a leader in response to them. The arrows that
extend out from each Tier 1 level join together as they reach *Tier
2 Strategic Choice Theory as a Strategy for Climate Change*.
As cultural expectations for leadership and one's understanding
of them develop, they give rise to this second tier where strategic
choice becomes a mechanism for climate change. In the
aforementioned example, for instance, by identifying the organizational expectation that devalues a group, while also understanding that one does not support that expectation, the leader
can begin to consider strategic ways to promote change.

In their study of cross-cultural ethical leadership, Resick,
Hanges, Dickson, and Mitchelson (2006) examined data from the
Global Leadership and Organizational Effectiveness (GLOBE)
project to determine what aspects of ethical leadership were important across various cultures (e.g., character/integrity; altruism; collective motivation; and encouragement). What the GLOBE data
refers to as Culture Clusters included societies in the following 10
categories: Anglo, Confucian Asian, Eastern European, Germanic
European, Latin American, Latin European, Middle Eastern,
Nordic European, Southeast Asian, and Sub-Saharan African.
Interestingly, Resick et al. (2006) found that the four aspects of
ethical leadership — often equated with Western societies — were
universally supported as important for ethical leadership.

Despite uniform support, however, there were differences
among cultures in terms of the degree to which each aspect was
endorsed. What the authors define as a variform universal refers
to circumstances in which "a principle is viewed similarly around
the world, however cultural subtleties lead to differences in the
enactment of that principle across cultures" (Resick et al., 2006,
p. 354). These four categories are included as factors that help
influence strategic choice for climate change as illustrated in Fig. 1.

Fig. 1 shows that the four variform aspects of ethical leadership in Tier 2 are followed by five specific skills Fullan (2003)
identified in the literature: "a deep sense of moral purpose,
knowledge of the change process, capacity to develop relationships across diverse individuals and groups, skills in fostering
knowledge creation and sharing, and the ability to engage with
others in coherence making amidst multiple innovations"
(Fullan, 2003, p. 35).

Fig. 1 depicts a dotted arrow that goes from Tier 2, through
the two levels of Tier 1, and back to Tier 2. This arrow illustrates
how strategic choice factors for the social justice organizational

leader play out given an understanding of self as leader and cultural expectations of the leader. The arrows that circle around Tiers 1 and 2 create a feedback loop effect.

Tier 3, Re-invigorating the Social Justice Organizational Leader, is the model's last component. Tier 3 refers to what happens to the social justice organizational leader after the decision is made. Fig. 1 depicts a double arrow pointing from Tier 2 to Tier 3. This arrow illustrates how the impact of the feedback loop created during Tier 1 and Tier 2 influences the experience of Tier 3, where the leader is encouraged to reflect upon his/her decision in order to understand the factors that went into the decision-making process. This is in contrast to research that found many leaders, while making decisions they felt good about, did not understand the processes by which their decisions were made (Klinker & Hackmann, 2004). The social justice organizational leader is reinvigorated in Tier 3 because s/he takes time to reflect upon the processes by which decisions were made.

Given that leaders must make decisions about complex issues every day, this level of self-reflection is important. Retrospective analysis may result in preemptive decision-making by providing a sense of competence at knowing when to move forward with a decision and, if not able to identify influencing decisional processes, to reach out to others for help in doing so. Thus, understanding one's process in determining outcomes can offer a sense of security in the face of future decisions.

The identified strategy of reaching out to others introduces the concept of networks as a Tier 3 factor. Beyond providing support and an influx of new ideas, networks can help build consensus in decision-making across constituencies (Santamaría, 2014). They can also help the social justice organizational leader engage in critical conversations across the network (Santamaría, 2014). Finally, understanding the decision-making process and having a network to provide support or engage in it can create a sense of preparedness for the next leadership decision.

REAL LIFE EXAMPLES OF THE SOCIAL JUSTICE ORGANIZATIONAL LEADER

At times, organizational and institutional cultures have a profound impact on the psychological well-being of those working within them. Whether due to political, structural, or institutional norms, what these cultures often have in common is that they foster moral distress (Pasquerella & Clauss-Ehlers, 2014). The phenomenon of moral distress was first described by philosopher Jameton (1984) to refer to instances where individuals who face a moral dilemma believe they know the correct course of action but are coerced into doing otherwise as a result of institutional or organizational constraints. Moral distress differs from distress involved when confronting a moral dilemma in that the latter, unlike the former, involves not knowing the right action to take. Social justice organizational leadership can help prevent instances of moral distress through the transformation of a culture.

For instance, a new administrator at a small liberal arts college found herself enmeshed in a culture that professed a commitment to equity and consistently rejected a system that would, in their view, create a hierarchy through merit pay. Since they regarded all faculty as equally valuable, merit pay was considered unnecessary and unjust. Nevertheless, members of the faculty routinely went to the administrator's predecessor requesting that special deals be made regarding teaching loads, research funding, retirement packages, and retention bonuses for those who had secured outside job offers and wanted them to be matched. The new administrator inherited a culture in which backroom deals were the norm. Those who were the beneficiaries lauded the previous administrator for his faculty advocacy, though it was a small subset who actually benefitted.

Recognizing that this approach to allocating resources undermines the very principles of justice the faculty espoused, the incoming administrator pointed to existing committee structures and policies, along with procedures for altering systems through the governance structure. However, she refused to engage in individual deal making. Instead, she sought movement toward consensus by setting up individual and group meetings to discuss how allowing for negotiations for salary and workload on a case-by-case basis disadvantaged those who were unlikely to advocate for themselves over others, potentially resulting in a disparately negative impact on women and those from underrepresented groups.

The new administrator invited pretenured faculty to sessions where their voices could be heard without fear of being judged by senior colleagues who would be voting on their tenure and promotion cases. Further, she identified faculty leaders who offered testimony focused on the fact that loyalty to an institution by not seeking outside job offers should not serve as a disadvantage. In the absence of a formal merit system, no amount of exceptional work was compensated through increased pay, but taking time away from work to get a position at another institution was almost always rewarded in this way.

Senior male faculty, the largest beneficiaries of the previous system, complained the most about attempts to change the culture, and threats of a vote of no confidence were floated on faculty listservs. In the end, the administrator's willingness to lead by example and include all voices in the discussion resulted in a faculty working group who took up the charge of examining whether a system of merit would better serve their proclaimed dedication to equity. Employing faculty leadership in shaping this conversation helped to build trust, erode suspicion, and erase the perception of top-down decision-making.

However, the process took time and was not without its challenges. Faculty who had the most invested in the culture of deal making, and who were often the loudest voices, accused colleagues who supported the administrator's position of being mere pawns of the administration. To effect change, it was necessary to empower those whose voices had been silenced to join the narrative around hidden biases implicit in the previous system.

Institutions containing more fixed hierarchies than traditional academic settings can generate even greater levels of moral distress. In fact, the concept of moral distress was initially identified in the context of nursing practice, where today, as many as 80 percent of nurses admit experiencing this phenomenon (Epstein & Hamric, 2009). Cases can range from situations where nurses witness the effects of health administrator mandates such as physicians seeing more patients for shorter periods of time, leading to more frequent re-hospitalization, to cases where nurses believe that prolonged treatment for terminally-ill patients is futile to the point of being more harmful than death. The most obvious cases are those in which nurses are given direct orders that contravene their values.

Consider, for instance, the case of a 40-year-old patient being treated for cancer of the palate who was brought to the emergency room, suffering from delirium. The patient, who was subsequently admitted to the Intensive Care Unit for treatment of an overdose, had an extensive history of alcohol and drug abuse. He reported cluster headaches and made very specific requests about the type of medication he wanted, along with the method of delivery —two injections, fifteen minutes apart, one in each buttock. The covering physician was not only concerned about what he identified as drug-seeking behavior, but also about the effects of the requested medication on the patient's already precarious respiratory status. As a result, the doctor ordered a nurse on the floor to administer a placebo. She adamantly refused, at which point the physician became belligerent.

The case was brought to the ethics committee of a community hospital by the nursing supervisor. In exercising social justice organizational leadership, the supervisor raised not only the issue of giving placebos but also the moral distress experienced by the nurse who was ordered to do something she believed was unethical. The supervisor had worked to train her staff to identify moral dilemmas as they arose, to determine the source of their moral distress, and to inventory the institutional barriers that might prevent someone from coming forward when distress occurred. This process resulted in policies and practices that shaped a culture in which people were expected to do the right thing and did not feel at risk in voicing their concerns regarding questionable behavior. This particular leader also understood that for the transformed culture to be maintained there needed to be support from both staff and supervisors, requiring ongoing assessment, conversation, and education.

At the center of many, if not all instances of moral distress, is the question of the extent to which a leader is willing to countenance individual injustice for the sake of long-term organizational reform. Social justice organizational leadership is key in undertaking successful reform, but implementing this type of leadership is not always straightforward, especially when there is a risk of violence. For example, a director of a community-based learning for a state's flagship university established a partnership with the Department of Corrections to place interns within a variety of facilities, ranging from juvenile detention to men's maximum security. Placement in the maximum security facility was restricted to working with prisoners seeking parole. However, on her way to a supervised meeting, one of the students in the program witnessed a shackled prisoner, face down on the floor, being kicked in the head by two correctional officers.

The student made a frantic call to the director wanting to know whether she should report the alleged abuse. In weighing the considerations, the director was mindful of an incident that had taken place a few months earlier when a correctional officer had "blown the whistle" on two of his colleagues. As the officer entered the prison's intake center, he saw his fellow officers kidney punching an accused child molester. The officer who reported the event had the windows blown out of his house and received death threats, causing him to leave his job under medical disability. The community-based learning director also knew that if this case were reported, both the student and the program would have been at risk.

The issue came down to whether the director should seek to protect this inmate's rights regardless of the consequences, or allow for a consideration of long-term consequences that might lead to lasting reform of an organizational culture that desperately needed reform. There was an understanding that to achieve the long-term reform necessary to eradicate this type of behavior, there must be buy-in from the correctional officers. While reporting the event in an attempt to uphold the inmate's rights may seem the correct course of action initially, it could ultimately lead to even greater injustice than the alternative.

At the level of the individual decision maker, the director must decide how much evil and injustice should be countenanced to accomplish lasting good. Then she must determine how to resolve conflicts between personal values and the dominant organizational culture (Pasquerella & Richman, 1996). In spite of a personal commitment to principles of justice and fairness, consistent with a course of action that would ultimately protect the rights of the individual inmate, the community-based learning director might not allow herself to do here what she would do in another context (Johns, 2006). The intricacies contained within this assessment highlight the critical importance of having a network of support and engaging in a comprehensive assessment of the decision-making process.

Conclusion: Theoretical Contributions and New Directions for Research and Theoretical Development

This chapter has undertaken an examination of the concept of effective leadership through the lens of strategic choice theory, which foregrounds the agency of leaders in shaping, as opposed to merely reacting to, institutional and organizational cultures. In the process, the concept of a *social justice organizational leader*, who makes leadership decisions focused on the promotion of social justice and ethical practice, was introduced. A model of social justice leadership, including key concepts related to it, was developed and applied to ethical dilemmas in three organizational settings. Each scenario contained a common element of moral distress, where the actor believed that s/he knew what was ethically correct but felt coerced into doing otherwise. These case studies illustrate the extent to which internal and external forces can influence cultures and create barriers to reform. Nevertheless, they also demonstrate how a commitment to social justice organizational leadership, with its emphasis on consensus, inclusion, and team building, is capable of transforming cultures in support of the notion of justice as fairness. This approach to leadership serves the needs of all members of an organization, in contrast with leaders who promote justice solely as utility.

Leaders across the country, including those who are enacting social justice organizational leadership, have been challenged recently around issues of race, class, gender, and heteronormativity. Much of the discourse involves attacks on leaders who, in virtue of their position, are viewed as part of a monolithic administrative structure incapable of fostering social justice. Moving forward, it will be important to address the impact of contemporary perceptions of leadership and calls for accountability in an emerging culture of protest and nonnegotiable demands. One specific component of this research should take into account the ways in which the advent of social media has resulted in an additional powerful external source influencing organizational and institutional cultures. Such work would contribute enormously to closing the continued gap on research related to the characteristics of good leadership as inextricably linked to effective, inclusive and ethical leaders.

Discussion Questions

1. The chapter presents a historical overview of ethical leadership characteristics. What model(s) of ethical decision-making resonate with your approach?
2. What are the three dimensions of justice presented in the chapter?
3. Having critical conversations was one of nine leadership characteristics identified in research conducted by Santamaría (2014). What critical conversations support the role of the social justice organizational leader in your organization? How can these conversations reinvigorate discussion about leadership?

4. How can you engage in actions that support either your role or that of others as social justice organizational leaders?

Acknowledgment

The first author would like to thank the Social Policy Research Unit at the University of York, UK for providing an academic home where much of her writing for this chapter took place.

References

Bentham, J. (1996). *The collected works of Jeremy Bentham: An introduction to the principles of morals and legislation.* Oxford: Clarendon Press.

Child, J. (1972). Organization structure, environment, and performance: The role of strategic choice. *Sociology, 6*(1), 1–22.

Cho, J., & Danseraau, F. (2010). Are transformational leaders fair? A multi-level study of transformational leadership, justice perceptions, and organizational citizenship behaviours. *The Leadership Quarterly, 21*(3), 409–421.

Clauss-Ehlers, C. S., & Pasquerella, L. (2014). Understanding retirement from a developmental perspective: The case of Mount Holyoke College. In C. Van Ummersen, J. M., McLaughlin, & L. J. Duranleau (Eds.), *Faculty retirement: Best practices for navigating the transition* (pp. 42–51). Sterling, VA: Stylus Publications.

Cropanzano, R., & Stein, J. H. (2009). Organizational justice and behavioral ethics: Promises and prospects. *Business Ethics Quarterly, 19*(2), 193–233.

Deutsch, M. (1985). *Distributive justice: A social psychological perspective.* New Haven, CT: Yale University Press.

Epstein, E. G., & Hamric, A. B. (2009). Moral distress, moral residue, and the crescendo effect. *The Journal of Clinical Ethics, 20*(4), 330–342.

Fehr, R., & Gelfand, M. J. (2012). The forgiving organization: A multilevel model of forgiveness at work. *Academy of Management Review, 37*(4), 664–688.

Feng-I, F. (2011). A study on school leaders' ethical orientations in Taiwan. *Ethics and Behavior, 21*(4), 317–331.

Fullan, M. (2003). *Change forces with a vengeance.* London: RoutledgeFalmer.

Glanz, J. (2010). Justice and caring: Power, politics, and ethics in strategic leadership. *International Studies in Educational Administration, 38*(1), 66–86.

Goldman, M., & Kirsch, G. E. (2005/2006). Women, leadership, and social change: Past and present. *International Journal of the Diversity, 5*(6), 125–131.

Jameton, A. (1984). *Nursing practice: The ethical issues.* Upper Saddle River, NJ: Prentice Hall.

Johns, G. (2006). The essential impact of context on organizational behavior. *Academy of Management Review, 31*, 386–408.

Kant, I. (1785). *Groundwork of the metaphysics of morals (Grundlegung zur metaphysik der sitten).*

Kant, I. (1993). *Grounding for the metaphysics of morals*. Translated by J. W. Ellington (3rd ed). Cambridge, MA: Hackett Publishing.

Klinker, J. F., & Hackmann, D. G. (2004). An analysis of principals' ethical decision making using Rest's Four Component Model of Moral Behavior. *Journal of School Leadership*, 14, 434–455.

Machiavelli, N. (1909–14). *The prince*, translated by N.H. Thomson. Vol. XXXVI, Part 1. The Harvard Classics. New York, NY: P.F. Collier & Son, Bartleby.com, 2001.

Martin, R. J., & Dagostino-Kalniz, V. (2015). Living outside their heads: Assessing the efficacy of a multicultural course on the attitudes of graduate students in teacher education. *Journal of Cultural Diversity*, 22(2), 43–49.

Mill, J. S. (1901). *Utilitarianism*. London: Longmans, Green and Company.

Ng, E. S., & Sears, G. J. (2012). CEO leadership styles and the implementation of organizational diversity practices: Moderating effects of social values and age. *Journal of Business Ethics*, 105, 41–52.

Pasquerella, L., & Clauss-Ehlers, C. S. (2014). Giving voice to intuition in overcoming moral distress. In J. Liebowitz (Ed.), *Bursting the big data bubble: The case for intuition based decision making* (pp. 135–146). Florence, KY: Taylor & Francis Group.

Pasquerella, L., & Killilea, A. G. (2005). The ethics of lying in the public interest. *Public Integrity*, 7(3), 261–273.

Pasquerella, L., & Richman, R. (1996). Breaking down barriers: Administrative reform of the organizational culture within a women's prison. In L. Pasquerella, A. G. Killilea, & M. Vocino (Eds.), *Ethical dilemmas in public administration*. (pp. 61–73). Santa Barbara, CA: Praeger Press.

Plato & Lee, H. (1974). *The Republic*. Harmondsworth: Penguin.

Resick, C. J., Hanges, P. J., Dickson, M. W., & Mitchelson, J. K. (2006). A cross-cultural examination of the endorsement of ethical leadership. *Journal of Business Ethics*, 63, 345–359.

Rhodes, C. (2012). Ethics, alterity, and the rationality of leadership justice. *Human Relations*, 65(10), 1311–1331.

Robicheau, J. W. (2011). Ethical leadership: What is it really? *AASA Journal of Scholarship and Practice*, 8(1), 34–42.

Santamaría, L. J. (2014). Critical change for the greater good: Multicultural perceptions in educational leadership toward social justice and equity. *Educational Administration Quarterly*, 50(3), 347–391.

Senge, P. (1990). *The fifth discipline*. New York, NY: Doubleday.

Shoho, A. R., Merchant, B. M., & Lugg, C. A. (2005). Social justice: Seeking a common language. In F. W. English (Ed.), *The Sage handbook of educational leadership: Advances in theory, research, and practice* (pp. 47–67). Thousand Oaks, CA: Sage.

Thibaut, J., & Walker, L. (1975). *Procedural justice: A psychological analysis*. Hillsdale, NJ: Lawrence Erlbaum.

10 Probing Leadership from Racio-Ethnic Perspectives in Higher Education: An Emergent Model of Accelerating Leader Identity

Jeanetta D. Sims, Ed Cunliff,
Atoya Sims and Kristi Robertson

Introduction

This study probes academic leadership through the intersection of authentic leadership with relational dialectics and organizational diversity. Authentic leadership places the origin of leader development on the selves of racio-ethnic leaders. The frameworks of relational dialectics and organizational diversity account for the depth and complexity of leadership identity from racio-ethnic perspectives.

This qualitative study involved interviews with distinguished educators from differing racio-ethnic and gendered backgrounds. Also, semistructured interviews with the educators' colleagues and mentees were conducted. The transcript data of nearly 300 pages were analyzed by a team of researchers using grounded theory.

Four areas emerged that lead to a model for accelerating leader identity. These leaders were guided by an internal sense of identity growing from their lived experiences and shaping their behavior as they faced challenges in their careers. The four areas of the model appear to hold constant though they manifest differently within the cultural contexts of the leaders.

Research findings can enable higher education to focus faculty development efforts on accelerating leader identity, particularly since this research is derived directly from distinguished educators who have enjoyed academic success.

While the context of higher education served as the impetus for this investigation, the four-faceted model has implications for and may be applied to other areas of nonprofit and corporate settings. This research offers a potentially new paradigm in leadership development. Further research is needed, particularly in terms of the impact of personality traits and situational variability.

Rationale

Conducting grounded theory research and collecting qualitative data as methods of inquiry are important to build a foundation of knowledge to minimize inherent bias from ethnocentric views in current theories of leadership. Future research is needed to confirm and expand the important questions about what we now know about diversity and leadership. (Chin & Trimble, 2015, p. 256).

Recent scandals in higher education have renewed the call for educational leadership that is trustworthy, transparent, and genuine. Similar to the corporate scandals of WorldCom, Enron, Bernie Madoff, Lehman Brothers, and BP, which have prompted public upheaval and a renewed interest in authentic leadership (Northhouse, 2010), the recent scandals in higher education in the United States (e.g., Jerry Sandusky allegations at Penn State University, Bernie Fine allegations at Syracuse University, SAE fraternity parties at Yale University and the University of Oklahoma, student protests at the University of Missouri, vandalism of African American professor portraits at Harvard Law School, etc.) have generated similar public disgust and a demand for research to examine the composition of authentic educational leadership. Northhouse (2010) explains that "people's demands for trustworthy leadership make the study of authentic leadership timely and worthwhile" (p. 205). A call for educational leadership that is genuine, respectable, and value-laden is in demand.

Our research integrates three bodies of interdisciplinary literature — authentic leadership (e.g., Gardner, Cogliser, Davis, & Dickens, 2011; Terry, 1993; Woods, 2007), relational dialectics (e.g., Baxter, 1990, 2004a, 2004b; Baxter & Montgomery, 1996), and organizational diversity (e.g., Nkomo & Cox, 1996; Parker, 2005; Sims, 2008) to probe academic leadership through the intersection of authentic leadership with relational dialectics and organizational diversity. Authentic leadership is the managerial concept that is warranted to combat public scandals and renew faith in educational institutions. Leaders who are considered to be authentic have "the will to be genuine and true to one's own beliefs, ensuring that words and principles are consistent with action" (Wilson, 2014, p. 483). The framework of relational dialectics affords an opportunity to account for the depth and complexity of leadership from racio-ethnic perspectives. The framework of organizational diversity offers the promise of having different identities not only present in organizational environments, but also making full contributions in those contexts. And, shifting to leader identity provides an opportunity to reframe past leadership approaches in a manner that encompasses the perspectives of racial/ethnic minority leaders (see Chin & Trimble, 2015, p. 40).

A key aspect of our inquiry is to conduct research in a manner consistent with Chin and Trimble's (2015), which is referenced in the above quote, to both support and extend the extant literature pertaining to diversity and leadership. Thus, from a racio-ethnic perspective, this investigation examines differences and similarities in the experiences of distinguished educators to provide clarity on the conceptualization of a model capable of accelerating leader identity. We use the term "racio-ethnic" to encompass in a single term various racial and ethnic groups. The resulting conceptual model can aid current and future racio-ethnic leaders in realizing their own leadership identity in the academy. We first explore theoretical insights associated with this investigation before offering the methods and discussing the model that emerged.

Theoretical Frameworks

The research we offer stems from three theoretical frameworks that are relevant to leadership inquiry in higher education. This section of the chapter briefly introduces a summary of each framework with an explanation of how each framework informs the present study.

AUTHENTIC LEADERSHIP

Since ancient Greek times, philosophers such as Plato, Socrates, and Aristotle have focused on authenticity, examining the goodness in people and moral societies. According to Gardner, Cogliser, Davis, et al. (2011), authentic leadership began with the idea of "authenticity" as linked with the ancient philosophies of Socrates (the examined life) and Aristotle (the pursuit of the "higher good"). Gardner et al. mention that the concept of authentic leadership emerged about 50 years ago and has continued to be researched and conceptualized with a greater focus this century, possibly due to the open frustrations with leadership. The scholars examine 91 publications on authentic leadership and conclude that there is a need for leadership with a greater emphasis on trust and values. They emphasize that this claim derived from disappointments of unethical behavior displayed by today's government and business leaders. Initial and recent definitions of authentic leadership often use differing and inconsistent language, but the fundamental ideas refer to the same root; concerns of ethics, self-analysis, and consistency between words and action are foundational elements that are evident in both early and recent literature.

In George and Sims' (2007) study, 125 authentic leaders were interviewed for the purpose of understanding their progression as leaders and to explain the aspects of their style. Through their qualitative process, multiple characteristics were identified that are consistent with previous studies. For instance, recognition and acceptance of self are pronounced attributes that were revealed. Other traits such as integrity and dedication were also identified, even during moments of adversity. Another discovery was that authentic leaders respond according to their beliefs. In other words, they "walk the talk."

Woods (2007) developed a comprehensive model around three areas of authenticity − personal, ideal, and social − and shared it in his article geared towards academic leaders. According to him, the authentic leader strives to focus on improving self in the midst of a bureaucratic system. To accomplish this successfully, the authentic leader should have a strong personal identity, a set of principles that reach outside of self, and an awareness of the need for social order. In focusing on self-evaluation, Wilson (2014) suggests that "a realistic and authentic understanding of self must be embedded in an individual's social background, context, culture and the influence of relationships, including those of family, friends, and work colleagues" (p. 484).

"Authentic leaders act in accordance with their personal values and convictions, earning respect, trust, and credibility for being genuine and true to their beliefs" (Wilson, 2014, p. 484). Authentic leaders can positively influence followers because of their admirable character traits, particularly values and ethics (Cusher, 2015). Leadership skills are determined by recognizing self, life experiences, cultural values, and beliefs (Pegues & Cunningham, 2010). From his research on previous leadership studies, Wilson (2014) compiled a series of virtuous traits that he considers to be the essence of authentic leaders. Virtuous traits unique to authentic leaders include "honesty," "humility," "perseverance," "courage," "honoring commitments," "sense of duty," "sense of justice," and "sacrificial service" (Wilson, 2014, p. 486). He emphasizes that harmony is an essential trait as well, especially when working with diverse people or in culturally diverse atmospheres.

Models are often created to visualize and help explain the concept of authentic leadership. To assist leaders with decision-making, Terry (1993) presents the Authentic Action Wheel. The authentic leader moves an issue through six variables (e.g., mission and power) in a circular motion to resolve a problem. George (2004) also uses a circular illustration to convey authentic leader attributes. In his model, he identifies styles and characteristics that influence the actions of authentic leaders. For instance, values determine behavior, purpose drives passion, compassion is compelled by the heart, consistency comes from self-discipline, and relationships stem from connectedness.

Chin and Trimble (2015) describe authentic leaders as "individuals in positions of responsibility who are trustworthy, genuine, believable, and reliable." They address challenges to authenticity for bicultural leaders: "while leaders can be more effective in conforming to the culture of their followers, they might also be questioned as to their authenticity (e.g., forgetting where they came from, trying to be White)" (p. 137). This view of questioning a bicultural leader's authenticity demonstrates the perceptual dilemma that often occurs when bicultural leaders are simply taking action to lead.

While themes, traits, and models have been developed to identify the concept of authentic leadership, a method of accelerating and sustaining leadership identities, particularly in higher education, is lacking (Sims et al., 2014). The framework of authentic leadership offers much as a foundation for probing this path to leader identities. It presumes a focus on the selves of leaders and places the origin of leader development within the racio-ethnic leaders themselves. Next, we turn to the framework of relational dialectics.

RELATIONAL DIALECTICS

Researchers have used dialectics to study communication between couples (Cools, 2006), between parents and their children (Toller & Braithwaite, 2009), on social media (Kim & Yun, 2008), and among African American female entrepreneurs (Anderson, Sims, Shuff, Neese, & Sims, 2015). However, research has not examined dialectics concerning the experiences of racio-ethnic educators for the development of leader identity. Collinson (2005) argues that "taking a dialectical perspective can facilitate new ways of thinking about the complex, shifting dynamics of leadership" (p. 1422). Though numerous approaches to dialectical inquiry exist, we draw from the work of Baxter and Montgomery's relational dialectics.

M.M. Bakhtin, a Russian cultural philosopher of the early 20th century (Holquist, 1990), significantly shaped the theoretical work of Baxter and Montgomery's (1996) relational dialectics. Bakhtin (1975/1981) suggests that any social discourse is "a contradiction-ridden, tension-filled unity of two embattling tendencies" (p. 272). His concentration on contradictions in social dialogue was the foundation that launched Baxter and Montgomery's work. His observations prompted Baxter and Montgomery to explore how the self influences and is influenced by the "other" through dialogue. The "other" refers to people, ideas, or institutions, and the dialogue is thought to be a deeper involvement of opposites and not just a simple conversation (Baxter, 2004b). Lollar (2013) also addresses the "other" in her study, referring to the "other" as a person present in the conversation. She discusses relational ethics in dialogue and concludes that people should respect the difference in others' identities and not "reduce their otherness to the sameness that is familiar" (p. 16). Relational dialectic ethics are especially important when discussing authentic leadership characteristics since a need exists to recognize the "other" by listening, seeing, and being there. This underscores the value of a more qualitative, grounded theory approach to research inquiry.

Another motivator for Baxter and Montgomery's (1996) development of relational dialectics is their dissatisfaction with the "theoretical one-sidedness and neglect of the 'both/and'-ness of relating" (p. 6) in previous studies. As a result, they began to re-evaluate the relational development concept and concentrate on the contradictions and inconsistencies (e.g., happiness/sadness, united/divided, etc.) in relational dialogue (Baxter, 1990). From this perspective, relational development does not consist of stages that go from beginning to end or have a goal of finding a balance or end state (Baxter, 2004a, 2004b; Baxter & Montgomery, 1996). Instead, the process involves the negotiation of the internal and external struggles, either between the self and the "other" or between the relationship and the larger community. Dialogue does not just occur in conversations, but in the contradictions in perceptions. Thus, the presence of dialogue suggests the presence of tensions, contradictions, and opposing tendencies. Relational balance would mean that opposing forces or tensions were not present, and "a state of nondialogue" (Baxter, 2004b, p. 19) would exist. Through the lens of relational dialectics, we can see how the leadership efforts among racio-ethnic educators are riddled with contradictions and destined for inconsistencies. This assertion is not meant to be problematic, but is instead designed to offer a true representation of the both/and-ness aspect of the leader's reality. In this way, relational dialectics serves as a framework for better understanding the messy complexities that are present in leadership experiences.

To be successfully functioning racio-ethnic leaders in a dominant-culture environment, Pegues and Cunningham (2010) argue that racio-ethnic groups engage in two opposing leadership approaches – avoidance and confrontation. They argue that ethnic minorities, such as African Americans and Hispanics, tend to avoid potentially unhealthy work environments and change their career path to deal with discrimination or get more involved by engaging in networking, mentoring, and risk taking. From this research, we see the benefit of dialectics in acknowledging the presence of both opposing approaches, rather than infusing a single approach, to explain the leadership experience.

"Leadership processes and interaction provide a particularly good case for exploring the tensions and paradoxes" (Parker, 2005, p. xix) associated with leader development and longevity in academia. The framework of relational dialectics offers a theoretical lens for viewing the complexity and the contradictions present in the leadership of accomplished educators. Next, we discuss the contribution that an organizational diversity framework provides.

ORGANIZATIONAL DIVERSITY

Organizational diversity is another framework that informs leadership practices in higher education. Diversity has been perceived as both a "big challenge and an opportunity of great value" (Ravazzani, 2006, p. 11) for organizations and for educational institutions. Davis (1963) predicted that companies would see an increase in minorities and older adults. He indicated that companies would be compelled to make the "greatest possible use of trained ability, regardless of race, religion, sex, age, or any other basis of ascribing status" (p. 135) because of the diverse cultural groups.

Scholars have used a variety of definitions for organizational diversity, and numerous definitional approaches exist within the context of the academy. Despite these variations, "the concept of identity appears to be at the core of understanding diversity in organizations" (Nkomo & Cox, 1996, p. 339). Consistency does exist among empirical studies that examine the circumstances, processes, and experiences related to *different identities* in the workplace. Nkomo and Cox (1996) provide a compilation of diversity research orientations to the experiences of *different identities* in the workplace. Sims (2005) summarizes in greater detail the primary methods associated with examining *different identities* within the context of organizational diversity.

In Heystek and Lumby's (2011) study of educational leadership, social identity theory, which suggests that social groups influence an individual's identity, is discussed in relation to identity formation. Just as people have their personal identities, personal identities are often linked to the social groups with which people associate (Chin & Trimble, 2015). Pegues and Cunningham (2010) add that ethnic minorities are often expected to conform to the leadership style of the dominant group, while simultaneously remaining true to their ethnic and cultural identities and values. In the context of academia, another aspect is that racio-ethnic educators are likely to have their leadership identities influenced by the institutional culture which may or may not differ from their personal and social identities. For these reasons, Pegues and Cunningham (2010) acknowledge the need for a leadership study from the perspective of individuals from different racio-ethnic backgrounds.

Though identity is shaped and influenced by others and other external aspects, individuals are at the forefront of their own identity formation. Thus, to manage diversity is not to manage *different identities* since individuals assume this primary role on their own; instead managing diversity involves managing the full contributions of people with *different identities* into the social, structural, and power relationships of an organization or institution (Sims, 2005). Scholars have investigated several areas of diversity that define the *different identities* in the workplace, which often include characteristics such as age, sex, race, ethnicity, social status, religion, sexual orientation, job tenure, and national origin (see Sims, 2008). This research probes leadership by focusing on the racio-ethnic dimension of diversity to examine the experiences of distinguished educational leaders. Race and ethnicity often serve as the most salient aspects of identity.

From the catalyst of authentic leadership conversations, we embrace the complexity and opposing tendencies associated with relational dialectics to explore the leadership of educators from different racio-ethnic identities. Amid the backdrop of public criticism from recent scandals in higher education, we see the need to explore a model capable of yielding insights on leader identity. Thus, the primary research aim is to identify a leadership development model capable of accelerating leader social and ethnic identity.

Method

In accordance with Chin and Trimble's (2015) call, a qualitative approach was used to examine the primary aim of this research. With the three theoretical underpinnings informing our work, interviews were conducted with educator leaders from differing racio-ethnic and gendered backgrounds. Consistent with Parker's work (2005), we employ life history interviews with racio-ethnic educators, and when possible, semistructured interviews with the educators' colleagues and mentees.

PARTICIPANTS AND PARTICIPANT RECRUITMENT

For inclusion in this study, educators had to meet the following criteria: (1) be leading and accomplished educators in their respective disciplines, and (2) be recognized as the "first" to achieve key accomplishments in their academic careers. Given the criteria for participant inclusion, identifying educators was done through Internet searches for "Hall of Fame" programs, through journal and newspaper archives that would reference significant "firsts," and through word of mouth discussion and recommendations from others. In addition, the authors used personal and professional networks to acquire recommendations of educators. Educators offered the names and contact information for the colleague and mentee interviews at the time of their interview as a snowball sampling technique.

Through these recruitment procedures, a total of 21 individuals participated in this study that included eight educators (five males; three females); six colleagues (five males; one female); and seven mentees (four males; three females). The groups included presidents, executives, distinguished faculty, and gifted researchers. Because of the mature age of these participants, the longevity of their academic careers spanned through significant historic events (e.g., civil rights movement, segregation, etc.).

DATA GATHERING TECHNIQUES

Three separate interview protocols for the educator, for the educator's colleague, and for the educator's mentee were developed for use in interviews with each of the types of research participants. After Institutional Review Board approval, participants who met the criteria were recruited, and researchers maintained the same interview protocol for each type of interview. However, probing questions were asked to clarify statements and gain a better understanding of participant responses.

After providing written consent, participants were interviewed in their respective offices or other desired location where they felt relaxed and that also provided privacy and convenience. One researcher conducted the interviews, using the same interview protocol, while another performed the videotaping. This method assured consistency among the interviews.

With consent, audio- and video-taped interviews were conducted with each educator and ranged in length from 1½ to 3 hours. The extensive interviews covered their history, their leadership approaches, and their perception of their responsibility as a leader.

Interviews with the educators' mentees and colleagues ranged from 30 to 45 minutes. Each of these types of interviews were conducted over the telephone and were audiotaped with the participants' permission. In total, the three sets of interviews translated to nearly 300 pages of transcript data from more than 20 interview participants. Pseudonyms were used in interview transcriptions to protect the identity of the participants, as many of them shared information that was sensitive. The racio-ethnic and gender identity descriptions for educators are shared based on the self-identification of each educator during interviews; when educators offered no racio-ethnic or gendered designation, none is offered in the description.

Additional data collected to enhance the interview processes includes samples of publications, media, internal and external communications, and daily calendars shared by the educators. This practice allows new ideas to develop during the research process (Strauss & Corbin, 1990).

DATA ANALYSIS

Grounded theory, a constant comparative analysis (Glaser & Strauss, 2006; Strauss & Corbin, 1990), was used as the primary method for data analysis and inductive theory development. Grounded theory development relies on coding processes where researchers immerse themselves in the documents in order to "identify the dimensions or *themes* that seem meaningful to the producers of each message" (Berg, 2001, p. 245). The process of induction allows researchers "to link or *ground* these categories to the data from which they derive" (Berg, 2001, p. 246).

After the interviews were transcribed, researchers engaged in open coding, which is the "analytic process through which concepts are identified and their properties and dimensions are discovered in data" (Strauss & Corbin, 1998, p. 101). Using grounded theory, each researcher analyzed data independently looking for key themes then together highlighting and recording notes. When using a grounded theory technique, these "different memoing, data coding, and data reduction processes [help] to construct, evaluate, add and later reduce" coding (Bridgewater & Buzzanell, 2010). Researchers discussed the main conceptual themes identified in transcript data. The coding and conversations extended over multiple semesters with research assistants and the faculty researchers discussing and comparing insights from coding. Through this process with the full research team, the faculty researchers achieved consensus on both the underlying approach to accelerating leader identity and the labeling of the four-faceted model that emerged.

Findings and Discussion

The findings of this study stem from the research team engaging in multiple hours and semesters of coding and conversation. Repeatedly, what was most impressive about each of the educators is their internal fortitude and self-identity. This aspect was much more striking than their titles, achievements, or external status, which were numerous and accomplished; truly the educators' understanding of themselves, their intentions, and their own sense of ownership of self is prominent and inescapable in transcript data. They owned their own identity, which is the germ of our findings that provides an excellent foundation for accomplishing the primary research aim of model development. Based on the analysis of transcript data, four areas emerged that researchers labeled as facets of a model for accelerating leader identity. As prompted from transcript data, the impetus for acceleration is to assist leaders in becoming more of who they are sooner and owning this identity for a very long time. Table 1 provides an overview of the four-faceted model with an introduction of each facet name and description along with key words associated with each facet. We now turn to a discussion about each of the four facets with supporting participant quotes.

FACET ONE: A SPIRITED SENSE OF SELF

Participants were unapologetically descriptive of themselves; they knew who they were and could articulate experiences or situations that shaped or molded their identity. This first facet was labeled *a spirited sense of self*, and it was present despite differences in race, ethnicity, and personality.

Fred described himself as "very ordinary" and "...a little bit more of a peacemaker than [his] father was" (male, Caucasian American educator). Martha described herself as a "protest carrying individual" (female, Native American educator) while at UC Berkeley. Nancy said, "I guess I was sort of an entrepreneur..." (female educator). And, Hannah repeatedly articulated that she was "frank" and often "straightforward" (female, Caucasian American educator) in her conversations with faculty and colleagues. All could articulate aspects of their personal style that translated into their approach to leadership situations.

> Primarily, I did that almost always by trying to be an example of what I wanted. You know, if I were going to

Table 1. Four-Faceted Model for Accelerating Leader Identity.

Facet Name	Facet Description	Key Words Associated with Facet
A spirited sense of self	Participants knew who they were, were content with themselves, and were grounded in an informal process of self-discovery from youth or adolescence	• Grounded • Reflective • Self-Discovery • Passionate
An in-process-oriented life	Participants had a commitment to life-long learning rather than perfection and were more interested in being active, engaged, and in-process rather than achieving a destination	• Active • Learner • Engaged • Permanent-Beta
A no-gritch mentality	Participants sought opportunities rather than leadership and service rather than titles; they preferred challenges for growth and botched experiments for greater learning	• Steadfast • Challenges • Opportunities • Obstacle-Free
A work-infused journey	Participants talked about their work more than their titles or their leadership; they were not workaholics, they were work-infused (meaning and purpose)	• Meaning in Work • Sacrificial • Deliberate • Articulation

Note: The term *"gritch"* was created for this model and refers *to speech acts that include complaints, excuses, griping, blaming, or whining.*

make the case for punctuality, I intended to be first there. I intended to always be there. If I wanted to make the case for hard work, I worked harder than anybody else. If I made a case for paying money, I paid first (male, African American educator).

The infused sense of self among these authentic leaders is also apparent in their responses to dealing with the demands of others. Often they were adamant in not allowing themselves to be pushed into what they perceived to be a misguided direction or undesirable portrayal of their identity and efforts. Martha firmly asserts:

I think I probably in the estimation of some of my Anglo sisters really represent all that a feminist is supposed to be, whatever that is supposed to be...and [they] get a little disillusioned and a little curt with me when I said 'No, I can't be a part of that. I'm supportive of you. I believe in that. I believe in equal pay. I believe that we should be

represented in the academy and higher education...
I believe in that, but I'm not going to get out there and
actively be involved in it.' I'll work from behind (female,
Native American educator).

Participants were unashamedly firm with their sense of self
and were secure in juxtaposing a rendering of themselves that
might run counter to others' expectations. Even in confrontational situations, these authentic educators remained firm as Fred
describes with one administrator:

And he said "Write me down what your belief is about
civil disobedience. What is your philosophy of civil disobedience?" Well, what I said [is] "I'm not applying this
to you...but it needs more time." What I did is I pushed
the tablet back to him and I said, "I am not going to
write you on the spur of the moment what I believe
about civil disobedience. I will take a little time and I'll
be glad to give you my views'...and I did. And I never
heard any more about it. But I just...I just refused to be
sucked into that" (male, Caucasian American educator).

There was evidence of shifts in self and adaptiveness in personal identity similar to Fred's reflection, "I have to say that.
Now, I am not nearly the person I was when I started out"
(male, Caucasian American educator). Despite the shifts, adapta-
tions and renewed sense of self that occurred over time, these leaders were still comfortable in their own skin.

Additional quotes associated with Facet One from educators,
colleagues, and mentees can be seen in Table 2. In summary, an
endearing aspect of the mindset for these authentic leaders is a
spirited appreciation of their sense of self. As Ben says, "So that
sense of putting your own self in perspective in terms of your own
importance is something that I've lived with. Sometimes it's hurt
me, sometimes it's helped me, but overall I think it's been helpful"
(male, African American educator). These authentic leaders were
resolute and content with attributes that comprise who they are.

FACET TWO: AN IN-PROCESS-ORIENTED LIFE

The second facet relates to participants' internal view of their
efforts, which was a mindset focused on pursuing, moving, and
growing. We labeled this internal facet, *an in-process-oriented
life*.

Table 2. Facet One: "A Spirited Sense of Self" Select Quotes.

Facet One Description: Participants knew who they were, were content with themselves, and were grounded in an informal process of self-discovery from youth or adolescence

"I would have to find diplomatically find a way to tell the captain, 'Do you want to say this?' and 'You didn't spell that right.' You have to have patience to do it."
~ Ben, African American educator

"...she is a very loving, a very kind, a very giving person. I laugh sometimes because even when I try to do something kind for her I tell her I can never out give her...if she gives you something...it's gone. She never expects you to do anything with it or pay it back, and she does it freely and with love."
~ Gloria, Colleague of Native American educator

"I think I learned over time to be contemplative...to think about it."
~ Martha, Native American educator

"And he is never a person who's wanting to jump on somebody what they are wrong about; he is just absorbing and wants to talk to you about it if you want to."
~ Mark, Colleague of Caucasian American educator

"And I think that is something that has really characterized me. I would prefer not being out in front. I would prefer being in a supportive role. I would prefer just being among and with the people."
~ Martha, Native American educator

"For a chemist and a scientist, he does have a fair amount of what I would say understanding of personality and character and how that influences decision making. But...he is very scientific in his approach and very logical and very fair and always open to any logical explanation or discussion or initiative."
~ Tony, Colleague of Asian American educator

"I look upon myself more as an organizer."
~ Sam, Asian American educator

"It goes back to the point that he is approachable; he is not intimidating, which is a very good quality to have for someone that is that established in his career."
~ Kimberly, Mentee of Asian American educator

"I try to keep a strong ethical base always."
~ Fred, Caucasian American educator

"He is also very humble. He does not like people to bring up his accomplishments. Or, if you try to put him in the spotlight, he endures it for other people's sake, but he doesn't like to be in the spotlight."
~ Kristy, Mentee of Caucasian American educator

> I think pursuing your personal and professional lives in as affirmational [a] way as you possibly can is very important, and humor is a part of that. Number two, don't accept a responsibility unless you're willing to follow through on it and you better define fulfilling that responsibility in a successful way as having the greatest good for the greatest number (Frank, male, Caucasian American educator).

The idea of pursuing life in an affirmational manner came across strongly in the interviews. There was a constant sense of movement and energy, consistently expressed. Paradoxically, the message was to take yourself and career seriously, but with a sense of humor, moving forward knowing that there would be times to step or fall backwards. The affirmational manner that Frank spoke of is affirming self, career and others, and all of these authentic leaders were focused on honesty and directness with colleagues and students — recognizing that they could support as they might also challenge.

There was also a strong message of learning as a never-ending and on-going process. Despite the fact that all of these individuals had "terminal degrees" there was no indication that they ever knew enough. At times the pursuit of learning was towards a particular goal as Martha describes it here:

> If I'm going to be directing a Native American studies program, I'm not going to be the weak link in the organization. If Doctorate degrees are what are looked at in the academy, in higher education, then I'm going to meet that academic level (female, Native American, educator).

Sometimes the educational pursuit was to open a door to be able to be in the same room as others. And, sometimes the learning was to be able to adapt to the surroundings. Instead of doing what the Romans do, Martha also spoke of learning to adapt to what was done at Harvard:

> I would have never carried a protest sign at Harvard. That's just something that people at Harvard, in my way of thinking at that time, didn't do. They seemed to look upon themselves as a little bit more cultured. And so, if I was going to succeed, I had to learn how they operated (female, Native American educator).

There was an understanding of the need to be flexible and to understand the cultures they dealt with at different times. This learning allowed them to go places and to talk with people that they might have missed or who might have deflected them from their pursuits. Education and learning were truly door openers.

The in-process orientation was not just utilitarian. There was passion in this facet as there is in all of the facets. In the passion to do something well, to teach or research or administrate, the option was always there to do just enough or to seek to do their best. They chose to do their best.

> But I view myself mainly as a researcher and I view that the student or post-doc came into my lab as a co-worker who eventually I like for them to become a scientist. So I view myself as a scientist whose job, my reason of existence, is to discover new knowledge in the biomedical field that may impact in doing something about the diseases and so eventually somebody will benefit and that makes it worthwhile (male, Asian American educator).

The process extended beyond themselves to the people that they worked with or taught. These were strong mentors with strong expectations of others, and always with a value of equanimity — the willingness to share with others. Martha expressed it succinctly as follows: "...my expectations of my students have been very high because I live with high expectations and have lived with exceptionally high expectations in my career...in my profession" (female, Native American educator).

For additional quotes related to this facet from educators, colleagues, and mentees, see Table 3. A summation that works well for this facet comes from Thomas: "Throughout my entire career, making discovery is the most important to me" (male, Asian American educator). Learning new aspects of one's field, and also of others is part of the drive to constantly learn. These authentic leaders are the perfect poster children for life-long learning.

FACET THREE: A NO-GRITCH MENTALITY

The third facet relates to the educators' view of obstacles, failure, challenges, and setbacks, which they tackled with minimal griping or complaining. We use the term "gritch" to refer to speech acts that include complaints, excuses, griping, blaming, and whining. This facet we labeled *a no-gritch mentality*, since these

Table 3.   Facet Two: "An In-Process-Oriented Life" Select Quotes.

Facet Two Description: Participants had a commitment to life-long learning rather than perfection and were more interested in being active, engaged, and in-process rather than achieving a destination

"I communicate almost daily with my key staff people and most of that communication is I go down in their office, sit down, and we talk about the issues that are at hand or the tasks that are coming down the pipeline or some of the decisions that we have to make and if it includes more people, then we have a meeting and we meet on different topics."
~ Sam, Asian American educator

"I would have never carried a protest sign at Harvard. That's just something that people at Harvard, in my way of thinking at that time, didn't do. They seemed to look upon themselves as a little bit more cultured. And so, if I was going to succeed, I had to learn how they operated."
~ Martha, Native American educator

"I always assume everybody in the group will be eventually an independent scientist, so I treat them that way...So I felt that my job — the first is to provide — to come up with new ideas..."
~ Thomas, Asian American educator

"You have to be able to communicate and you have to be able to talk to folk you don't want to talk to."
~ Ben, African American educator

"She has a bunch of camps that she uses to get middle schoolers to get interested in science, and she is the one that pushes for that and makes that happen. There is just, she is the one that makes all the activities that the students are able to get involved in possible. That allows us to get experience and um, just be able to do those little things to build your career and confidence. So without her, I feel like nothing really happens."
~ Karrie, Mentee of Caucasian American educator

"He very rapidly went from one of our senior colleagues to the chair to the provost and then to the Vice Chancellor, but it seems like at every stage he advanced...he was very happy with what he was doing; he wasn't looking to move up...Each time someone else would approach him and try to convince him that they needed his skills in the next position. And each time they did convince him, he succeeded in the next position and they moved him to a higher level. He kept advancing but he was happy with where he was each time."
~ Jacob, Mentee of Asian American educator

"He is a meticulous preparer for class and he always, he is always feeling like, there is always one more thing to do before class starts and uh, he is always thinking he is behind. He has been, he has always put his preparation for class ahead of other things. So, the joke is that things get left undone."
~ Mark, Colleague of Caucasian American educator

"He never let us get out of our assignments because you thought you were cool people or anything, you know. He kept us to our tasks."
~ Kristy, Mentee of Caucasian American educator

authentic leaders spent virtually no time making excuses or grumbling about circumstances or people; instead they were firm, resilient, and steadfast.

> [Obstacles] were present all the time, and in many cases there were so many you just didn't pay attention to them. You just kind of built it into the way you were thinking. It's going to happen. So it's not such a big thing that you got to get upset if it happens over here; it's going to happen over here. So you just kind of built it into the way you do business (male, African American educator).

These authentic leaders struggled to offer specific examples of setbacks or obstacles that they experienced as they pursued and accomplished "firsts" in their careers. The truth is not that their experiences in academia were void of challenges; instead their perspective on the difficulties overshadowed the challenges themselves. Thomas said:

> Within your own lab, it's always easier because if certain people have personality difficulties...you learn how to deal with this sort of thing. I learned how to deal with this sort of thing quite early, because number one, in any human endeavor or organization, you first establish leadership. If you do not have leadership, nothing gets done (male, Asian American educator).

Often, challenges are acknowledged but are re-framed as Sam suggests, "Okay. So these are different difficulties. I think it's — by far I prefer the difficulties that have to do with the enormity of a scientific challenge because it is intellectual and a scientific challenge" (male, Asian American educator). Ben, too, offers a mindset on difficulties, "Getting degrees approved is just a process, a difficult process. But I learned it can be done and that I could do it" (male, African American educator). And, Martha demonstrates this emphasis of perspective taking despite differences:

> There was always that kind of tension, although I would say that we worked together well enough that I decided that I'd rather not have to deal with that kind of a situation and I began looking around for schools that had Native American Studies as a standalone program (female, Native American educator).

Despite disagreements, these educators were focused on moving forward to embrace new opportunities, seek new challenges, and fail fast through botched experiments. Often, they side-stepped engaging in conflict altogether in route to their desired aim. As Frank suggests, "So there are certain arguments that you just don't get in to" (male, Caucasian American educator). And occasionally, they opted to tackle challenges head-on with optimism:

> You can always have an impact. But you've got to do something. I've always had the feeling that there was a possibility that I could always make something happen if I wanted to. Maybe not exactly what I wanted but human effort, human behavior, has the possibility of changing some things (Ben, male, African American educator).

See Table 4 for additional evidence of this facet from educators, colleagues, and mentees. Frank's summation is:

> But I found out if you work hard enough and you are persistent enough, that finally you get accepted. And I think that's what life is all about. It's okay to be different, but you have to...and the way you overcome...you don't, I think, pull into yourself and quit trying...I think you just try harder (male, Caucasian American educator).

Trying harder, persisting more, and digging in a little deeper were all plausible paths associated with the resilience of these authentic leaders.

FACET FOUR: A WORK-INFUSED JOURNEY

The final facet acknowledges that the career paths of all of the authentic leaders we spoke with were not without a personal cost. This facet was labeled, *a work-infused journey*, since the interviews were permeated with stories of each educator's emphasis on meaningful work and the frequent sacrifices associated with this journey. Several of them acknowledged giving up time with family and community:

> To accomplish things in my career, I have been willing to risk or give up...unfortunately, valuable time with my children and my family and have had to spend time away

Table 4.   Facet Three: "A No-Gritch Mentality" Select Quotes.

Facet Three Description: Participants sought opportunities rather than leadership and service rather than titles; they preferred challenges for growth and botched experiments for greater learning.

"I don't fight if I can at all avoid because when you fight, you spend your energy in the most nonproductive way."
~ Thomas, Asian American educator

"And so when the pressure is on and it's the midnight hour before the board of regents, she is very willing to say let me do that for you and you do something else. She doesn't sit in her office and twiddle her thumbs or worry or fret that we won't get it done but she wants to help us get it done. She is not uh, she doesn't spaz out when the pressure is on. She is very comforting; we might be spazzing out but she doesn't."
~ Gloria, Colleague of Native American educator

"You can eventually get to folk. It just takes you a long time to do that and so the frustration level is often higher because you had to work so hard to get to where you should have been able to get to it with almost nothing."
~ Ben, African American educator

"...one thing I can count on from Nancy is....her tenacity, her tenacity to make sure certain things are accomplished."
~ Dennis, Colleague of Caucasian American educator

"...anymore, I don't dally with students if they're in class or unruly or anything, I ask them to come in and I'll ask them to leave. Either drop it or conform. I don't have to listen to this. If you've got a problem, come to me and talk about it...that's fine. If I feel like someone is not doing a good job of listening, paying attention, I just really won't talk with them about it."
~ Fred, Caucasian American educator

"But in academics, problems and issues can be very complicated. There are always two sides to every story but whenever you have Sam there and he is assisting in judgment, you always know he is going to make the logical decision and it's going to be for the ultimate good of the department or academic unit or university. You never have to worry about hidden agendas or big personality differences coming in. He is someone you could trust ultimately."
~ Jacob, Mentee of Asian American educator

"We had to make our own road... when it comes to conflict, to not react with a knee-jerk reaction. You think about it. And then, to be as firm and gentle as you possibly can."
~ Martha, Native American educator

"I could safely say there is no one in our biology department that had a tenth of the knowledge of evolutionary theory that he does. A 90-year-old music teacher and he got that because of his own willingness to individually study to devour these books"
~ Mark, Colleague of Caucasian American educator

from my tribal community (Martha, Native American educator).

For Martha it was not just time with family, but also time away from the tribal community that she held so dearly. There is something a bit ironic in her comment as her commitment was very strongly connected to her tribal community, yet the work she engaged in kept her from being fully present in that community.

It was a choice these educators made, to spend time at their work. But their work was one of their passions, and some might suggest it was their calling. They measured time spent in their careers differently than some would at a "job." "I think you develop your career wherever you are. Because, to me, a career is something that you do and enjoy. A job is something you do to make a living" (Nancy, female). Nancy clearly made a distinction between a job and a career; she spent time doing what she loved in a fulfilling career, in contrast to working to make money to live. Some Generation Xers have suggested that Baby Boomers live to work while they, as Generation Xers, work to live; these authentic leaders lived within their work. Their sense of meaning within the world was living their work.

While the sacrifice on one hand had to do with spending time away from family, all of our authentic leaders had been strongly influenced by family role models. A devotion to doing one's job was not a new idea, but something that had been instilled within them by parents or community. Ben's comments regarding his efforts in a particular fraternal organization are instructive in this regard, going so far as describing his work commitment as a debt to his father:

> Part of my work was just in reference to paying off my debt in remembrance of my dad who spent 65 years in that organization. And I remember telling them, I said, "Anything that was important enough for my dad to spend 65 years of his life in is important for me" (male, African American educator).

We must acknowledge that these leaders were active in careers at the times of great social change within the United States. While some are still working today, in 2017, others have retired. But the early years of their careers were the 1960s and 1970s. Within that context it is worth noting that some of their activities, for those involved in education and social change efforts, came with an actual physical risk. Ben references risking his safety and told a story about putting clear tape on his car door before going into a meeting, and if the tape was gone when he returned then he would go home with someone else for fear of a car bomb. That devotion to work is much greater than one normally encounters.

See Table 5 for additional quotes from educator, colleagues, and mentees related to this facet. Thomas summarized well the work-infused journey: "You have to love what you're doing. If you do not love what you're doing, you don't last very long" (male, Asian American educator). A scientist, Thomas talked about making one significant discovery early in his career. For much of the rest of his career there were no "big discoveries," just the hard scientific search with an understanding that there would be many more trials and "failures" than there would be glory. This is the work-infused journey, and this is the passion that carries authentic leaders forward — if they are lucky enough to seek it out and find it.

Conclusion

Leader identity is "self-defined and can be varied and complex" (Chin & Trimble, 2015, p. 88). The central premise of our findings is that racio-ethnic identities can lead better from a vantage point of accelerated identity, which suggests they should have *a spirited sense of self, an in-process oriented life, a no-gritch mentality,* and *a work-infused journey.* These four facets represent an internal fortitude that links lived experiences and family upbringing to shape behavior in leadership situations, in the face of challenges, and in interactions with others. No distinctions at the racio-ethnic level exist among this group of distinguished educators as all were conscious of their leader identity. This leads us to believe that variations in cultural distinctions will manifest themselves differently within the four facets, but the four facets still remain.

Findings of this research are consistent with existing conceptualizations of authentic leadership. With its focus on trust, values, and other internal attributes, authentic leadership provides a key mechanism for exploring the internal manifestations that contribute to an accelerated leader identity. The results of this research also extend the contextual applicability of relational dialectics and organizational diversity — both of which offer a

Table 5.   Facet Four: "A Work-Infused Journey" Select Quotes.

Facet Four Description: Participants talked about their work more than their titles or their leadership; they were not workaholics, they were work-infused (meaning and purpose).

"I've always been expected to, and usually of my own self, to work 200 percent...there are many today who think I'm a workaholic and maybe I am, but you know what you have to do in higher education."
~ Martha, Native American educator

"Under his leadership, we started writing many more grants and acquiring more equipment and building our infrastructure for teaching and doing research with students. So that's been a huge impact on not just the department but the university across the board and just his continued interest on academic excellence."
~ Jacob, Mentee of Asian American educator

"I think you have to have a serious dose of stupidity. Now I think if you had said, a certain person has a serious dose of ambition, he'll never work. Because ambition is something that you try to — behind ambition is perhaps fame, monetary wealth, position of respect, people look up to you. And these are wrong ends...you have to have something you want to drive yourself there but those are not goals."
~ Thomas, Asian American educator

"He has this quality that is great, he can't play the piano like he used to but he would organize various things on campus like he wrote and helped direct music, student musicals for years. He would write original music for it or he would adapt songs to those programs and call them songs America sings. A student reviewer went on every other year for about 25 years. He also put together a faculty glee club, a men's/boy's faculty glee club and he would direct that and arrange music for it."
~ Mark, Colleague of Caucasian American educator

"...the academic enterprise is of no value, in my opinion, to the teacher...real value to the teacher, unless the teacher is prepared to grow and to develop as a dynamic part of accepting the responsibility to teach in the classroom. And I've got to think that it's infinitely less fun not to grow".
~ Frank, Caucasian American educator

"Nearly overnight he reorganized the administration so as to open up communication with the president. He really saw the presidency as isolated and he wanted to make it open and connected. When people say that they have an open door policy, no one can say that more honestly than Frank. I mean he wanted faculty, administrators, staff, and students to come by and share their thoughts with him."
~ Russell, Mentee of Caucasian American educator

"I think you develop your career wherever you are. Because, to me, a career is something that you do and enjoy. A job is something you do to make a living."
~ Nancy, Caucasian American educator

"It's a big deal now even in the department, for a number of the colleagues are participating and promoting the idea of undergraduate research. She is really one of the faculty members early on that initiated that."
~ Dennis, Colleague of Caucasian American educator

platform to explore the richness and complexities of academic leadership among different racio-ethnic identities.

This research has taken the charge of exploring new paradigms or alternative views of leadership rather than exclusively retaining the approaches already present in the literature. Drawing from authentic leadership, relational dialectics, and organizational diversity, we offer four facets capable of enhancing an educator's staying power in higher education through supporting leader identity.

Discussion Questions

1. Discuss what you learned about leader identity through the four facets. Did they lead you to a new understanding or awareness of your own leader identity? If so, how? If not, why not?
2. Think of someone you would consider a leader. Compare the leadership style of that person to the authentic leaders described in this chapter. Discuss the similarities and differences among the leaders and whether your opinion of that person as a leader changed.
3. Authentic leaders are known for being true to their beliefs. Do you think the authentic leaders in this chapter might conform to circumstances and still be authentic? If so, how? If not, why not?
4. Discuss how ethnic minority leadership identities can be influenced by a dominant-culture institution. How can having an accelerated leader identity be effective in that environment?

Acknowledgment

This research was funded from interdisciplinary grants received in 2013 and 2015 from the Office of Research & Grants at the University of Central Oklahoma.

References

Anderson, P., Sims, J. D., Shuff, J., Neese, S., & Sims, A. (2015). A price-based approach to the dialectics in African American female entrepreneur experiences. *Journal of Business Diversity, 15*(2), 46–59.

Bakhtin, M. M. (1981). *The dialogic imagination: Four essays by M. M. Bakhtin* (C. Emerson & M. Holquist, Trans.). Austin: University of Texas Press (Original work published in 1975).

Baxter, L. A. (1990). Dialectical contradictions in relationship development. *Journal of Social and Personal Relationships, 7*, 69–88.

Baxter, L. A. (2004a). A tale of two voices: Relational dialectics theory. The Journal of Family *Communication, 4*, 181–192.

Baxter, L. A. (2004b). Distinguished scholar article: Relationships as dialogues. Personal *Relationships, 11*, 1–22.

Baxter, L. A., & Montgomery, B. M. (1996). *Relating: Dialogues and dialectics.* New York, NY: Guilford.

Berg, B. L. (2001). *Qualitative research methods for the social sciences.* Boston, MA: Allyn and Bacon.

Bridgewater, M. J., & Buzzanell, P. M. (2010). Caribbean immigrants' discourses: Cultural, moral, and personal stories about workplace communication in the United States. *Journal of Business Communication, 47*(3), 235–265.

Chin, J. L., & Trimble, J. E. (2015). *Diversity and leadership.* Thousand Oaks, CA: Sage Publications.

Collinson, D. (2005). Dialectics of leadership. *Human Relations, 58*(11), 1419–1442.

Cools, C. A. (2006). Relational communication in intercultural couples. *Language and Intercultural Communication, 6*, 262–274.

Cusher, B. E. (2015). Leaders in conversation: The dialectic model of leadership education in Plutarch's Lives. *Journal of Leadership Education, 14*(2), 198–208.

Davis, K. (1963). The corporate image in social context - the problem of demographic change. In J. W. Riley, Jr. (Ed.), *The corporation and its publics: Essays on the corporate image* (pp. 107–136). New York, NY: Wiley.

Gardner, W. L., Cogliser, C. C., Davis, K. M., & Dickens, M. P. (2011). *Authentic leadership: A review of the literature and research agenda in* 'The Leadership Quarterly'. Thousand Oaks, CA: Sage Publications.

George, B. (2004). *Authentic leadership: Rediscovering the secrets to creating lasting value.* San Francisco, CA: Jossey-Bass.

George, B., & Sims, P. (2007). *True north: Discover your authentic leadership.* San Francisco, CA: Jossey-Bass.

Glaser, B. G., & Strauss, A. L. (2006). *The discovery of grounded theory: Strategies for qualitative research.* New Brunswick, CT: Aldine Transaction.

Heystek, J., & Lumby, J. (2011). Identity and diversity: A case study of leaders in a South African primary school. *Education as Change, 15*(2), 331–343.

Holquist, M. (1990). *Dialogism: Bakhtin and his world.* New York, NY: Routledge.

Kim, K. H., & Yun, H. (2008). Cying for me, Cying for us: Relational dialectics in a Korean social network site. *Journal of Computer-Mediated Communication, 13*, 298–318.

Lollar, K. (2013). Dialogic ethics. Leadership and the face of the other. *Journal of the Association for Communication Administration, 32*(1), 15–26.

Nkomo, S. M., & Cox, T. Jr. (1996). Diverse identities in organizations. In S. R. Clegg, C. Hardy, & W. R. Nords (Eds.), *Handbook of organizations* (pp. 338–356). Thousand Oaks, CA: Sage.

Northhouse, P. G. (2010). *Leadership: Theory and practice* (5th ed.). Thousand Oaks, CA: Sage Publications.

Parker, P. S. (2005). *Race, gender, and leadership: Re-envisioning organizational leadership from the perspectives of African American women executives.* Mahwah, NJ: Lawrence Erlbaum Associates, Inc.

Pegues, D. A., & Cunningham, C. J. (2010). Diversity in leadership: Where's the love for racioethnic minorities? *Business Journal of Hispanic Research, 4*(1).

Ravazzani, S. (2006, November). Communicating for diversity, with diversity, in diversity: Main implications and summary of the contents. Paper presented at the 2nd World Public Relations Festival, Milan, Italy.

Sims, J. D. (2005, May). Dialogue on organizational diversity: Academic conceptions and approaches to different identities. Paper presented at the meeting of the International Communication Association, Organizational Communication Division, New York, NY.

Sims, J. D. (2008). Communicating value-in-diversity campaigns: The role of reactance and inoculation in accomplishing organizational aims. Unpublished doctoral dissertation, University of Oklahoma.

Sims, J. D., Cunliff, E., Floyd, L., Neese, S., Shuff, J., & Sims, A. (2014). Lessons on longevity: Achieving staying power as a servant leader. Conference presentation at the 24th Annual International Conference of the Robert K. Greenleaf Center for Servant Leadership. Atlanta, GA.

Strauss, A., & Corbin, J. (1990). *Basics of qualitative research: Grounded theory procedures and techniques.* Newbury Park, CA: Sage.

Strauss, A., & Corbin, J. (1998). *Basics of qualitative research: Techniques and procedures for developing grounded theory* (2nd ed.). Newbury Park, CA: Sage.

Terry, R. W. (1993). *Authentic leadership: Courage in action.* San Francisco, CA: Jossey-Bass and Action Wheel Publishing.

Toller, P. W., & Braithwaite, D. O. (2009). Grieving together and apart: Bereaved parents' contradictions of marital interaction. *Journal of Applied Communication Research, 37*(3), 257–277.

Wilson, M. (2014). Critical reflection on authentic leadership and school leader development from a virtue ethical perspective. *Educational Review, 66*(4), 482–496.

Woods, P. A. (2007). Authenticity in the bureau-enterprise culture. *Educational Management Administration & Leadership, 35*(2), 295–320.

11 Campus Unrest in American Higher Education: Challenges and Opportunities for Strategic Diversity Leadership

Ralph A. Gigliotti, Brighid Dwyer and Kristina Ruiz-Mesa

Introduction

In response to a wide array of challenges and concerns, we have seen a surge of student protests across college and university campuses. This is arguably part of a larger watershed moment — a moment punctuated by increasingly vocal students and protests, administrative responses to issues of institutional racism and insensitivity, and community-wide efforts to mobilize the pursuit of a more inclusive campus climate. In order to create more inclusive campus climates that value diverse voices, experiences, and perspectives, this chapter highlights the importance of strategic diversity leadership (Williams, 2013) in higher education. Moreover, this chapter provides an overview of these campus protests and syntheses of the scholarly literature in the areas of crisis leadership, diversity and inclusive leadership, and crisis diversity leadership. Distilling various lessons from recent diversity crises across higher education, this chapter concludes with five suggested practices for taking a coordinated, proactive, and intentional approach to leading during these tumultuous times. The authors argue that proactively incorporating strategic diversity leadership into everyday leadership practices is essential for colleges and universities to be successful in this current environment.

Chapter Objectives

1. To identify strategies for effective crisis diversity leadership in higher education.
2. To understand the contemporary landscape of student protests and campus unrest related to issues of diversity and inclusion in higher education.
3. To synthesize the intersecting literature in the areas of crisis leadership, diversity leadership, and crisis diversity leadership.

In their text *Occupying the Academy*, Clark, Fasching-Varner, and Brimhall-Vargas (2012) encouraged the higher education community to "disconnect from your devices, and instead plug into your community face-to-face, hand-in-hand, heart-to-heart" (p. 209). In 2015, many heeded this call as protests against racial injustice erupted on college and university campuses across the United States. This is arguably part of a larger watershed moment – a moment punctuated by increasingly vocal students and protests, administrative responses to issues of institutional racism and insensitivity, and community-wide efforts to mobilize the pursuit of a more inclusive campus climate. While protests are not unique to college campuses, and in fact, it is arguable that they are frequent occurrences on colleges and universities, the actions in pursuit of justice that have defined the present moment are national and international in scope. These protests have united college students across the United States, and in many ways they have connected students to national and international policies that transcend higher education and relate to broader issues of justice. This call to action demands that institutions of higher education acknowledge, value, and reflect a diversity of voices, experiences, and perspectives.

Within the context of this growing unrest, there is a need for all leaders in higher education to enact strategic diversity leadership (Williams, 2013), a proactive approach to organizational diversity and inclusion which foregrounds diversity efforts in leadership decisions and practices. Although diversity is widely recognized as an important value for institutions of higher education, crises and subsequent crisis responses have challenged these broader institutional diversity efforts. In many instances, there is a tendency for university officials to "behave most often like cheetahs...acting in a reactionary burst of energy but often doing only what is immediately needed to resolve a diversity crisis" (Williams, 2013, p. 7). For example, Parker (2015) described the response by some institutions to immediately appoint chief diversity officers as a swift, but shallow, response.

Of the many incidents to occur at colleges and universities across the United States,[1] some widely publicized examples include high-profile events that have occurred at the University of Oklahoma, the University of Missouri, Yale University, the University of Louisville, and elsewhere. While much of the unrest on campuses has focused on the experiences of Black students, it is equally important to highlight the experiences of others who have been marginalized, such as women, Latina/os, LGBTQ students, undocumented students, and others. Given the range of exclusionary experiences and incidents which have occurred on college campuses, it is important to situate unrest within broader national and organizational contexts in order to create appropriate and effective responses from campus leadership. Distilling various lessons from recent college and university diversity crises, this chapter will also highlight suggested practices for taking a coordinated, proactive, and intentional approach to leading during these tumultuous times – an approach that considers the deeper structures of inequity and calls for collaboration to discover systemic solutions. This chapter closes with a discussion about ways of proactively incorporating strategic diversity leadership into everyday leadership practices (Williams & Wade-Golden, 2013).

---

[1]In addition to the domestic cases offered in this chapter, the scope of international student protests in recent years is fairly extensive, including student-led protests in China, Spain, South Africa, Nigeria, and India. The reasons for these protests are widespread; yet in all instances, college and university students demonstrated a willingness to stand up for issues of collective concern. A more extensive summary of domestic and international protests is beyond the scope of this chapter, but deserves increased attention in future scholarly treatment of this topic.

The Context: Violations of Campus Inclusion and Community at U.S. Colleges and Universities

Over the past year, institutions of higher education have seen considerable unrest and student protests. These protests echo in many ways the student movements of the 1960s — demonstrations in response to a wide array of public policies and decisions, including the Civil Rights Movement, the Free Speech Movement, and the Vietnam War (Lipset & Altbach, 1966; Thelin, 2013). Many of the contemporary examples of campus unrest have been in response to a series of racist, sexist, xenophobic, and other prejudiced incidents that have occurred at numerous institutions.[2] These incidents, paired with the increase in reports of campus hate crimes in the United States (Robers et al., 2015), require campus leaders to be proactive in adopting policies and practices that strengthen and enhance diversity and inclusion efforts. An examination of all of the cases of student protest are beyond the scope of this chapter; however, the following overview of high-profile cases provides a context for this exploration into the intersections between crisis leadership and diversity leadership in higher education.[3]

Of the many diversity-related incidents to occur since 2015, the situation at the University of Missouri served as a seminal moment for much national conversation. The multifaceted case at Missouri included a history of complex race relations at the flagship campus (Landsbaum & Weber, 2015; Pearson, 2015; Woodhouse, 2015), a series of racially charged incidents, the failure of the University president to address a group of protestors at the annual Homecoming parade, and widely publicized responses

---

[2]This chapter focuses primarily on recent racially charged events that led to student protests. As an anonymous reviewer rightfully pointed out, a number of colleges and universities are eliminating their ethnic studies programs; yet, in nearly all of these cases, there has been little demonstration by the students. Future research should consider what factors contribute to student unrest, and whether or not the unrest is specific to one or more ethnic groups.
[3]For more examples and details of campus incidents and hate crimes, see Jaschik (2015) and Robers, Zhang, Morgan, and Musu-Gillette (2015).

from students, including a hunger strike by a graduate student and the football team's boycott to play in their upcoming game — a decision that would have resulted in a loss of at least $1 million for the institution.

Beyond the events at Missouri, many other institutions experienced events that can be characterized as diversity-related crises. For example, on March 7, 2015, a video appeared of members of the Sigma Alpha Epsilon (SAE) chapter at the University of Oklahoma singing a song with extremely offensive racial language that referenced lynching and implied that students of color would never be admitted into the fraternity. Two students involved in the case were immediately expelled by President David Boren for their leadership role in creating "a hostile learning environment for others" ("OU President Boren").

At Yale University, there were claims of a fraternity brother saying "white girls only" at the entrance to a party. Although this event remains disputed, Yale continues to deal with a racially charged environment following a series of public debates over the right to wear offensive Halloween costumes and the naming of a residence hall for alumnus John C. Calhoun, a 19th-century politician and outspoken White supremacist. In an open letter, students at Yale acknowledged that "To be a student of color on Yale's campus is to exist in a space that was not created for you" (Yale Students, 2015, para. 7). Other examples include the excessive use of force by campus police in breaking up a party of mostly Black students at an off-campus student housing complex at the University of Maryland, the hosting of a "ghetto party" by students at Fairfield University, and an episode on a panel at Ithaca College where two white male alumni called a Black alumna a "savage," following her claims of having a "savage hunger" to succeed (Logue, 2015, para. 2).

Violations of campus safety and inclusion are not limited to race, but also occur across gender, ethnicity, religion, sexual orientation, and other social identities. Additional examples include the president of the University of Louisville appearing in a photograph with a group of University staffers at a Halloween party dressed in sombreros mimicking Mexican culture (Grinberg & Hassan, 2015). There have been sex scandals involving athletes and coaches at the University of Louisville, where women were paid for sex with players and recruits (Barr & Goodman, 2015); and at Baylor University, where the president was demoted, and the head football coach was fired over his mishandling of reported sexual assaults (New, 2015; Tracy, 2016). These divisive incidents and others occurring across the nation must also be considered within the broader context of changing national rhetoric surrounding issues of diversity and inclusion. For example, the 2016 U.S. presidential election normalized denigrating language about marginalized groups and previewed political changes that could further marginalize underrepresented groups.

Corrective institutional responses to such acts of racial intolerance are widespread. For example, the University of Missouri implemented several corrective actions, including the appointment of new senior leaders in the roles of president and chancellor, the hiring of a diversity, inclusion, and equity officer, the creation of a task force to develop strategies for improving diversity and inclusion, the mandate of a new diversity and inclusion training program for all faculty, staff, and incoming students, and the establishment of a system to provide support to students, faculty, and staff who experience discrimination (Addo, 2015; Eligon & Perez-Pena, 2015; Fortunato, Gigliotti, & Ruben, 2017; Stripling, 2015). In the case of the University of Oklahoma, President David Boren received praise for his prompt and bold response to the crisis, He called the students "disgraceful" and expelled the students "because of [their] leadership role in leading a racist and exclusionary chant which has created a hostile educational environment for others" (Stripling & Thomason, 2015, para. 3).

We are at a critical point in the United States, where there is long overdue attention to the violence and racial profiling against Black people, and especially Black men. This recognition is changing the way people understand race in the United States, and yet diversity-related offenses are in no way limited to the Black community. In addition to drawing attention to the plight of Black Americans, we must also be outraged when anyone's cultural traditions are dismissed and diminished. For example, in 2010, a first-year student at Rutgers University, Tyler Clementi, took his own life after being filmed kissing another man (Pilkington, 2010). This incident generated greater conversation and preventative action about cyberbullying, as well as additional advocacy to support LGBTQ youth. Effective campus leaders need to proactively engage in conversations about diversity, learn about complex issues of identity, and remain abreast of emerging best practices related to inclusion in higher education before campus incidents occur.

Presently, many campuses are having extensive conversations on campuses about sexual assault, however, in many instances, these conversations still fall short. As noted by di Bartolo (2015), transgender and gender-nonconforming students have not been adequately supported by campus policies and practices. Greater recognition is being given to transgender students and students who do not identify with the gender binary, but simply recognizing that gender-nonconforming students exist does not sufficiently solve issues related to access and inclusion. Rather, leaders of colleges and universities must urge their campuses to become more accepting, and to adapt the learning environment to more intentionally embrace students with a wide range of gender identities and expressions.

The ongoing array of assaults based on race, ethnicity, gender identity, and sexual orientation on college campuses are not trivial. Rather, the disturbing acts that occur at our institutions become representations and reflections of the campus community more broadly. These exclusive and violent acts have the potential to cast individual colleges and universities as intolerant and unaccepting of nondominant groups. These acts simultaneously quietly label people of color, LGBT individuals, and gender-nonconforming community members as "others," who are outside the norm of the college community. In many instances, these events may be seen as personal and institutional crises that threaten not only the reputation of higher education, but more importantly, the lives of those most directly involved.

The complexity of the cases noted above and their impact on the lived experiences of the many students, faculty, and staff involved with these situations, coupled with the very public nature of the leadership responses (or lack thereof), provide a foundation for our exploration into the intersections between crisis leadership and diversity leadership. Of the many competencies required for effective leadership (Ruben, 2012), an understanding of and proficiency in crisis diversity leadership is critical for senior-level leaders in higher education. When recruiting and hiring these leaders, it is important for crisis diversity leadership to be a critical competency in this current environment − a competency that is not tangential, but central, to one's leadership experience. These cases stress the exigency for organizational leaders who are knowledgeable of, and prepared for, the challenge of creating, supporting, and sustaining inclusive and diverse college campuses. The following section examines how the crisis and diversity leadership literature can serve as a resource for leading today's institutions of higher education.

Literature Review

CRISIS LEADERSHIP

Events that are characterized as crises have the potential to threaten the reputation of an organization. In many instances, these periods of disruption test the very core of an institution, and they challenge leaders to manage an array of uncertain and unpredictable elements in an environment of heightened scrutiny. Adding to the challenges of these moments are the varying expectations and needs of key organizational constituencies, including students, faculty, staff, alumni, members of the community, and the media. An understanding of crisis leadership requires one to not only explore the current incident or set of incidents impacting the institution, but to also understand the history of an institution, the preparation of its leaders, and the actions moving forward beyond the incident (Gigliotti, 2017; Gigliotti & Fortunato, 2017).

The notion of crisis has been defined by a wide array of scholars and practitioners, yet the central characteristics of the concept remain similar across all definitions. Crises are understood to be "untimely but predictable event[s]" that have the potential to impact stakeholders and the organization's reputation more broadly (Heath & Millar, 2004, p. 2). Sohn and Lariscy (2014) built upon this idea of the impact on stakeholders in their definition of crisis as "a major event that has the potential to threaten collective perceptions and estimations held by all relevant stakeholders of an organization and its relevant attributes" (p. 24). These incidents often tend to have a "negative effect" on the organization as a whole (Coombs, 2015), unlike mere routine incidents or nuisances that tend to have a minor, localized impact (Pauchant & Mitroff, 1992). This distinction between incidents and crises is important given the focus of this chapter. Recent diversity-related incidents in higher education may appear to some to be isolated examples that are limited to the scope of one particular office on campus; however, a more comprehensive understanding of these issues points to the systemic, institution-wide impact of what may be perceived to be ongoing "crises" in higher education.

There has been a tendency for many institutions, both within higher education and beyond, to adopt a reactive approach to crisis management planning. Despite the seemingly pervasive nature of crises across organizations, institutional learning in this area appears to be somewhat limited. As Booker (2014) posited, "Research is limited on crisis management planning in higher education because many institutions of higher education have written their crisis management plans *after* a crisis event occurred; a reactive approach to crisis that seems to typify crisis management" (p. 17). He went on further to warn that "This reactive posture is creating environments unequipped to handle either man-made or natural disasters that ultimately threaten safety on college campuses" (pp. 17, 18). We would extend this logic further to explore the under-researched area of crisis leadership as it relates to diversity-related issues and campus protests on college and university campuses.

There is still much to learn about crises in higher education. The types of crises that are most germane to colleges and universities range from natural disasters and cyberattacks to widespread plagiarism scandals and campus shootings (Gigliotti, 2017). In their study of the Virginia Tech shooting and the subsequent actions following the incident, for example, Wang and Hutchins (2010) noted that "While it is impossible to prepare for every conceivable type of crisis, the best-prepared organizations have learned how to develop a crisis portfolio that reflects the institution's complexity and that can change over time" (p. 570). As campus communities, policies, laws, and demographics around the nation continue to change, new issues related to culture, race, gender, religion, sexuality, and social class will emerge and add complexity to this required portfolio for leaders in higher education.

Crises within colleges and universities are particularly challenging moments for institutional leaders given the many stakeholders involved in higher education, along with the often competing missions of higher education (Gigliotti & Fortunato, 2017; Ruben, De Lisi, & Gigliotti, 2017). For those involved in the leadership of these institutions, events that are characterized as crises can dramatically impact all aspects of organizational leadership. As Weick (1993) suggested, "What makes such an episode so shattering is that both the sense of what is occurring and the means to rebuild that sense collapse together" (p. 633). Leaders in higher education often wrestle with the tensions of leader-as-performer and leader-as-human in the face of these crises (Gigliotti, 2016), and these crises present a unique opportunity for institutional leaders to build credibility, cultivate trust, and demonstrate the ability to effectively resolve a given issue. Given this surge in diversity-related incidents and crises on college and university campuses across the country, the importance of understanding diversity competencies as an integral part of higher education leadership remains a critical topic for scholarly investigation and applied leadership practice.

DIVERSITY LEADERSHIP

In order to demonstrate leadership in the area of diversity and inclusion, colleges and universities must validate their commitment to diversity in very tangible ways. This involves having a diverse student body, as well as a faculty and staff who reflect the racial, socio-economic, and gender identities within the nation; and ensuring that campus professionals have resources available to give support and to enact change when needed. According to Jenkins (2010), "universities verbally espouse a commitment to these issues but do very little to ensure staff can effectively manage, replicate, and create culture on a contemporary college campus" (p. 138). Instead of employing diversity as "window dressing," colleges and universities must trust their campus diversity professionals, and help them to employ best practices in their field to effect change. Student affairs professionals, and specifically cultural practitioners,[4] must be supported in their work (Jenkins, 2010).

Moreover, leadership in the area of institutional diversity should not come solely from centers of multicultural affairs or institutional diversity offices. As Sutton and McCluskey-Titus (2010) acknowledged,

> A perception held by most campus administrators is that the concerns of ethnic/racial minority students should be the sole responsibility of the MACC [Multicultural Affairs and Cultural Center] professional ... Although MACC professionals' positions cause them to assume institutional leadership for achieving ethnic/racial minority student retention goals, for instance, caution should be exercised to prevent other institutional staff from ignoring their professional responsibilities to underrepresented students. (p. 161)

Therefore, rather than relying entirely on the leadership of professionals in diversity-related offices, understanding the

---

[4]This includes the wide array of practitioners who work in multicultural or intercultural affairs offices.

importance of diversity should be a competency for all campus leaders.

Over the past decade, institutional diversity has begun to receive much needed and overdue attention. Many university's diversity efforts include initiatives for increased recruitment and retention for staff and faculty, programming that brings attention to underrepresented communities, as well as university-wide initiatives that work to foster diversity and inclusion across all aspects of campus, not just students. Research published by Williams et al. has helped to generate conversations and research about institutional diversity and the necessity for strategic diversity leadership (Wade-Golden & Matlock, 2007; Williams, 2008, 2013; Williams & Clowney, 2007; Williams & Wade-Golden, 2013). Additionally, the importance of strategic diversity leadership has been highlighted by a number of prominent institutional and organizational leaders (Williams & Wade Golden, 2013). One of these leaders, William Tierney, stated that "for diversity to succeed necessitates 'strategic diversity' – it does not just organically happen" (Williams, 2013, p. xi). Williams (2013) argued that diversity is an essential and integral part of the modern college and university, but also that fostering inclusion and success among people of all backgrounds is a moral obligation, and one that is essential to the growth of the nation. By addressing diversity needs on campuses, colleges and universities must tend to the campus climate and promote inclusion so that students, faculty, and staff from a variety of backgrounds feel welcomed and supported. Our collective hope should be that all higher education leaders are proactive and supportive of a campus community that encourages diversity and inclusion, leading to a reduction or elimination of violations to community. However, we know that these negative incidents do occur; therefore, campus leaders need to be prepared to engage in effective crisis diversity leadership.

Crisis Diversity Leadership

Crisis diversity leadership works to disrupt diversity-related crises, such as hate crimes and discrimination lawsuits, through rapid crisis communication and by hiring individuals to address diversity and inclusion for the organization. In recent years, corporations, such as Coca-Cola and Bank of America, have faced lawsuits related to racial discrimination that have led to those companies engaging in crisis communication to reduce negative media attention and consumer backlash related to organizational diversity issues (Temin, 2011). Williams (2008) calls this reactive approach the "diversity crisis model," and that it "usually involves stakeholder responses, a high-profile declaration of support from senior leadership, the commissioning of a planning group, deliberation and discussion by diversity planning teams, and the development of a diversity plan" (p. 27). The crisis model of diversity and inclusion has been criticized for creating superficial and symbolic organizational diversity and inclusion efforts and results, such as creating a position to support institutional diversity without providing adequate resources for this position to make policy and structural changes for inclusion and equity (Williams, Berger, & McClendon, 2005). These largely symbolic practices associated with the diversity crisis model are often implemented to quell negative publicity stemming from racial discrimination lawsuits or campus hate crimes.

The diversity crisis model is not limited to corporations; institutions of higher education and nonprofit organizations also have experienced the pressure to act as a result of diversity-oriented crisis situations (Williams, 2008). Williams (2008) argued that diversity missteps by college leadership, as well as an increase in racist-themed campus parties and campus hate crimes are leading more U.S. institutions of higher education to employ the diversity crisis model. The increase in racist campus incidents (Garcia & Johnston-Guerrero, 2015), paired with the increasing politicization and polarization of access and funding for U.S. higher education (Jaschik, 2014), are making campus leaders feel the pressure to answer for their diversity and inclusion policies and practices.

Strategies for Effective Crisis Diversity Leadership

Through our review of the intersecting literatures in the areas of crisis leadership, diversity leadership, and crisis diversity leadership, it is increasingly apparent that proactive and inclusive policies and organizational communicative practices designed to increase transparency and inclusion of diverse ideas and perspectives are needed to advance organizational leadership in higher education. More importantly, these principles and practices can further enhance and enrich the experiences of underrepresented students, faculty, and staff involved in the organization. Within the context of the many complex diversity-oriented crises facing institutions of higher education, what follows is a host of theory-informed strategies that strengthen and enhance crisis diversity leadership.

CRISIS DIVERSITY LEADERSHIP AS AN INSTITUTION-WIDE IMPERATIVE

As previously noted, diversity offices, plans, and personnel, are not a "magical fix" for the various diversity challenges on college and university campuses. Rather, changes in campus climate require multidimensional, collaborative, and intentional processes at an institutional level. Many diversity initiatives tend to focus primarily on two areas of campus to further their diversity efforts: (1) Chief Diversity Officers or other high-level diversity administrators, and (2) staff members in Cultural Centers or Multicultural Affairs Offices. Although they are not usually the focus of diversity change efforts, department chairs and deans play a critical role in campus diversity efforts. For example, deans and department chairs can influence faculty members' inclusion of diversity within the curriculum and recruitment efforts to employ a diverse faculty (Chun & Evans, 2015). Additionally, other senior-level administrators play an important role in fostering inclusive excellence in their respective divisions. Thus, if taken seriously, crisis diversity leadership extends across units and must be recognized as an institution-wide imperative.

DIVERSITY AUDITS

Despite having a well-formulated diversity process, there remains an opportunity for leaders to learn that what they once perceived to be effective is not producing the anticipated results. Therefore, as Patton (2010) suggests, performing periodic audits is critical. Much like the societies in which we live, colleges and universities are not static. Terminology and best practices change frequently and it is important that our policies and plans remain updated and flexible in order to keep up with changes in the environment. For example, the 2016 U.S. presidential election has raised questions and concerns regarding changes in immigration policy and federal financial assistance, both of which may require new practices or policies to support organizational members, such as undocumented students, and increase equity and access to higher education.

PROTEST PROTOCOLS

According to a recent Cooperative Institutional Research Program (CIRP) study, nearly 1 in 10 incoming first-year students expect to participate in student protests while in college (Higher Education Research Institute, 2016). Given this trend, "institutional leaders will continue to be called on to create campuses that are more equitable and inclusive of an increasingly diverse population" (Frye & Morton, 2016, p. 4). Creating campus diversity initiatives provides institutions with an opportunity to "articulate their values and goals related to diversity ... [Moreover] strategic diversity planning has emerged in higher education as an important step toward fostering organizational change" (Frye & Morton, 2016, p. 4). Higher education leaders must be aware of protocols for dealing with student protests, and these protests should be recognized for their value in encouraging student leadership and creating opportunities for campus and community improvement.

CREATE AND SUPPORT PIPELINES

One of the ways that organizations have increased diversity and changed their climate is through the creation of pipeline programs for faculty, staff, and administration that are designed to recruit, mentor, and guide individuals into specific career paths (McCarty, Hukai, & McCarty, 2005). Creating and supporting pipelines into organizations, can subsequently lead to targeted training, orientation, and dialogue programs that are designed to increase all employees' knowledge, awareness, and inclusion efforts surrounding issues of diversity and inclusion. Pipeline, training, orientation, and dialogue programs are utilized in concert by organizations to increase diversity by changing the population, creating new social and communicative organizational norms, and, eventually, creating a more inclusive organizational culture.

DIALOGUE EXPERTISE

Rather than avoiding conflict during challenging diversity-related crises, the most effective leaders engage in sustained conversation and dialogue with students and other campus constituents. Engaging in dialogue does not mean having a single conversation, rather, it is thoughtfully listening, expressing compassion, and engaging in a long-term relationship with people who are disenchanted, yet committed to seeing change (Dwyer, Gigliotti, & Lee, 2014). Crisis diversity leadership requires an acknowledgment of past wrongs and a genuine commitment to improve in the future. Many campuses have dialogue programs that teach students the communication skills necessary to engage authentically and thoughtfully across lines of difference (Maxwell, Dessel, Dwyer, Bowen, & Nance, 2016). In addition, some campuses have even made it their goal to transform their chilly campus racial climate into a hospitable one through the use of intergroup dialogue programs (BizEd, 2015; Lang, 2014). Intergroup dialogue programs help manage campus conflict, improve campus climate, bolster town—gown relationships, and support other diversity-oriented leadership initiatives across the institution (Gurin, Dey, Hurtado, & Gurin, 2002; Lang, 2014).

Conclusion

The five suggested practices noted above — an institution-wide commitment, diversity audits, protest protocols, pipeline programs, and dialogue expertise — are not the only strategies available for effective diversity leadership, but they provide an excellent foundation upon which to move forward in mending campus divisions and supporting inclusion. Additional institutional strategies may be pursued depending on the type of institution and its mission. For example, public state institutions may require leaders to engage in similar diversity and inclusion discourse that are in use by the governor and legislature and to address diversity-related issues that are most germane to the state or region where the institution is located. Moreover, leaders at religious institutions may find it useful to engage with the religious leaders of their particular tradition and to deliver congruent messages about the ethical, moral, and religious teachings of diversity and inclusion that reflect the specific religious tradition.

While these strategies are not a fait accompli, they are a starting point. There is a clear need for further consideration of additional strategies that may help leaders to navigate the complex terrain of diversity-oriented crises in higher education. Consistent with the other chapters in this volume, the necessity for effective leadership practices – particularly inclusive practices that meet the challenges of crises associated with issues of diversity – are critical to contemporary organizations. These practices can help leaders to grapple with the challenges of a rapidly changing, diverse, and global society. The strategies for effective diversity leadership are multidimensional and inclusive, and leaders must attend to the nuances of this approach to leadership in preparing for, responding to, and learning from the inevitable crises that may occur in the future. The focus on diversity and leadership remains critical to cultivating environments of inclusive excellence across all institutions of higher education.

The board of directors of the American Association of Colleges and Universities (AAC&U) has affirmed and reaffirmed inclusive excellence as an essential pillar of higher education, stating that liberal education must be "global and pluralistic" (AAC&U, 2013, para. 3). Moreover, AAC&U (2013) defines inclusive excellence as

> attending both to the demographic diversity of the student body and also to the need for nurturing climates and cultures so that all students have a chance to succeed. Commitment to student success in these terms requires broad-based, compassionate leadership and equity-minded[5] practice—not only within individual institutions, but also across states and systems and in policy circles that make decisions affecting the nation. (para. 5)

AAC&U goes so far as to suggest that inclusive excellence is essential not only for institutions of higher education, but also for creating productive citizens across society more broadly. The organization purports, "Without inclusion, there is no true excellence" (AAC&U, 2013, para. 6). From this application, we see that the principles and concepts raised in this chapter are transferrable across sectors. We hope that leaders outside of higher education may choose to also adopt the strategies offered in this chapter to improve and enhance their workplaces.

---

[5]"Equity-mindedness" means that educational leaders, faculty, and staff demonstrate an awareness of and a proactive willingness to address their institution's equity and inequity issues (Bensimon, 2007).

Discussion Questions

1. What are the common themes and areas of concern that contributed to recent student protests on college and university campuses?
2. In what ways can the literature in the areas of crisis leadership, diversity leadership, and crisis diversity leadership inform our understanding of campus unrest related to issues of diversity and inclusion?
3. How does the institutional identity of a college or university change when it makes diversity and inclusion an institutional imperative?
4. Which of the five suggested crisis diversity leadership practices offered in the conclusion of this chapter do you find most valuable? Of the five suggested crisis diversity leadership practices presented in the conclusion of this chapter, which might be the most challenging for leaders in higher education to implement?

References

Addo, K. (2015, November 8). Mizzou football players say they won't play until president is ousted over race issues. St. Louis Post-Dispatch.

American Association of Colleges and Universities (2013). Board statement on diversity, equity, and inclusive excellence. Retrieved June 30, 2016 from https://www.aacu.org/about/statements/2013/diversity

Barr, J., & Goodman, J. (2015, October 20). Former Louisville recruit about his visit: 'It was like I was in a strip club.' *ESPN.com*. Retrieved from http://espn.go.com/espn/otl/story/_/id/13927159/former-louisville-cardinals-basketball-players-recruits-acknowledge-stripper-parties-minardi-hall

Bensimon, E. M. (2007). The underestimated significance of practitioner knowledge in the scholarship on student success. *The Review of Higher Education*, 30(4), 441–469.

BizEd (2015, December 21). New course at Cornell teaches students to manage conflict http://www.bizedmagazine.com/archives/2016/1/ideas-in-action/new-course-cornell-teaches-students-manage-conflict

Booker, L. (2014). Crisis management: Changing times for colleges. *Journal of College Admission*, 222, 16–23.

Chun, E., & Evans, A. (2015). *The department chair as transformative diversity leader: Building inclusive learning environments in higher education*. Sterling, VA: Stylus Publishing.

Clark, C., Fasching-Varner, K. J., & Brimhall-Vargas, M. (Eds.). (2012). *Occupying the academy*. Lanham, MD: Rowman & Littlefield Publishers.

Coombs, W. T. (2015). *Ongoing crisis communication: Planning, managing and responding*. (4th ed.). Thousand Oaks, CA: Sage.

di Bartolo, A. N. (2015). Rethinking gender equity in higher education. Association of American Colleges and Universities. Retrieved from https://www.aacu.org/diversitydemocracy/2015/spring/dibartolo

Dwyer, B., Gigliotti, R. A., & Lee, H. H. (2014). Mindfulness & authentic leadership development for social change: The intergroup dialogue program at Villanova University. In K. Goldman Schuyler, J. E. Baugher, K. Jironet, & L. Lid-Falkman (Eds.), *Leading with spirit, presence, and authenticity* (pp. 125–146). San Francisco, CA: Jossey-Bass/Wiley.

Eligon, J., & Perez-Pena, R. (2015, November 10). Campus protests at Missouri spur a day of change. *New York Times*.

Fortunato, J. A., Gigliotti, R. A., & Ruben, B. D. (2017). Racial incidents at the University of Missouri: The value of leadership communication and stakeholder relationships. *International Journal of Business Communication*, *54*(2), 199–209.

Frye, J. R., & Morton, C. S. (2016). Strategic planning for higher education: Insights from a multiinstitution research project. *Insight Paper* National Center for Institutional Diversity: Ann Arbor, MI. Retrieved on June 16, 2016 from.

Garcia, G. A., & Johnston-Guerrero, M. P. (2015). Challenging the utility of a racial microaggressions framework through a systematic review of racially biased incidents on campus. *Journal of Critical Scholarship on Higher Education and Student Affairs*, *2*, 50–66.

Gigliotti, R. A. (2016). Leader as performer; Leader as human: A discursive and retrospective construction of crisis leadership. *Atlantic Journal of Communication*.

Gigliotti, R. A. (2017). The social construction of crisis in higher education: Implications for crisis leadership theory and practice. Unpublished doctoral dissertation, Rutgers University, New Brunswick, NJ.

Gigliotti, R. A., & Fortunato, J. A. (2017). Crisis leadership: Upholding institutional values. In B. D. Ruben, R. De Lisi, & R. A. Gigliotti (Eds.), *A guide for leaders in higher education: Core concepts, competencies, and tools*. Sterling, VA: Stylus Publishing.

Grinberg, E., & Hassan, C. (2015, October 31). University of Louisville president sorry for photo of staff in Ponchos, Sombreros. *CNN*. Retrieved from http://www.cnn.com/2015/10/31/living/university-louisville-racist-staff-party-feat/

Gurin, P., Dey, E. L., Hurtado, S., & Gurin, G. (2002). Diversity and higher education: Theory and impact on educational outcomes. *Harvard Educational Review*, *72*(3), 330–366.

Heath, R. L., & Millar, D. P. (2004). A rhetorical approach to crisis communication: Management, communication processes, and strategic responses. In D. P. Millar & R. L. Heath (Eds.), *Responding to crisis: A rhetorical approach to crisis communication* (pp. 1–17). Mahwah, NJ: Erlbaum.

Higher Education Research Institute. (2016). The American freshman: National norms of Fall 2015. Retrieved May 3, 2016 from http://heri.ucla.edu/monographs/TheAmericanFreshman2015.pdf

Inside Higher Ed. (2015, October 21). Former recruit: Louisville visit was like "strip club." Inside Higher Ed. Retrieved from https://www.insidehighered.com/quicktakes/2015/10/21/former-recruit-louisville-visit-was-strip-club

Jaschik, S. (2014, January 31). *Obama vs. art history*. Retrieved from Insider Higher Ed website: https://www.insidehighered.com/news/2014/01/31/obama-becomes-latest-politician-criticize-liberal-arts-discipline

Jaschik, S. (2015, November 9). Racial tensions escalate. *Inside Higher Ed*. Retrieved from https://www.insidehighered.com/news/2015/11/09/racial-tensions-escalate-u-missouri-and-yale

Jayakumar, U. M. (2008). Can higher education meet the needs of an increasingly diverse society and global marketplace? Campus diversity and crosscultural workforce competencies. *Harvard Educational Review*, 78, 615–651.

Jenkins, T. S. (2010). Viewing cultural practice through a lens of innovation and intentionality: Strategies for student personnel administrators in cultural centers. In L. D. Patton (Ed.) *Cultural centers in higher education: Perspectives on identity, theory, and practice* (pp. 137–156). Sterling, VA: Stylus.

Landsbaum, C., & Weber, G. (2015, November 9). What happened at the University of Missouri? *Slate*. Retrieved June 28, 2016 from http://www.slate.com/blogs/the_slatest/2015/11/09/timeline_of_u_of_missouri_protests_and_president_resignation.html

Lang, S. S. (2014, March 12). Intergroup dialogue project course wins Perkins Prize. Retrieved July 1, 2016 from http://chronicle.cornell.edu/stories/2014/03/intergroup-dialogue-project-course-wins-perkins-prize

Lipset, S. M., & Altbach, P. G. (1966). Student politics and higher education in the United States. *Comparative Education Review*, 10, 320–349.

Logue, J. (2015, October 30). Racial tensions erupt at Ithaca. Inside Higher Ed. Retrieved June 28, 2016 from https://www.insidehighered.com/news/2015/10/30/racial-tensions-ithaca-college

Maxwell, K., Dessel, A., Dwyer, B., Bowen, S., & Nance, T. A. (March, 2016). *Intergroup Dialogue: Shifting paradigms toward student-centered learning*. Association of American Colleges and Universities, Philadelphia, PA.

McCarty Kilian, C., Hukai, D., & Elizabeth McCarty, C. (2005). Building diversity in the pipeline to corporate leadership. *Journal of Management Development*, 24, 155–168.

New, J. (2015, August 26). Black eye for Baylor. *Inside Higher Ed*. Retrieved from https://www.insidehighered.com/news/2015/08/26/baylor-u-facing-questions-over-handling-sexual-assault-involving-football-player

Parker, E. T. (2015, December 3). Hire a Chief Diversity Officer, check! *Diverse Education*. Retrieved December 21, 2015 from http://diverseeducation.com/article/79300/.

Patton, L. D. (2010). Best practices for examining and evaluating campus culture centers and multicultural affairs offices. In L. D. Patton (Ed.), *Cultural centers in higher education: Perspectives on identity, theory, and practice* (pp. 194–200). Sterling, VA: Stylus.

Pauchant, T. C., & Mitroff, I. I. (1992). *Transforming the crisis-prone organization: Preventing individual, organizational, and environmental tragedies*. San Francisco, CA: Jossey-Bass.

Pearson, M. (2015, November 10). A timeline of the University of Missouri protests. *CNN*. Retrieved June 28, 2016 from http://www.cnn.com/2015/11/09/us/
missouri-protest-timeline/

Pilkington, E. (2010, September 10). Tyler Clementi, student ousted as gay on
internet, jumps to his death. *The Guardian*. Retrieved June 24, 2016 from
https://www.theguardian.com/world/2010/sep/30/tyler-clementi-gay-student-
suicide

Robers, S., Zhang, A., Morgan, R. E., & Musu-Gillette, L. (2015, July).
Indicators of school crime and safety: 2014 (NCES Report No. 2015-072/NCJ
248036). Retrieved June 29, 2015 from http://nces.ed.gov/pubs2015/2015072.
pdf

Ruben, B. D. (2012). *What leaders need to know and do: A leadership competencies scorecard*. (2nd ed.). Washington, DC: National Association of College
and University Business Officers.

Ruben, B. D., De Lisi, R., & Gigliotti, R. A. (2017). *A guide for leaders in higher
education: Core concepts, competencies, and tools*. Sterling, VA: Stylus
Publishing.

Sohn, Y. J., & Lariscy, R. W. (2014). Understanding reputational crisis:
Definition, properties, and consequences. *Journal of Public Relations Research*,
26(1), 23–43.

Stripling, J. (2015, November 10). Thrust into a national debate on race, 2
Missouri chiefs resign. *Chronicle of Higher Education*. Retrieved December 13,
2016 from http://chronicle.com/article/Thrust-Into-a-National-Debate/234131

Stripling, J., & Thomason, A. (2015, March 11). Oklahoma president's swift
action on racist video carries risks. *Chronicle of Higher Education*. Retrieved on
December 13, 2016 from http://chronicle.com/article/Oklahoma-President-s-
Swift/228389/

Sutton & McCluskey-Titus (2010). Campus culture center director's perspectives
on advancement, current issues, and future directions. In L. D. Patton (Ed.),
*Cultural centers in higher education: Perspectives on identity, theory, and prac-
tice* (pp. 157–177). Sterling, VA: Stylus.

Temin, D. B. (2011). How to handle a diversity crisis. *Talent Management*.
Retrieved June 29, 2015 from http://www.talentmgt.com/articles/how-to-handle-
a-diversity-crisis

Thelin, J. R. (2013). *A history of American higher education*. (2nd ed.).
Baltimore, MD: Johns Hopkins University Press.

Tracy, M. (2016, May 26). Baylor demotes President Kenneth Starr over handling of sex assault cases. *The New York Times*. Retrieved June 29, 2016 from
http://www.nytimes.com/2016/05/27/sports/ncaafootball/baylor-art-briles-ken-
neth-starr-college-football.html

Wade-Golden, K., & Matlock, J. (2007). Ten core ingredients for fostering campus diversity success. *The Diversity Factor*, 15(1), 41–48.

Wang, J., & Hutchins, H. M. (2010). Crisis management in higher education:
What have we learned from Virginia Tech? *Advances in Developing Human
Resources*, 12(5), 552–572.

Weick, K. E. (1993). The collapse of sensemaking in organizations: The Mann
Gulch disaster. *Administrative Science Quarterly*, 38(4), 628–652.

Williams, D. A. (2008). Beyond the diversity crisis model: Decentralized diversity planning and implementation. *Planning for Higher Education, 36*(2), 27.

Williams, D. A. (2013). *Strategic diversity Leadership: Activating change and transformation in higher education.* Sterling, VA: Stylus.

Williams, D. A., Berger, J. B., & McClendon, S. A. (2005). Toward a model of inclusive excellence and change in postsecondary institutions. Washington, DC: Association of American Colleges and Universities. Retrieved June 29, 2016 from https://www.aacu.org/sites/default/files/files/mei/williams_et_al.pdf

Williams, D. A., & Clowney, C. (2007). Strategic planning for diversity and organizational change: A primer for higher-education leadership. *Effective Practices for Academic Leaders, 2*(3), 1–16.

Williams, D. A., & Wade-Golden, K. C. (2013). *The Chief Diversity Officer: Strategy, structure, and change management.* Sterling, VA: Stylus.

Woodhouse, K. (2015, November 13). What's next for Missouri? *Inside Higher Education.* Retrieved June 28, 2016 from https://www.insidehighered.com/news/2015/11/13/university-missouri-looks-ahead-it-tries-combat-race-issues-campus

Yale Students. (2015, October 31). Open letter to Associate Master Christakis [open letter]. *Down Magazine.* Retrieved June 29, 2016 from http://downatyale.com/post.php?id=430

12 Inclusive Leadership and the Dynamics of Multinational Military Operations ☆

Yvonne R. Masakowski

This chapter focuses on the development of military leaders who are inclusive and capable of forging a cohesive coalition command structure in multinational military operations. Multinational military operations require military leaders to develop an inclusive organizational structure that affords coalition partners the opportunity to participate equally in command decision-making processes. Such partner participation further supports the development of a command with unity of purpose and unity of command that will ensure military operational success.

The chapter examines some of the challenges associated with becoming an effective leader of multinational military teams. Among these, military leaders are tasked to develop a coalition

---

☆ Note: The author currently serves as the U.S. Chair for a NATO HFM RTG 286 panel focused on Leader Development for NATO Multinational Military Operations. This panel is examining the education, training, experience, and personal development for all future military leaders.

The views expressed in this panel are those of the author and do not necessarily represent those of The United States Naval War College.

team that works together in a collaborative and cooperative manner. Given the complexities of cultural diversity among the disparate military forces and civilian organizations, inclusivity plays a pivotal role in leadership effectiveness. This chapter will explore the importance of establishing rapport and building relationships based on respect and trust. Inclusive leaders empower those under their command and facilitate the team's mission success. Global security requires leaders to be effective in establishing teams with unity of command. This discussion will highlight the path to achieving these objectives.

Primary Objective: The primary objective of this chapter is to increase awareness of the importance of becoming an inclusive and culturally competent military leader of multinational military operations.

Secondary Objective: The secondary objective is to emphasize the critical role that cultural diversity plays in multinational military operations. It is essential for military leaders to understand how cultural diversity influences multinational military operations.

Introduction

The 21st-century global security environment poses a broad range of operational challenges for military leaders, especially for those leading multinational military operations. NATO faces numerous challenges with regard to the range of multinational military operations being conducted on a global scale. This range of military operations requires leaders who are competent and capable of leading culturally diverse military forces. Effective military leaders are those who are good communicators, able to build relationships based on trust and respect. In this regard, leadership requirements are shaped by sociopolitical events and the cultural values of each nation (Masakowski, 2008). The coalition team represents a diverse spectrum of beliefs, values, and varying organizational structures. Thus, it is essential for leaders of NATO military operations to be culturally aware and inclusive leaders with coalition partners.

As American military officers are prone to acknowledge, contemporary militaries are operating in a volatile, uncertain, complex, and ambiguous environment (Greene Sands & Greene-Sands, 2014; McFate & Laurence, 2015). Global security challenges range from counterterrorism and cyberwarfare to humanitarian and immigration crises. Therefore, there is a need to develop leaders who are inclusive and capable of working across military forces and civilian agencies composed of culturally diverse teams.

NATO multinational military operations mandate the need to develop military leaders who are capable of building and leading culturally diverse multinational military teams (Masakowski, 2008; Soeters & Manigart, 2008). NATO military leaders are especially challenged, as each military or civilian organization has its own set of ranks, roles, and responsibilities. NATO military leaders are also held to a higher standard of moral and ethical behavior on the global stage. This is especially true in the 21st-century digital age, where YouTube, Facebook, Twitter, and other social media generate group responses that are radical if military leaders fail in their command.

This chapter also characterizes several constraints that military leaders face when operating in diverse operational environments, such as Afghanistan and Iraq. This discussion will examine the ways that military leaders might address these issues as they strive to establish unity of purpose and command among multinational military teams. For example, leaders who excel in communication are better able to inspire and motivate their teams by sharing their visions of the missions and achieve consensus among their teams (Bass, 1990). These leaders instill a sense of confidence and trust among those they are leading and are much more effective in shaping coalition teams that will achieve success. In so doing, leaders build meaningful and effective interpersonal relationships with all those in their command. Thus, becoming an inclusive leader paves the path for building teams that will work together more efficiently and effectively. The balance between leader development and leadership effectiveness is a sensitive one that requires leaders to be self-aware and inclusive. The cost of failure is significant in that the leader may not only have failure in the mission; the leader's failure may have implications for the 21st-century security environment.

Creating an Inclusive Command Environment

Contemporary military leaders are presented with increased challenges as they build cross-functional teams with military teams and civilian representatives from the United Nations and non-governmental organizations, such as the Red Cross and

Médecins Sans Frontières (Doctors without Borders), that support humanitarian and peacekeeping missions. Today's leaders are required to adapt rapidly to the demands of the operational environment. It is essential that leaders gain experience in a variety of operational environments if they are to succeed in leading a multinational military operation. There are critical experiences that help shape leaders' awareness and cultural perspectives, as well as influence their decision-making abilities.

Traditionally, military leaders are provided with operational briefings prior to beginning operations in foreign nations. These information briefings prepare them for the physical and security environments but more often fail to address the cultural aspects of the environment. Emphasis is placed upon language skills, political climates, and the topography of the landscape. Indeed, the Intelligence Preparation of the Battlespace is a primary step in understanding the military operation. However, this approach fails to fully prepare leaders to deal with the diversity of the people whom they will lead. Leaders are often assigned to positions based on their familiarity with a region without consideration of the cultural environment. Indeed, there have been occasions when the US military has overlooked local cultural concerns with negative consequences. For example, during the Iraq War, there was a need to establish a medical center for Sunni women to have access to medical care for their families. The US Army selected a region to build a hospital based on its proximity to the village, without cultural considerations. For the Sunni women, this land was sacred, as their husbands, sons, and other loved ones had died there. They would not go to this hospital and chose to make the journey to a medical center far from their homes rather than cross that land (Dorough-Lewis, 2015; Laurence, 2015; McFate, 2005, 2015; McFate & Laurence, 2015; Meyer, 2014). This incident demonstrates the importance of a military leader's awareness of the human terrain and the cultural beliefs, customs, and values of those in the leader's region of command (Petraeus, 2015).

Effective Leadership: Qualities of an Inclusive Leader

Professor Edwin Hollander was the first person to coin the phrase *inclusive leadership* and define the role of inclusive leadership in the development of effective leaders. He suggested that *inclusive leadership* is about relationships that can accomplish things for mutual benefit (Hollander, 1978, 1979, 1992). On the basis of this view, an inclusive leader is someone who is equipped with interpersonal skills and an understanding of the unique perspectives of each individual based on the individual's culture, knowledge, and experience. Inclusive leadership in multinational military operations is indispensable for building effective relationships and achieving mission success.

Professor Bruce Avolio has conducted research dedicated to leader development and leadership effectiveness (Avolio, 2009; Avolio & Gardner, 2005; Eberly, Johnson, Hernandez, & Avolio, 2013). He has examined the role of self-awareness, moral perspectives, and transparency as part of the development of authentic leaders. Avolio (2009) suggests that it is important to provide a positive and ethical environment that fosters growth and development.

Similarly to Hollander's theory, this approach promotes the development of a relationship between leaders and followers. This interactive relationship is highly relevant for the development of military leaders as mentors and role models. This is especially true in foreign military operations, where those in command set the example for their followers by their decisions and actions.

Today's leaders who weigh their decisions and actions within the context of the cultural environment achieve greater success in building cohesive military teams (Morrow, 2016). Skills in negotiation and conflict resolution rely on a leader's sensitivity to the cultural, social, and political aspects of the environment (Earley & Ang, 2003; Eisen, 2015; Terlizzi, 2014). For example, the contemporary mass migration of Syrian refugees serves as an illustration of some of the challenges that each nation faces with regard to managing the physical, psychological, and cultural impacts of such events. There is no established plan for such events, nor is there any consensus among nations as to how each nation should approach each crisis. Indeed, it is impossible to develop a fixed plan of action, as each crisis has its own unique set of issues (Greene Sands & Greene-Sands, 2014; McFate & Laurence, 2015; Soeters & Manigart, 2008; Terlizzi, 2014). In addition, these events do not occur in isolation but rather occur in the context of unique cultural environments.

Educators who develop leaders can help leaders gain a perspective in this regard by helping them to understand the potential consequences of their decisions and actions (Abbe & Gallus, 2012; Abbe, Gulick, & Herman, 2008). Cultural ideologies, beliefs, and values contribute to the way that military teams interact with each other as well as with the local population. Failure to understand these factors may give rise to unintended consequences of greater proportion and at a cost to mission success (Abbe et al., 2008; Gurstein, 1999; Klein, Pongonis, & Klein, 2000). Inclusive leaders understand the importance of examining the situation through a cultural lens and making decisions that support both the culture and the mission (Abbe & Gallus, 2012; Bennett, 2009; Masakowski, 2008).

Cultural intelligence contributes to a leader's effectiveness and is an important component of cultural competency (Earley & Ang, 2003; Van Dyne et al., 2012). Cultural intelligence is the framework used by leaders to view and understand culturally diverse people (Bentley, 2016). Stella Ting-Toomey reminds leaders to be "mindful" of their own personal assumptions, ideas, and emotions, as well as others' perspectives (Ting-Toomey, 1985, 1988, 1999). Our task is to develop military leaders who understand the importance of each individual's cultural perspective. This information is vital for the leader to grasp before entering into negotiation and/or conflict resolutions.

The human terrain is an essential component of multinational military operations, as culture influences the execution of operational plans, as experienced by those in Iraq and Afghanistan (Petraeus, 2015).

Effective leaders are those who first seek to understand the people with whom they are working and whom they are leading before attempting to move ahead with the mission (Earley & Ang, 2003; Livermore, 2010). What makes matters even more difficult is that leaders are often presented with emerging crises for which there is no blueprint or set of rules. During tsunamis, typhoons, and hurricanes, military leaders address these challenges by reaching out to neighboring nations. For example, the US Navy ship *Mercy* came to the aid of the Philippines and other nations in the aftermath of Typhoon Haiyan (LaGrone, 2013). The crew's task was to organize a team of medical and emergency personnel to assist those in crisis. The crew quickly rose to the occasion, modifying a ship that normally held a limited crew and converting it into a 1,000-bed hospital with a crew of 1,200 Navy physicians, nurses, and corpsmen to assist wherever needed (Steele, 2016). The crew also reached out to neighboring nations for assistance. As a result of these actions, regional partnerships formed into a team called Pacific Partnership (2014), organized to address future crises in the area. This team assists during crises ranging from earthquakes to tsunamis that hit the Pacific region and surrounding nations (Sander & Solomon, 2014; Steele, 2016). This is but one example of the importance of achieving an awareness of the capabilities that each nation has to offer during times of crisis. Crises often yield opportunities for nations to build and strengthen relationships as they offer their support and aid.

Leadership has always required moral courage and remains a critical capability in today's complex global environment. The news media are replete with moral failures among our military leaders (Jaffe, 2012). The U.S. Navy's "Fat Leonard scandal" (Grazier & Hempowicz, 2016) highlights the need for developing leaders of character who can uphold the high moral and ethical standards that society demands (Abbe, 2014; Brooks, 2015; Grazier & Hempowicz, 2016; Livermore, 2010). Today, social media are quick to report on a military leader's moral and ethical failures. The immediacy of this notoriety highlights the importance of maintaining a high caliber of character, morals, ethics, and values. Leadership behaviors are scrutinized by those in the leader's command and organization, as well as by the people living in the region. Character relies on a leader's inner strength and a core sense of integrity and honesty that builds trust among those in the leader's command. Thus, military leaders who reflect on their strengths and weaknesses are often more successful in understanding how their decisions might impact culturally diverse people (Klein et al., 2000; Matsumoto, Grissom, & Dinnel, 2001). Communication plays a pivotal role in leadership effectiveness. Leaders convey their individual beliefs, ethics, and values as they interact with those in their command (Abbe, 2014; Greene Sands & Greene-Sands, 2014; Gudykunst, 2003; Livermore, 2010; Macaulay & Arjoon, 2013; Ting-Toomey, 1999). Researchers have shown that people who are valued for their unique talents and have a voice in decision making feel valued as members of the team. For example, the pioneering work of Triandis highlights the importance of culture and its impact on social norms. Triandis argued that culture plays a crucial role in people's attitudes, beliefs, expectations, etc., and that the way that others "categorize" information is unique within a cultural group (Triandis, 1972, 1982, 1984, 1995). He presented the construct of a cultural assimilator as a means of achieving an understanding of cultural diversity. Accordingly, these dimensions of behavior may be anchored by either associative (e.g., cooperative, supportive, helpful) or dissociative (hostile, avoidance) behaviors. These dimensions constitute a theory of cultural differences in social behavior that may be used to develop culture assimilators (Triandis, 1982, 1984). This framework affords the military leader a means of understanding cultural differences that have implications for social interactions and organizational functioning (Triandis, 1982, 1984). There has been a considerable amount of research done on cross-cultural competence over the years and there are specific constructs that have emerged over time, such as the need to understand general and culture-specific differences (Abbe, 2014; Deardorff, 2009; Greene Sands & Greene-Sands, 2014; Hofstede, 2001; Triandis, 1982, 1984).

It is important for leaders to understand how power is distributed and accepted by various cultures as described by Hofstede's power distance theory (Hofstede, 2001). Power distance defines one's tolerance and distance from powers, such as subordinates and superiors in an organization (Hofstede, 2001; Hofstede, Hofstede, & Minkov, 2010).

Various cultures perceive interactions with other cultures differently dependent upon how they view their own level of power (e.g., high- vs. low-power distance; Hofstede, 2001; Hofstede et al., 2010). For example, those in low-power-distance nations (e.g., United States, France, Denmark, etc.) accept that power is distributed equally, whereas those in high-power-distance nations accept and expect a higher degree of inequality in the distribution of power (e.g., Bulgaria, Iran, Iraq).

Understanding the unique cultural characteristics of a society is central to a leader's success. For example, General Douglas MacArthur served as the supreme commander for the Allied Powers in Japan from 1945 until his departure in April 1951. Prior to this time, General MacArthur had gained experience with other cultures, as his father had served as a military governor of the Philippines after the Spanish-American War. General MacArthur had also served as the military adviser to the Commonwealth Government of the Philippines prior to taking command. These cultural experiences in the region gave him an appreciation for the Asian culture that he applied during his time as supreme commander. This was clearly evidenced by the Japanese at the end of the war.

Japan was in a state of chaos following the war. Upon General MacArthur's departure from Japan in 1951, the Japanese people and their leaders paid tribute to him and accorded him the honor and respect for helping their country emerge from a critical and desperate time in their history. Many Japanese expressed their love and support for him upon his departure; indeed, the Japanese government cited MacArthur as the person who helped the nation prevail following the war. These actions are a testament to his cultural competency and sensitivity to the needs of the Japanese people to sustain their dignity during a time of national crises.

MacArthur's decisions and actions during this time serve as an example for future leaders. If a leader is going to be effective, then that person should first appreciate the cultural values of those in the leader's command and region. While there are numerous challenges in setting up a multicultural military force, leaders who are culturally competent will prove to be more effective in gaining the cooperation and loyalty of those in their command. Successful military leaders will be those who are capable of adapting to the cultural and organizational requirements of the region in which they are leading.

Organizational and Cultural Challenges

There are many challenges regarding achieving an understanding of each nation's organizational hierarchy and functionality across multinational military forces. The organizational structure of each nation's military team varies in roles and levels of responsibilities, which often presents barriers for individuals from different countries. Leaders from the Iraq and Gulf Wars have reported on problems arising from varying organizational structures of their coalition partners that often present barriers to the mission itself (Nobel, Wortinger, & Hannah, 2007).

Leaders who can create a bond between culturally diverse teams ensure mission success. An inclusive leader is one who is aware of the gaps in ideology, structure, and organization, yet helps to build cohesive teams focused on the objectives of the mission.

Developing Inclusive Leaders

Traditionally, leadership theory has focused on the development of character traits, whereas more-contemporary models have shown that behavior, cognition, and attitude play increasingly more-important roles in leader development (Arvey, Zhang, Avolio, & Krueger, 2007; Zhang, Ilies, & Arvey, 2009). As Sinek (2014) alludes in his book *Leaders Eat Last*, leaders should build an environment of trust and confidence for everyone to feel safe, confident, valued, and a full member of the team. Team members will perform their best in this environment and ensure the success of the entire team. Senge (1990), Drucker (1992), and Covey (1998) have highlighted the importance of humility and support the concept of *servant leadership*. According to researchers, servant leadership facilitates the building of organizations that enrich the individual's life, as well as that of society and the world. (Covey, 1998; Greenleaf, 1977; Sinek, 2014).

A leader who shares the vision with partners inspires and motivates the team to achieve the military objectives. Leaders with humility and confidence inspire those around them to work harder and more effectively. Leaders require the experience, education, training, and personal development that are essential for them to become effective in foreign environments (Rayner, 2007, 2008). This is not an intuitive exercise but one that requires that they be educated in cultural competency, diplomacy, and communication skills to prepare them for their future assignments. Leaders who are decisive, inclusive, and confident will win the confidence and support of their teams and subordinates.

One of the first steps toward becoming an effective leader is to understand oneself. Today, there are numerous tools for personal assessment that are currently in use for this purpose. These include the Hogan assessment, the "360 assessment," the Myers–Briggs Type Indicator, and the Mental Complexity assessment. Each of these tools is used to cultivate the personal development and professional growth of future leaders.

Every nation has its unique sociopolitical and cultural perspectives that contribute to the development of operational plans (Masakowski, 2008). Inclusive leaders who achieve an understanding of these differences open the door for others to contribute effectively to the mission.

Successful leaders are those who have mastered the art of being inclusive. They recognize the capabilities and competencies of their partners. Leaders who understand the organizational and cultural diversity of their military forces also need to learn how to leverage their partners' abilities effectively. However, it is left to the educators to help leaders gain an appreciation of the benefit and importance of being inclusive.

One of the central characteristics of effective leadership is the ability to communicate. As educators, we can enhance a leader's communication skills and teach ways to engage with others and share vision. Communication is more than speaking the local language. Rather, it requires an understanding of the cultural nuances, traditions, values, and beliefs that are essential for building rapport and relationships.

Education is central to teaching leaders how to succeed by gaining an understanding of their teams' cultural perspectives. Leaders can gain insight into how they are perceived as leaders by the local population. Educators can develop inclusive leaders with the capacity for effective communication and relationship building. In this way, leaders can win the trust of those in their command through their authentic leadership.

The Changing Operational Environment: Implications for Inclusive Military Leaders

Today's military operational environment is dynamic, volatile, and uncertain. In contrast to the Second World War or the Cold War today's leaders defend against an invisible adversary who creates chaos on a global scale, without a single shot. Today's enemies conduct cyberwarfare, Psyops, and terrorist recruiting using the internet and social media. The internet and social media have become a force multiplier for the terrorist community and a cultural weapon of war. Their members are adaptive and distributed over a global network. In response, it is essential for our military to be equally adaptive and agile if we are to defeat the enemy (Heifetz, Grashow, & Linsky, 2009).

McChrystal recognized the importance of flexibility and the value of building a *"Team of Teams"* composed of individuals with the knowledge, skills, and abilities in teams similar to the Navy SEALs. These groups are tightly organized and highly focused on the military objectives and share a sense of trust with each other. They rely on each other's level of competency, knowledge, and capability. These capabilities afford the team the ability to provide a flexible and agile response to any crisis (McChrystal, 2015). Small teams, however, are not exempt from cultural challenges. Indeed, working with foreign translators as part of the team may present a unique set of challenges for trust building within the group. Thus, the cultural composition of the small team may prove to be even more challenging for leaders. Thus, regardless of whether you are leading a large, multinational military operation or a small team of military professionals, leader inclusivity is an essential ingredient in mission success. The inclusive leader recognizes the critical role each individual team member plays and strives to develop the best balance of skills required for the operation. Inclusive leadership needs to be taught to our leaders and reinforced by their experiences throughout their careers.

Conclusion

The 21st-century operational environment is complex and complicated for all military leaders. Multinational military operations will continue to emerge and our leaders should be prepared to deal with the cultural diversity of the battlespace environment. The operational environment will continue to be unpredictable. Military leaders who are inclusive and consider the cultural diversity of their teams will successfully harness the capabilities of their military force (Elron, Shamir, & Ben-Ari, 1999; Matsumoto et al., 2001). Multinational military operations are increasing in demand and no one nation can manage all of these crises alone. Nations are bound to each other and need to work together to face future crises together as a team. Multinational military missions require cooperation among leaders and teams. Regardless of the mission, future multinational teams will be culturally diverse and there is a need to educate and prepare our leaders. Nations need to take the time to prepare their leaders to be inclusive in order to build consensus, and establish cooperation and collaboration among the coalition teams.

Inclusive leadership will ensure that culturally diverse nations can work together to achieve military objectives and mission success.

As we move forward in the future, the world is becoming more complicated with the addition of autonomous systems and robotics. Advances in technology, artificial intelligence, and autonomous, unmanned systems will add to the complexity of managing a military operation (Masakowski, 2008, 2015a, 2015b). There will continue to be debate regarding the role of autonomous systems and whether these should be independent and weaponized. However, the role for the inclusive leader will remain a primary one, as it will be the inclusive leader who will make the decisions regarding how these systems will be integrated in the mission plan. There will be an even greater need for leaders who can discern and decide on the ethical application of these systems in the future. Perhaps leaders from each nation will have to work together to decide whether to use such systems.

The dialogue has begun and as educators, we are certain that leaders will continue to rise to the challenges presented in the global security environment. Military leaders who are successful in forging inclusive, international relationships with their allied partners will be better prepared to respond effectively to global threats and security challenges. Now, more than ever before, there is a need for inclusivity among nations and military partners to lay the foundation for a secure future.

Discussion Questions:

1. What are some of the challenges that leaders of multinational military operations must address in their leadership role with culturally diverse military teams?
2. From a leader's perspective, how does cultural diversity help to shape your perspectives, thinking and decision making?
3. How can cross-cultural competence facilitate leadership effectiveness?
4. How can a leader help to ensure inclusion of all members of a multinational military operation? Why is this important?
5. Why is character a critical component for leadership effectiveness in multinational military operations?

Acknowledgments

The author thanks her colleagues whose personal counsel and direction have been indispensable:

First, she extends her appreciation to CAPT John C. Meyer, USN (Ret.), Assistant Dean for Leadership and Ethics, College of Operational & Strategic Leadership, U.S Naval War College, for his encouragement and support of this NATO research effort.

She also thanks Professor Timothy J. Demy, ThD, PhD, Former Navy Chaplain and Professor of Military Ethics, U.S. Naval War College for graciously sharing his expertise and invaluable insights into leadership and ethics.

Finally, she expresses her gratitude to Mr. Paul Chatelier, Office of Naval Research, for his support and guidance throughout the NATO research effort.

References

Abbe, A. (2014). The historical development of cross-cultural competence. In R. Greene Sands & A. Greene-Sands (Eds.), *Cross-cultural competence for a twenty-first-century military* (pp. 31–42). Lanham, MD: Lexington Books.

Abbe, A., & Gallus, J. A. (2012). *The socio-cultural context of operations: Culture and foreign language learning for company-grade officers.* Technical Report 1316. Arlington, VA: U.S. Army Research Institute for the Behavioral and Social Sciences. (DTIC No. ADA565311).

Abbe, A., Gulick, L. M. V., & Herman, J. L. (2008). *Cross-cultural competence in army leaders: A conceptual and empirical foundation.* Study Report 2008-01. Arlington, VA: U.S. Army Research Institute for the Behavioral and Social Sciences. (DTIC No. ADA476072).

Arvey, R. D., Zhang, Z., Avolio, B. J., & Krueger, R. F. (2007). Developmental and genetic determinants of leadership role occupancy among women. *Journal of Applied Psychology, 92*(3), 693–706.

Avolio, B. (2009). Pursuing authentic leadership development. In N. Nohria & R. Khuria (Eds.), *Handbook of leadership theory and practice.* Boston, MA: Harvard Business School Publishing.

Avolio, B. J., & Gardner, W. L. (2005). Authentic leadership development: Getting to the root of positive forms of leadership. *Leadership Quarterly, 16*(3), 315–338.

Bass, B. M. (1990). From transactional to transformational leadership: Learning to share the vision. *Organizational Dynamics, 18*(3), 1990. Retrieved from: http://discoverthought.com/Leadership/References_files/Bass%20leadership%201990.pdf

Bennett, J. (2009). Cultivating intercultural competence: A process perspective. In D. Deardorff (Ed.), *The Sage handbook of intercultural competence.* Thousand Oaks, CA: Sage.

Bentley, W., (2016). *The leader development framework,* Canadian Defence Academy, Canada. Joint Staff J7, Joint Education and Doctrine Meeting.

Brooks, D. (2015). *The road to character.* New York, NY: Random House.

Covey, S. R. (1998). Servant-leadership from the inside out. In L. Spears (Ed.), *Insights on leadership: Service, stewardship, spirit, and servant-leadership.* New York, NY: Wiley.

Deardorff, D. (Ed.). (2009). *The Sage handbook of intercultural competence.* Thousand Oaks, CA: Sage.

Dorough-Lewis, J. (2015). The human terrain system. In M. McFate & J. H. Laurence (Eds.), *Social science goes to war* (pp. 291–316). Oxford, UK: Oxford University Press.

Drucker, P. F. (1992). *Managing for the future*. New York, NY: Truman Talley Books/Dutton.

Earley, P. C., & Ang, S. (2003). *Cultural intelligence: Individual interactions across cultures*. Palo Alto, CA: Stanford University Press.

Eberly, M. B., Johnson, M. D., Hernandez, M., & Avolio, B. J. (2013). An integrative process model of leadership: Examining leadership loci, mechanisms and event cycles. *American Psychologist, 68*(6), 427–443.

Eisen, S. (2015). Raumschach negotiations. In M. McFate & J. H. Laurence (Eds.), *Social science goes to war* (pp. 331–354). Oxford: Oxford University Press.

Elron, E., Shamir, B., & Ben-Ari, E. (1999). Why don't they fight each other? Cultural diversity and operational unity in multinational forces. *Armed Forces and Society, 26*(1), 73–98.

Grazier, D., & Hempowicz, L. (2016, June 28). The U.S. Navy's "Fat Leonard scandal" highlights the need for whistleblower protection [Blog post]. Retrieved from http://nationalinterest.org/blog/the-buzz/the-us-navys-%E2%80%9Cfat-leonardscandal%E2%80%9D-highlights-the-need-16751

Greene Sands, R., & Greene-Sands, A. (Eds.). (2014). *Cross-cultural competence for a twentyfirst-century military*. Lanham, MD: Lexington Books.

Greenleaf, R. K. (1977). *Servant leadership: A journey into the nature of legitimate power and greatness*. Mahwah, NJ: Paulist Press.

Gudykunst, W. B. (2003). *Cross-cultural and intercultural communication*. Thousand Oaks, CA: Sage.

Gurstein, M. (1999). Leadership in the peacekeeping army of the future. In J. G. Hunt, G. E. Dodge, & L. Wong (Eds.). *Out-of-the-box leadership: Transforming the twenty-first century army and other top-performing organizations*. Stamford, CT: JAI Press.

Heifetz, R. A., Grashow, A., & Linsky, M. (2009). *The practice of adaptive leadership: Tools and tactics for changing your organization and the world*. Boston, MA: Harvard Business Press.

Hofstede, G. (2001). *Culture's consequences* (2nd ed.). Thousand Oaks, CA: Sage.

Hofstede, G., Hofstede, G. J., & Minkov, M. M. (2010). *Cultures and organizations: Software of the mind* (3rd ed.). New York, NY: McGraw-Hill.

Hollander, E. P. (1978). *Leadership dynamics: A practical guide to effective relationships*. New York, NY: Free Press.

Hollander, E. P. (1979). The impact of Ralph Stogdill and the Ohio State leadership studies on a transactional approach to leadership. *Journal of Management, 5*(2), 157–165.

Hollander, E. P. (1992). The essential interdependence of leadership and followership. *Current Directions in Psychological Science, 1*(2), 71–75.

Jaffe, G. (2012, November 30). Petraeus: Not a hero, but not a failure. *The Washington Post*. Retrieved from https://www.washingtonpost.com/opinions/

petraeus-not-a-hero-but-not-afailure/2012/11/30/8b9e46d8-3a57-11e2-b01f-5f5
5b193f58f_story.html

Klein, H. A., Pongonis, A., & Klein, G. (2000). *Cultural barriers to multinational C^2 decision making*. Presentation at the 2000 Command and Control Research Technology Symposium, Naval Postgraduate School, Monterey, CA. (DARPA Report No: DAAH01-00-CR094).

LaGrone, S. (2013). Navy activates hospital ship Mercy for Philippines disaster relief. *USNI News*, November. Retrieved from https://news.usni.org/2013/11/14/navy-activates-hospital-ship-mercy-philippines-disaster-relief

Laurence, J. H. (2015). The human terrain system. In M. McFate & J. H. Laurence (Eds.), *Social science goes to war* (pp. 291–316). Oxford: Oxford University Press.

Livermore, D. (2010). *Leading with cultural intelligence*. New York, NY: American Management Association.

Macaulay, M., & Arjoon, S. (2013). An Aristotelian-Thomistic approach to professional ethics. *Journal of Markets and Morality, 16*(2), 507–527.

Masakowski, Y. R. (2008). *Multinational military operations and intercultural factors*. NATO Report TR-HFM-120: Research Task Group 120. Neuilly-sur-Seine, France: NATO.

Masakowski, Y. R. (2015a, September). *Leader development for twenty-first century multinational military missions*. Paper presented at and published in the proceedings of the International Military Testing Association, Stockholm, Sweden.

Masakowski, Y. R. (2015b, October). *Leadership and multinational military operations*. Paper presented at and published in the proceedings of the International Leadership Association Meeting, Barcelona, Spain.

Matsumoto, D., Grissom, R., & Dinnel, L. (2001). Do between-culture differences really mean that people are different? *Journal of Cross-Cultural Psychology, 32*, 478–490.

McChrystal, S. (2015). *Team of teams*. New York, NY: Portfolio.

McFate, M. (2005). The military utility of understanding adversary culture. *Joint Force Quarterly, 38*(Third Quarter), 42–48.

McFate, M. (2015). Mind the gap. In M. McFate & J. H. Laurence (Eds.). *Social science goes to war* (pp. 45–89). Oxford: Oxford University Press.

McFate, M., & Laurence, J. H. (Eds.). (2015). *Social science goes to war*. Oxford: Oxford University Press.

Meyer, E. (2014). *The culture map*. New York, NY: Public Affairs.

Morrow, C. (2016). Moving the dial: Measuring inclusive leadership. *The Diversity Journal*. Retrieved from http://www.diversityjournal.com/13313-moving-dial-measuring-inclusiveleadership

Nobel, O. B.-Y., Wortinger, B., & Hannah, S. (2007). *Winning the war and the relationships: Preparing military officers for negotiations with non-combatants*. Research Report 1877. West Point, NY: U.S. Army Research Institute for the Behavior Sciences, U.S. Military Academy.

Petraeus, D. (2015). Foreword. In M. McFate & J. H. Laurence (Eds.), *Social science goes to war* (pp. vii–xi). Oxford: Oxford University Press.

Rayner, S. (2007). *Managing special and inclusive education.* London: Sage.

Rayner, S. (2008). Complexity, diversity and management: Some reflections on folklore and learning leadership in education. *Management in Education, 22*(2), 40–46.

Sander, D., & Solomon, W. (2014). Pacific Partnership 2014. Developing skills is key to improving medical care. *Navy Daily*, Retrieved from http://news.navy.gov.au/en/Jun2014/Fleet/1153/Pacific-Partnership-2014–Developing-skills-is-key-to-improving-medical-care.htm

Senge, P. M. (1990). The leader's new work: Building learning organizations. *Sloan Management Review, 32*(1), 439–457.

Sinek, S. (2014). *Leaders eat last: Why some teams pull together and others don't.* New York, NY: Portfolio.

Soeters, J., & Manigart, P. (2008). *Multinational peace operations: Managing cultural diversity and crisis response.* London: Routledge.

Steele, J. (2016). Navy's floating hospital to sail again. *The San Diego Union-Tribune*, May 9, 2016.

Terlizzi, A. (2014). Cross-cultural competence and civil-military operations. In R. Greene Sands & A. Greene-Sands (Eds.), *Cross-cultural competence for a twenty-first-century military* (pp. 131–139). Lanham, MD: Lexington Books.

Ting-Toomey, S. (1985). Toward a theory of conflict and culture. In W. Gudykunst, L. Stewart, & S. Ting-Toomey (Eds.), *Communication, culture, and organizational processes* (pp. 71–86). Beverly Hills, CA: Sage.

Ting-Toomey, S. (1988). Intercultural conflicts: A face negotiation theory. In Y. Y. Kim & W. B. Gudykunst (Eds.), *Theories in intercultural communication* (pp. 213–238). Newbury Park, CA: Sage.

Ting-Toomey, S. (1999). *Communicating across cultures.* New York, NY: Guilford Press.

Triandis, H. C. (1972). *The analysis of subjective culture.* New York, NY: Wiley.

Triandis, H. C. (1982). Dimensions of cultural variation as parameters of organizational theories. *International Studies of Management & Organization, 12*(4), 139–169.

Triandis, H. C. (1984). A theoretical framework for the more efficient construction of culture assimilators. *International Journal of Intercultural Relations, 8*(3), 301–330.

Triandis, H. C. (1995). *Individualism and collectivism.* Boulder, CO: Westview.

Van Dyne, L., Ang, S., Ng, K.-Y., Rockstuhl, T., Tan, M. L., & Koh, C. (2012). Sub-dimensions of the four-factor model of cultural intelligence: Expanding the conceptualization and measurement of cultural intelligence. *Social and Personal Psychology Compass, 6*(4), 295–313.

Zhang, Z., Ilies, R., & Arvey, R. D. (2009). Beyond genetic explanations for leadership: The moderating role of the social environment. *Organizational Behavior and Human Decision Processes, 110*(2009), 118–128.

PART 4
Future Directions…

13 A New Perspective towards Leadership Paradigm

Damini Saini

Introduction

This chapter explores leadership from the perspective of the leader's value set and its effects upon the organizational commitment of the employees and the perceived productivity of the firm in an Indian context.

This research study employed a quantitative method using a cross-sectional survey design to assess the effect of value-laden leadership on organizational commitment and employee productivity. A nonprobability, convenience sample was obtained from the population group, which was managers and employees in the Indian service sector industry and was based on our accessibility to them.

The research study examined whether integrity, benevolence, and responsibility are found to be the most factors most effective in fostering higher levels of organizational outcomes. It found that employees led by highly ethical leaders reported greater organizational productivity.

Generalization of this study's results to circumstances in other countries may not be possible because the target population constituted employees in Indian corporations.

The study can be helpful in addressing the gap of empirical analysis in relation to all-inclusive leadership (managerial context) in the Indian service sector corporations.

The business world and the humankind over the ages had suffered from transgressions. The shocking period of corporate scandals in the world during the last decade shook the assurance and trust of the people as to the integrity of corporate leadership. From Enron to Anderson, Satyam to the 3G scam, each outrage exposed the offenses and exploitative exercises of business leaders and their political counterparts (Datta, 2012; Shirur, 2011). The corporate manipulations of Enron, WorldCom, Arthur Andersen, Adelphia, Satyam brought corporate double-dealing out in the open (Shirur, 2011). Senior chiefs, bookkeepers, business pioneers were found to be misassigning costs in the monetary explanations, confusing arrangements, misrepresentation of figures, control of information, false valuation, and so on (Chandler, 2009; Shirur, 2011).

Earlier Trevino (1986) speculated that dishonest practices cost the commercial enterprises billions of dollars a year and harmed partnerships, which led to the increased emphasis on moral behavior in organizations, and these practices increased in recent years. WorldCom's Bernie Ebbers and Enron's Ken Lay epitomize the leaders who neglected to provide the confidence and moral administration in their associations and so confronted the monetary outrage that brought about the biggest financial disaster (Shirur, 2011; Trevino & Brown, 2005). Further, Andrew Fastow and Jeffrey Skilling of Enron, Dennis Koslowski of Tyco, and Ramalinga Raju of Satyam are some other names in the rundown of leaders who were effective but failed to provide responsible leadership (Bhasin, 2013; Chandler, 2009).

This crisis in the field of leadership today is not only a crisis of ethics but a crisis of humankind. Much of this crisis stems from insufficiencies in human thinking, like self-centeredness and self-involvement (Gini & Marcoux, 2009; Murtaza, 2011), which results in unethical behavior and greed. Prominent researchers and practitioners have predicted that the prevalent leadership practices are not able to cope up with the challenges of these times. Most leadership theories are based on linear and generalized theories, thinking, and models, which cannot meet up with the complexities of business transgressions. The inquisitiveness of understanding the central aspects of leadership has been rapidly growing, which can help to observe leadership from all-inclusive dimensions. To resolve the ecological, economic, or humanitarian catastrophe, we should focus on the underlying beliefs and mind sets that guide the leadership decisions and actions.

Immoral Leadership: The Crisis Offers a Prospect for Positive Change

> In the hands of a mature, healthy human being—one who has achieved full humanness—power ... is a great blessing. But in the hands of the immature, vicious, or emotionally sick, power is a horrible danger. (Maslow, 2000, p. 146)

Ford professor emeritus, Donald Schon (1971) stated that society is changing, and these changes are highly visible and broadly recognizable but inadequately understood. The changes carry with them inconsistencies that disrupt the stability of societal regulations and structures as well as the individuals. Further, he suggested that we need to develop institutional structures, ways of knowledge, and an ethics for the process of change. The management literature is full of discussions about the need for not only individual but also organizational and global transformation is required (Neal, Benyamin, Bergman-Linchtenstein, & Banner, 1999). In the context of business and corporations, this is the phase where the intricate cognizance has been going through several complexities that are yet to be illuminated.

One can see that corporate leaders are struggling with ethical dilemmas that are not only black or white areas but the gray, and to compete and revive from these situations, they need an expanded and holistic view. For instance, in 2005, according to *Fortune Magazine*, Bear Stearns was one of the "most admired" securities firms (*Fortune Magazine* Names, 2005), yet it collapsed in mid-2007. The CEO of the company, James Cayne, was charged with betting the firm on risky home loans, and two of its extremely leveraged hedge funds shrank ("25 People to Blame," n.d.). In early 2008, Bear Stearns was sold to JP Morgan. More than 7500 Bear Stearns employees lost their jobs. A year before, in 2006, Cayne took home US$34 million and became the first Wall Street chief to own a company stake worth more than US$1 billion. He created a huge fortune for himself and perhaps he knowingly insulated himself from the reality of his risky business venture (Oliver & Goodwin, 2010, p. 173).

In 2007, at a time when Bear Stearns was on the brink of collapse, he exemplified irresponsible leadership, as he was out of town taking part in a bridge competition for more than three days and causing the misfortune to the company (Oliver & Goodwin, 2010). Individuals and groups both can be lead to unethical conduct, and the causes could be the pressures of loyalty vs. truth, for example (Maheshwari & Ganesh, 2006). There could be many reasons behind behaving immorally and irresponsibly, it could be the complexity of the issues being dealt with, and the difficulty in many instances of determining what action to take.

In a similar discussion, George (2011) stated that we often characterize the leaders tangled in the scams or scandals as the "immoral people," but in reality they often yield to attractions in their path that lead them to neglect their values, and they set themselves on a slippery slope called *ethical failure*. No recent leadership theory has succeeded in addressing the complications and entangled mind set of the leaders in organizations. An abundance of literature is founded on empirical research directed at a huge variety of leadership theories; however, no agreement has been made regarding what constitutes an effective leader precisely. And, no agreement has been made regarding what constitutes an effective leader. Conversely behavioral theories were successful in providing useful information about what leaders do. Many of the existing theories of leadership provide the patterns of leadership needed for the long-term success of organizations. Nevertheless, these approaches are in general based on linear (Razik & Swanson, 2001), fragmented, and often oversimplified (Bolman & Deal, 2003) leadership thinking, theories, and models. Such oversimplified approaches were unable to cope up with the complexities of today's organizational context. Some leadership scholars have recognized the need for the conceptualization of a coherent leadership framework that can clarify what leadership means; explain how the existing leadership knowledge base, theories, and models relate and interconnect with one another; and improve the ability to determine leadership practices (Razik & Swanson, 2001). There is a need for additional thinking and analysis of the strengths, weaknesses, and the gaps in the existing knowledge base with respect to the existing leadership practices.

Recent Leadership Models and Theories — A Quick Glance

Leadership is the fundamental drive that works and motivates the work of employees in associations, and this theory implies the unavoidability of the moral - and worth-based behavior by the top authority. Marcy, Gentry, and McKinnon (2008) suggested that a leader ought to support a particular system to have an upright impact on the system's followers. Leadership theory can be examined from no less than five viewpoints: the quality approach, the behavioral methodology, possibility approaches, the part approach, and developing speculations. The conventional speculations speak to the initial four theories.

The behavioral methodology endeavors to decide the sorts of authority practices that lead to effective assignment of tasks. Specialists at Ohio State University played out a broad arrangement of initiative studies in building this theory. Work done at the University of Michigan on pioneer conduct arrived at comparative conclusions. The methodology relies on the behavioral style of pioneers as opposed to identity characteristics (Blake & Mouton, 1965). The possibility or situational approach holds that there is no all-inclusive way to deal with authority; however, reasonably successful initiative conduct relies on situational variables, which may change after some time (Vroom & Yetton, 1973). Current leadership theories are constructed intensely in the light of this methodology, which expresses that powerful authority is liable to three variables: the leader, the follower, and the circumstances. Another two possibility models of authority, House's Path-Goal model (1971) and Hershey and Blanchard's Situational Leadership model, hold a unique spot in situational hypothesis. Unlike the conventional authority models, which portray leadership conduct as leaders-supporter connections — setting objectives, giving guidance and backing, and fortification practices — the new initiative models underscore typical leadership conduct: visionary, rousing messages; passionate sentiments; moral and good values; individualized consideration; and scholarly incitement. That which has been known as the *new type administration* considers what constitutes a charming, helpful, and visionary initiative. In the next section, we provide a brief description of new genre leadership theories.

CHARISMATIC LEADERSHIP

Prior to studying transformational and transactional leadership, researchers focused on what constitutes charismatic and visionary leadership. The term *charismatic leadership* was first coined by Max Weber (1968). Bass (1985) stated that charismatic leadership arises when crisis is chronic. Yet, there is prevalent confusion about the meaning of *charismatic leadership*, due to the differences among theorists (Bryman, 1993). Most charismatic leadership theories emphasize attributions by followers of extraordinary qualities to the leader. Conger (1998) and Conger and Kanungo (1987) proposed that the attributions are determined jointly by characteristics of the leader, subordinates, and situation. In contrast, House (1977) and Shamir, House, and Arthur (1993) defined charismatic leadership in terms of how the leader influences followers' approaches and inspiration, regardless of whether the followers consider the leader extraordinary. In that perspective there is need for more clarity and consistency in how the term *charismatic* is defined and used.

According to Shamir et al. (1993), theories of charismatic leadership highlight such effects as emotional attachment to the leader on the part of the followers; emotional and motivational stimulation of the followers; follower self-esteem, trust, and assurance in the leader; follower morality; and follower intrinsic motivation. The group perspective considers not only the leader's influence on individual members, but also the leader's influence on how well the work is organized to utilize personnel and resources and how well group activities are coordinated. Yukl (1999) also specified that group processes are largely ignored in most theories of charismatic leadership, and these theories do not explicitly incorporate leadership behaviors such as organizing, coordinating, team building, and facilitating group decisions. Further, he extended that some theories of charismatic leadership describe organizational-level processes, but only in relation to selected topics. In summary, charismatic leaders are believed to have a tremendous influence on organizations, which can be negative as well as positive. The distinction between charismatic and transformational processes and between positive and negative charisma is one of the most interesting subjects of the research and theory (e.g., Bass, 1985; de Vries & Miller, 1985; Harrison, 1987; Kuhnert & Lewis, 1987).

TRANSACTIONAL LEADERSHIP AND TRANSFORMATIONAL LEADERSHIP

Burns (1978) was the first to present the concepts of transformational and transactional leadership. He considered leaders to be either transformational or transactional. Burns (1978) described transactional leaders as those who lead others in exchange for something of value. Transactional leadership involves an exchange process to motivate follower compliance with leader requests and organization rules. Yukl (1989, 1999) stated that transactional leadership includes contingent reward behavior, passive management by -exception, active management by exception, and clarification of the work, too, for obtaining rewards. Evaluating the conceptual weaknesses, Yukl (1999) stated that the theory fails to forge a strong link between this process and each of the transactional behaviors, as transactional leadership includes a diverse collection of leader behaviors that lack any clear common denominator; and contingent reward behavior includes things that are clearly involved in an impersonal exchange process, which also includes providing recognition to subordinates, a distinct type of behavior (Yukl, 1999). If praise and acknowledgment are usually more personal, this may involve transformational leadership and transactional leadership both. Transformational leadership, according to Bass (1985), occurs when leaders widen and raise the welfare of their employees, when they generate awareness and acceptance of the purposes and mission of the group beyond their own self-interest for the good of the group. Transformational leadership is usually viewed as a shared process involving the actions of leaders at different levels and in different subunits of an organization (Burns, 1978). Porter and Bigley (1997) proposed that transformational leadership can have some unfavorable consequences for the organization. For example, if members of an organization are influenced by different leaders with contending visions, the result will be increased role uncertainty and role conflict, and excessive competition may arise among organizational units.

The underlying influence progression for transformational leadership is still not clear and not considered in a systematic way. Influence processes that involve a series of dyadic interactions over time include instrumental compliance, personal identification, and internalization (Kelman, 1958). The moderately overlapping content and the high intercorrelation found among the transformational behaviors raise doubts about the legitimacy of the concept. The content of intellectual stimulation is diverse and ambiguous as there is no clear description of what the leader actually says or does to influence the cognitive processes or behavior of subordinates. Yukl (1999) has defined the differences thus: Instrumental compliance is most important for transactional leadership, internalization is central for transformational leadership, and personal identification is essential for charismatic leadership

Leader's Responsibility and Values

Bozesan (2010) found that most of today's organizations are working essentially from obsolete corporate qualities and an unwillingness to glimpse at the shadow side of business. There is a moderate profound quality in the corporate part and a developing number of shallow Enron-style projects being accounted for in the midst of late corporate outrages. Moreover Driscoll and McKee (2007) articulated that a hefty portion of the stories in business associations center around topics such as "the client is best," "the shareholder rules," and "the manager is constantly right" (p. 210). In this way, the straightforward terms like *awareness and consciousness in business* are very reasonable and ethically focused on. Leadership effectiveness is the successful exercise of personal influence by one or more people that results in accomplishing organizational objectives consistent with a mission while earning the general approval of the stakeholders. Marcy et al. (2008) often found a disconnection between what the leaders saying and doing in organizations, then they recommended that a leader should develop a specific strategy for ethically influencing followers.

Corporate leaders have a natural responsibility toward the stakeholders, society, and the environment. Maccoby (2005) clearly stated that organizational values and leadership are the areas that are important in judging and creating moral organizations. If employees observe ethical indiscretion by the leader, in all likelihood, they will soon begin to emulate such unethical behavior (Seshadri, Raghavan, & Hegde, 2007). So it becomes important for leaders to be mindful of personal values, ethics, and morals as they stimulate the selections they make and the behaviors in which they indulge (Grojean, Resick, Dickson, & Smith, 2004). In a similar vein, Upadhyay and Singh (2010) concluded that leadership is ultimately responsible for setting the course by which business operations succeed or fail in meeting the moral expectations of society. Maslow (1970) also considered values like wholeness and goodness as a part of the human self. Similarly, Roe and Ester (1999) stated that, in direct contrast to basic needs, such values are integrated in their daily lives by people who bring to work the values that drive their behavior. For an example, Jack Welch, one of the successful CEOs of GE, asserted that the leaders of his organization should be oriented toward the organizational value more than being highly result oriented.

Researchers and practitioners discovered different resolutions to help inculcate morality specifically identified with the top-level authority and ties them to follow most astounding moral norms. It is not so simple, as it appears to apply on a more elevated amount. Enjoying the inebriation of influence and cash, frequently the best leaders refuse to see the truth and free association with their own selves. Business, being a fundamental piece of our lives, deliberately is a key part of living intentionally, and a cognizant business leader brings a consciousness of truth, humanity, and moral goals to the business and advances care. As Avolio and Gardner (2005) stated, "Through increased self-awareness, self-regulation and positive modelling, authentic leaders foster the development of authenticity in followers, in turn followers authenticity contributes to their well-being and attainment of sustainable and veritable performance"(p. 317).

Professors James Kouzes, Barry Posner, and W. H. Schmidt asked 1500 managers, "What values do you look for and admire in your superiors?" Integrity (being truthful and trustworthy and having character and conviction) was the most frequently mentioned characteristics (Kirkpatick & Lock, 1991). Values are conceived of as guiding principles in life that transcend specific situations, which may change over time, guide selection of behavior and events, and are part of a dynamic system with inherent contradictions (Debats & Bartelds, 1996). Burns (1978) also said that "transforming" leaders inspire followers by aligning their own and their followers' value systems toward important moral principles.

Treviño, Hartman, and Brown (2000) acknowledged this, mentioning that an ethical executive leader must also find ways to focus the organization's attention on values and to infuse the organization with principles that will guide the actions of all the employees. At the core of effective leadership is the creation of values that inspire, provide meaning for, and instill a sense of purpose in an organization's members. Revealing a series of eloquent and inspiring exhortations on the importance of caring, responsive leaders and empowering leaders who serve the common good, Gardener said, "We should hope that our leaders will keep alive values that are not so easy to embed in laws — our caring for others, about honor and integrity, about tolerance and mutual respect, and about human fulfillment within a framework of values" (Gardner, 1990, p. 77).

Values are the main concepts of transformational, spiritual, servant, and ethical leadership theories. Also, in this chapter, we discuss that the recent downturn of the organizations is due to the decline in the value sets of the leadership. The idea here is to charge the operator for the moral breaches in the associations. Yet, at the same time, a more all-encompassing methodology is required for the leadership, which may mean utilizing numerous practices to guarantee on all bases that are social, ecological and financial. For the mapping of a value-laden leadership, we tried to develop a questionnaire that encompasses all the values relevant to measuring an all-inclusive leadership. It contains items related to ethics, integrity, responsibility, empathy, compassion, and inspiration. Based on a review of the literature and theories and concepts derived from the literature, certain issues have emerged that warrant further investigation. The research issues for this study have been outlined as (1) to assess the leadership paradigm based on values and to explore its dimensions; (2) to assess the existence and levels of various dimensions of a leadership paradigm (in an Indian context); and (3) to assess its influence on organizational outcome variables. These issues prompt the research questions: Does the value-laden approach to leadership, which is being examined with the help of various dimensions of a leadership paradigm, help to intensify the organizational commitment and productivity.

Empirical Analysis

The purpose of this study was to observe the leadership of managers according to the value-laden leadership style in the workplace and how this independent has an impact on the organization's commitment and the productivity of its employees. A quantitative research methodology with a correlational design was used to collect data. Depending on the nature of the questions and these themes, the scaling technique used was the Likert scale of 4, where the respondents indicated the amount of agreement or disagreement with the statements. The Likert scale, frequently called the *method of summated ratings*, is a widely accepted and adopted technique and is highly reliable.

SAMPLE

The respondents were chosen randomly from the service sector so that every member of the population had similar chance of being selected. Respondents were in cross-functional departments, from finance, logistics, HR, IT, Sales, and so forth. This brought heterogeneity to the sample. The choice of the service sector was due to its large representation in the Indian corporate world, because India became a positive outlier not only in terms of the share of services in value addition but in terms of the industry's share in employment. The service sector was also a good choice due to the availability of managers for a leadership survey. The population of interest for this research is the government-regulated Indian service sector. Convenience sampling, which is a type of nonprobability sampling was used to select respondents who meet the criteria. The population criteria requested included (1) both genders, (2) ages 21–60, (3) only organizational managers and supervisors, and (4) all educational levels. For the research, a self-administered questionnaire instrument was selected as the most appropriate approach, due to quickness and ease in getting data lots of information from respondents in a nonthreatening mode, ease of administration to many people, and inexpensiveness. The questionnaire had five sections. Section 1 covered general information and demographics about the respondent and respondent's organization, section 2 included items related to value-laden leadership (perceived), and sections 3 and 4 had items related to organizational commitment and productivity.

VALUE-LADEN LEADERSHIP SCALE

For this research, we developed an instrument to measure value-laden leadership using 15 items. It included four items from the ethical leadership questionnaire (Brown, Trevino, & Harrison, 2005); two item from spiritual climate questionnaire of Pandey Gupta and Arora (2008); one item from the ECQ of Victor and Cullen (1987, 1988); four items from LPI of Kouzes and Posner (2003); and the rest were developed. Development of the instrument inventory was completed in three major steps; (1) item creation, (2) validity check, and (3) reliability testing. All items were positively keyed. Response descriptions against items were given on a 4-point Likert-type scale: "strongly disagree" (1), "disagree" (2), "agree" (3), "strongly agree" (4). Managers were asked to indicate to what extent each statement was true regarding their immediate superior.

ORGANIZATIONAL COMMITMENT SCALE

Twelve items were taken from the Allen and Meyer (1990) commitment scale to measure organizational commitment, in which five items were positively keyed and the sixth item was, "I do not feel emotionally attached to this organization," which was reverse coded. The alpha reliability for this scale was 0.85. Higher scores indicated high reliability. Response descriptions against items were given on a 4-point Likert-type scale.

PERCEIVED PRODUCTIVITY SCALE

Productivity basically is the efficiency in producing results, benefits, or profits. Four items were taken from Nyhan productivity scale (2000) to measure productivity. Productivity was measured through the four items: effort, work quality, eventfulness, and maximum output. All items were positively keyed. The alpha reliability of the scale was 0.76.

Findings

Approximately 350 employees, who were working in senior managerial posts were asked to participate in this survey, as the survey was about leadership; and 263 responded to this survey (responding rates = 75.1%). Finally, 221 cases were analyzed; there were 46 missing cases. The reliabilities of the dimensions of the questionnaire were found to be acceptable, and the Chronbach alpha of the consolidated scale was 0.78.

All 15 items consisted of questions to judge the leadership skills of the managers on the basis of their values: *humanism, ethics, benevolence, integrity, responsibility, trust, honesty,* and so on The assessments of the questionnaires were subjected to exploratory factor analysis using principal component analysis (see the appendix). The outcome was that six components provided a KMO measure of sampling adequacy of 0.68, which according to Field (2005) is considered good. Six factors emerged having eigenvalues more than 1. These factors jointly explained 68.18% of the total variance of the scale. To provide a meaningful interpretation of the factor loadings, they were rotated using the varimax procedure. The first and third factors loaded significantly on four and three items and the second, fourth, fifth, and sixth on two items, respectively. Observation of the item content of the first factor unfolded the "sympathetic" dimension of holistic leadership, as sympathy has been found to be related to a wide range of prosocial behaviors (Eisenberg & Miller, 1987). While talking about conscience Greenleaf (2002) said that it relates us to world of relationships, it causes sincere caring for others, a combination of sympathy and empathy, where pain is shared and received. Sympathetic strategies of the leader responded to subordinates' needs to be encouraged, protected, and garner concern. The second factor, having two items, focused on the ethicality of the leader. Ciulla (2003) stated that, in leadership, we see morality magnified; and that is why the study of ethics is fundamental to our understanding of leadership. Further, she says that the study of ethics is about human relationships, about what we should do and what we should be like as human beings, as members of a group or society, and in the different roles that we play in life. Leaders that have an ethics-oriented attitude cultivate moral teachings and values and share them with subordinates. The third factor describes the approach toward "benevolence and responsibility" of the leader. Research on benevolent leadership has received growing interest in Asia because of its desirability for followers (Farh & Cheng, 2000; Wu, Hsu, & Cheng, 2002). According to Pellegrini and Scandura (2008):

> *Benevolence* refers to an individualized concern for subordinates' personal well-being. This type of leadership is still prevalent and effective in many business cultures, such as in the Middle East, Pacific Asia, and Latin America. *Benevolence* refers to leader behaviors that demonstrate individualized, holistic concern for subordinates' personal and family well-being.

Responsibility should have been an important dimension of global leaders — leaders with responsible mind sets care for the needs of others and act as global and responsible citizens. *Responsible leadership* can be defined as the art and ability involved in building, cultivating, and sustaining trustful relationships to different stakeholders, both inside and outside the organization, and in coordinating responsible action to achieve a meaningful, commonly shared business vision (Maak, 2007).

The contents of the fourth factor reveals the "innovative" dimension of leadership scale. Innovative behavior is increasingly important for organizations' survival (Pieterse, van Knippenberg, Schippers, & Stam, 2010). Theories of transformational leadership emphasize stimulating innovation as a core leadership function (e.g., Bass, 1985; Conger, 1999); and transformational leadership, in contrast to transactional leadership, has been argued to be a particularly effective way to engender innovative behavior (Basu & Green, 1997). More specifically, the inspiring and motivating nature of transformational leadership should be more effective in engendering innovative behavior when followers feel better able to proactively influence their work role and environment, that is, when psychological empowerment is high (Pieterse et al. 2010).

Many leadership theories emphasize the need for the leader to articulate an inspiring vision, but what is important is not so much words but actions: the level of ethics demonstrated, the respect and compassion shown to others. The fifth factor exposes this. Leaders must also create enthusiasm among their people, inspiring and motivating subordinates to make the leader's vision a reality (Conger & Kanungo, 1987).The sixth factor, having two items, examines the leader's attitude toward honesty. Honesty and integrity are virtues in all individuals but have special significance for leaders. Survey research frequently links perceived leadership effectiveness with the leader's honesty (i.e., truthfulness), integrity (i.e., principled behavior), or trustworthiness (i.e., can be trusted) (Brown et al., 2005). A leader's honesty and integrity form the foundation on which that leader gains followers' trust and confidence; without honesty and integrity, the leader would not be able to attract and retain followers (Kirkpatick & Lock, 1991).

Means and standard deviations of all the factors used in this study were computed to examine the distribution of scores within each set of variables. Means were rank ordered to underline their order of endorsement by the executives and managers. It should be noted that responses were made on a Likert scale. Higher scores on each dimension denoted greater affirmation with the dimension description. Table A3 reveals that integrity ranks first in the order of endorsement shown by the managers. The mean and SD of this dimension clearly indicate that most managers considered their supervisor's approach based on sympathy. Benevolence and responsibility and inspiring approach ranked second and third, respectively. The least endorsed approaches included integrity, which holds the fourth rank, and innovative and ethical attitude, holding the fifth and sixth ranks, respectively. Therefore, it can be concluded on the basis of Table A3 that findings indicating a sense of benevolence and responsibility, empathy, and inventive approaches were more frequently and positively endorsed by the senior managers than those that consider integrity and risk taking. Then, we strived to find out the percentage of leaders who showed the traits of different dimensions of assessed leadership and the intercorrelation among these factors.

In correlation analysis, the purpose is to assess the degree of familiarity in the linear relationship between the defined variables. The correlation coefficient shows how closely the data fit a linear pattern. Each of the factors had a significant zero-order correlation with the other factors, which shows the association. Finally, we had to see the impact of these leadership traits on subordinates' commitment and perceived productivity.

To check the strength of the causality, regression analysis was performed on the dependent variables. In the regression model, a manager's commitment is predicted from all six dimensions of the leadership instrument. The instrument used for this study was a closed-ended questionnaire that consisted of some questions related to leadership (independent variables) and the dependent variables of organizational commitment and perceived productivity. Total scores of the leadership questionnaire were correlated with organizational commitment and productivity, in which some factors came out as significantly correlated with outcome variables. Factors two, three, and four had a significant relationship with the organizational commitment (see Table A5); and factors two, three, four. and six had significant associations with productivity.

To check the strength of the causality, regression analysis was performed on the dependent variables. A summary of the regression model for the first dependent variable, organizational commitment, is given in Table A6. In the regression model, a manager's commitment is predicted from all the six dimensions of leadership questionnaire. Leadership factors explain only 22.9% of the variance in organizational commitment for this sample. The results of Table A6 concludes that, among the six dimension of leadership scale, only the third factor, benevolence and responsibility, is one of the best predictors of the commitment of the managers. For the next dependent variable, productivity, according to the model summary (Table A7), leadership factors explain only 21.7% of the variance in productivity for this sample. Meanwhile the p value is less than 0.05, (see Table A7), which shows that at least one independent variable is a significant predictor of productivity. Table A7 concludes that the second factor, ethical, is a significant predictor of the productivity of managers.

The results indicate significant correlation among all six factors of the leadership construct, organizational commitment, and productivity. Further, the analysis of data show that the third factor, responsibility and benevolence of the leader, most exemplifies the organizational commitment of the surveyed managers; moreover, the second factor, which is related to ethical attitude of the supervisor, was found significant for perceived productivity. The rest of the factors were rather insignificant to the manager's commitment and perceived productivity or had no significant impact on the dependent variables.

Discussion and Implication

These results provide a different picture of the prerequisite leadership for the organizations. In the items under the "benevolent and responsible" factor, we found constructs related to empathy, generosity and responsibility in the behavior of the supervisor or leader create an impact over the organizational commitment of managers (Deci & Ryan, 2000; Fry, 2005). Commitment is basically a force that binds an individual to a course of action that is of relevance to a particular target (Meyer & Herscovitch, 2001). Commitment encourages discretionary behaviors that will result in positive goal outcomes and hence reinforce employee commitment to the organization (Collier & Esteban, 2007). Organizational benevolence based on intentions attributed to genuine concern and care is stronger predictor of commitment (Ganesan & Hess, 1997). A study by Cullen, Parboteeah, and Victor (2003) also supports the fact that the benevolent climate of an organization has a positive relationship with organizational commitment. The willingness of the company involved to define its responsibility to society in terms of a wider global focus (Collier & Esteban, 2007). Brammer, Millington, and Rayton

(2007) suggest both that social responsibility is positively related to organizational commitment and that the contribution of responsibility to organizational commitment is at least as great as job satisfaction.

The behavior of leaders (empathy, generosity, and responsibility) can be of immense help for practitioners, who often identify the appropriate behavior that can enhance commitment in employees. Further, the ethical approach of the leader is the next factor that affected the dependent variable in a positive manner. The ethical factor of the construct has items related to ethical conduct in daily work with subordinates. Ethical leadership is fundamentally the employment of a moral workplace and also the leadership that supports it. Burke and Black (1990) suggest that ethics interventions can be a critical strategy for improving organizational productivity. Berman and West (1998) also add that the relationship between ethics and productivity is not surprising, because ethics is strongly associated with norms of responsiveness, efficiency, and professionalism, all of which are associated with productivity improvement strategies.

Conclusion

The chapter begins by identifying the necessity for a new paradigm of leadership and reviews the relevant social scientific literature relating to the prerequisite leadership paradigm. Further, the author describes the contemporary theoretical conceptions of the leadership phenomena and displays real-life examples of immoral and unethical acts committed by top leaders and tries to identify the reasons behind these wrongdoings. The chapter contributes to the contemporary debate on the leadership crisis, focusing on the level of values. The work investigates the existence of value-laden leadership traits in the Indian service sector, with an emphasis on whether virtues, sympathy, and responsible management affects the job-related outcomes. Values imbibed in a global representation of leadership would allow newer conceptualizations of leadership based on this schema to look for and incorporate similar phenomenon in the leadership domain. The study identifies the impact of the leader's ethical behavior on subordinates' commitment and the organization's perceived productivity. Integrity, benevolence, and responsibility are found to be the most effective factors for the output according to this survey. These findings indicate that the dimensions of value-laden leadership have a significant impact on the workplace in the form of job-related outcomes of commitment. Additionally, the scale should be tested further, as the studies differ in nature of subjects as well as the methods of plotting the values in leadership, so there are some disagreements on generality of findings. The specific nature of relationship between value-laden leadership and organizational outcomes is at best only partially established.

References

Allen, N. J., & Meyer, J. P. (1990). The measurement and antecedents of affective, continuance and normative commitment to the organization. *Journal of Occupational Psychology, 63*(1), 1–18.

Avolio, B. J., & Gardner, W. L. (2005). Authentic leadership development: Getting to the root of positive forms of leadership. *The Leadership Quarterly, 16,* 315–338. Retrieved from http://www.keyleadership.com/Downloads/Authentic%20Leadership%20Development%20.pdf

Bass, B. M. (1985). *Leadership and performance beyond expectations.* New York, NY: The Free Press.

Basu, R., & Green, S. G. (1997). Leader-member exchange and transformational leadership: An empirical examination of innovative behaviors in leader-member dyads. *Journal of Applied Social Psychology, 27*(6), 477–499.

Berman, E. M., & West, J. P. (1998). Productivity enhancement efforts in public and nonprofit organisations. *Public Productivity and Management Review,* 207–219.

Bhasin, M. (2013). Corporate accounting scandal at Satyam: A case study of India's Enron. *European Journal of Business and Social Sciences, 1*(12), 25–47.

Blake, R. R., & Mouton, J. S. (1965). A 9, 9 approach for increasing organizational productivity. In E. H. Shein & W. E. Bennis (Eds.), *Personal and organizational change through group methods* (pp. 169–183). New York, NY: Wiley.

Bolman, L. G., & Deal, T. E. (2003). *Reframing organizations—Artistry, choice, and leadership* (3rd ed.). San Francisco, CA: Jossey-Bass.

Bozesan, M. (2010). *The making of a consciousness leader in business: An integral approach.* Published PhD Dissertation, ITP Palo Alto. Redwood City, CA: Sageera.

Brammer, S., Millington, A., & Rayton, B. (2007). The contribution of corporate social responsibility to organizational commitment. *The International Journal of Human Resource Management, 18*(10), 1701–1719.

Brown, M. E., Trevino, L. K., & Harrison, D. A. (2005). Ethical leadership: A social learning perspective for construct development and testing. *Organizational Behavior and Human Decision Processes, 97,* 117–134.

Bryman, A. (1993). Charismatic leadership in organizations: Some neglected issues. *Leadership Quarterly, 4,* 289–304.

Burke, F., & Black, A. (1990). Improving organizational productivity: Add ethics. *Public Productivity & Management Review,* 121–133.

Burns, J. M. (1978). *Leadership*. New York, NY: Harper & Row.

Chandler, D. J. (2009). The perfect storm of leader's unethical behavior: A conceptual framework. *International Journal of Leadership Studies, 5*(1), 69–93.

Ciulla, J. B. (2003). *The ethics of leadership*. Wadsworth, OH: Thomson Learning.

Collier, J., & Esteban, R. (2007). Corporate social responsibility and employee commitment. *Business Ethics: A European Review, 16*(1), 19–33.

Conger, J. A. (1999). Charismatic and transformational leadership in organizations: An insider's perspective on these developing streams of research. *The Leadership Quarterly, 10*(2), 145–179.

Conger, J. A., & Kanungo, R. (1998). *Charismatic leadership in organizations*. Thousand Oaks, CA: Sage Publications.

Conger, J. A., & Kanungo, R. N. (1987). Toward a behavioral theory of charismatic leadership in organizational settings. *Academy of Management Review, 12*(4), 637–647.

Cullen, J. B., Parboteeah, K. P., & Victor, B. (2003). The effects of ethical climates on organizational commitment: A two-study analysis. *Journal of Business Ethics, 46*(2), 127–141.

Datta, D. (2012). Spectrum auction and investment in telecom industry: A suggested policy. *Vikalpa, 37*(1), 19–30.

Debats, D. L., & Bartelds, B. F. (1996). The structure of human values: A principal components analysis of the Rokeach Value Survey (RVS). Retrieved from http://www.dissertations.ub.rug.nl/FILES/faculties/ppsw/1996/dlhmdebats/c5.pdf (Erişim: 05.12. 2011).

de Vries, M. F. K., & Miller, D. (1985). Narcissism and leadership: An object relations perspective. *Human Relations, 38*(6), 583–601.

Deci, E. L., & Ryan, R. M. (2000). The "what" and "why" of goal pursuits: Human needs and the self-determination of behavior. *Psychological Inquiry, 11*(4), 227–268.

Driscoll, C., & McKee, M. (2007). Restoring a culture of ethical and spiritual values: A role for leader storytelling. *Journal of Business Ethics, 73*, 205–221.

Eisenberg, N., & Miller, P. A. (1987). The relation of empathy to prosocial and related behaviors. *Psychological Bulletin, 101*(1), 91.

Farh, J. L., & Cheng, B. S. (2000). A cultural analysis of paternalistic leadership in Chinese organizations. In J. T. Li, A. S. Tsui, & E. Weldon (Eds.), *Management and organizations in the Chinese context* (pp. 84–127). Palgrave Macmillan UK.

Field, A. (2005). *Factor analysis using SPSS*. Retrieved from http://users.sussex.ac.uk/~andyf/factor.pdf. Accessed on February 16, 2013.

Fortune magazine names Bear Stearns 'most admired' securities firm. (2005, February 25). Retrieved from http://www.businesswire.com/news/home/20050225005422/en/FORTUNE-Magazine-Names-Bear-Stearns-Admired-Securities. Accessed on July 15, 2014.

Fry, L. W. (2005). Toward a theory of ethical and spiritual well-being, and corporate social responsibility through spiritual leadership. In R. A. Gicacalone,

C. L. Jukiewicz, & D. Craig (Eds.), *Positive psychology in business ethics and corporate responsibility* (pp. 47–84). Greenwich, CT: Information Age Publication.

Ganesan, S., & Hess, R. (1997). Dimensions and levels of trust: implications for commitment to a relationship. *Marketing letters*, 8(4), 439–448.

Gardner, J. W.(1990). *On leadership*. New York, NY: The Free Press.

George, B. (2011, June 6). Why leaders lose their way. Retrieved from http://hbswk.hbs.edu/item/6741.html. Accessed on 16 June, 2014.

Gini, A., & Marcoux, A. M. (2009). Malden Mills: When being a good company isn't good enough. *Proceedings of the Good Company. Sixth International Symposium on Catholic Social Thought and Management Education*. Rome, Italy.

Greenleaf, R. K. (2002). *Servant leadership: A journey into the nature of legitimate power and greatness*. Paulist Press.

Grojean, M. W., Resick, C. J., Dickson, M. W., & Smith, D. B. (2004). Leaders, values, and organizational climate: Examining leadership strategies for establishing an organizational climate regarding ethics. *Journal of Business Ethics*, 55, 223–241.

Harrison, R. (1987). Harnessing personal energy: How companies can inspire employees. *Organizational Dynamics*, 16, 4–21.

House, R. J. (1971). A path goal theory of leader effectiveness. *Administrative Science Quarterly*, 16, 321–339.

House, R. J. (1977). A 1976 theory of charismatic leadership. In J. G. Hunt & L. L. Larson (Eds.), *Leadership: The cutting edge* (pp. 189–207). Carbondale, IL: Southern Illinois University Press.

Kelman, H. C. (1958). Compliance, identification, and internalization: Three processes of attitude change. *Journal of Conflict Resolution*, 1, 51–60.

Kirkpatick, S. A., & Locke, E. A. (1991). Leadership: Do traits matter? *The Executive*, 5(2), 48–60.

Kouzes, J. M., & Posner, B. Z. (2003). *The leadership practices inventory (LPI): Participant's workbook* (Vol. 47). Hoboken, NJ: John Wiley & Sons.

Kuhnert, K. W., & Lewis, P. (1987). Transactional and transformational leadership: A constructive/developmental analysis. *Academy of Management Review*, 12(4), 648–657.

Maak, T. (2007). Responsible leadership, stakeholder engagement, and the emergence of social capital. *Journal of Business Ethics*, 74(4), 329–343.

Maccoby, M. (2005). Creating moral organizations. *Research Technology Management*, 48(1), 59–60.

Maheshwari, S., & Ganesh, M. P. (2006). Ethics in organizations: The case of Tata Steel. *Vikalpa*, 31(2), 77–87.

Marcy, R. T., Gentry, W. A., & McKinnon, R. (2008). Thinking straight: New strategies are needed for ethical leadership. *Leadership in Action*, 28(3), 3–7.

Maslow, A. (1970). *The farther reaches of human nature*. New York, NY: The Viking Press.

Maslow, A. (2000). *The Maslow business reader*. D. C. Stephens (Ed.). New York, NY: John Wiley & Sons.

Meyer, J. P., & Herscovitch, L. (2001). Commitment in the workplace: Toward a general model. *Human Resource Management Review, 11*(3), 299–326.

Murtaza, N. (2011). Pursuing self-interest or self-actualization? From capitalism to a steady-state, wisdom economy. *Ecological Economics, 70*(4), 577–584. doi: 10.1016/j.ecolecon.2010.10.012

Neal, J. A., Benyamin, M., Lichtenstein, B., & Banner, D., (1999). Spiritual perspectives on individual, organizational and societal transformation. *Journal of Organizational Change Management, 12*(3), 175–186.

Nyhan, R. C. (2000). Changing the paradigm trust and its role in public sector organizations. *The American Review of Public Administration, 30*(1), 87–109.

Oliver, J., & Goodwin, T. (2010). *How they blew it: The CEOs and entrepreneurs behind some of the World's most catastrophic business failures* (1st ed.). Philadelphia, PA: Kogan Page.

Pellegrini, E. K., & Scandura, T. A. (2008). Paternalistic leadership: A review and agenda for future research. *Journal of Management, 34*(3), 566–593.

Pieterse, A. N., van Knippenberg, D., Schippers, M., & Stam, D. (2010). Transformational and transactional leadership and innovative behavior: The moderating role of psychological empowerment. *Journal of Organizational Behavior, 31*(4), 609–623.

Porter, L. W., & Bigley, G. A. (1997). Motivation and transformational leadership: Some organizational context issues. Unpublished paper, University of California at Irvine.

Razik, T. A., & Swanson, A. D. (2001). *Fundamental concepts of educational leadership* (2nd ed.). Upper Saddle River, NJ: Prentice Hall, Inc.

Roe, R. A., & Ester, P. (1999). Values and work: Empirical findings and theoretical perspective. *Applied Psychology, 48*(1), 1–21.

Schön, D. A. (1971). *Beyond the stable state: Public and private learning in a changing society.* Maurice Temple Smith Limited.

Seshadri, D. V. R., Raghavan, A., & Hegde, S. (2007). Business ethics: The next frontier for globalizing Indian companies. *Vikalpa, 32*(3), 61–79.

Shamir, B., House, R. J., & Arthur, M. B. (1993). Motivational effects of transformational leadership: A self-concept based theory. *Organization Science, 4*(4), 577–594.

Shirur, S. (2011).Tunneling vs. agency effect: A case study of Enron and Satyam. *Vikalpa, 36*(3), 9–20.

Trevino, L. K. (1986). Ethical decision making in organizations: A person-situation interactionist model. *Academy of Management Review, 11*(3), 601–617.

Trevino, L. K., & Brown, M. E. (2005). The role of leaders in influencing unethical behavior in the workplace. In R. Kidwell & C. Martin, (Eds.), *Managing organizational deviance* (pp. 69–96). Thousand Oaks, CA: Sage.

Treviño, L. K., Hartman, L. P., & Brown, M. (2000). Moral person and moral manager: How executives develop a reputation for ethical leadership. *California Management Review, 42*(4), 128–142.

Twenty five people to blame for the financial crisis. (n.d.). *Time.* Retrieved from http://content.time.com/time/specials/packages/article/0,28804,1877351_1877350_1877327,00.html

Upadhyay, Y., & Singh, S. K. (2010). In favour of ethics: The linkage between ethical behaviour and performance. *Journal of Human Values, Management Centre for Human Values*, 16(1), 9–19.

Victor, B., & Cullen, J. B. (1987). A theory and measure of ethical climate in organizations. *Research in Corporate Social Performance and Policy*, 9(1), 51–71.

Victor, B., & Cullen, J. B. (1988). The organizational bases of ethical work climates. *Administrative Science Quarterly*, 33, 101–125.

Vroom, V. H., & Yetton, P. W. (1973). *Leadership and decision-making* (Vol. 110). Pittsburgh: University of Pittsburgh Press.

Weber, M. (1968). *On charisma and institution building*. Chicago, IL: University of Chicago Press.

Wu, T. Y., Hsu, W. L., & Cheng, B. S. 2002. Expressing or suppressing anger: Subordinate's anger responses to supervisors' authoritarian behaviors in a Taiwan enterprise. *Indigenous Psychological Research in Chinese Societies*, 18, 3–49.

Yukl, G. (1989). Managerial leadership: A review of theory and research. *Journal of Management*, 15(2), 251–289.

Yukl, G. (1999). An evaluation of conceptual weaknesses in transformational and charismatic leadership theories. *The Leadership Quarterly*, 10(2), 285–305.

Appendix

Table A1.   Reliability.

Questionnaire Factors	Cronbach's Alpha
Leadership	0.74
Organizational commitment	0.85
Productivity	0.76
Consolidated	0.78

Table A2.   Item Content and Factor Structure of Leadership Scale (Factor Analysis).

Item*	Component	FL**	V%***	EV*
	Factor 1, Sympathy		25.04	3.75
8	Concerned about people's personal and professional problems	0.73		
9	Discusses business ethics or values with employees	0.71		
4	Shows cooperation to a higher degree	0.77		
6	Conducts life in a moral way	0.79		
	Factor 2, Ethics		12.52	1.87
20	Has a sense of responsibility to the outside community	0.89		
17	Sets a high standard of accountability	0.91		
	Factor 3, Benevolence and Responsibility		11.14	1.67
12	Speaks with genuine conviction about the higher meaning and purpose of the organization's work	0.57		
17a	Makes sure that his or her decisions also benefit the wide community along with the organization	0.85		
18	Shows kindheartedness, humility, and thought to everybody	0.80		
	Factor 4, Innovativeness		10.46	59.17
5	Believes that followers need breaks to reenergize themselves.	0.88		
6a	Searches outside the formal boundaries of his or her organization for innovative ways to improve what they do	0.89		
	Factor 5, Inspiring		8.11	1.21

Table A2.   (*Continued*)

Item*	Component	FL**	V%***	EV*
14	Seeks out challenging opportunities that test his or her own skills and abilities	0.83		
16	Appeals to others to share an exciting dream of the future	0.87		
	Factor 6, Honesty		7.36	1.10
7	Defines success not just by results but also by the way they are obtained	0.89		
19	Makes sure that his/her decisions also benefits the wide community along with the organization	0.81		

*Eigen value; **Factor loading; ***Variance percentage.
Note: The serial number of the items in the questionnaire is put in parenthesis.

Table A3.   Descriptive Statistics for Factors.

Variable	Mean	SD
Sympathy	11.9	2.26
Ethics	5.8	1.49
Benevolence and Responsibility	9.4	1.94
Innovativeness	5.9	1.62
Inspiring	6.4	1.08
Honesty	6.2	1.28
Organizational commitment	12.34	2.52
Perceived productivity	36.63	5.81

Table A4.   Factors Correlations ($N = 221$).

	Sympathy	Ethics	Benevolence and Responsibility	Innovativeness	Inspiring	Honesty
1. Sympathy		.17**	.20**	.24**	.11	.24**
2. Ethics			.18**	.34**	.11	.33**
3. Benevolence and Responsibility				.28**	.14*	.09
4. Innovativeness					.17**	.20**
5. Inspiring						.14*
6. Honesty						

*Correlation is significant at the 0.05 level (2-tailed); **Correlation is significant at the 0.01 level (2-tailed).

Table A5. Correlations.

Variables	Organizational Commitment	Productivity
1. Sympathetic	0.09	0.005
2. Ethical	0.16*	0.22**
3. Benevolent & Responsible	0.23*	0.15*
4. Innovative	0.13	0.15*
5. Inspiring	0.04	0.02
6. Honest	0.09	0.19**

N = 221
*Correlation is significant at the 0.05 level (2-tailed); **Correlation is significant at the 0.01 level (2-tailed).

Table A6. Standard Regression Analysis Predicting Organizational Commitment.

	R	R^2	β	SE	B	T	Sig
Benevolence and Responsibility	22.9	0.05	0.68	0.19	0.22	3.47	0.001

Table A7. Standard Regression Analysis Predicting Productivity.

	R	R^2	β	SE	B	T	Sig
Ethics	21.7	0.47	0.35	0.10	0.21	3.29	0.001

14

A Sustainable, Culturally Competent Approach to Academic Leadership

Sherwood Thompson, Timothy Forde
and Tom Otieno

T he purpose of this chapter is to discuss the role that sustainable, culturally competent leadership plays in higher education settings. The literature supports our belief that characteristics such as civility, ethical behavior, data-driven decision-making, and cultural sensitivity provide the grounding for effective culturally competent leadership in higher education settings according to Porath (2012).

This chapter presents a review of the literature on cultural competency in relation to leadership in higher education by focusing on the philosophy that sustainable cultural competence serves as a catalyst for sustainable leadership excellence.

The authors propose that sustainable culturally competent leadership on campuses is a catalyst for diversity leadership excellence. This chapter concludes that a sustainable, culturally competent leadership paradigm for academic leaders on campuses benefits the entire campus, especially other academic leaders.

This new paradigm presents evidence that a structured sustainable, culturally competent approach to academic leadership works. A combination of passionate connections on campus forges relationships that design a functional leadership model that improves and preserves the diversity and inclusive excellence on campuses.

Introduction

In this chapter, we explore the necessity of creating a sustainable, culturally competent approach to academic leadership for advancing campus diversity. To this end, we examine the role of sustainable, competent leaders: assessing their insights, characteristics, and leadership styles among diverse groups on college and university campuses. The specifics of what constitutes this diverse group will vary by institution, depending on the ways in which the student population served by the institution, as well as the employee population, differs. In general, however, these differences will include visibly apparent characteristics such as ethnicity, gender, age, and physical ability, as well as less obvious characteristics such as marital status, sexual orientation, socioeconomic status, national background, and religion.

We have developed the term *sustainable, culturally competent leadership* as our working model to indicate the lasting role academic leadership plays when working in educationally diverse environments. We have forged together definitions of the terms sustainable, and culturally competent to develop the term sustainable, culturally competent leadership. The first aspect of our model adopted the seven principles of sustainability established by Hargreaves and Fink (2006) to devise and clarify this term. In so doing, we tailored our definition by using the following characteristics for effective sustainable education leadership.

1. Depth
   Sustainable leadership matters. "The first principle of sustainable leadership is leadership for learning and leadership for caring for and among others" (p. 18).
2. Length
   Sustainable leadership lasts. "It preserves and advocates the most valuable aspects of life over time, year upon year, from one leader to the next" (p. 18).
3. Breadth

Sustainable leadership spreads. "It sustains as well as depends on the leadership of others" (p. 19).

4. Justice

Sustainable leadership does no harm to and actively improves the surrounding environment. "Sustainable leadership is not self-centered; it is socially just" (p. 19).

5. Diversity

Sustainable leadership promotes cohesive diversity. "Sustainable leadership, in contrast, fosters and learn from diversity in teaching and learning and moves things forward by creating cohesion and networking among its richly varied components" (p. 19).

6. Resourcefulness

Sustainable leadership develops and does not deplete material and human resources. "Sustainable leadership is prudent and resourceful leadership that wastes neither its money nor its people" (p. 20).

7. Conservation

Sustainable leadership honors and learns from the best of the past to create an even better future. "Amid the chaos of change, sustainable leadership is steadfast about preserving and renewing its long-standing purpose" (p. 20).

Next, we incorporated the three qualities of critical cultural competence to denote what Cooper, He, and Levin (2011) refer to as transforming educational setting "through thoughtful, innovative, and responsible practices that enhance equity in education for all" (p. xvi). Our definition of sustainable, competent leadership similarly involves using the following characteristics from the critical culturally competent model to ensure that sustainable leadership has the ability to:

1. Engage in self-reflection about its cultural identities and experiences. Additionally, sustainable leadership must engage in critical reflection on its own surface and personal biases and develop visions and beliefs that guide and even transform educational practices in diverse settings.
2. Explore the cultural background of its students, families, and the communities (i.e., internal and external stakeholders). Furthermore, sustainable leadership must find ways to negotiate its role as teachers and administrators to leverage student's strengths and assets to maximize learning.

3. Transform its individual practices in classroom, schools (campuses), and other educational settings by using systematic, thoughtful, and innovative practices and collaborations (p. 5).

Our intent is to transform these two practices into a framework on sustainable culturally competence leadership with diversity strengths that will have a lasting impact on higher education.

Toward Sustainable, Culturally Competent Leadership

The second aspect of our models led us to focus on three categories including (a) cultural competence as a catalyst for leadership excellence: this explores how the awareness and activation of culturally competent leadership practices galvanize academic leaders' achievement in internal and external administrative duties; (b) multidimensional constructs of sustainable cultural competence on college and university campuses: this describes the development of productive, lasting campus relationships and how leaders incorporate collaboration and partnerships among diverse groups; (c) the use of inclusive excellence in shaping diversity strategic plans: these categories encompass best practices for preparing and presenting strategic planning for diversity, internationalism, and sustainable institutional diversity goals.

The sustainable, culturally competent leader works with other administrators to promote knowledge about cultural competence and diversity awareness among population in diverse settings.

Promoting Cultural Competence

In some studies, the literature supports the belief that characteristics such as civility, ethical behavior, data-driven decision-making, and cultural sensitivity provide the groundwork for effective culturally competent leadership in higher education settings (Porath, 2012). Kumagai and Lypson (2009) described cultural competence in education settings as a categorized set of learning outcomes. Kumagai and Lypson maintained that these outcomes specifically indicate that cultural competence may be characterized as focusing on the acquisition of knowledge, skills, and attitudes; a philosophy that mirrors the belief that a baseline of cultural competences is crucial to transforming a college or university.

Fostering a common understanding of cultural competence advances the commitment to broaden, grow, and strengthen individuals' appreciation and perspective about diversity and inclusive excellence. Furthermore, it appears that a culturally competent paradigm benefits the entire campus, particularly in how it equips leaders with the resources, awareness, education, skills, and training to advance cultural competence (Gasman, Abiola, & Travers, 2015).

Regarding diversity on campus, the culturally competent leaders focus on the intellectual and social development of students while academically engaging the campus in key diversity learning outcomes. Thus, we assert that highly visible academic leaders are better able to model intellectual and social development traits for students when they are practicing cultural competence in every aspect of their responsibilities. Again, we maintain that the entire leadership team of a campus must participate in promoting diversity and inclusive excellence on campus.

Admittedly, this is a daunting challenge for many academic leaders – especially those accustomed to thinking of diversity as the sole responsibility of the chief diversity officer. However, a change in mindset is needed to accommodate the increasing diversity of student populations forecasted by demographers (Pascarella, Edison, Nora, Hagedorn, & Terenzini, 1996; Swail, 2002; Williams, 2014). Mounting campus cultural diversity requires greater cultural diversity leadership development among key academic leaders.

The Changing Landscape of U.S. College Campuses

The student populations of U.S. institutions of higher education (IHEs) are becoming more racially and ethnically diverse (Williams, 2014). While White students' enrollment is projected to increase by only 7% between 2012 and 2023, the anticipated growth rates among Hispanic, Black, and Asian/Pacific Islander students are 34%, 25%, and 11%, respectively (Hussar & Bailey, 2016). This demographic shift requires IHEs to (a) improve access to higher education for groups that have been historically underrepresented and (b) address entrenched inequitable practices that inspire vastly different outcomes for low-income and racial and ethnic minority students.

Changes in the student populations of IHEs reflect the mounting diversity of the United States as a whole. According to the U.S. Census Bureau's 2014 National Population Projections (Colby & Ortman, 2015), the non-Hispanic White population is currently the largest racial and ethnic group with a 62% (198 million) share of the nation's total population as of 2014. However, this group's share is projected to drop to 44% by 2060 as its population declines to 182 million. During the same period, the populations of racial and ethnic minorities are projected to rise. Furthermore, social, political, and technological changes have spurred a greater interdependence between countries and, by extension, fostered a more mobile and competitive workforce. Consequently, American IHEs are responsible for graduating students who can function effectively in a multicultural workforce and a global economy – particularly by imbuing them with cross-cultural awareness, intercultural communication skills, and an international perspective.

In order to achieve the above goals, IHEs must establish structures that support a sustainable and culturally competent approach to academic leadership. To aid this process, this chapter presents a number of recommendations regarding the characteristics and leadership styles that culturally competent leaders might adopt. We also discuss the central role of leaders' social responsibility in advancing campus diversity. In particular, the rest of the chapter examines (a) the dimensions of cultural competency and different leadership styles; (b) the characteristics of culturally competent leaders; (c) the methods in which IHEs can demonstrate their commitment to diversity and inclusive excellence; and (d) sustainable leadership practices.

Dimensions of Cultural Competency Starting with Culture

A proper understanding of culture is the first step in creating a culturally competent environment. While culture maintains several connotations, we have grounded our discussion on the work of Kagawa-Singer, Dressler, George, and Elwood (2014) in a report titled *The Cultural Framework for Health: An Integrative*

Approach for Research and Program Design and Evaluation. This model was selected because it provides a reliable and scientifically valid framework using six steps that can be tested for research purposes. We realize that there is no one assessment that an individual can take to accurately become culturally competent; however, we believe that Kagawa-Singer et al.'s (2014) work offers some relevant principles that we can use in discussing the role of culture.

The findings in their report provide a comprehensive research-based framework that is designed to assist educators and researchers from all academic disciplines in designing culturally competent practices using culture as a starting point. The authors in their Executive Summary listed five applications of culture titled *The Cultural Framework for Health* (CFH). Among the five applications included in the CFH, we focus on application two, which states, "Identifies why culture is fundamental for understanding human behavior and the impact of cultural ways of life on mental and physical health and well-being" (p. 5). This application covers a broad range of perspectives that relate to the growing issues of ethnic, cultural, linguistic, and global awareness on campuses.

Unquestionably, a person's culture, its practices, and customs play a fundamental role on the individual's overall character. We agree with the authors' notion that social and cultural identity is a culmination of the shared traits and assigned cohesion of particular groups with cultural and social attributes (p. 29). In other words, we agree that who individuals are is the collection and sum total of one's background, norms, and traits. When discussing culture, individuals are left with these questions: "What is culture? What are the necessary aspects and characteristics of culture? What fundamental role does culture play among Homo sapiens?

Culture as a concept can serve as an umbrella used to give individuals an identity within a group or society – comprehensively identifying their beliefs and values. The authors take special care to define culture by indicating that it is dynamic and vibrant, causing individuals to "each respond, evolve, and differ due to individual, ecologic, social, political, and historical circumstances" (p. 31). Notwithstanding, the authors caution that there are some inconsistencies in the research that emphasize the focus on an individual's intergroup cultural norms. External conditions such as political and social factors may influence the realms of individual's own cultural identity. Culture in social group identity can be hampered by social categories and a person's own self-concept. Social identity researchers purport that individuals' social identities (which capture their cultural alliances) belong to their personal identities and idiosyncratic characteristics (p. 21).

In response to the question, "What is culture?" Kagawa-Singer et al. (2014) maintained that culture provides an individual with tools to survive in society. In part, they address the definition of the concept of culture as "an essential pan-human process that ensures survival, endurance, and wellbeing for a given group of people (p. 31). The authors concluded that culture is not "a single item or variable, but a multidimensional, multilevel process that constantly evolves and encompasses all levels of the human condition" (p. 31).

As to what culture does, Kagawa-Singer et al. (2014) posited that culture provides patterns that enable individuals to function in society in an organic manner interacting with other members of their group with comfort and ease. Most notably, the authors indicated that "much of how cultural processes function is implicit rather than explicit and often subconscious in the minds of its members" (p. 33). Nieto (2008) maintained, "culture is complex and intricate" (p. 129). She also discussed how culture is dynamic and multifaceted and how cultures influence one another. Banks and Banks (2009) maintained that culture "consists, of the shared beliefs, symbols, and interpretations within a human group" (p. 8).

Kim and Matthews (2015) believed that "culture refers to patterns of thoughts, beliefs, and values that distinguish members of a particular social group and that are acquired through social interaction rather than being based on biology" (p. 172). According to Surbone (2004), culture interacts with identity formation in three ways: (a) it provides a framework for interpreting the external world, (b) it helps us make sense of the events that happen to us, and (c) facilitates our reliance on our own sense of self and connectedness. Furthermore, Morton and Atkinson (1983) and Helms (1990) suggested that there are several phases of growth during identity development, including: (a) internalization of the culture's negative imagery, (b) expression of anger, (c) immersion, and (d) integration of life. These phases can also apply to institutions, which may develop new community identities in response to diversification. During this transition, it is important to realize that negative reactions and judgments may surface.

However, institutions must commit to moving beyond the trials of the early stages and ultimately change the landscape. In order to do so, institutions must employ new models of leadership – in particular, the cultural competence model. In this framework, leaders recognize that understanding culture is the first step toward better outcomes.

Hofstede's (1980) research supported the theory that an organization's behavior is impacted by its cultural values. This idea gained prominence in the healthcare industry as well, where providers realized the significant impact of culture on people's health (Coris, 2003; Kagawa-Singer et al., 2014; Lee, 1991; Sutton, 2000). This inspired the notion of cultural competence, which Davis (1997) defined (in the context of health outcomes) as the integration and transformation of knowledge about individuals and groups of people into specific standards, policies, practices, and attitudes used in appropriate cultural settings to increase the quality of services (Phan, Vugia, & Jones, 2015; Reich & Reich, 2006). After surveying the literature on culture, we must ask ourselves, how does cultural influence culture competence?

Orlandi (1992) argued that cultural competence is a concept that involves cultural knowledge, attitude, and skill development.

Several milestones are identifiable on the journey to becoming culturally competent. Trimble (2003) stated that cultural competence is not linear. He argued that cultural competence is "a life long journey ... the journey begins with self-exploration and self-reflection" (p. 18). He also maintained that cultural competence is not a license examination process where a candidate completes a set of requirements and demonstrates some level of proficiency and skill and then is awarded a certificate of completion (p. 18).

On the other hand, Thompson and Cuseo (2009) characterized cultural competence as an ascending stairway with the lowest steps displaying the most extreme forms of resistance to diversity, and as the steps escalate, they display progressively higher levels of diversity appreciation and culminate in cultural competence. As described in the table below, Thompson and Cuseo (2009) advanced that cultural competence is a process that moves individual beyond the extreme rejection of acceptance and tolerance to a genuine appreciation of diverse cultures (Table 1).

Saunders, Haskins, and Vasquez (2015) believed that "To develop cultural competence, one must undertake an elusive journey that likely has no destination" (p. 19). The focus of cultural

Table 1.   Staircase to Cultural Competence.

Steps to Cultural Competence	Stairway of Attaining Cultural Competence
Cultural competence	Cultural competence is moving beyond mere acceptance or tolerance of diversity to a deeper and genuine appreciation of people from diverse cultural backgrounds
Cultural action	Recognizing differences and responding to them in a positive manner; this represents an advanced step in the process of becoming culturally competent
Cultural acceptance	Valuing cultural differences and similarities and viewing the differences as positive
Cultural acknowledgement	Acknowledging the differences that exist between individuals, races, and entire cultures and viewing those differences as positive rather than negative
Cultural awareness	An awareness of your own cultural biases and the effect they may have on yourself and others
Cultural sensitivity	An understanding that our internal biases have affected those around us (both those we know personally and those we do not)
Bias	Characterized at the lowest and most extreme forms of resistance to diversity
Stereotyping	Characterized at the lowest and most extreme forms of resistance to diversity
Prejudice	Characterized at the lowest and most extreme forms of resistance to diversity
Discrimination	Characterized at the lowest and most extreme forms of resistance to diversity
Genocide	Characterized at the lowest and most extreme forms of resistance to diversity

Note: This table advances the concept that escalated progressive levels are the desired levels of achieving cultural competence.

competence in businesses, schools, colleges, and civic organizations has increased over the last decade – it is truly a journey.

Commitment to Inclusive Excellence

Ideally, the acquisition of cultural competence will foster inclusive excellence. A sibling to diversity, inclusive excellence suggests that all individuals should have the opportunity to achieve academic excellence. Institutions that abide by this idea should strive to outfit individuals with the resources they need to advance their talents and participate in civil discourse. College and university campus leadership should embrace the vision that inclusive excellence is the process of developing access, student success, and high-quality learning, according to the Association of American Colleges and Universities (AAC&U, 2016). AAC&U maintains that addressing diversity, inclusion, and equity is the bedrock of a democratic culture. Of course, accomplishing inclusive excellence requires institutional support, research, and planning related to student profiles, campus climate, cultural competences, resource prioritization, and active learning – especially among historically underserved populations. Additionally, institutions must go beyond the numerical representation of diversity and assist all members of the campus community with achieving their goals. By embedding diversity into their educational opportunities, institutions can facilitate excellence in student development, research, teaching, institutional functioning, local and global community engagement, and workforce development (AAC&U, 2016).

Reframing the organizational structure in higher education begins with considering two levels: the unit (teacher) level and the administrative level. On the unit level, the teacher must be aware of not only his or her personal values and cultural background but also the values and backgrounds of students and peers. In 2013, the Interstate Teacher Assessment and Support Consortium (In TASC) 2016 released its new education standards. Among the 10 standards that underscore teachers helping students as learners, InTASC Standard #2, Learning Differences, recommends that teachers, "use(s) understanding of individual differences and diverse cultures and communities to ensure inclusive learning environments ..." (p. 1)

On the administrative level, the following factors should be considered:

- Having a defined set of values and principles, while demonstrating behaviors, attitudes, policies, and structures that enable administrators to work effectively cross-culturally
- Having the capacity to (a) value multiple perspectives, (b) honestly evaluate self-bias, (c) manage the dynamics of difference, and (d) acquire and institutionalize cultural knowledge

Administrators need to consider three areas in order to better promote cultural competence and encourage educators to develop and leverage their cultural assets.

1. Leaders should look for ways to integrate the multiple perspectives of their faculty and staff into the decision-making perspective.
2. Leaders should consider how to build a community where all faculty feel empowered and valued.
3. Leaders should constantly question the status quo and work closely with their colleagues to create goals that promote inclusiveness, equity, and empowerment among diverse faculty and staff.

Creating Culturally Competent Leaders

THE PURPOSE OF LEADERSHIP

Culturally competent academic leadership involves understanding the culture of diverse populations served by the university. Equally important here is critical thinking, which provides an epistemological framework for assessing acquired knowledge and translating it into culturally competent administrative decisions (Williams, 2006). Culturally competent administrators should obtain three types of skills:

1. Process skills: Process skills refer to the development of strategy via reflection and interpretation of environments and situations.
2. Conceptualization skills: Conceptualization skills include understanding contextualized meanings, subtle nuances, and nonverbal cues, as well as engaging in innovative thinking.
3. Personalization skills: Personalization skills that function in learning the behaviors of the diverse population, encouraging multiple perspectives, and taking responsibility for acquiring specialized knowledge and skills.

On a majority of college and university campuses, the chief diversity officer is the primary person responsible for planning, implementing, and monitoring diversity initiatives. Therefore, this individual is considered the institutional diversity leader. However, all university administrators, including department chairs, college deans, and university vice presidents, should partner with the chief diversity officer in the responsibilities of creating an inclusive campus environment. Having all institutional administrators work together in this way has several benefits including (a) sending a clear message to the campus community that diversity is an institutional priority; (b) ensuring that the momentum of the diversity agenda is maintained even if there is a change in the position of the chief diversity officer; and (c) providing the chief diversity officer greater access to the various campus constituencies. For example, while curriculum is the primary purview of the faculty, it can also be a place where institutional diversity goals and learning outcomes can be articulated, implemented, and assessed. However, this cannot be done without the cooperation of administrators from academic affairs (provost, deans, and chairs).

Characteristics of a Diversity Leader

The chief diversity officer is the primary person responsible for creating a diverse campus through programs, initiatives, and building collaborative relationships. This title oftentimes comes with the responsibility to be the guardian for the common good of the campus in regards to institutional diversity and social justice. According to Thompson (2012), the chief diversity officer has many responsibilities. Among the responsibilities are the following:

1. Serve as the primary representative for the institution regarding diversity/multicultural and inclusive excellence issues.
2. Advise the president, provost and vice president for academic affairs, and deans while working collaboratively with all institutional officials to enhance the campus climate by advancing diversity as the chief spokesperson on virtually all issues involving diversity.
3. Be responsible for and serve as a consultant providing innovative leadership, guidance, and direction for all campus diversity initiatives including the development and implementation of diversity strategic plans as well as the establishment of diversity committees, study groups, and work teams focused on diversity issues.
4. Work with campus offices to serve as the university liaison and diversity ombudsperson to mediate situations of ethnic and cultural tensions before they become serious problems or enter into the grievance system.
5. Monitor all aspects of the institution's effort toward diversity with emphasis placed on the advancement of faculty, staff, and students of color.

6. Examine existing academic programs and develop new programs to ensure equitable opportunities for all members of the university community.
7. Provide leadership for academic and curricular changes that encourage cultural, language, and racial diversity.
8. Provide frequent reports depicting the progress and status of the diversity efforts ongoing at the university (p. 164).

We believe that characteristically, the term "diversity leader" refers to all campus leaders who seek to uncover what works on a given campus regarding diversity and inclusion and are caring leaders. This leader develops an acceptable diversity paradigm and invites all members of the campus community to support this mission and vision. However, educating the campus on diversity topics is not a simple task. This step requires bold and predictable leadership from a leader who is able to "build a community of shared values" (Kouzes & Posner, 1996, p. 105) – usually referred to as the "leader of the future" approach. In order to foster shared values on campus, the diversity leader must model the characteristics and personality that make change possible, as well as acutely align all activities and programs with the campus mission and vision statements.

Chin and Trimble (2015) argued that "a paradigm for diversity leadership is important ... We need to ask new questions, create new paradigms, and identify new dimensions to expand our thinking about how leadership is perceived, enacted, and appraised" (p. 17).

The Diversity Leader as Promoter of Cultural Competence

Diversity leadership, which is central to advocating and caring about people, involves motivating and inspiring individuals through a clear vision and agenda that serves the organization's needs. The diversity leader can come from many different racial and ethnic backgrounds and is often the point person for cultural competence leadership on campuses and may see their role in the organization as a person with a mission or a calling to give himself or herself to the work of the university and its members. The diversity leader works in concert with all other campus leaders to ensure that cultural competence is aligned with the institution's strategic goals.

One of the characteristics of a diversity leader is an individual who has higher expectations and greater anticipation of things to come than a leader who only relies on the mechanics of management techniques to move people to action. The diversity leader must understand the reality of the campus chain of command and should use this knowledge to assign roles to individuals, which complement their interests and talents and addresses the activities, projects, and needs of the diversity agenda. Chin and Trimble (2015) discussed reframing leadership to be "inclusive of diversity, to be responsive to broad social contexts and systems, and to be relevant to rapid changes occurring in the 21st century" (p. 54).

The diversity leader can be characterized as a caring individual who does not want to hurt another person. He or she would never want to be mean, cruel, or insensitive. The diversity leader inspires trust and confidence in the people by reshaping the purpose of the group and helping the group invest in the outcome of their actions. The diversity leader should always treat people with kindness and generosity and promote the greater good for those whom he or she directs – this leader has the responsibility to serve as an advocate and to be open to all constituents on campus. This characteristic is unique – leading by showing concern for others and being responsive to the needs of others – and exemplifies a high level of leadership competency.

By practicing the principals of caring, promoting the campus diversity agenda, and working with all other campus leaders, the diversity leader can make a difference, be successful, and gain the support of the campus community and external stakeholders. The best qualities in diversity leadership resonate with the attitude of caring and compassion; these are the right qualities to have in order to advance the strategic goal of cultural competence. These relational qualities enhance the internal and external collaboration among and between the university and its stakeholders.

An individual who is ready to assist others in finding solutions to complicated matters that involve the university community is one way to characterize the diversity leader and all other cultural competent leaders. The diversity leader works as a forerunner, contemplating the outcomes of every action, every word spoken, and every decision made pertaining to diversity issues. The diversity leader frames the reality of particular situations in a sensible, understandable manner using past successful experiences as a guide to present day solutions. It can be said that diversity leaders on college and university campuses are in the diversity business because they have a notion that their work is a calling and their commitment to advancing diversity is more than a job. The chief diversity officer, as one of the institutional diversity leaders and all other administrators who have the mandate to work on diversity issues, bring to this work different leadership styles. Here are a few that are common in education.

Different Leadership Styles

We identified five leadership styles common in higher education: (a) sustainable leadership (Hargreaves & Fink, 2006); (b) servant leadership (Greenleaf, 2007; Greenleaf & Spears, 1996); (c) collaborative leadership (Hallinger & Heck, 2010; Veal, Holland, Johnson, McCarthy, & Clift, 1995); (d) transformational leadership (de Poel, Stoker, & Van der Zee, 2014; Thoonen, Oort, Peetsma, Geijsel, & Sleegers, 2011; and (e) visionary leadership (Brown & Anfara, 2003; Nanus, 1992). While culturally competent leaders should ultimately employ the leadership style that works best for them, we would like to highlight the following leadership styles that reflect leadership traits that employ cooperation from both the leader and the followers.

SUSTAINABLE LEADERSHIP STYLE

Sustainable diversity leadership emphasizes civility on campus, which is enacted by a leader who offers an alternative to the status quo, based on diversity and inclusion. The sustainable leadership style, like the other leadership styles, displays vision and commitment to relationship building. The sustainable leader understands and puts a premium on civility, diversity, and global awareness. However, effective leaders do not expect to improve the organization simply by acting as the gatekeeper. Instead, diversity leaders using the sustainable leadership style must work to improve the campus, craft partnerships, and build collaborations with relevant units on campus to promote the strategic diversity plan. To do this, sustainable leaders must inspire followers to become involved in facing the challenges inherent to the organization's objectives, mainly by teaching purpose and values to the campus community. In short, they lead by example. In summary, sustainable leadership, according to Hargreaves (2007), is: "sustainable educational leadership and improvement preserves and develops deep learning for all that spreads and lasts, in ways that do no harm to and indeed create positive benefit for others around us, now and in the future" (p. 224).

SERVANT LEADERSHIP STYLE

Servant leadership is a style in which the leader operates as a servant and puts people first. Greenleaf and Spears (1996) recognize the importance of doing the will of the people and promoting people to makes a difference. They stated:

> The difference manifests itself in the care taken by the servant-first to make sure that other people's highest priority needs are being served. The best test and difficult to administer is: Do those served grow as persons? Do they, while being served, become healthier, wiser, freer, more autonomous, more likely themselves to become servants? And, what is the effect on the least privileged in society? Will they benefit or at least not be further deprived? (p. 6)

Greenleaf recommended that individuals should "convert themselves into affirmative builders of a better society" (p. 4). The servant leader has to have a burning desire to want to help others. In fact, other people are the servant leader's highest priority. Motivating followers to want to lead reflects the purpose of the servant leader.

COLLABORATIVE LEADERSHIP STYLE

The collaborative leadership style is inclusive and sustainable. Hargreaves and Fink (2004), who studied eight U.S. and Canadian high schools across three decades, uncovered seven principles of sustainable leadership that correlate well with a model of collaborative leadership:

1. Design learning environments that engage the mind intellectually, socially, and emotionally.
2. Plan and prepare for succession from the beginning and not as an afterthought.
3. Ensure that others share and help develop the vision.

4. Develop fair and equitable practices so all persons feel included.
5. Provide resources that attract and retain the best and brightest.
6. Promote diversity of thought and practices to achieve stated goals and activities.
7. Create an environment of innovation and support.

TRANSFORMATIONAL LEADERSHIP STYLE

The transformational leader is proficient in transforming the beliefs and attitudes of individuals for them to perform beyond what they are expected to do. This leader works to stretch the abilities of the followers to get the necessary task done (de Poel et al., 2014). Transformational leaders are like athletic coaches; they give directions, inspire, possess the vision for success, and they are impassioned leaders who expect accomplishments and results.

An example of such exemplary leadership can be found in former Tennessee women's basketball coach Pat Summitt. The late Coach Summitt won more games than anyone in college basketball history, man or woman. She was truly a transformation leader. One memorable quote from the late coach Summitt, which illustrates her belief that the right attitude can spell success, was: (2014). "I can't score for you, or get a rebound for you; I can only give you the information to be successful," (p. 1), she told her players

The transformational leader inspires individuals and lays out the blueprints for the future. They appeal to each employee to work hard and go beyond what is expected (Judge & Bono, 2000). They list three traits of transformational leaders that demonstrate their charismatic and transformative style:

1. Increase followers' self-efficacy by providing a sense of direction.
2. Increase followers' social identification with their group.
3. Influence followers through value internalization and self-engagement with projects and work. (pp. 754–755)

The transformational leader depends on the followers' commitment to the assignment and their willingness to work together with the leader to accomplish the goal at hand.

VISIONARY LEADERSHIP STYLE

Visionary leadership has many different forms, and it relies on ideas, communication, and action. Westley and Mintzberg (1989) defined visionary leadership using three dimensions:

> First, visionary leadership is a dynamic, interactive phenomenon, as opposed to a unidirectional process. Second, we assume that the study of strategic vision must take into consideration strategic content as well as the strategic contexts of product, market, issue, process, and organization. Third, we assume that visionary style can take on a variety of different forms. (p. 18)

One unique trait of the visionary leader is that this leadership style empowers those the leader works with and empowers himself or herself. The visionary leaders convert goals and strategies into a vision and promote the significance of the vision. An essential trait of this leadership style is that the leader and the followers hold each other responsible for getting things done and work together to ensure that the goals are accomplished. "… Integrity – this sense of being truly genuine – which proves crucial to visionary leadership" (p. 21) (Table 2).

Culturally Competent Practices

Culturally competent leaders perform the duties of sustainability, servant-focus, collaboration, and transformative and visionary leadership interchangeably – all of which help to foster and justify accountability. The servant leadership style can be employed by culturally competent leaders to make an organization wholesome; however, the servanthood "needs to be felt, understood, believed, and practiced if it is to be faithful" (DePree, 1992, p. 10). This sort of leader creates order, instills democratic values, adapts to controversial situations, takes risks, promotes others, and bolsters passion and commitment among the students, faculty, and staff. Ideally, the culturally competent leader sees himself or herself as a steward, placing service over self-interest. The above-mentioned leadership styles are a companion to and complement the sustainable leader.

Diversity leaders are responsible for upholding both the common good of people and the best interests of the university. Those who are culturally competent express genuine care for individuals and advocate for their ability to make the most

Table 2.   Leadership Styles that Relate to Sustainable
Leadership.

Leadership Styles	Description	Key Sustainable Traits
Sustainable leadership	Sustainable leadership spreads and lasts. It shares responsibility and does not unduly deplete human or financial resources. It cares and avoids exerting negative damage on the surrounding educational and community environment	Endures and secures success over time; it shares and cares. It pays attention to relationship building.
Servant leadership	Servant leadership focuses on those in the organization, and shows no sense of self-interest on the part of the leader. The leader steps back and supports only the interests of the followers	Provides guidance, empowerment, and commitment to growing people and growing community. Makes sure that other individuals' highest priority needs are being served
Collaborative leadership	Collaborative leadership is a humanistic principle that encourages individuals to get involved with a venture and work together	Encourages buy-in and ownership of the organization, project, or venture. Involves everyone in decision-making and problem solving
Transformational leadership	Transformational leadership takes a broad view of the issues surrounding leadership and then uses viewpoints as driving forces for meeting the overall goals of the organization	Shows a deep sense of shared purpose, motivates others, and gives support. Provides a sense of direction to followers. Encourages self-engagement among followers working on projects
Visionary leadership	Visionary leadership displays a capacity to communicate a view of a desired state of affairs that clarifies the current situation and induces a commitment to an even better future	Actively works to realize the goals and objectives of the organization. Creates a shared vision. Empowers those whom the leader works with and empowers oneself

Note. These five leadership styles are common among cultural competent leaders and among educators who care about diversity and equity issues.

significant contributions possible. Thus, they practice constantly seeking to motivate individuals via a clearly articulated vision of the campus diversity agenda. For this reason, such leaders are central to underrepresented populations on campus and may even see their role as an agent of change – an individual with an urgent mission to improve the university and all its members.

Culturally competent leaders do not simply rely on management techniques to move people to action; rather, they communicate high expectations and a greater anticipation of future prospects. The cultural competent leader bundles several leadership styles among other similar leadership styles and juxtaposes these styles in order to accomplish high-impact goals. As with the servant (and the sustainable, collaborative, transformational, and visionary leader), the culturally competent leader is a sustainable leader who uses many of the same techniques. One example of this practice is the transformational leader, who uses high levels of communication to motivate individuals to follow through on goals. The same is true with the culturally competent leader; he or she communicates effectively the needs of the organization and always keeps the big picture in mind. With a deep commitment to collaborate with the campus chain of command, the culturally competent leader assigns individuals to roles that complement their interests and talents while addressing the activities, projects, and needs of the diversity initiatives. In short, the culturally competent leader builds relationships by understanding the campus culture and its myriad personalities.

The culturally competent leader is a caring individual who would never deliberately project insensitive behavior but instead aims to treat people with kindness and generosity. These leaders radiate a distinct and predictable demeanor that promotes empathic listening and the greater good for all whom he or she directs. The culturally competent leader understands that positive intergroup relations produce positive results; therefore, they always strive toward intergroup fairness, rights, and positive outcomes. Imbued with a compassionate interpersonal attitude, these leaders foster a climate of inclusion on campus, thereby enhancing the amount of internal and external collaboration among the university and its stakeholders.

The culturally competent leader works tirelessly to elevate the campus personality from monoculture to multiculturalism, largely by inspiring idealism and positivity about the values of diversity and social justice. In their efforts to reshape the old culture, such leaders must inspire trust and confidence in campus members by promoting interpersonal congruence among groups, which tends to improve group relations and social integration (Polzer, Milton, & Swann, 2002). By aligning the positive values of diversity with the institution's strategic plan, diversity leaders are better able to locate resources for diversity awareness training and education, which can help to focus members' attention to the specifics of institutional diversity goals.

Culturally competent leaders strive to find solutions to complex campus problems, they maintain high accountability, and they are especially considerate of past experiences, historical wrongs, and ancestral lessons. Therefore, such leaders seek to frame particular situations in a sensible, understandable manner, using past successful experiences as a guide to present-day solutions. This leadership style does not hide the truth, but rather ensures that facts are open to examination by all members of the campus community. Such honesty should be rooted in the leaders' belief that advancing diversity and social justice on campus is their calling – a source of personal fulfillment that stems from performing deeply meaningful work (Bunderson & Thompson, 2009; Duffy, Bott, Allen, Torrey, & Dik, 2012; Hirschi, 2012).

The image portrayed by culturally competent leaders is paramount to their success. Campus members want to know that their diversity leaders model high standards for civility, ethical behavior, critical thinking, data-driven decision-making skills, and cultural sensitivity. The culturally competent leader is additionally expected to express the values of self-worth, dignity, and passion, as well as a sense of courage, belonging, responsibility, accountability, equality, community, and positive identity. In short, these leaders are the face of the institution regarding the important work of advancing diversity and social justice. Thus, they should possess the maturity and emotional intelligence expected of a top-ranking administrator. Whether that person is the president, chancellor, provost, vice president, dean, chair, director, or chief diversity officer, the culturally competent leadership style seeks to promote the ethics of cultural competence, inclusive excellence, and global awareness.

Undoubtedly, this leadership style poses significant challenges. However, despite its demands, it has proven to be effective in producing positive outcomes and advancing higher levels of diversity appreciation on campus. In order to be effective, however, such leaders must be fully aware that respect and affirmation are the keys to acceptance among and between all individuals, and that every member of the campus must exercise his or her own ability to build mutuality, which is the benchmark for diversity's perceived success.

Conclusion

A sustainable, culturally competent approach to academic leadership is a new paradigm, which requires a combination of passionate connections on campus to achieve the diversity imperative. By forging the practices of sustainable leadership and culturally competent leadership, we were able to design a functional leadership model that improves and preserves the diversity and inclusive excellence on college and university campuses. To this end, we developed roles and traits of the sustainable, culturally competent leader, and identified three central themes: (a) the sustainable, culturally competent leader helps solve problems related to campus diversity issues; (b) he or she builds trust among diverse campus populations, and (c) he or she involves all members of the president's leadership team and the academic community in working to meet the institution's diversity mission. To perform these tasks, the institution's diversity leader (often called the chief diversity officer) must be empowered to execute the goals of the diversity initiatives on campus in concert with the institution's strategic plan. Each member of the president's leadership team has a role to play in making sure these diversity goals are operational, through working collaboratively with the chief diversity officer.

Culturally competent IHE leaders are acutely aware that in higher education settings, bias, disagreement, resistance, and tension will naturally occur. The culturally competent leader and campus partners recognize that dealing with bias thinking, tokenism, acts of intolerance, and narrow viewpoints are opportunities for teachable moments on campus. For example, some culturally competent leaders establish a multilevel bias response team. The bias response team consists of administrators and faculty who are available to support and guide individuals seeking assistance in determining how to handle an alleged bias incident. A culturally competent leader in partnership with the president and senior campus leadership continually strive to find mutual understanding of opposing points of view in dealing with unacceptable behaviors while building a diverse and inclusive learning community.

Professionally, the chief diversity officer aims to ensure that every member of the campus community enjoys a welcoming, safe, and supportive learning environment. The chief diversity officer in concert with the senior leadership team works to satisfy the aspirations and goals of the campus and ensure the enforcement of the strategic diversity plan. Philosophically, such leaders aspire to right wrongs and inspire others to seek the truth – building a united commitment to diversity and inclusion excellence.

We maintain that the chief diversity officer would be effective if he or she adapts the sustainable, culturally competent styles and traits. This practice requires high standards and, thus, reveals higher accomplishments. The chief diversity officer on campus should be the role model among all sustainable, culturally competent leaders.

It is our belief that sustainable, culturally competent practices yield comprehensive results. The emphasis is placed on empowering people and encouraging buy-in from a broad sector of the campus.

The very soul of the diversity leader is exposed in the commission of serving as an advocate of the campus; this necessitates transparency, maturity, and a steadfast belief in the virtues of goodness and fairness. To some, this type of leadership may seem rather complicated, but nonetheless, critics aside, this leadership style produces positive outcomes, beginning with increased civility and respect among the entire campus community. By sufficiently supporting these human values and through building relationships, the campus can move in the direction of establishing cultural competence and inclusive excellence among its faculty, staff and students. By taking these steps, institutions can make significant gains in advancing cultural competence and inclusive excellence on campus in all its dimensions.

References

Association of American Colleges and Universities (2016). Making excellence inclusive. Retrieved from http://aacu.org/making-excellence-inclusive.

Banks, J. A., & Banks, C. A. M. (2009). *Multicultural education: Issues and perspectives*. Wiley.

Brown, K. M., & Anfara, V. A. (2003). Paving the way for change: Visionary leadership in action at the middle level. *Nassp Bulletin, 87*(635), 16–34.

Bunderson, J. S., & Thompson, J. A. (2009).The call of the wild: Zookeepers callings and the dual edges of deeply meaningful work. *Administrative Science Quarterly, 54*(1), 32–57. doi: 10.2189/asqu.2009.54.1.32.

Chin, J. L., & Trimble, J. E. (2015). *Diversity and leadership*. Los Angeles, CA: Sage.

Colby, S. L., & Ortman, J. M. (2015). Projections of the Size and Composition of the US Population: 2014 to 2060. US Census Bureau, *Ed*, 25-1143.

Cooper, J. E., He, Y., & Levin, B. B. (2011). *Developing critical cultural competence: A guide for 21st-century educators.* Thousand Oaks, CA: Crowin.

Coris, E. E. (2003). *Cultural competency in the management of obesity. A paper presentation for the Netcast Lectures on Obesity.* Tampa, FL: U.S. Department of Health and Human Services and the University of South Florida, College of Public Health.

Council of Chief State School Officers (2016). The interstate teacher assessment and support (inTASC). Retrieved from ccsso.org/Resources/Programs/Interstate_Teacher_Assessmemnt_Consortium_(InTASC).html

Davis, K. (1997). *Exploring the intersection between cultural competency and managed behavioral health care policy: Implications for state and county mental health agencies.* Alexandria, VA: National Technical Assistance Center for State Mental Health Planning.

de Poel, F. M., Stoker, J. I., & Van der Zee, K. I. (2014). Leadership and organizational tenure diversity as determinants of project team effectiveness. *Group and Organization Management, 39*(5), 532–560.

DePree, M. (1992). *Leadership jazz.* New York, NY: Doubleday.

Duffy, R. D., Bott, E. M., Allen, B. A., Torrey, C. L., & Dik, B. J. (2012). Perceiving a calling, living a calling, and job satisfaction: Testing a moderated, multiple mediator model. *Journal of Counseling Psychology, 59*(1), 50–59.

Five core values behind Pat Summitt's legendary leadership (2014). Retrieved from https://mollyfletcher.com/5-core-values-behind-pat-summitts-legendary-leadersh

Gasman, M., Abiola, U., & Travers, C. (2015). Diversity and senior leadership at elite institutions of higher education. *Journal of Diversity in Higher Education, 8*(1), 1–14.

Greenleaf, R. K. (2007). The servant as leader. In *Corporate Ethics and Corporate Governance* (pp. 79–85). Berlin: Springer.

Greenleaf, R. K., Frick, D. M., & Spears, L. C. (1996). *On becoming a servant-leader.* No. D10 297.

Hallinger, P., & Heck, R. H. (2010). Leadership for learning: Does collaborative leadership make a difference in school improvement? *Educational Management Administration and Leadership, 38*(6), 654–678.

Hargreaves, A. (2007). Sustainable leadership and development in education: Creating the future, conserving the past. *European Journal of Education, 42*(2), 223–233.

Hargreaves, A., & Fink, D. (2004). Seven principles of sustainable leadership. *Educational Leadership, 61*(7), 8–13.

Hargreaves, A., & Fink, D. (2006). *Sustainable leadership.* San Francisco, CA: Jossey-Bass Publishers.

Helms, J. E. (1990). An overview of black racial identity theory. In J. E. Helms (Ed.), *Black and white racial identity: Theory, research, and practice* (pp. 9–33). New York, NY: Greenwood.

Hirschi, A. (2012). Calling and work engagement: Moderated mediation model of work meaningfulness, occupational identity, and occupational self-efficacy. *Journal of Counseling Psychology, 59*(3), 479–485.

Hofstede, G. (1980). Culture and organizations. *International Studies of Management and Organization*, 10(4), 15–41. Retrieved from http://www.jstor.org/stable/40396875.

Hussar, W. J., & Bailey, T. M. (2016). *Projections of Education Statistics to 2016 Washington. DC*. NCES 2008-060. National Center for Education Statistics, Institute of Education Sciences.

Judge, T. A., & Bono, J. E. (2000). Five-factor model of personality and transformational leadership. *Journal of Applied Psychology*, 85(5), 751.

Kagawa-Singer, M., Dressler, W. W., George, S. M., & Elwood, W. N. (2014). The cultural framework for health: an integrative approach for research and program design and evaluation.

Kim, K. H., & Matthews, M. S. (2015). Cultural background. In S. Thompson (Ed.) *Encylopedia of diversity and social justice* (p. 172). New York, NY: Rowman & Littlefield.

Kouzes, J. M., & Posner, B. Z. (1996). Seven lessons for leading the voyage to the future. In Hesselbein, F.; Goldsmith, M., & Beckhard, R. (Eds.), *The leader of the future* (p. 105). San Francisco, CA: Jossey-Bass Publishers.

Kumagai, A. K., & Lypson, M. L. (2009). Beyond cultural competence: Critical consciousness, social justice, and multicultural education. *Academic Medicine*, 84(6), 782–787.

Lee, C. C. (1991). *Multicultural issues in counseling: New approaches to diversity*. Alexandria, VA: American Association for Counseling and Development.

Morton, G., & Atkinson, D. R. (1983). Minority identity development and preference for counselor race. *Journal of Negro Education*, 52(2), 156–161.

Nanus, B. (1992). Visionary Leadership: Creating a Compelling Sense of Direction for Your Organization. Jossey-Bass Inc., 350 Sansome Street, San Francisco, CA 94104-1310.

Nieto, S. (2008). Chapter 9: Culture and Education. *Yearbook of the National Society for the Study of Education*, 107(1), 127–142.

Orlandi, M. A. (1992). Defining cultural competence: An organizing framework. *Cultural competence for evaluators: A guide for alcohol and other drug abuse prevention practitioners working with ethnic/racial communities* (pp. 293–299).

Pascarella, E. T., Edison, M., Nora, A., Serra Hagedorn, L., & Terenzini, P. T. (1996). Influences on students' openness to diversity and challenge in the first year of college. *Journal of Higher Education*, 67, 174–195.

Phan, P., Vugia, H., & Jones, T. (2015). Cultural competence for college students: How to teach about race, gender and inequalities. Retrieved from http://www.nea.org/home/65432.htm.

Polzer, J., Milton, L., & Swann, W. (2002). Capitalizing on diversity: Interpersonal congruence in small work groups. *Administrative Science Quarterly*, 47(2), 296–324. Retrieved from http://www.jstor.org/stable/3094807 doi: 1.

Porath, C. L. (2012). The oxford handbook of positive organizational scholarship. In K. S. Canerib & G. M. Spreitzer (Eds.), *Civility* (pp. 439–448). New York, NY: Oxford University Press.

Reich, S. M., & Reich, J. A. (2006). Cultural competence in interdisciplinary collaborations: A method for respecting diversity in research partnerships. *American Journal of Community Psychology, 38*(1-2), 51−62.

Saunders, J. A., Haskins, M., & Vasquez, M. (2015). Cultural competence: A journey to an elusive goal. *Journal of Social Work Education, 51*(1), 19−34.

Surbone, A. (2004). Cultural competence: Why? *Annals of Oncology, 15,* 697−699.

Sutton, M. (2000, October). Cultural competence: it's not just political correctness. It's good medicine. *Family Practice Management, 7*(9).

Swail, W. S. (2002). Higher education and the new demographics: Questions for policy. *Change, 34*(4), 14−23.

Thompson, A., & Cuseo, J. B. (2009). *Diversity and the college experience.* Dubuque, IA: Krndall Hunt.

Thompson, S. (2012). *Views from the frontline: Voices of conscience on college campuses.* Champaign, IL: Common Ground Publishing.

Thoonen, E. E. J., Oort, F. J., Peetsma, T. T. D., Geijsel, F. P., & Sleegers, P. J. C. (2011). How to improve teaching practices: The role of teacher motivation, organizational factors, and leadership practices. *Educational Administration Quarterly, 47*(3), 496−536.

Trimble, J. E. (2003). Cultural sensitivity and cultural competence. In *The Portable Mentor* (pp. 13−32). Springer US.

Veal, M. L., Holland, P., Johnson, M., McCarthy, J., & Clift, R. T. (1995). *Collaborative leadership and shared decision making: Teachers, principals, and university professors.* NY: Teachers College Press.

Westley, F., & Mintzberg, H. (1989). Visionary leadership and strategic management. *Strategic Management Journal, 10*(S1), 17−32.

Williams, C. C. (2006). The epistemology of cultural competence. *Families in Society, 87*(2), 209−220.

Williams, J. P. (2014). College of tomorrow: The changing demographics of the student body. U.S. News and World Report. Retrieved from http://www.usnews.com/news/college-of-tomorrow/articles/2014/09/22/college-of-tomorrow-the-changing-demographics-of-the-student-body.

15 Addressing Race and Culture within a Critical Leadership Approach

Jennifer L. S. Chandler and
Robert E. Kirsch

Introduction

The chapter offers tenets for conducting critical leadership studies drawn from critical race theory and uses those tenets to assess a recent critical leadership study as an example.

In this theoretical essay, the authors draw from critical race theory to formulate and propose tenets for addressing race and culture within a critical leadership approach.

The authors use the framework of critical race theory to display how a critical orientation in leadership studies can yield new insights about patterns of oppression and domination. They find that without such a critical lens, the power relations and social processes of leadership are not challenged, and cannot be changed. To challenge those processes, leadership must be critically analyzed in its broader social, political, and cultural contexts.

The tenets proposed in this chapter can be employed in conducting critical leadership studies and can also be applied in assessing leadership research results.

Goals of the Chapter

This chapter has two goals. One is to provide tenets addressing race and culture for use in designing critical leadership research.

Our tenets can also be used in assessing critical leadership research. Thus, the second goal of this chapter is to deliver an example assessment of a recent critical leadership study. We conclude with some normative considerations of how to build a body of critical leadership literature.

What Makes Theory Critical?

Defining critical analysis is challenging. In the current context, to think critically is to think deeply, use reason, or otherwise think well with the aim to make citizens into an inquisitive, innovative, and lean workforce. We believe that this ambiguous and highly instrumentalized conceptualization will not do. There is much brush to be cleared away to delineate what it means to undertake critical analysis, so a brief etymological discussion of critique and what it means to be critical is appropriate. Only at that point will we be able to lay out our tenets of integrating critical race theory into analyzing critical leadership theory, and then use them to critique an empirical study to highlight their use.

The word critique originates from the Greek *krisis*. It is a medical concept that assessed whether the body's self-healing properties would be enough for recovery; if the harm exceeded the body's capacity for self-healing, the body was in crisis, necessitating an external intervention (Habermas, 1975). The socialized concept of crisis uses the body politic as a metaphor, and the critical intervention is a recognition of the need to act in order to preserve the body politic. The necessity of action recognizes that the body politic cannot heal itself through normal operations (Brown, 2005). A crisis can therefore be construed as a two-part process: (1) recognizing that there is a grave risk at a given point in society, and (2) taking some sort of corrective action. To say that one should pursue a critical leadership theory is to say that there is something disordered about the current regime of leadership theory; and corrective action must be applied.

With this understanding of crisis, the role of critical theory itself comes into sharper focus. The goal of critical theory is not only to diagnose but to offer an alternative vision that alleviates the disorder. Diagnosing the disorder requires showing the disconnect between how a theory says the world works, and the actual lived experiences of people in the world. Further, the alternative vision shows how reason might be unified in theory and in practice, toward the goal of human flourishing (Marcuse, 1968).

Any critical theory then, in any given area (such as race, politics, philosophy, or leadership), means working toward the goal of human flourishing by revealing the inadequacies of orthodox theories. Thus, the inadequacies of existing critical leadership theory are explored in the next section.

The Current Terrain of Critical Leadership Theory

With this working definition of critical theory, there is little in the academic literature on leadership that meets this threshold. The most important work in critical leadership theory that meets our conception of critical theory is from Alvesson and Spicer (2014). Their findings incorporate the inadequacies of leadership studies as currently constructed, by breaking the field of leadership studies into two camps: functionalist and interpretivist. Functionalists accept the leader–follower structures in organizations, and assess them empirically, assuming that the model itself is valid. Interpretivists try to incorporate a more diverse array of voices within organizations to elucidate effective leadership, but often miss the ideological dimension of that assessment including how forms of domination may still be reinforced even if participation is expanded (Alvesson & Spicer, 2014).

In both cases, by employing the leader–follower structure, the status quo is reaffirmed. For Alvesson and Spicer (2014), this is inappropriate, because by avoiding the ideological dimension of leadership studies, or assuming given power relations as natural or otherwise given, orthodox leadership studies foreclose on the critical insight that leadership in contemporary society is badly flawed in some way. By making that critical intervention, Alvesson and Spicer (2014) fulfill our first requirement listed above for critical inquiry. Their work attempts to fulfill our second requirement by offering a vision of "critical performativity" which builds an ethic of care that extends in and outside of the organization, affirming participants' voices by explicitly surfacing power relations, and focuses on participants' potential in the organization. Critical performativity thus gives voice to the ideological dimension of organizational and leadership relations. This growing notion of "performativity" in leadership studies is taken from feminist philosopher Judith Butler, and is most clearly explained by Cabantous, Gond, Harding, and Learmonth (2016) as a way to remedy the deficiencies in leadership studies and reorient them along the lines of human flourishing.

There is still a question of whether, and to what extent, critical performativity achieves the human flourishing part of critical theory. The concept of critical performativity is itself under critical scrutiny. There have been challenges to critical performativity on the basis of political usage of language, essentially suggesting that it is too easy to lump together old relations of domination and call it an ethic of care. The aims of Alvesson and Spicer (2014) may be to the good in an abstract sense, but if the structures or institutions through which they frame critical performativity are not changed, then altering language is merely cosmetic, and does not sufficiently engage in a critique of leadership (Fleming & Banerjee, 2016; Cabantous *et al.* 2016). Rest of this essay will explore these constructs further and offer tenets drawn from critical race theory for conducting critical leadership studies.

Critical race theory is an important lens for assessing leadership studies. It demands that the object of investigation, such as leadership, not be divorced from the complex web of its social, ethical, cultural, and political relations. Leadership cannot be abstracted out of these embedded relations, nor can it be isolated from them. We drew from critical race theory because it makes those webs of relationships the focus of analysis, and is therefore an apt lens through which to analyze the critical element in critical leadership studies. This is not to suggest that critical race theory is a panacea that can solve all the ills of leadership studies and it is beyond the scope of this chapter to provide a review of critical race theory.

Three Tenets for Addressing Race within a Critical Leadership Approach

The goal of this section is to crystallize the importance of the embedded structures, norms, and flows of power in leadership from the insights of critical race theory. Below, we offer our three tenets for addressing race and culture in critical leadership research. Our tenets are drawn from a body of academic literature concerning critical race theory (Crenshaw, Gotanda, Peller, & Thomas, 1995; Matsuda, Lawrence, Delgado, & Crenshaw, 1993). Our critical approach creates a theoretical space that highlights the ideological imperative to studying leadership as emergent phenomena within a social culture that is inherently inequitable. A critical examination of the cultural, racial, social, ethical, political, and gendered assumptions embedded in leadership practices, values, and principles, is necessary for building a theory of leadership that is inclusive and integrative. We argue that embedded in the habits of leadership are meanings and practices of racial domination and oppression. Therefore, our tenets demand a leadership approach whose normative goals include the elimination of oppression and progress toward human flourishing.

Tenet 1 − *Critical leadership studies act on the recognition that systemic racial oppression exists in all societies and that power is used in the service of maintaining that racial oppression. Critical leadership studies examine processes that contribute to the perpetuation of social inequities by race.* In other words, the assumption in critical leadership studies must be that racial oppression is ubiquitous, and steps to examine it must be a part of every critical leadership research study. This approach challenges claims of racial objectivity, neutrality, and meritocracy espoused in dominant leadership narratives by examining leadership goals, initiatives, and impacts by race using methods recommended by Blank, Dabady, and Citro (2004). The themes of neutrality and meritocracy and the narrative uses of them have been discussed extensively by researchers (Bonilla-Silva, 2010; Hill, 2009; Leonardo, 2002; San Juan, 2002; Sue, 2010) examining how dominant discourses perpetuate racism. Their body of work provides conclusions that the dominant racial ideology in the United States is a

> loosely organized set of ideas, phrases, and stories that help whites justify contemporary white supremacy; they are the collective representations whites have developed to explain, and to ultimately justify, contemporary racial inequality. Their views then are not just a "sense of group position" *but symbolic expressions of whites' dominance.* [emphasis in original] (Bonilla-Silva, 2010, p. 262)

Because the themes of meritocracy, objectivity, and neutrality are mainstays in leadership discourses, to explain the deficiencies in these assertions, we return to the insights of critical theory discussed above. A key contention of Marcuse's (1968) is that advanced industrial society has effectively neutralized opposition by flattening out rationality in such a way that all practical thought and action ends up serving the existing order. The result, Marcuse (1968) argues, is that all countercultural claims, or alternatives to the existing order are either irrational or are co-opted to the extent that they actually reinforce instead of challenge the existing order. Marcuse's (1968) one-dimensionality thesis presents the abstract concepts of neutrality, objectivity, and meritocracy as rationality itself, and so critical voices that challenge this regime are therefore irrational. To follow race as an example through Marcuse's (1968) argument: one-dimensional society sees that racial equality has been codified in law in some way, however incomplete. Organizations in this society have statements that say they comply with non-discrimination. Therefore, to suggest that racism persists is irrational. Marcuse (1968) argues that a society without opposition is impossible, but a one-dimensional society produces its own puppet of opposition in a way that ultimately reinforces the established order. Thus, the existing system is maintained.

The result is an instrumentalized rationality, a concept Marcuse (1968) offers to mean that the lived experiences and goals of humans are stripped away or deemed unimportant, and social analysis reduces subjects and objects to material that can be manipulated: "rationality assumes the form of methodological construction; organization and handling of matter as the mere stuff of control" (p. 156). Such an attitude means that social context need not be explored and the consequence of one-dimensional thought is that the supposedly scientific rationalities of meritocracy, objectivity, and neutrality reinforce patterns of domination. The everyday lives and lived experiences of people in social structures cannot matter because it is not readily quantifiable. We argue that any sufficiently critical examination of leadership as a process in organizations must grapple with and work to overcome the myths of meritocracy, objectivity, and neutrality to see the underlying relations of domination.

Tenet 2 – *Critical leadership studies accepts that leadership is an emergent property of human relations and takes a holistic view that does not focus on practices of only certain individuals by labeling them leaders and labeling some individuals followers.* Embracing a definition of leadership that eliminates hierarchical positioning of individuals shifts the focus to their interactions. Furthermore, rather than simply asking the people labeled "leaders" what they do, this tenet requires the abandonment of the leader–follower labels and requires that the embedded, unspoken, and intractable social rules be given primacy instead. This concept is addressed somewhat in the Alvesson and Spicer (2014) discussion above, especially in the deficiencies of the functionalist approach, but our tenet pushes their insight beyond research into the study of leadership itself.

Liberating leadership from the leader–follower prison also highlights that who tells the story is as important as whose story is being told. The weight of dominant narratives can drown out stories even when people of color tell their own stories of racial oppression meted out through meritocratic, neutral, and objective leadership practices. This tenet stresses a need for transparency regarding the identity components of the researchers conducting leadership studies. A cursory and complacent review of common biases during one's graduate work is insufficient to counter the constant hegemonic forces pressuring leadership researchers to collude with dominant norms. Therefore, this tenet compels leadership researchers, educators, and practitioners to undergo ongoing self-reflexive analysis to divulge their own implicit assumptions or blind spots. Inherent in conducting critical leadership studies is an ever-present acknowledgement of one's own enmeshed involvement in the very processes one attempts to study.

To address the need for such self-reflexive analysis, Hanold (2013) recommends that researchers engage in a three-part somaestheic analysis of their bodily feelings. While we agree with Hanold's (2013) analysis that "current views of the body in the leadership literature are based in naturalist and essentialist notions and that a social constructionist view of the body is needed" (p. 90), we recommend an approach that also recognizes Salancik, Calder, Rowland, Leblebici, and Conway's (1975) definition of leadership. They argue that leadership is a social process within social networks. Their relational understanding of leadership demands an analytical approach unlike a linear calculus or a binary categorization. Attending to what is created *between* people rather than parroting the hegemonic culturally embedded meanings assigned *to* people, forces one to assess the ways in which organizational norms are perpetuated. Thus, examining the norms within social networks is an alternative avenue for examining leadership.

That brings us to the distributed understanding of leadership advanced by Spillane, Halverson, and Diamond (2004) which presents the organizational context, location, and meanings as not simply a backdrop for leadership processes. The meanings and practices embedded and re-enacted in the organization are as powerful in the leadership process as the actual people. Those practices are the social norms of the organization and as such they are like lines of code or DNA segments waiting to be executed by the current crop of players (i.e., people) coming through the organization. Analyzing dominant social norms operating in organizations provides one avenue for revealing the norms and assessing one's own participation with those norms.

Tenet 3 – *Critical leadership studies aims to more fully and more deeply understand the processes of leadership rather than developing more efficient ways to teach people to be leaders.* Recognizing that existing critical leadership theory is limited also demands that those purporting to advocate a critical leadership approach attend to the purpose of studying leadership. Part of the insistence on our more holistic approach that addresses the social, cultural, and political embeddedness of the emergent processes of leadership is to recognize where relations of domination or oppression exist in the broader contexts of everyday lives and social relations. It also understands that oppression is not an isolated incident that can separated from what leadership is. Oppression seen in leadership cannot be solved simply by rearranging who is in what position in a particular leadership structure. Such attempts to isolate and "fix" instances of oppression apart from their broader embeddedness is one-dimensional as we described above. One-dimensional approaches assume that there is nothing that one can or should do about the underlying organizational norms because they are natural. The result is that attempts to alleviate oppression often end up enacting the same tactics and strategies of that very oppression, and the "improvement" is simply shifting the oppression from one group, to another group. "Lean In" feminism, for instance, reifies the corporate mode of social relations. Instead of challenging the harms modern capitalism disproportionately visits to lower socioeconomic status populations, it removes a certain class of woman from those harms and ignores or villainizes people who cannot afford day care, or who otherwise do not work in the C-suite (Williams, 2014). Such strategies do not address the underlying structures of domination because they do not begin with an acceptance that they exist nor do that accept the necessity for explicating and examining them.

Examining a Recent Critical Leadership Study

This section uses the three tenets we offered above to analyze a recent study that is self-identified as a critical leadership study. The qualitative study we chose to assess was conducted by Evans, Hassard, and Hyde (2013) who analyzed an organization comprising 99 elected officials located in the north of England. The aim of their study was to "examine the influence relationships between leaders and followers in a public-sector organization and how these relationships inform social influence processes" (p. 83). Through an ethnographic methodology, Evans *et al.* (2013) find that in the public sphere, the leader–follower dynamic is ambiguous, and determined by flows of power and game-playing for position. We chose this study to use as our example because it was published recently by a major publisher and it is titled and advertised as critical leadership. Our determinations of whether this one research example adhered to each of our tenets is intended to further illustrate the tenets themselves by demonstrating how they apply. We do not seek to establish the truth-value of the study under consideration, only to use it as an example of how our tenets derived from critical race theory can be employed to assess the critical content of critical leadership studies.

Tenet 1 – *Critical leadership studies act on the recognition that systemic racial oppression exists in all societies and that power is used in the service of maintaining that racial oppression. Critical leadership studies examine processes that contribute to the perpetuation of social inequities by race.* We assessed the degree to which Evans et al. (2013) research moved forward with the assumption that *because* race-based oppression exists within all organizations, they had a duty to transparently study it. This is especially so given that they suggest their study will "widen the scope of contributive voices" (Evans et al., 2013, p. 187).

We find that Evans et al. (2013) did not acknowledge the ubiquitous nature of race-based oppression in their study. In fact, they made no mention of race-based, or cultural-based, or identity-based oppression. In this sense, their analysis shifts into one-dimensionality, where structures are taken as given and the precepts of the power relations of various leader/follower dynamic go underanalyzed. This is significant because by not addressing the structural embeddedness of oppression *within* power relations of the leader—follower dynamic, the analysis can no longer be considered critical. Such an analysis is simply a question of which individuals are entitled through the enactment of dominant social norms to occupy positions of power and which individuals have only one option to collude with the dominant social norms further marginalizing people with whom they share identity characteristics. In other words, ignoring these vectors of oppression reifies the modes of domination that determine these power relations by ignoring their existence or taking a position of neutrality by omission. We further find this omission noteworthy since the 2000 Amendment to the Race Relations Act (RRA) (Commission for Racial Equality, 2001) created a "general statutory duty on a wide range of public authorities to promote racial equality and prevent racial discrimination" (p. 6). In other words, public organizations in Great Britain have no presumed neutrality with regards to race relations under the law. The law demonstrates that the nation accepts that current dominant social norms perpetuate race-based inequities and public organizations are bound by law to take positive action to dismantle oppressive processes and ameliorate inequities.

Tenet 2 — *Critical leadership studies accept that leadership is an emergent property of human relations and take a holistic view that does not focus on practices of only certain individuals by labeling them leaders and labeling some individuals followers.* We find that Evans et al. (2013) attempted to address power by putatively injecting their study of leadership with a dose of what they call political theory. They identified a political theory of leadership that hews too closely to the leader-centric model of leadership. We find this unsatisfactory because it defines leadership as only the behaviors, actions, and assessments of those individuals who occupy specific positions or roles within organizations. While their argument that a political theory should not leave out groups of people under consideration may sound convincing, their critique does not offer a new or better definition of politics. Politics in their text are simply assumed, and they are never clearly defined anywhere. Thus, the reader is left to infer that politics in organizations, and hence as a theory of leadership, is how people jockey for and exercise the levers of power in these already-existing organizations. Furthermore, by leaving the mechanisms of power unexamined, their interpretation is apolitical and uncritical. Their unwillingness to engage in political theories of sovereignty or structural analysis, which would be helpful in establishing a political theory of leadership, instead offers a warmed-over conception of politics that offers very little for critical leadership theory. All this stems from their unfounded commitment to the leader–follower hierarchy.

For these reasons, we find that the Evans, Hassard, and Hyde (2103) study did not comply with Tenet 2. In fact, it does the exact opposite of what our Tenet 2 recommends. In explaining the significance of their study, Evans et al. (2013) point to Critical Theory as a "perspective [which] has been generally neglected with leadership studies and could be utilized to develop a more holistic appreciation of leadership process" (p. 11), and yet they state that their study "seeks to illuminate the dynamics of the relationship between leaders and followers" (p. 4) as if this is a novel construct. They are completely wed to the leader-follower structure as revealed by their claim that all leadership scholars agree with the leader-follower structure "the essence of leadership therefore, is followership; there can be no leader without followers" (p. 24). Rather than clinging to a structure that contributes little to the understanding of leadership as a process except generating a great deal of what Evans et al. (2013) referred to as ambiguity, we recommend discarding the leader–follower labeling entirely. Such an approach ends the continuing need for classifying the interactions as "ambiguous" as Evans et al. (2013) did. Furthermore, it obviates the need for statements like this: "leaders and followers need each other and, due to complex multiple identities and observances, they can at times be the same thing" (p. 134).

Tenet 3 – *Critical leadership studies aim to more fully and more deeply understand the processes of leadership rather than developing more efficient ways to teach people to be leaders.* Our tenet 3 requires that critical leadership research explicate the intricate processes of leadership rather than searching for tips and tricks to teach those who want to climb their respective organizational ladders. This requires researchers to eschew a functional approach that perpetuates the status quo and instead cast a wider net that includes and examines the counterstories that exist within organizations alongside the dominant ones. The counterstories function not only to reveal the dominant norms, they offer the starting points for modifying those norms. The dominant norms must be examined as a part of critical leadership studies and critical leadership researchers must also examine their participation with those norms.

Assessing Evans et al. (2013) along this tenet for addressing race and culture within a critical leadership approach was muddled because Evans et al. (2013) addressed four possible definitions for leadership. In their first possibility, they did not consider leadership as a process. This definition simply considers the people in power as "leaders" and whatever those individuals do is then labeled leadership. This overly simplistic definition fails to meet the critical guidelines put forth by Alvesson and Spicer (2014), noted above, to say nothing of its inadequacy to our tenets. In other words, their first definition is both functionalist and one-dimensional. The second leadership definition that Evans et al. (2013) presented was that leadership is what is accomplished. Again, in this definition, only the people in power are the focus as they are labeled "leaders" and the collective efforts of everyone else involved were attributed to those "leaders." This reified vision of leadership normalizes certain modes of power relations, leaving them unexamined. This second definition falls into the interpretivist category laid out by Alvesson and Spicer (2014). Even if this kind of leadership takes into account the attitudes and contributions of a more cohesive organizational unit, it fails to critically examine the underlying structures that produce those power relations at the start. The third definition Evans et al. (2013) presented considers the actual position of power as leadership regardless of who fills that position. Using this definition acknowledges that the actual people may come and go, but leadership still is not framed as a process; it is simply a position atop the essentialized hierarchy of the leader-follower model. All three of our tenets show the inadequacy of assuming that power hierarchies are natural, or that people who are in those positions do so because of some blind, objective, or meritorious process. Our tenets push past this level of analysis because instead of asking the rules by which certain people may or may not be invited to hold certain positions of power, we ask how the dynamics whereby these unequal power relations can be abolished toward a better society. Lastly, leadership is defined as a process. However, Evans et al. (2013) only focus on *how* things are done. No mention is made of what is done or what is not done, or the context in which things are done. By addressing only the how, they leave aside the most important argument and are unable to formulate a critical leadership study that takes those contexts into account. The shortcomings of these definitions of leadership bring into sharp focus the effects of one-dimensional thought. The commitment to the hierarchically organized leader–follower dynamic as inherently rational shows Evans, Hassard, and Hyde's (2103) inability to use a truly critical lens when examining the behaviors and interactions in the organization they studied. Even more so, that this is billed as a critical engagement lends strength to the hypothesis that in a one-dimensional society, opposition is generated internally but only in a way that is easily absorbed by, and to the benefit of, the status quo. To say that Evans et al.'s (2013) work is one-dimensional is to suggest that their work has not met the threshold for critical analysis, and we have highlighted places where they have fallen short.

We have little to say about the Evans et al. (2013) study on its own merits. In fact, we believe the findings are valid, and are well-positioned in the orthodox theory of leadership studies. Our critique finds its footing on the fact that this is a self-positioned "critical" study. Using our tenets, we have found that while this is a valuable contribution to leadership studies, it is not a contribution to *critical* leadership studies.

Conclusion

Those advocating critical leadership approaches must do more than simply offer criticisms; critique offers not only a diagnosis of social illness, but the necessity of corrective action. As a result, they must do more than dress up leadership using new fashionable adjectives as Western (2013) does with the label "eco-leadership." Western (2013) claims to take a critical approach to leadership and yet describes that in his own consulting practice with CEOs of multinational organizations that his goal is to "begin at the beginning" and "approach the organization without pre-ordained ideas of what leadership should *look like*" [emphasis added] (p. 312). We suggest that critical leadership theorists and practitioners like Western (2013) must be less concerned with what leaderships looks like and more invested in the foundational definition of critical leadership itself. To warrant the critical moniker, that definition must be more than a facile reference to influence among people that permeates existing leadership texts. The reason for this is simple. Without a definition of critical leadership that sets it apart, the frame through which we examine the social processes called "leadership" has not changed. If the frame has not changed, how can we discover as-yet undiscovered constructs? Our goal as leadership researchers is to discover, and a critical frame of race and culture is one lens to begin the examination of leadership processes more critically. Using a critical leadership approach must offer opportunities for discovering new things. In this essay, we offered three tenets for addressing race and culture within a critical leadership approach. Thus, we have expanded, transformed, and defined segments of the frame called critical leadership to support such opportunities. Using those tenets to assess a recent critical leadership study, we have demonstrably advanced the utility of taking such a critical leadership approach. As critical leadership research accumulates, the degree to which that research adheres to the tenets we provided can be assessed. Such work will benefit the research as the tenets themselves can be refined for critical leadership research must address all forms of oppression for it to truly have an aim of liberation and human flourishing.

Discussion Questions

- How are leadership researchers and theorists rewarded, or conversely sanctioned, for employing a critical lens addressing race and culture in their work that reveals structural organizational inequities?
- How does a one-dimensional society deploy concepts of neutrality, objectivity, and nondiscrimination as a way to perpetuate race-based oppression?
- What might a leadership study that eschews the leader-follower dichotomy look like?

References

Alvesson, M., & Spicer, A. (2014). Critical perspectives on leadership. In D. V. Day (Ed.), *The Oxford handbook of leadership and organizations* (pp. 40–57). New York, NY: Oxford University Press.

Blank, R. M., Dabady, M., & Citro, C. F. (Eds.). (2004). *Measuring discrimination: Panel on methods for assessing discrimination*. Washington, DC: The National Academies Press.

Bonilla-Silva, E. (2010). *Racism without racists* (3rd ed.). Lanham, MD: Rowman & Littlefield Publishers, Inc.

Brown, W. (2005). *Edgework: Critical essays on knowledge and politics*. Princeton, NJ: Princeton University Press.

Cabantous, L., Gond, J., Harding, N., & Learmonth, M. (2016). Critical essay: Reconsidering critical performativity. *Human Relations, 69*(2), 197–213.

Commission for Racial Equality. (2001). The General Duty to Promote Racial Equality: Guidance for Public Authorities on their Obligations under the Race

Relations (Amendment) Act 2000. Commission for Racial Equality. London, England: Commission for Racial Equality.

Crenshaw, K., Gotanda, N., Peller, G., & Thomas, K. (Eds.). (1995). *Critical race theory: The key writings that formed the movement.* New York, NY: The New Press.

Evans, P., Hassard, J., & Hyde, P. (2013). *Critical leadership: Leader–follower dynamics in a public organization.* New York, NY: Routledge.

Fleming, P., & Banerjee, S. (2016). When performativity fails: Implications for critical management studies. *Human Relations, 69*(2), 257–276.

Habermas, J. (1975). *Legitimation crisis.* (T. McCarthy, Trans.) Boston, MA: Beacon Press.

Hanold, M. (2013). (De/Re)Constructing leading bodies. In L. R. Melina, G. J. Burgess, L. L. Falkman, & A. Marturano (Eds.), *The embodiment of leadership* (pp. 89–107). San Francisco, CA: Jossey-Bass.

Hill, J. H. (2009). *The everyday language of White racism.* Chichester: Wiley-Blackwell.

Leonardo, Z. (2002). The souls of White folk: Critical pedagogy, whiteness studies, and globalization discourse. *Race Ethnicity and Education, 5*(1), 29–50.

Marcuse, H. (1968). *One-dimensional man.* Boston, MA: Beacon Press.

Matsuda, M. J., Lawrence, C. R., Delgado, R., & Crenshaw, K. W. (1993). *Words that wound: Critical race theory, assaultive speech, and the First Amendment.* Boulder, CO: Westview Press.

Salancik, G., Calder, B., Rowland, K., Leblebici, H., & Conway, M. (1975). Leadership as an outcome of social structure and process: A multidimensional analysis. In J. G. Hunt & L. L. Larson (Eds.), *Leadership frontiers* (pp. 81–101). Kent, OH: Kent State University.

San Juan, E. (2002). *Racism and cultural studies: Critiques of multiculturalist ideology and the politics of difference.* Durham, NC: Duke University Press.

Spillane, J. P., Halverson, R., & Diamond, J. B. (2004). Towards a theory of leadership practice: A distributed perspective. *Journal of Curriculum Studies, 36*(1), 3–34.

Sue, D. W. (2010). *Microaggressions in everyday life: Race, gender, and sexual orientation.* Hoboken, NJ: Wiley.

Western, S. (2013). *Leadership; A critical text* (2nd ed.). London: Sage Publications.

Williams, C. (2014). The happy marriage of capitalism and feminism. *Contemporary Sociology: A Journal of Reviews, 43*(1), 58–61.

Epilogue

Ian O. Williamson

Today, almost every aspect of life is shaped by global factors. The advancements in communication technology, the rise of multinational companies, the proliferation of global trade agreements, and widespread migration means that how we live, how and where we work, and how we enjoy our leisure time are all influenced by the action or inaction of people on a global scale. The pervasive impact of globalization is evident, yet it remains largely underrepresented in dominant theories of leadership. Leadership is still researched and taught, for the most part, from an Anglo-Western-male capitalistic perspective. But the existing paradigm of leadership must be challenged if leadership research and training is to remain relevant and impactful. This book is that challenge.

The writers in this book highlight the value of Indigenous cultural perspectives of leadership. They push existing boundaries by providing new tools to consider the role of religion, culture, and race in developing leadership models. They provide valuable information to help guide the training and development of leaders by educational institutions and organizations, and explore leadership across a variety of settings, including business, military, educational, and civic organizations.

Leadership is most often defined as a set of actions by an individual or individuals that facilitate the accomplishment of a predetermined goal. Building on this definition, contemporary research has focused on examining the actions that leaders can take to increase the likelihood of achieving a goal. Indeed, many leadership theories have been developed to code and articulate the different behaviors leaders can undertake (e.g., transformational leadership, servant leadership, transactional leadership, charismatic leadership). These theories can be very effective in helping individuals address the question of "*how* to lead." But a less examined question is *"what* goals should leaders attempt to accomplish." The answer to that question is often not straightforward, particularly in a world characterized by increased globalization and greater interaction between dissimilar individuals and groups.

Numerous factors are contributing to the increased difficulty leaders face when answering the "what should we do question." The activities of a global organization can be hugely impacted by shifts in the areas of economic growth (e.g., the ASEAN region), the increased expansion of non-western multinational companies (e.g., Chinese firms), political calls for protectionism and reservations about global trade, and ongoing debates about environmental concerns. All of these issues mean that leaders must first give thorough consideration to what the goal is before they can focus on how to achieve it. This will invariably require great skill in balancing numerous and potentially conflicting interests. For example, in a corporate setting, how should leaders weigh the issues of employee well-being, financial performance, customer satisfaction, civic community engagement, and investor returns? In a government or not-for-profit setting, how should leaders weigh the issues of community economic well-being, respect for traditional culture and religion, or support for diversity and efficient allocation of resources? Much of the literature and training on leadership starts with the assumption that the appropriate goal has been selected by the leader(s). But if the goal is suboptimal or inappropriate, then there is no value in efficiently executing it using highly developed skill sets and behaviors. The choice of the goal is a critical aspect of leadership and leaders are not always equipped to make this decision.

To some extent the navigation of this choice is shaped by the leader's personal values. Organizations do, however, play an important role in shaping the values of their members. It is particularly incumbent upon educational institutions to develop and offer curricula that support students in answering foundational questions such as: What is a culturally appropriate goal? What are economically, socially, and environmentally sustainable goals? Addressing these issues will require a strong interdisciplinary approach to leadership training, and educational institutions will need to experiment with new approaches to training future and current leaders.

One such experiment is the Melbourne Business School's (Australia) Asia Pacific Social Impact Center. The Center's goal is to examine the intersection between business and social interests in order to solve intractable social issues. Its activities consist of research projects on social impact issues, the creation of community engagement projects to alleviate social challenges, and the development of innovative pedagogy to expose students to the nexus between economic and social concerns. For example, students have the opportunity to intern with Australian Indigenous businesses to gain insight into the development of a culturally appropriate business. The center has also created cross-sector alliances to deliver unique classes to students, such as the partnership between the business school, the chamber of commerce from a rural Australian community, and a leading global consulting firm. This partnership allows MBA students, in close consultation with community representatives, to develop and implement a community economic growth strategy. In addition, the Full-time MBA and Executive MBA students are required as part of their respective curriculum to provide consulting services to social enterprises. The Asia Pacific Social Impact Center is just one example of innovation in education that expands leadership development to both the "how" and "what" questions surrounding business decisions.

Another issue to consider when determining what makes a "good leader" is whether that person needs to be a leader of all or a leader of a few. This will directly impact "who the followers should be" and accordingly, "what the goal should be." Much of the academic research on diversity highlights the benefits that organizations and social systems receive from the presence of diverse experiences, thoughts and beliefs. Leadership research and training largely builds on this idea and often starts with an assumption that good leaders can bring together individuals from diverse backgrounds to accomplish a task. However, this assumption is somewhat inconsistent with the actual behaviors observed in groups globally. In many countries, leaders have publicly embraced a targeted approach of leading groups composed of similar others, whether this similarity be based on religion, political belief or ethnic background. Leaders who have uncompromising positions on issues or leaders who adopt "fundamentalist" labels (irrespective of the cause or issue) have been publicly praised because they have a focused message that resonates with a defined audience, even if the message overtly excludes others. By simplifying who they lead, this approach to leadership attempts to navigate the complexities of a global environment by simplifying the goals to which leaders aspire.

The pragmatic benefits of tailoring goals to targeted audience are obvious, but are not ideal for supporting global leadership. Traditional Western-based leadership theories have been appropriately criticized for homogenizing or dismissing the diverse experiences of others. This book appropriately calls for newer and more heterogeneous models of leadership to be developed that are built upon the values, beliefs, and experiences of specific groups. Yet, it is possible for the pendulum to swing too far the other way. Does exercising Maori leadership mean you can only lead Maori's? Does exhibiting Muslim leadership mean you can only lead Muslims? If the answer to these questions is yes, then a heterogeneous or diverse approach could create just as many limitations to global leadership as a homogeneous approach. It is unlikely that avoiding complexity makes the world less complex.

The insights in this book provide an important counterpoint to traditional perspectives on leadership and bring legitimacy to perspectives that have been under-researched or misunderstood. These new insights should be used to help people develop skills that allow them to be more effective and impactful across a wider range of situations. However, the practical insights must be coupled with a reflection on the broader picture of leadership in a truly global context. I encourage the readers of this book to reflect on these insights as well as how the research presented can be used to encourage all leaders to consider a larger set of goals and engage in a broader repertoire of behaviors. This will provide a strong foundation for developing excellence in global leadership.

About the Authors

Marco Aponte-Moreno is an Assistant Professor of Global Business at Saint Mary's College of California. His research focuses on leadership and cross-cultural management. He also researches the role of the arts in leadership development and communication. He has written extensively about political leadership in Venezuela, his native country. He has lived abroad most of his life in France, the United Kingdom, and the United States. He is fluent in English, Spanish, and French.

Christie Caldwell is a Senior Consultant with Aperian Global. She conducts research and writes regularly on topics related to globalization, with particular focus on leadership development for high potentials in fast-growth markets. Originally from the United States, she has spent over 14 years as an expatriate in Asia and Europe. She holds an MA degree from Harvard University and also completed an MA program in Chinese Studies at Johns Hopkins School of Advanced International Studies in Nanjing, China.

Jennifer L. S. Chandler, PhD, is a Lecturer in the Leadership and Interdisciplinary Studies Program at Arizona State University. Her current research examines leadership in a National Science Foundation (NSF) Engineering Research Center (ERC) comprising researchers at Arizona State University, UC Davis, New Mexico State, and Georgia Tech. Her previous research has used critical race theory in the examination of Whiteness norms employed across the United States.

Po Chung, SBS, OBE, JP, is Co-founder of DHL International and Chairman of Hong Kong Institute of Service Leadership & Management. He has dedicated his professional life in large part to understanding how to provide superb service, how to educate others as superior service leaders, and how to design and operate service sector organizations. He is also author of the Service Masters Editions: *The First Ten Yards, Service Reborn, The 12*

Dimensions of a Service Leader, and *25 Principles of Service Leadership.*

Caroline S. Clauss-Ehlers is an Associate Professor in the Department of Educational Psychology at the Graduate School of Education, Rutgers, The State University of New Jersey. She is a New York state licensed psychologist. She has been appointed by the New York State Board of Regents to serve as a member of the New York State Board for Psychology to assist them in the regulation of licensure, conduct, and the practice of psychologists in New York State. She is dedicated to public education efforts that promote awareness of mental health and educational equity. She has written, co-authored, and/or authored four books that focus on topics that include cultural resilience among children and families, culturally responsive school mental health, and cultural competence. She currently serves as the Chair of the American Psychological Association's Task Force on Re-envisioning the Multicultural Guidelines for the 21st Century.

Ed Cunliff is an innovative and reflective educator who facilitates organizational and individual growth. He teaches courses in program evaluation and transformative learning as a professor of adult and higher education in the College of Education and Professional Studies at the University of Central Oklahoma. He also serves as the Co-Editor of the *Journal of Transformative Learning* and the *Transformative Learning Conference Proceedings.*

Brighid Dwyer (PhD) is the Director of the Program on Intergroup Relations at Villanova University. She is also an Assistant Professor in the Communication Department and Department of Education and Counseling. Her research explores dialogue, diversity and inclusion, leadership, Minority-Serving Institutions, and students' cross-racial interactions in college. Her work has been published in several edited books and journals including *Creating Inclusive Campuses for Cross-cultural Learning and Student Engagement* (NASPA, 2007), *Today's College Students: A Reader* (Peter Lang, 2014), *Educational Foundations,* and the *Journal of Peace and Justice Studies.*

Rob Elkington is the CEO, and President, of Global Leadership Initiatives (www.globalleader.ca). Rob holds a PhD from North West University, and an Advanced Certificate in Intercultural Management from Notre Dame University. He is an Adjunct Professor at the University of Ontario Institute of Technology serving in both the Business and IT faculty and the Education faculty where he teaches undergraduate courses in Critical Thinking and Ethics, Collaborative Leadership, Leadership Negotiation and Teamwork, Business Ethics, and graduate courses in Foundations of Leadership, Leadership and Technology, and Ethics and Leadership. He is also an *Associate Professor* at the Yorkville University serving with the Faculty of Education, *Senior Lecturer* with the Stellenbosch University School of Public Leadership and Good Governance (http://www. sun.ac.za/english/faculty/economy/spl/centres-institutes/sggf),   a *Facilitator* with the UOIT Management Development Centre (http://mdc.uoit.ca) where he has been asked to facilitate one day seminars on Foundations of Leadership, Critical Thinking and Problem Solving, Critical Decision Making, Diversity and Leadership, Advanced Leadership, and Leadership & Customer Service. He serves as *Community Liaison and Mentor* with the Durham Community Innovation Lab (http://communityilab.ca), an Entrepreneurship incubator that develops Not Employed or Educated or Trained (NEET) youth in start-up ventures. Durham Co-ILab also supports Social Entrepreneurship.

Timothy Forde is the Chief Diversity Officer and Special Assistant to the Executive Vice President at Eastern Kentucky University (EKU). He is also an Associate Professor in the Department of School of Clinical Educator Preparation at EKU. He completed his PhD at Vanderbilt University and had written and presented extensively over the past ten years on the topics of diversity, cultural competence, and the use of emerging instructional technologies to facilitate higher order thinking skills.

Kem Gambrell is an Associate Professor in the Doctoral Program in Leadership Studies at Gonzaga University. She holds a doctorate from the University of Nebraska in Leadership and Human Sciences. Her research interests include understanding Alaska Indian and Native Americans, underrepresented groups, cultural competency, and constructive development as they relate to leadership and leadership development.

Ralph A. Gigliotti (MA, MPA) is Assistant Director for the Center for Organizational Development & Leadership at Rutgers University, where he oversees a number of faculty and staff leadership development initiatives and leads several research projects related to leadership and communication in higher education. He also serves as the co-director of the Rutgers Leadership Academy and co-director of the Distinction in Leadership in Academic

Healthcare Program. His research interests explore the intersection of organizational communication, leadership, and crisis communication, particularly in the context of higher education. His research appears in numerous books and journals, including the *Journal of Leadership and Organizational Studies, Journal of Leadership Education*, and the *Atlantic Journal of Communication*. He is also the co-author of *A Guide for Leaders in Higher Education: Core Concepts, Competencies, and Tools* (Stylus Publishing, 2017).

Nyasha M. GuramatunhuCooper, PhD, is an Assistant Professor of Leadership Studies at Kennesaw State University. She earned a doctorate from Gonzaga University in Leadership Studies, with a focus on leadership in Southern African armed liberation movements. Living in Zimbabwe, Germany, and the United States, as well as travelling around the world, heavily (and happily) informs her work and passion: examining leadership as a culturally and socially mediated practice. Additional teaching and research interests include examining current events and global issues to understand the historical, cultural, social, and political contexts of leadership and the lived experiences and identities of leaders and followers.

Robert E. Kirsch, PhD, is an Assistant Professor in the Leadership and Interdisciplinary Studies Program at Arizona State University. His current research focuses on leadership approaches toward overcoming institutional inertia to implement changes that value broadening participation efforts. He is a principal investigator on a National Science Foundation (NSF) grant on GEO Opportunities for Leadership in Diversity, along with researchers at the University Corporation for Atmospheric Research, Kansas State University, San Diego State University, and University of the Virgin Islands.

Lina Klemkaite holds a degree in sociology (University of Vilnius, Lithuania), an MA in Migrations, Conflicts, and Social Cohesion in the Global Society (University of Deusto, Spain), and a University-specific degree in Human Rights (Universidad del País Vasco, Spain). Currently, she is enrolled in the Doctoral Programme on Migration Studies (University of Granada). She is experienced in project management and evaluation, specializing in social innovation and diversity management. SYLFF (The Ryoichi Sasakawa Young Leaders Fellowship Fund Program) fellow and co-author of *"Local Initiatives to the Global Financial Crisis"* (Deusto Digital, 2012).

Konstantinos Koulouris graduated with an MSc in management from University College London. His dissertation, which analyzed the impact of personal stories on leadership communication, inspired this chapter. He is originally from Athens, Greece, where he graduated with a BA in communication studies. He has lived in four different countries and has travelled extensively. He is currently a research associate with the Gerson Lehrman Group in London.

Hema A. Krishnan is a Professor of Strategy and Global Business at Xavier University, Cincinnati. She also has several years of business experience at the managerial level in the petroleum industry in India. She conducts research in the areas of mergers/ acquisitions, top management teams, and corporate restructuring, and has published over 35 articles in premier journals of business, including *Strategic Management Journal, Journal of Management Studies, Oxford University Press, and Business Horizons*. She teaches International Management, Strategic Management, Strategic Leadership, and Global Strategic Thinking.

Hildie Leung, PhD, is an Assistant Professor at the Department of Applied Social Sciences in The Hong Kong Polytechnic University. Her research centers on positive youth development and its application to the promotion of healthy adolescent development and the prevention of problem behaviors among children and adolescents.

Li Lin, PhD, is a Research Assistant Professor in the Department of Applied Social Sciences at The Hong Kong Polytechnic University. Her research interests involve positive youth development, family and parenting, service leadership, and program evaluation.

Yvonne R. Masakowski is an Associate Professor of Strategic Leadership at the U.S. Naval War College with a distinguished career spanning over 20 years. Her leadership and scientific research have made a significant impact on the national and international scientific community. She has been the recipient of the *Czech Republic's Cross of Merit*, France's *Ministère de la Défense Sciences medal*, the *Civilian Meritorious Service Award*, and the US *Navy Achievement Award*.

Afsaneh Nahavandi is Professor of Leadership at the University of San Diego and Professor Emerita at Arizona State University.

She is the author of the *Art and Science of Leadership*, now in its 7th edition. She has several additional books including *Ancient Leadership Wisdom, Organizational Behavior*, and *Organizational Behavior: The Person–Organization Fit, Organizational Culture in the Management of Mergers*, as well as many publications about leadership, culture, teams, and ethics in journals such as the *Academy of Management Review*, the *Journal of Management Education*, and the *Journal of Business Ethics*.

Eddie Ng, PhD, is a Research Assistant Professor in the Department of Applied Social Sciences at The Hong Kong Polytechnic University. His research focuses on positive youth development, particularly from the community psychology perspective. He is also interested in the area of spirituality and well-being.

Tom Otieno, PhD, is Interim Dean of the College of Science and Professor of Chemistry at Eastern Kentucky University. His research involves the synthesis of various classes of transition metal complexes, determination of their physical and chemical properties, and the correlation of these properties with the structures of the complexes. In addition to numerous scientific publications, he has published articles in the areas of academic leadership, faculty development, diversity, and university/K-12 partnerships.

Lynn Pasquerella is President of the Association of American Colleges and Universities and former president of Mount Holyoke College. A philosopher whose career has combined teaching and scholarship with local and global engagement, she is committed to championing liberal education, inclusive excellence, and the ideal of colleges and universities as civic missions. She has written extensively on medical ethics, metaphysics, public policy, and the philosophy of law and is the host of Northeast Public Radio's *The Academic Minute*.

Ethan Prizant is a Project Manager at Aperian Global. He supports clients in the design and implementation of leadership development programs and conducts research on global leadership. Originally from the United States, he has spent five years as an expatriate in China. He holds a BA degree in Asian Studies from the University of California, Berkeley and a Graduate Certificate in Chinese Studies from the Johns Hopkins School of Advanced International Studies in Nanjing, China.

Kristi Robertson is a graduate student pursuing a master's degree in adult and higher education from the University of Central Oklahoma. At the time this research was being conducted, she worked as a graduate research assistant for Dr. Jeanetta D. Sims and Dr. Ed Cunliff through their funded interdisciplinary grant. She has co-authored several research conference presentations, and this is her first publication.

Kristina Ruiz-Mesa (PhD) is an Assistant Professor of Communication Studies and serves as the Basic Course Director of Oral Communication at California State University, Los Angeles. Her research interests involve critical communication pedagogy, and improving communicative practices for diversity and inclusion in U.S. institutions of higher education. Her previous research on the academic impact of experiencing racial microaggressions in higher education has been used to create pre-college bridge programs and improve support services for under-represented students. She teaches a variety of courses including Instructional Communication, Sex Roles in Communication, Oral Communication, Research Methods, and Feminism in Communication.

Damini Saini is currently an Assistant Professor and a key member of Library and Research committee at IMS, University of Lucknow. She has earned her PhD from Faculty of Management Studies (FMS), University of Delhi and availed Junior and Senior Research Fellowship in HRM (OB). She has qualified the NET and has been awarded UGC's Research Fellowships. She has been awarded for the Best research paper award twice, including PRMEs Conference "Responsible Management Education, Training and Practice" (2015). She has also contributed to nationally and internationally acclaimed journals including Springer and in various conferences.

Daniel T. L. Shek, PhD, FHKPS, BBS, SBS, JP, is Chair Professor of Applied Social Sciences and Associate Vice President at The Hong Kong Polytechnic University. He is the Editor in Chief of *Applied Research in Quality of Life* and *Journal of Youth Studies*. His research interests include leadership, mental health, youth development, and family processes.

Jeanetta D. Sims is an assistant dean in the Jackson College of Graduate Studies and a professor in the Marketing Department of the College of Business at the University of Central Oklahoma. She is accredited in public relations, and her program of research includes strategic communication, workforce diversity, and persuasion and social influence. She founded Diverse Student Scholars, an undergraduate research engagement program, now in its tenth year. Her sole- and co-authored research appears in multiple book chapters and journals.

Atoya Sims holds a master's degree in adult and higher education from the University of Central Oklahoma and works as a human resources administrator with Ford Audio-Video Systems, LLC. As an undergraduate and graduate student, she worked as a research assistant in Diverse Student Scholars. She has multiple publications and research conference presentations related to various aspects of workforce diversity, and she has earned two Top Paper Awards at conferences for her co-authored research.

Sherwood Thompson is a professor at Eastern Kentucky University. He has three edited books: *Views From The Frontline: Voices of conscience on College Campuses, Coping With Gender Inequities: Critical Conversations of Women Faculty*, and a two-volume Encyclopedia of Diversity and Social Justice. He published 64 articles, essays, and papers all variously concerned with education and social justice. He has attained distinction through a lengthy and productive career in an array of leadership positions that served the academic needs of diverse students, faculty, and staff.

Elizabeth A. Tuleja, PhD, is an Associate Professor at the Mendoza College of Business, University of Notre Dame, where she teaches intercultural communication and global leadership. She also has had the honor to serve as a Fulbright Scholar in China. Prior to Notre Dame, she taught at the Wharton School and the Chinese University of Hong Kong. She holds a Master's degree in Intercultural Communication and a Doctorate in Education from the University of Pennsylvania, graduating with distinction. She consults with clients such as Boeing, U.S. Marines, U.S. Army, Merrill Lynch, Morgan Stanley, Bank of America, AXA, Marriott International, Verizon, China Development Bank, and HSBC. She is the author of two books: *Intercultural Communication for Business* (GlobeComm, 2015) and *Intercultural Communication for Global Leadership: How Leaders Communicate for Success* (Routledge, 2017). She has also developed a popular online executive certificate course (http://goo.gl/fM0XoN) in Advanced Intercultural Management through the University of Notre Dame/University Alliance.

Melba J. T. Vasquez is in independent practice in Austin, TX. She is a former president of the American Psychological Association, and of APA Divisions 17 (Society of Counseling Psychology), 35 (Society for the Psychology of Women), and the Texas Psychological Association. She has an extensive record of scholarship in the areas of ethics, multicultural psychotherapy, psychology of women, counselling, and psychotherapy. She has received awards for distinguished professional contributions, career service, leadership, advocacy, and mentorship.

Ian O. Williamson is the Pro-Vice Chancellor and Dean of the Business School at Victoria University, Wellington (New Zealand). His research focuses on how the development of effective "talent pipelines" can enhance organizational and community outcomes. In particular, he examines strategic human resource management issues, talent management in SMEs, diversity management, and firm innovation. He received his PhD from the University of North Carolina at Chapel Hill (USA) and a bachelor's degree from Miami University (USA).

About the Editors

Jean Lau Chin (EdD, Columbia University, Teachers College) is a psychologist and Professor at Adelphi University. Her career of more than 40 years of experience includes significant leadership roles within academia as dean at Adelphi University and Systemwide Dean at Alliant International University, and within health service delivery systems as Director of the Thom Clinic and Executive Director of the South Cove Community Health Center. Currently, she is Council Leadership Team Chair and on the Board of Directors of the American Psychological Association, President of the International Council of Psychologists. In addition to her clinical and consulting practice, she has published 18 books and numerous publications and professional talks on diversity, leadership, Asian American, and women's issues. She was editor of the Special Issue on Diversity and Leadership in the *American Psychologist* (April 2010), author of *Women and Leadership* (2007), and co-author of *Diversity and Leadership* (2015). She is a Fulbright Scholar as Distinguished Chair in Cultural Competence at the University of Sydney in Australia and has engaged in leadership development training for women and ethnic minorities.

Joseph E. Garcia (PhD, University of Utah) is Professor of Management and formerly founding Director of the Morse Leadership Institute at Western Washington University. His career focus is on building healthy communities in organizations, with publications spanning topics of leadership, diversity, managerial skills, management education, and change management with information technology. His service includes being a lead faculty member for the Society for the Advancement of Chicano/a and Native American Scientists (SACNAS) Leadership Institute. He is a member of the Academy of Management, OBTS: Teaching Society for Management Educators, and the Management Faculty of Color Association. He currently serves as member of the Editorial Board for the *Journal of Management Education, Management Teaching Review, and the Journal of Leadership and Organizational Studies.*

Joseph E. Trimble (PhD, University of Oklahoma) has over 35 years of experience conducting social and behavioral research with ethnic populations primarily American Indians and Alaska Natives and has played significant roles in leadership within the multicultural communities and within the profession. For the past 35 years he has served on over 15 different scientific review panels for the National Science Foundation and the National Institutes of Health. He has generated over 150 publications on cross-cultural and ethnic topics in psychology including 21 edited, co-edited, and co-authored books. His recent books include (with Celia Fisher), the *Handbook of Ethical Research with Ethnocultural Populations and Communities,* and (with Miguel Gallardo, Christine Yeh, and Thomas Parham) *Working culturally and competently with persons of African, Asian, Latino, and Native Descent: The culturally adaptive responsive model of counseling.* and (with Paul Pedersen, Juris Draguns, Walt Lonner, and Maria Scharron-del Rio) *Counseling Across Cultures,* 7th Edition, and (with Jean Lau Chin) *Diversity and Leadership.*

Index